AN ECONOMIC HISTORY
OF KENYA AND UGANDA
1800–1970

AN ECONOMIC
HISTORY OF
KENYA AND UGANDA
1800-1970

R. M. A. van ZWANENBERG
with
ANNE KING

First published 1975 by
THE MACMILLAN PRESS LTD
London and Basingstoke
Associated companies in New York
Dublin Melbourne Johannesburg and Madras

SBN 333 17671 5

Printed in Great Britain by
THE BOWERING PRESS LTD
Plymouth

Contents

Contents

Foreword

This book is one of the first attempts to write an integrated economic and social history of Kenya and Uganda covering the nineteenth and twentieth centuries. We have chosen to limit our discussion both in time and length for a number of reasons. We realise that to pick up the story at the beginning of the nineteenth century is, in many ways, to plunge into it in midstream and that we run the risk of implying that nothing much happened in the preceding period. That is far from being our view. Changes and developments – the stuff of history – are a part of the human condition and no period can be truly described as static. However, at this stage of historical research in Africa our knowledge of earlier periods is limited. As one approaches the present day the volume of material available, both raw data and academic studies, becomes greater: thus we know more about the twentieth century than the nineteenth, more about the nineteenth than the eighteenth and so on. We have decided, therefore, to restrict ourselves to a period about which we have relatively abundant material. Even so, attempting to account for some aspects of the nineteenth century has proved difficult. Our knowledge of nineteenth-century agricultural production, for example, is woefully inadequate. As a consequence readers will find that we have been unable even to give the nineteenth-century sections in most chapters the emphasis which we think they deserve. The exception to this neglect is in the chapters on trade. Here we have been fortunate in having at our disposal a richer field of published sources which we have been able to supplement with our own research; the reader will notice that we have been able to devote two chapters to nineteenth-century trade alone.

We could, of course, have further limited our discussion and dealt with only the twentieth century, about which there is not a lack but an overwhelming amount of material. In our view, however, this would have given a false picture. Although there are many sharp contrasts between nineteenth- and twentieth-century history in Kenya and Uganda, the colonial period does not mark a sharp break with the pre-colonial past. Rather, many of the developments which took place in the nineteenth century continued into the twentieth, and conversely, many developments of the twentieth century cannot be understood without a knowledge of their pre-colonial roots.

We have chosen to discuss Kenya and Uganda rather than the whole of Eastern Africa for two reasons. First, a study of Kenya and Uganda makes for interesting comparison and contrast in a discussion of change and development. In the nineteenth century, we can contrast southern and western Uganda's centralised systems of social and political authority with decentralised systems of northern and eastern Uganda and most of Kenya. Economically, we can compare and contrast between the systems of production of these areas; both were geared for subsistence production, but centralised systems existed which had the additional burden of providing a livelihood for the administrators and court officials not directly engaged in agriculture. During the colonial period the contrast between Kenya and Uganda as economic units comes into clearer focus : here we can contrast Uganda, developed predominantly through the production of peasant-grown export crops, and Kenya, developed predominantly through the production by expatriates of plantation export crops. The differences in the economic systems have important repercussions on the societies involved.

Our second reason for concentrating on Kenya and Uganda is a practical one : to have included Tanzania or to have ranged further afield in Eastern Africa to consider Zambia, Malawi, Ethiopia, Somalia and Malagasy would have multiplied the number of points of comparison and contrast to a bewildering degree and would probably have resulted in the production of either an unwieldy tome or a short book of generalities. At this stage in research into the social and economic history of Africa it seemed more practical to limit our ambitions and deal with a smaller area which could be treated in some detail.

As a result of the rapid increase in academic specialisation in African history in recent years there are now a large number of books and papers on topics relevant to this study. However, the nature of this increase itself poses problems for the general reader. These recent works are often studies of short periods or of small geographical areas so that while we may have a wealth of information on a particular topic in one area, we may have little comparable information on a neighbouring area, or on the same area at a different time. Inevitably, therefore, the present book will tend to reflect the unevenness of available material. Again, some aspects of historical study have received more attention than others. Economic history in particular has been tragically neglected and social history has often to be extracted with great difficulty from timeless anthropological and sociological accounts and from oral traditions. As a consequence, material on economic and social history has to be collected from a wide variety of (at present) disparate sources. A related problem is that even where there is adequate material on a wide area or over a long timespan, the detail of the primary studies may make it difficult for the general reader to grasp the essentials of the situation. Our aim in this book is to attempt to synthesise recent research on economic and social history in Kenya and Uganda in such a way that the important processes of change and development over the last hundred and fifty years or so can be understood. Specialists, therefore, will find little new material here, but they may perhaps find the integrated discussion of some value. In drawing up lists for further reading we have attempted to show where material can be found to supplement the discussion of topics in this book.

Finally, we have placed the emphasis on topics rather than on chronology in order to show more clearly the changes and developments which have occurred in specific areas of study. Each section of the book deals with a group of related topics (population, society, manpower, production, exchange and distribution, new institutions) while the chapters themselves break down the topics into themes, discussing each more or less chronologically, and where necessary, according to geographical area. This approach inevitably leads to some duplication and cross-referencing but we hope that it will have the advantage of allowing both historians and other social scientists to find information and discussion on a given subject conveniently and efficiently.

Acknowledgements

Most of this book was written in Nairobi while Dr van Zwanenberg was a member of the History Department of the University and Dr King was a member of the sister History Department at Kenyatta University College. Thanks are due to our colleagues in both places who, led by Professor B. A. Ogot and Dr O. J. E. Shiroya respectively, provided much inspiration and stimulation for the work. We were also much assisted by colleagues at Makerere University, Kampala; in particular we would like to mention Professor J. B. Webster, Mr Oliver Furley, Dr Phares Mutibwa and Dr Keith Rennie of the History Department and Professor B. Langlands of the Department of Geography whose assistance, hospitality and readiness to make their work and ideas available to us during our visits to Uganda did much to make our time there agreeable and productive. At both universities the help of the library staff, particularly in the Special Collection in Nairobi and in the Africana Collection at Makerere, was freely given and greatly valued.

Various chapters of this book have been read at early stages by a number of people, all of whom we thank for their helpful and constructive criticism. In particular we would like to mention Professor S. H. Ominde, Miss W. Muiruri, Dr Gachuhi, Dr Judith Heyer, Mr John King, Dr Gideon Mutiso, Dr Philip Mbithi, Dr James Fordyce, Mr Muinde, Mr Michael Cohen and Dr Robert Chambers. Responsibility for the opinions and ideas in each chapter rests, of course, on the shoulders of the authors.

A number of people have been involved in the typing of the manuscript, many of whom had a great deal of trouble with our handwriting and for this we apologise and offer grateful thanks for their efforts. Two ladies in particular deserve mention for their time and trouble: the efforts of Betty Kaume and Esther Fine were beyond the call of duty. Mrs Fine has, in many places, altered our turgid prose into something more respectable. We hope that our readers will be as grateful to her as we are ourselves.

The authors and publishers wish to thank the following for their permission to reproduce copyright material: Controller of Her Majesty's Stationery Office, for use of the map from *Kenya: Report of the Northern Frontier Commission*, Cmd. 1900; International

Acknowledgements

African Institute, for use of an extract from *The Bantu of Western Kenya* by G. Wagner; East African Institute of Social Research, for statistics taken from B. W. Langlands, 'On the Disparities of Economic Development in Uganda', East African Social Science Conference paper; and M. Safier, for use of the map from 'Patterns of Industrial Location and Urban Growth in East Africa, 1945–1985', EASSC paper.

Introduction: Change and Growth

If a man born one hundred and seventy years ago were still alive and looked back at the East African society of his youth it is quite likely that he would recognise some aspects of the present scene. He would feel familiar at the sight of the women bent in the fields or carrying water; he might not recognise the shape of the imported Japanese *pangas* or the tin *debbis* they used but the scene itself would be familiar enough. He would probably find some of the square houses a bit odd, and he would certainly not feel at home in today's clothing or transport. If he was brave enough to travel to Kampala or Nairobi he would be entirely lost; he would be left gasping with wonder, as such sights would have been beyond his or any other person's imagination one hundred and seventy years ago. Here in this book we hope to explain how and why some of these changes have come about.

In many respects throughout the book we will be dealing with two different economic systems which each have their own internal dynamics of change and growth. The first system could be described as pre-colonial, pre-capitalist and predominantly African-oriented; the second system can be characterised as colonial and post-colonial, capitalist and predominantly western-oriented.

Although we have distinguished between these two systems chronologically, it will rapidly become apparent that there was no sudden ending to the first system; rather, the two systems have gradually grown into each other. As we shall illustrate, the new dynamic of colonial capitalism in the twentieth century has, in one way or another, affected everyone in East Africa and thus affected the first of our two systems. In this introduction we shall treat the two systems separately in order to analyse the distinctive characteristics of each more clearly.

1 The pre-capitalist economic system

Nineteenth-century production and trade was pre-capitalist in the sense that neither activity was undertaken primarily for profit but for need : the dominant concern was to produce sufficient commodities for existence. Production was concerned with the control and adaptation of nature to man's conscious, or felt, needs. In the introductory chapter on agriculture and in the chapter on pastoralism we have been particularly concerned to illustrate the mechanics of this *adaptation to the limitations provided by the physical environment*. In the chapters on industrial production and African trade in the nineteenth century we show how people *manipulated their physical environment* in order to produce and distribute the goods which they needed.

We show that the peoples of East Africa adapted themselves to environmental limitations by a wide range of methods. Man was able to exploit the resources of the semi-arid regions of Karamoja and Turkanaland through stock-keeping and seasonal migration while in the more fertile areas around Lake Victoria and elsewhere man was able to exploit the environment through the development of agricultural technologies.

However, man is more than an adapter; he has also the ability to manipulate his environment to meet his needs. East African people produced iron tools, cleared forests and practised shifting agriculture and careful stock management. These technical developments were of great importance because they allowed many more people to exist on a given piece of land than was possible when technology was based on the digging stick of agricultural communities or the bow and stone- or bone-tipped arrow of hunting and gathering communities. Let us add that hunting and gathering technologies were, within their own sphere, highly sophisticated methods of production and an extremely successful example of man's adaptation to his environment. The making of stone tools and arrow-heads was in itself an attempt to manipulate nature : the making of the iron hoe and knife was a further technical development which allowed even more control of nature and guaranteed increased productivity.

Nature was, however, far from being completely conquered. The variability of nature (of soil fertility, water supply and sun) remained the major factor affecting people's lives. Famine remained a constant hazard which technical change had not been able to overcome. It is possible that famine was a cause of many of the major movements of people in East Africa. Famine led people to search for new land. In very bad years agricultural people would often exchange animals and in extreme cases, people, for food; they would migrate and seek refuge among better-off neighbours. Pastoral peoples in semi-arid regions always allowed stricken neighbours to use their grazing on the basis of future reciprocity. Despite technological developments, therefore, man's ability to produce and the dynamics of change and growth were still closely tied to the rhythm of nature.

2 The capitalist economic system

The colonial era was the period of major alterations in the dynamics of the old society. Three interrelated areas in which these alterations occurred are of particular interest to us here. First, the introduction of western technology; secondly the introduction of colonial capitalism; and thirdly the integration of the colonial economy into the world economic system.

The introduction of western technology

The first major significance of the introduction of western technology was that it had enormous destructive as well as productive potentialities. We outline some of the destructive aspects of western technology in the chapter on population growth. The productive potentiality of western technology can be seen in the possibility it offered for controlling nature to the extent of eliminating famine and producing a variety and quantity of goods undreamt of in the precolonial era. The productive aspect was not uniform in its effect on East Africa : new techniques have taken a long time to reach the people, but speaking generally change in the twentieth century has been less closely tied to the rhythm of nature than hitherto. Some people at least can expect an annual increase in production and wealth, unlimited by such natural disasters as famine, flood and drought. The rhythm of nature still plays an important part in people's daily lives, but this part has become smaller and smaller as man's control over water and soil fertility has become greater and spread to more areas.

The second major significance of the introduction of western technology has been the changing modes of production. In the nineteenth century the main form of production was small-scale subsistence production which was concerned with the supply of daily needs. Closely associated and integrated with this mode of production was that of the small-scale craftsman – iron-maker, pot-producer and so on – and the small-scale itinerant trader (see the chapters on nineteenth-century industry and trade). During the colonial era many of the old craft and trade skills became irrelevant as new imported goods supplanted those produced locally and new patterns of distribution replaced the old trade networks.

Colonial capitalism

The extent to which new institutions and technologies have been infused into the old economic systems has been determined by the characteristics of colonial capitalism and its integration into the world economy. Colonial capitalism was a variant of the European capitalism of the nineteenth and twentieth centuries. Capitalism is a system of production which historically has shown itself to be progressive because the techniques of production have consciously developed in order (a) to maximise profits and (b) to increase the output of goods for consumption. The classic example of the growth of a capitalist system occurred in Britain. British capitalism grew from *within* the old society and in the process destroyed the old precapitalist society. Rapidly, neighbouring European societies followed suit, also developing capitalist economies from within.

As the techniques of production have been developed further and further, and as the old society has been destroyed, so the system of production has expanded into the rest of the world. During the nineteenth and twentieth centuries capitalist forms of production have been *imposed* through conquest on the African and Asian peoples of the world. Thus while European capitalism originates from *within* the old society, colonial capitalism originates from *without*. One of the dominant characteristics of colonial capitalism in both Kenya and Uganda has been that as a system of production it was initially introduced into a limited geographical and agricultural area in both territories: into the Highlands of Kenya and into Buganda and Eastern Province in Uganda. In these areas there has been a rapid growth in output as new economic institutions and crops have been introduced; today they represent the richest rural areas in each country. The two chapters on agriculture illustrate the geographically uneven growth of production in both countries. The chapters on marketing, banking and urbanisation explain the domestic mechanics by which uneven growth of the economy (in geographical terms) has taken place, while the chapters on the East African common market and twentieth-century industrialisation show that the geographical unevenness of growth is repeated when we compare East African countries with each other. The differences between levels of growth in different regions have been given particular prominence in the chapter on pastoralism. There we are mainly concerned with the semi-arid areas where there has been little or no growth of production during the last seventy years and where it is possible that people have actually become poorer. While all forms of capitalism have always produced unevenness in wealth between geographical regions and inequalities between people, the levels of unevenness and inequality appear to be much greater in colonial capitalism than in the European parent. One of our more important aims has been to show how these economic differences have arisen.

Besides creating unevenness, the dynamics of colonial capitalism have also altered the pre-existing balances of wealth of the regions without destroying the older systems of production as in classical capitalism. To give one example, the islands of Mfangano and Rusinga in Lake Victoria were relatively wealthy in the old days. Cattle imports from the mainland were forbidden in order to keep the islands free from cattle disease. As a result they were rich in animals. Today the islands are far away from the main centres of commerce and trade, the young people leave home for the towns as soon as they are able, and so the islands' economic growth is limited in comparison with more fortunate regions which have access to towns and markets. This example illustrates that although Mfangano and Rusinga *appear* superficially to be little affected by colonial capitalism (the people continue to follow the occupations and techniques of production of their forefathers) the relative wealth of the islands has declined by comparison with their pre-colonial position.

A second consequence of the introduction of colonial capitalism has been an alteration in the means of accumulating wealth. In the pre-colonial period the means of accumulation of wealth was through obtaining cattle or stores of grain. Not only were cattle vitally important economically in resisting drought but they were the major means of social exchange (to obtain wives) and economic exchange (to obtain land-use and the labour of other people). Hence a man rich in cattle was likely to be a man with considerable social and political prestige.

The colonial capitalist system introduced a new means of accumulation, money. Like cattle, money can be exchanged for the goods and services of others, but unlike cattle there is no limit to the amount that can be accumulated. Moreover, the processes of classic or colonial capitalist production are specifically designed so that monetary accumulation can occur. In both systems production and trade are undertaken with financial accumulation as the *primary purpose,* whereas previous production and trade were undertaken for immediate use. Of course it was always pleasant to receive better value in any exchange of one good for another, but that was not the primary purpose of pre-colonial producers and traders. In the colonial period the Europeans introduced the idea, and the means to fulfil this idea, that production and trade were primarily for profit.

One particular aspect of colonial capitalism was that the invaders restricted ownership in the areas of greatest profit to themselves. Until the early 1950s Africans were almost entirely kept out of trade in both Kenya and Uganda and severely limited as to the extent of their production for profit. Europeans and Asians were allowed to produce and trade for profit, but as the chapters on agriculture show these attitudes have changed from 1954 so that in principle we are all now 'free' to compete for the profits of capitalist production.

Nevertheless, the introduction of a monetary economy did have the effect of drawing a wider and wider section of the population into the capitalist production system, either by cash cropping or by selling their labour to employers for a cash income. The process of integrating the peoples of East Africa into the capitalist economy is still far from complete; as already mentioned the old forms of subsistence are still widely practised. Yet over this century peasant farming has become more capitalistic as land has come into short supply and has been given a monetary value and crops have been grown more and more with the market in mind. The development of modern communications systems (principally roads and railways) had also aided the process of integration as people and goods have become able to travel over long distances – although as mentioned above the degree of integration has been geographically most uneven.

In both Kenya and Uganda a subsidiary mode of agricultural production has been the plantation system, which is geared solely to the production of a commodity for the market. In this sense the plantation system is a more fully capitalist system than that of peasant farming. Like factories in an industrial production system, plantations have capital stock, require paid wage labour, demand a regular work discipline and have annual accounting systems for determining profit and loss. In many senses the plantation mode of production operates in competition with the peasant production system. In Kenya and Uganda they have competed for access to the land and labour of the peoples as well as for the cash resources of the governments.

On top of these producing agencies and in many ways controlling them are the public and private corporations : banks, marketing agencies, co-operative organisations and foreign industries. All of these large-scale institutions were new to East Africa in the twentieth century and we shall examine their growth in some detail in this book. They are essentially monopolistic in the sense that as organisations they are giants beside the peasant farms, ensuring by their superior competitive power that small-scale trading, banking or initiative of any kind is limited. In principle they are organised on impersonal lines with profit as their criterion for success, and they represent the dichotomy of the growth of East African societies : the immense wealth of the few is reflected in the power of their monopoly beside the comparative poverty of the many which is in turn symbolised by the self-sufficient *shamba*.

Finally the introduction of capitalism has led to a widespread consciousness that economic growth can be a continuous process. Capitalist production has expanded the output of goods in both territories. Growth has therefore become a matter of public concern, and as such, a matter for government policy. Here again we see the colonial aspects of the system, as the decisions on the character and direction of growth were taken by the invaders. In the early colonial period up to 1929 there was little consistent thought given by the British government to the development of their colonies except for the introduction of new export crops. Apart from the original grants-in-aid, emergency relief and the guaranteeing of the interest on colonial loans raised in London, economic aid was severely limited. During this period there was a great deal of argument over such development concepts as native paramountcy, trusteeship and dual policy but in practice these policies had little effect on the direction of economic development. The direction of resources for development was determined by the ability of vested interests (e.g. farmers' associations) to have access to government decision-making.

In 1929 the first Colonial Development and Welfare Act was passed in London which heralded the earliest attempt to systematise ideas about development loans from the United Kingdom. The essential idea behind the act was that money should be made available from the United Kingdom for use in the colonies but that goods bought with that money would have to be bought in Britain; the loans were to be mutually beneficial. In Kenya and Uganda most of the loans were spent on infrastructure : communications, health facilities, water supplies and so on. Very little of the cash made available between 1929 and 1936 (six per cent in all) was spent directly on agriculture.

The Second World War demonstrated the immense importance of her colonies to Britain (see Chapter 11 on marketing) and their economic development began to be considered more important. New industrial schemes were begun in both Kenya and Uganda and more public and private investment flowed in. By 1954-5 the East African Royal Commission was thinking in terms of developing all the resources of the area rather than limiting developments on a racial basis. The Commission's report was a milestone in the economic thinking on East Africa in that it represented the first consistently thought-out plan for the economic growth of the whole of East Africa.

Since the time of the Royal Commission the structure of the economy has been developed rapidly along a few of the lines recommended by the report, particularly the removal of the old racial privileges of the Europeans. Foreign-financed industrial growth has become the corner-stone of development in the 1960s, while access to job opportunities has been firmly directed towards indigenous Kenyans and Ugandans. As we shall illustrate again and again in the forthcoming chapters the basic inherited economic structure has not been altered in a major sense, except that the personnel in charge have changed.

Integration into the world economy

The forceful imposition of capitalism from outside Kenya and Uganda led to the integration of the economies into the world system. Initially this integration occurred only within the small geographical areas already mentioned which produced cash crops. Apart from maize, the cash crops produced in these areas – coffee, cotton, sugar, sisal, etc. – were entirely *exported* (see Chapter 10). Thus the *growth* of the Kenya or Uganda economy, up until 1945 and in many respects up to the present day, has been *dependent* on the export of agricultural cash crops. The growth of European capitalism has never in the past been so entirely dependent on prices received from the already more developed economies. It is this aspect of capitalism, the aspect which leaves economic growth dependent on *foreign trade*, which provides another crucial characteristic of colonial capitalism.

It is particularly important to understand that the economic relationship between Europe and Africa has never been one of mutual dependence. East Africa's export crops were only a small portion of the world supply of these commodities, thus the East African producers could not influence the world prices quoted on the London market although the entire economy was dependent on these prices for growth. Not only that but the demand in Europe for East Africa's exports tended to fluctuate so that the income from sales and consequently the general state of the economy went up and down according to the conditions of demand in Europe, as is shown below :

Economic fluctuations based on international economic conditions

1904–14 Initial period of colonisation: experiments in suitable crops for export undertaken. Inflow of cash from settlers and imperial government.

1914–17 Check on export crops by the East African and European war, thus check on inflow of cash so economic growth virtually stationary.

1918–20 End of war and immediate demand in Europe for crops from East Africa, so prices rose very rapidly and the export economy expanded, i.e. growth.

1920–2   Demand in Europe for East African goods collapsed, part of a world depression in prices. Export prices therefore declined and growth of economies at a standstill.

1922–9   Demand in Europe recovered and prices rose annually; thus as output of settler farmers in Kenya and peasants in Uganda increased in quantity, so amount of cash entering the country rose rapidly too. Economy growing again.

1929–36   Demand for East African and world exports in Europe and United States declined drastically. World's greatest slump hit the East African miniature export economies very hard. Economic growth halted and went into decline.

1936–9   European demand again began to pick up slowly, and by 1939 money and export prices roughly back to their 1929 level.

1940–55   Rapid inflow of cash and boom conditions in both economies. Demand for East African and world produce increased in Europe and United States so that world prices rose rapidly, due to (a) demand for food during 1939–45 war, (b) post-war expansion and reconstruction in Europe, (c) demand for food and raw material during Korean war and (d) inflow of cash in Kenya, 1952–5, due to Mau Mau Emergency.

1955–66   Demand for East African products, e.g. sisal, declined due to growth of synthetics, and near saturation of demand for products like coffee; prices declined; level of growth declined somewhat.

1965–73   Prices of East African products in Europe neither declined nor increased, due to international product agreements which attempted to control the quantity of each product placed on world market.

We can see the demand conditions in Europe for East African produce vitally affect the economic health of the member territories. As is illustrated above, if Europe or the United States are at war, or if their population stop drinking tea or coffee, or if they decide to stop using cotton cloths and move into synthetic fibres, then the growth of East African economies is affected; colonisation tied East Africa to world economic fluctuations in such a way that it has become dependent on world demand. This is what we mean when we talk about the integration of East Africa into the world economy.

Integration of course means more than this. Because East Africa has joined the world economy comparatively late (only seventy years ago) the character of the exchange has been that cheap food and raw materials have travelled out of East Africa, while she has imported in return finished goods, motor cars, machines and so on. This is the typical transaction between rich and poor countries.

The rich countries with their head-start had by 1900 a comparative technical advantage over people in East Africa. Through the mechanics of colonisation (as we show throughout this book) the rich have maintained and even widened their technical industrial advantage. In a sense colonisation fossilised the division of production functions between themselves and poor countries.

If we return then to our old man comparing Kenya or Uganda now with the situation a hundred and seventy years ago, it is quite possible that he may not understand why some things have changed, why some people have been able to grow rich while so many remain probably as poor as they ever were. An old man will of course notice how many people there are now, but will not understand why a few can step out of their highly polished chauffeur-driven cars into large jet aeroplanes while others continue to live all their lives in huts and to dig the soil with their *jembes*. If our old man will read with us we will attempt to explain these differences to him.

Part One

PEOPLE

1 A History of Population Growth in Kenya and Uganda

Introduction

Economic history is the study of people and their way of life; it is concerned with *all* the people, not simply the rulers or decision-makers, and it is therefore very important that economic historians should know about the number of people in the community they are studying; in other words, they must concern themselves with the size of the population. As historians they also need to know how the size of the population has changed over time; has it increased in size, or decreased, and even more important, why and how have the increases or decreases occurred? This chapter will attempt to answer some of these questions.

Over the last one hundred years or so the size of the populations of Kenya and Uganda has been of more than academic interest to students of history. Since 1948 demographers (demography is the study of population) have shown that the population in both countries has grown at the rate of between 2·9 per cent and 3·5 per cent per year. As we shall illustrate in this chapter, this rate of growth is at least as high as that of any other known population growth rate at any time in history, anywhere in the world. Such a rate is unprecedented and we need to try to discover the factors which have led to this situation.

Changes in the rate of population growth before 1890

We know very little about the growth or decline in population size in Kenya and Uganda before 1890; we lack statistics and all we can do is to presume that the East African population behaved like other pre-industrial populations of which we have greater knowledge. However we do know a considerable amount about the economic and social mechanisms of East Africa which must have affected the rate of growth or decline of the number of people

One of the most important economic mechanisms which affected the growth of the population was the method used for food production. The more *technically* developed a society was, the more food could be produced from a given area of land, and the larger the number of people who could be fed. Thus, generally speaking, hunters and gatherers obtained less food off a given area of land than did pastoralists, while agriculturalists could obtain even larger quantities of food off the same area (providing of course that the land was sufficiently fertile). The technology of food production therefore, was a major factor governing population growth before the 1890s. We should add of course that the relationship between food production and population growth is still important; it does not however assume quite the importance now that it once did.

In the late nineteeth century East Africa accommodated a smallish number of hunters and gatherers in the forest zones and pastoralists used wide areas of land with an agricultural potential. Many fertile parts of the Rift Valley, for instance, were used by the Samburu or the pastoral Maasai. For both groups, land was important as the place which accommodated their major means of livelihood—wild animals or cattle—was of little value in itself. The growth of population among pastoralists over hundreds of years had led to shortages of pasture and in some cases had caused migration into more fertile areas where the people had settled, absorbed earlier populations and become agriculturalists or semi-agriculturalists; the agricultural Maasai and Pokot, the Kenya Luo and Kalenjin are examples. For the agriculturalists on the other hand, land was of vital importance and had a more direct relationship with population growth. However, even as late as the end of the nineteenth century land was in plentiful supply: almost everywhere there was virgin land waiting to be taken up and cultivated so that the availability of land did not act as a constraint on population growth even for agriculturalists. This process of settlement involved clearing the forests for agriculture and integrating with hunting and gathering peoples. The Kikuyu, for example, had expanded in this way in Central Kenya and were still in the process of settling Kiambu during the nineteenth century. Generally the technologies of the agriculturalists were replacing the technologies of the hunter-gatherers, either by conquest or absorption, and thus exploiting the production potential of the land to a greater extent; thus in turn it is probable that the potential for population growth increased.

While there were probably few economic constraints on population increase because there was, in general, plenty of land available, it is likely that communities did limit the size of increase through social mechanisms. One set of mechanisms which was particularly significant was marriage customs. By controlling the age at which people married, the number of children any woman could bear would be limited. In both Kenya and Uganda the age of marriage was determined by initiation and the times of initiation were decided on by the Elders. In times of dire emergency, for instance after a war or a famine when many young men or children had died, the age of initiation could be brought forward in order to encourage the earliest possible marriage and replenish the people lost. In one sense therefore the timing of initiation ceremonies was a sensitive mechanism which regulated the age of marriage and so affected the number of children born into the community.

Because there was no land shortage in the pre-colonial period, there were no major *economic* constraints on the age of marriage. Marriage could therefore be regulated according to *social* rather than economic needs of the community. These social criteria were decided by the Elders, and included such considerations as whether the season had been plentiful, or whether the young men were showing the Elders their due respect. It is likely that the periods between one initiation ceremony and the next fluctuated; some people may have been initiated as early as the age of twelve while others may have had to wait until they were thirty or so. It is likely overall that most people married before they were twenty years old, but we lack detailed evidence on this point.

There were other social customs which affected the rate of growth of the population. Birth control, in the form of sexual abstinence, seems to have been widely practised, particularly during the period after the birth of a child while it was still feeding at the breast. As a consequence the births of one woman's children were usually spaced at two-yearly intervals at least.

Giving birth before marriage was a practice severely frowned upon and often seems to have led to social ostracism. Birth control after marriage and sanctions against conception outside marriage therefore were both ways in which the community placed social constraints on the extent of population growth.

Other checks on the rate of increase of population included famines, diseases and wars. Again we have little exact data on these occurences as checks on population. It is still widely accepted by many demographers that these factors were some of the most important in keeping population growth rates at a low level. Certainly colonialists have argued that tribal wars, starvation and disease were rampant in the nineteenth century. However, as we lack the necessary careful empirical investigation of these factors, we need to treat generalisations of this nature with great care.

It seems to be true that there were *occasional* wars which decimated one group of people or another. For instance the Purko

Maasai seem to have destroyed nearly all the Uasin Gishu Maasai in the middle of the nineteenth century. But while we can pinpoint a few destructive wars of this nature, they were very few indeed. For the most part wars do not seem to have been concerned principally with killing people, but rather with the capture of women and livestock. If war did lead to the deaths of as few as five or six young men the Elders of both sides usually came together to sort out the argument.

The same type of argument can be applied to the problem of famine. Famine was a constant problem due to the irregularity of the rains, but most famines did not last for long. Moreover as our own research has shown, people who lived in potential famine areas developed widespread trade relations with surrounding peoples. So long as famine only affected a small area, as was generally the case, goats or goods like hoes could be exchanged for food from elsewhere. It was also often possible for people to migrate from a famine-stricken area to areas where conditions were better. As in the case of warfare there seem to have been occasional widespread famines which affected people over large areas and which tended to kill large numbers of people. A great deal more information is required before we can make more specific statements or before it will be possible to justify or deny the assertions of the colonialists.

What therefore can we conclude about the behaviour of the population of East Africa before about 1900? We can make the following tentative conclusions :

1. That the more advanced forms of production tended to be taking over from the less advanced forms during the nineteenth century. This process should have led to increases in the number of people who could live in the area.
2. That land, the major factor of production for the agriculturalists, was not in short supply overall, so that the *potential* for population increase was not held in check by the pressure of population on the land.
3. That it is likely that East African populations, like those of other pre-industrial societies, suffered from a high death rate due to ill-health and inadequate nutrition and that the death rate was likely to be highest among young infants.
4. That social customs tended to control population growth rates to some extent.
5. That warfare and famine were no doubt common enough, but probably they were not the major factors in limiting the rate of growth of the population.

Thus while the *potential* for rapid population growth was present it is likely that the overall number of people was fairly stable. During the occasional emergency (famine, drought, war) population is likely to have declined temporarily in certain localities. After such disasters however it was possible for social adjustments to be made so that the number of people could be made up to its previous level. On balance it is likely that there was a slow increase in the size of the population overall as agriculturalists extended their activities into hitherto uncultivated areas. In the twentieth century this pattern of slow population growth has been drastically altered. We must therefore now look at what happened to growth rates in the twentieth century and try to determine what were the major causes of the changes.

1890–1923

Early estimates of the size of the populations of Kenya and Uganda were as follows:

	Kenya	Uganda
1878 (Stanley)	–	780,000
1897 (Hardinge)	2,500,000	–
1897 (Portal)	450,000	–
1902 (Official estimates)	4,000,000	3,500,000

Clearly these figures provide us with no useful information; they cannot be proved or disproved, they were merely guesses based on limited and unsystematic observations.

From the beginning of the colonial period the method of estimating the extent of the population was somewhat better than these guesses, but not much so. Population estimates were at first based on tax returns. The earliest tax was a Poll Tax which was levied on every able-bodied male over the age of sixteen. Of course the collecting officers did not know whether a youth was sixteen years of age or not, and one rough method of estimating age was to look under his arms to see if there was any growth of hair in the arm-pit. All British colonial estimates were based upon the assumption that adult men made up 49 per cent of the adult population and that the number of children under the age of fifteen years was 37 per cent of the total adult population. As the Poll Tax returns were supposed to represent all the adult men, the number of women and then the number of children under fifteen could then be calculated. This was the method used for estimating populations in East Africa up to 1948.

When the first regular census was taken in 1948 it was discovered that the population *estimates* prepared in 1947 on the basis of the

Poll Tax figures were too low by about 25 per cent: they were wrong by over one million people in each of the three East African territories.

Part of the reason for this error was that the proportion of children to adults was much higher than the earlier estimators had thought. They had estimated that the number of children in the society would be about 37 per cent of the total population; the 1948 census showed that 48 per cent of the population were children. Many demographers have concluded that little can be usefully said about the population of East Africa before 1948 as all the earlier estimates were too low by 25 per cent or possibly more.

Certainly any population statistics based on tax collection figures are open to considerable and unknown error. Taxes were collected by the District Officer who would tour his district annually. In every village or area the headman would advise the DO on who should be exempted from taxation as aged or infirm. Venal headmen were open to straight-forward bribery and it is likely that many able-bodied men slipped through the tax net with the headman's favour and were thus not counted. Secondly, a paid government hut-counter was supposed to count all the huts in the area in preparation for the DO's visit and the collection of hut tax. Very often the hut-counter made errors in adding up his totals; 'Here are great and even absurd errors', remarked one DO who attempted to check the arithmetic. Thirdly, as men were moving back and forth as migrant labour it was sometimes very difficult to get hold of them at tax-paying time, and once again, the payment and the concomitant counting could be avoided. In Uganda the authorities attempted to get round this problem by appointing special tax collectors to collect from specific ethnic groups employed on contract labour in Kampala and Jinja but this was a cumbersome solution and rather ineffective. It is therefore almost impossible to assess the nature or degree of error in the early population estimates based on tax returns. However, we should not give up at this point; there are a number of other population estimates for this period which are based only partly on tax figures, and more importantly on the experience and observations of medical and administrative officers which can provide, if not absolute figures, at least some evidence of population trends.

Apart from the rough estimates based on tax returns the first trained observers to comment on demographic conditions were medical men. They argued that between about 1890 and 1922–3 the population of both Kenya and Uganda had been declining in size. It is important to remember that these men argued from observation and not from racial prejudice; a medical doctor is a trained scientific observer and should be less likely to succumb to the wildly prejudiced statements of unscientific observers who were abundant and vociferous in East Africa at the time. It is likely therefore that the observations on population made by medical men would have had greater validity than those of almost any other group of people. It is worth noting too that a few members of the administration's medical department had a professional interest and concern with the indigenous population's welfare, a concern rare at a time when even most of the medical welfare resources went into protecting Europeans at risk in tropical climates.

What is the evidence that population was declining in size during this period? First let us examine what was happening in East Africa between roughly 1890 and 1924. This was a period in which many people died from causes other than old age. Around 1890 there were (a) widespread wars in Uganda and (b) widespread famines, and epidemic diseases which followed the famines, throughout East Africa. Famine began in 1889 and in some areas continued sporadically until the end of the century. Rinderpest decimated cattle; drought and locust invasions upset crops; smallpox and dysentery killed people.

Following close on the heels of these disasters came the 'pacification' campaigns waged by the Europeans in which more people died, and accompanying the adventurers and traders who were 'opening up' East Africa, and the colonial administration, came a number of diseases new to East Africa which reached epidemic proportions because the African population had no immunity against them. Smallpox, chickenpox, measles, poliomyelitis, plague, influenza and whooping-cough all seem to have made their appearance in East Africa by at least 1890. Many of these diseases were killers. Jiggers, relapsing fever and sleeping sickness were introduced for the first time in the 1890s. As one medical historian has written :

> 'Jigger' infection and sleeping sickness, both introduced into Uganda at the same time . . . are probably but the most striking and obvious examples of a much more widespread migration . . . of many disease-producing parasites, that resulted from the 'opening up' of the country and increased intertribal communication that took place during the last quarter of the nineteenth century.

Jiggers was probably introduced into Uganda by Stanley's Emin Pasha Relief Expedition which travelled through Zaïre. At first it afflicted many people so seriously that they lost one or more toes. Relapsing fever probably came in by way of the east coast and rapidly became a serious danger to anyone travelling and resting at the regular camps on the trade routes. Sleeping sickness was by far the most serious of the new diseases : it seems that it originally entered Uganda with Emin Pasha's troops in the early 1890s.

By 1898 sleeping sickness had reached epidemic proportions in Busoga and in the next few years (until about 1905) it was rife around Lake Victoria and then continued to occur sporadically up to the early 1920s. Between 1900 and 1905 sleeping sickness alone is estimated to have killed at least 200,000 people on the western side of the Lake, about two-thirds of the estimated population at that time. Plague followed and smallpox was prevalent up to 1914. In 1913 a severe epidemic of cerebral spinal meningitis broke out and affected people from the Kikuyu in the south to the Lugbara in the north-west. Finally war once more appeared as a major killer. Many people died during or immediately after the 1914–18 war : 350,000 porters were said to have been recruited from East Africa; 46,618 were officially recorded as having died on duty and another 40,645 were untraced at the end of the war, many of whom must have died. For Kenya alone it has been estimated that 144,000 people died in the course of the war or from the famine immediately after, but this figure is sheer guess-work and the real figure is likely to be much larger. In late 1918 and 1919 famine, influenza and plague struck the people of the whole of East Africa and a long epidemic of yaws began as well.

If we add these events together – the famines, disease, colonial pacification, the European war and then more famines and disease, all happening within a thirty-year period – it would seem to be correct to suggest that the population of the whole area probably declined in numbers from its 1890 level. But it would be foolish to attempt to estimate the *size* of the decline. Estimates by demographers based on inadequate information have a tendency to be proved utterly wrong when fresh evidence comes to light. At present all we can say is that there seems to have been a downwards trend in the population from the 1890s until the middle of the 1920s.

Other more detailed observations of population trends support this. In the early 1930s S. H. Fazan, a District Officer in Kenya, tried to work out the history of population in the Kikuyu Province. He found that the only reasonably accurate figures on population provided by tax returns were the hut counts. He checked the work of the hut-counters, in some cases by going round the countryside himself to see whether the number of huts counted was correct. He discovered that the errors in the counts were not in the original counting but in the adding up, and that they could therefore be used as a basis of estimating population. But counts of course only provided information about the numbers of women, and can only tell us anything about the male population by implication.

Between 1909 and 1923, Fazan discovered the number of wives and widows living in the Kikuyu Reserve was as follows :

	Kiambu	Fort Hall	Nyeri	Total
1909	23,400	61,200	35,100	119,700
1923	23,900	44,050	34,890	102,840

Between these years, therefore, the number of married and widowed women was declining. Fazan thought that a part of the explanation of this decline was that from 1913–14 people began to migrate onto the European farms as squatters. He thought that by 1921 17,700 Kikuyu women had left their homelands and moved onto the adjacent white farms. Between 1916 and 1921 the emigration was particularly high from Fort Hall, probably as a result of the severity of famine and epidemic in this area. A more detailed look at Fazan's figures shows that between 1909 and 1916 there was an increase in the number of adult females of 0·5 per cent per annum; between 1917 and 1921 there was an annual rate of decrease of 3·2 per cent (these were the really bad years), and then an annual rate of increase of 0.75 per cent between 1921 and 1931. Clearly if the figures for the men had been available the decreases in the size of population in the Reserves would probably have been considerably greater, as it was they who died during the war and who suffered most from the diseases which followed. Unfortunately for historians, such detailed investigations into population trends were not carried out in other areas at the time. The Kikuyu case may be an extreme one, in that the rates of decline include migration out of the reserves into the White Highlands. However the constraints on population growth which affected the Kikuyu also operated in every other society in East Africa, and it seems that we can assume that the general trend was one of declining population before the mid-1920s.

To sum up, therefore, although we can say little about the exact size of the population in these thirty-odd years in Kenya and Uganda, we can see that conditions affecting population size had changed drastically. Wars were a major cause of deaths instead of a minor and incidental cause; new and lethal diseases had been introduced and as yet little had been done to counteract their effect, except for the case of sleeping sickness in Uganda which had been treated as a national emergency.

However it would seem that by the mid-1920s the population had begun to rise. The men had borne the major share of the wartime losses and probably suffered most from the diseases which followed; the women who survived this period to bear more children, and then their children themselves, were able to begin to make up the deficiency.

Population growth since 1924

From the middle of the 1920s it is likely that the population began to grow, slowly in the late twenties and thirties and thereafter more rapidly. The following table, based on research carried out by D. A. Lury in 1969, seems to bear this out.

Backward projections of population growth in Kenya and Uganda
(millions of people)

	1921	1931	1939	1948	1962	1969
Kenya	3·7	4·1	4·8	5·7	8·8	10·9
Uganda	3·4	3·6	4·2	4·9	7·2	9·5

Certainly the amateur demographers mentioned in the previous section of this chapter all commented on what appeared to be a rising rate of growth from around 1924–5. And this was to be expected. The aftermath of the war was beginning to recede as a major constraint on growth by the mid- to late-1920s, and certain of the diseases which had hitherto been so important were beginning to be held in check. Smallpox control was beginning to be effective. From the end of the eighteenth century in Europe the possibilities of vaccinating against smallpox had been known : by the early twentieth century the vaccination was cheap and widely available. In the second decade of the twentieth century medical officers in East Africa began wholesale vaccination campaigns; in Kenya alone between 1916 and 1918 1,702,000 people were vaccinated. A second widespread disease which was now held in check was yaws. Yaws was not a killer by itself but it caused serious disfiguration and lowered people's resistance to other diseases. Up to the early 1920s the cure for yaws was expensive to administer, but with the development of a cheaper method of cure, yaws was virtually eliminated in East Africa by the mid-1930s.

Diseases which were not being held in check were malaria, tuberculosis and dysentery, which continued to be suffered widely, often carried into the rural areas by workers returning from periods of wage employment on estates or government works. Of course it is not possible to assess whether the removal of smallpox and yaws as major scourges compensated for the growing prevalence of

malaria, dysentery and tuberculosis in terms of effect on population : we must wait for a medical historian to comment on this subject.

The continuing presence of diseases like malaria, dysentery and
tuberculosis accounted in part for the relatively slow rate of growth
of the population in the late twenties and thirties. Another important constraint was poor diet. Inadequate diet tends to lower resistance to disease and thus render diseases more effective as constraints
on population growth themselves. Of course any diet can only
be described as 'poor' in relative terms; here we mean 'poor'
in comparison to the standards worked out as the basis of adequate
nutrition by the United Nations – diets which include regular meat,
fish, green vegetables and fruits. By these standards it seems that
many East Africans were taking inadequate diets in this period.
The first major investigation of dietary habits was carried out by
two doctors, Dr Gilk and Dr Orr, between 1926 and 1927. They
examined the normal diets of some 12,000 Kikuyu and Maasai and
concluded that both groups' diets suffered from nutritional defici-
encies. Other less detailed surveys in different areas came to much
the same conclusions. Whether the low levels of nutrition were due
to the aftermath of the war and famines, or simply reflected inadequacies of traditional diets, is difficult to say.

Nevertheless, in the 1920s and 1930s the population of Kenya
and Uganda was probably growing at a rate of between 1 and 1·5
per cent every year, and largely as a result of natural increase (i.e.
slightly more babies were being born every year than there were
people dying). In Uganda however, there was a subsidiary reason
for population increases. Unlike Kenya, Uganda's population was
also increased by a flow of immigrants, mainly from Ruanda and
Burundi, who were looking for wage labour. This influx really
began to make itself felt from the second half of the 1930s : between 1936 and 1951 it is estimated that between 50,000 and
100,000 men and women from Ruanda and Burundi entered
Uganda to find work. Some stayed, while others returned home
after only a short work period.

While the inadequacies of the population estimates of this period
(up to 1948) make it difficult to establish what was happening to
the African population with any great accuracy, there is one area
where we do have satisfactory statistics. The European and Asian
populations were counted separately in four censuses in 1911, 1921,
1926 and 1931, as well as, of course, in the later censuses of
1948, 1959, 1962 and 1969. The figures for these groups were as
follows :

TABLE 1.1

European and Asian populations in Kenya and Uganda

	EUROPEANS		ASIANS	
	Kenya	Uganda	Kenya	Uganda
1911	3,175	1,269	12,000	2,216
1921	9,650	1,269	23,000	5,000
1926	12,529	2,001	41,140	5,000
1931	16,812	2,001	57,135	14,150
1948	29,660	3,448	97,528	35,767
1959	–	10,866	–	71,933
1962	55,759	–	176,613	–
1969	40,593[a]	–[b]	139,039[a]	–

[a] European figure includes 3889 Kenya citizens
Asian figure includes 60,994 Kenya citizens

[b] By August 1973 only vol. i of the report on the 1969 census was available and this only provided details by age and sex

Sources: 'Census of the Non-Native Population', 1911 through to 1948;
Statistical Abstracts, Kenya, 1971 and Uganda, 1969

These figures reflect quite clearly the differences of colonial occupation in the two countries. Not until 1948 did Uganda have as many Europeans in her population as Kenya had had in 1911, thirty-seven years before. However even in Kenya European farmers made up only a small proportion of the white population: the majority of Europeans were employed in a whole range of services which sprang up to support the settlers, in particular government, professional and commercial services (doctors, lawyers, land agents and so on). By 1931 over 5000 Europeans (twice the number of the agricultural population) were occupied in these services, trades and industries. The growth of the Asian populations can be accounted for with similar reasons. By 1921 over 3000 Asians in Kenya and Uganda were employed in government services, although this number decreased in Kenya as government jobs became the preserve of the whites. Industrial and commercial activities at first, and later the professions, were the major occupations for the Asian community.

Population growth since 1948

In 1948 the first reasonably accurate census was held throughout East Africa. C. J. Martin, the government demographer, planned the census like a military exercise. No full census had ever been taken before in East Africa and many Europeans doubted that it was possible.

Long and detailed planning over eighteen months went into the 1948 census; three-and-a-quarter million huts were counted in an area of 640,000 square miles. In many respects it was a great achievement to have carried it out at all. Martin reckoned that the results were accurate within a margin of plus or minus 5 per cent. Despite many problems in taking the census it would probably be safe to assume that a 5 per cent error, probably 5 per cent on the low side, was a reasonable estimate.

The census of 1948 was the beginning of detailed knowledge of the population of East Africa. In Uganda a second major census was taken in 1959 and in Kenya the next full-scale one was in 1962. Both countries carried out third censuses in 1969. With this data it should be possible to say with greater accuracy what has been happening to the population of Kenya and Uganda. We can see straight away, for instance, that both populations have increased rapidly between censuses (see Table 1.2, p20) and we can work out the average annual rates of increases from these figures. However if we want to find out how the increases have come about and why the rates of increase are changing, we need more information than the crude overall population totals can give us. In particular we need to know what proportion of the population are children, adults or old people, and to find this information we obviously need to know people's ages.

The problem facing the census takers in 1948, 1959 and 1962 was that the majority of people did not know exactly how old they were nor even how old their children were. The enumerators were therefore trained to estimate ages by reference to local historical events. This is a difficult task at the best of times. All three censuses relied on the common convention of placing people in age groups. But the groups here had to be fairly broad to take account of the difficulties of determining age. In the 1948 census, for example, children and adults were grouped as 'under one year old', one to five years, six to fifteen and sixteen to forty-six years old. In the 1962 census in Kenya an attempt was made to make the age groups more specific by using five-year periods : one to five, six to ten, eleven to fifteen, and so on.

Even so, problems arose over the accuracy of the age grouping. In the 1962 Kenya census it has been suggested that there were serious distortions in the estimates of the size of the various age groups. The under-fives seem to have been under enumerated; the size of the boy population between the ages of eleven and fifteen years seemed disproportionately large, while the girl population of the same age group seemed to be disproportionately small. There are several good reasons why ages should be misrepresented in this way. First, it is possible that parents might have been reluctant to count their very young children for fear of bad luck. Secondly it was very likely that boys of just sixteen may have been declared younger, in order to avoid their liability to pay tax, while with the girls, the situation was reversed and many fourteen-year-olds were probably declared to be fifteen-plus to make them appear to be of marriageable age. At the other end of the population too there were distortions. It seems that many old people tended to overstate their ages. The results of these distortions had a serious effect on the accuracy possible for any detailed analysis of population growth : they meant that all the statistics on mortality and fertility, with the exception of the crude overall totals, might be wrong. But wrong by how much? The margin of error here was difficult to judge, and attempts to 'correct' the figures could possibly lead to even further distortions.

The results of the 1948 census showed that in Uganda 41 per cent of the population were children below the age of fifteen years, while in Kenya the proportion of children to the total population was 48 per cent. Martin has argued that the Kenya figure is likely to be too high; probably the true figure would be nearer the Uganda percentage. Yet in 1962 the proportion of children under fifteen years in Kenya was around 46 per cent; still a very high figure. As we know that the girls tended to overstate their age and that the boys tended to understate, the overall figure is probably near enough correct. The figure for England and Wales in 1950 for under-fifteens was only 22 per cent of the total population, which gives Kenya a comparatively very high proportion of children.

Not only was the proportion of children in the East African populations very high in comparison with European populations, but birth rates were also of the same high comparative order. In 1948 the Kenya material is too poor to show an accurate birth rate but one demographer, Goldthorpe, did work out from the available data that the rate of births was in the region of 49 to 50 for every thousand people, an unprecedentedly high rate. As the crude birth rate in 1962 was still in the region of 47 to 51 per thousand of the population, when better data was available, the 1948 figures would seem to be correct. In Uganda the overall birth rate in 1948 and in 1959 was 42 births per thousand, rising to 49 by 1969. The overall Uganda figures for 1959 would have been higher but for the exceptionally low birth rate in Buganda Province (30 per thousand). Nonetheless both Kenya and Uganda had comparatively high crude

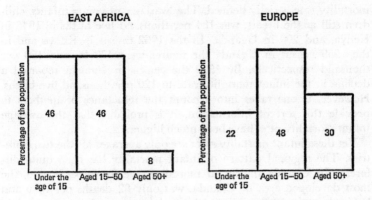

FIG. 1. *Chart illustrating the comparison between European and East African population structures, c. 1970*

birth rates when compared with other areas. In Asia the crude birth rate between 1965 and 1970 was 38 per thousand, while in Europe it was only 18 per thousand of the population.

The fertility rate in both countries was also comparatively extremely high, being well over double the rate for Europe. The fertility rate is the mean number of births to each woman currently in the reproductive period of her life. Censuses for both countries showed that women on average produced five *living* children during their lifetime. Clearly many women produce many more than five surviving children, while others produce fewer or none : the figure is an overall average for women between the ages of say, fifteen and forty-five. Moreover the total fertility rate appears to be increasing. In Uganda it rose to 6·5 in 1959 and 7·1 in 1969. A small proportion of urban-based women would seem to be moving towards family planning but this fact does not appear to have affected the overall picture.

These three factors, the proportion of children in the community, the relatively high birth rate and the high number of births per woman all point to the likelihood of a very high increase in population in the future. Another contributory factor would appear to be the possibility of declines in the infant mortality rate and the crude death rates.

The infant mortality rate is the number of children who die before the age of one year for every thousand children born. As the age statistics for the very young have been poor, the proportion of deaths among 'young infants' provides better statistics than infant mortality rate, strictly defined. The 'wastage' of young infants, children still at the breast, was 184 per thousand live births in 1948 in Kenya, and 200 in Uganda. In the 1962 census in Kenya and in the 1959 census in Uganda the figures were 170–80 and 160 per thousand respectively. By 1969 the census in Uganda reported a decline in the infant mortality rate to 120 per thousand live births. However, if one takes into account the reluctance of mothers to provide this sort of information, it is probable that the average infant mortality rates have been much higher.

Yet these infant mortality rates are only averages for the two countries. The regional pattern of infant mortality has been quite different. In Uganda the infant mortality rate for West Mengo, the most developed area of Uganda, was only 82 deaths per thousand babies born in 1969, while in the outlying areas the rate was close to 200 per thousand. The same wide regional differences were found in Kenya during the 1969 census. The richer the area in which one was born, therefore, the better were one's chances of surviving early infancy. Moreover, as is the case everywhere, girls tended to survive infancy better than boys. The explanation for the regional differences probably lies in (a) the availability of medical services, (b) the educational level of the mothers and (c) the presence of an adequate diet. If we compare the overall infant mortality levels with those of Western Europe, the difference is startling. In Europe in 1970 infant mortality was roughly 20 per thousand. Yet only seventy years ago, in 1900, infant mortality rates in Europe were much the same as those in East Africa today. Then Sweden had a rate of 196, Belgium 153 and Russia 260. Thus although by contemporary standards East Africa appears to have a very high infant mortality rate, it was not long ago that this was a fairly common rate in most areas of the world where statistics were available. We can assume that the infant mortality rate can, therefore, fall very quickly, given improvements in standards of living. Already, if we look back to East Africa in the 1920s, it is possible to argue that infant mortality rates between then and now have fallen dramatically. Estimates in the 1920s were around 500 per thousand live births, and these estimates may not have been inaccurate. Martin worked out from the 1948 statistics that 40 per cent of all children born were dead by the age of fifteen, while in the 1962 census the comparable figure for Kenya was 30 to 32 per cent of the total population.

One of the consequences of the low chances of survival for the very young was that the expectation of life at birth was only 42 years in Uganda in 1959 and 39 years in Kenya in 1962.* One con-

* The difference between the two figures is small enough to be due to statistical error.

clusion is that it would be relatively simple, with improved medical facilities and more extensive education among women, to reduce the chances of death for the very young very rapidly indeed. If this happened the potential rate of increase of the population would rise very quickly.

Finally we need to examine the death rates; the number of people who die each year per thousand of the population. This figure includes the deaths of the very young. Again, it has been difficult to get accurate information in this area as people are reluctant to tell of deaths. In 1948 there were relatively reliable figures for Kenya, but only tentative figures for Uganda. In 1962 the death rate for Kenya was given as between 18 and 24 per thousand of the population; it was probably nearer 24 than 18. Compared with figures for other areas in the world (15 per thousand in Asia and 10 per thousand in Europe), the East African figures appear very high.

More important than the crude, overall death rate is the proportion of old people living in the community : the more old people there are, in proportion to the total population, the lower the adult death rate will be. In 1962 in Kenya only 8 per cent of the population was over fifty years of age. In Uganda in 1959 the comparable percentage was 10. The proportions had hardly changed since the 1948 census. By comparison, 30 per cent of the population was over fifty years of age in England and Wales, and Sweden. Here again the possibilities of lowering the adult death rate through improving medical facilities and standards of living would have a significant effect on the level of population growth.

From this analysis we can conclude that in recent years the East African population has been growing very rapidly. The 1948 census showed Kenya's total population to be 5,407,599; by 1962 the population had grown to 8,365,942; by 1969 it was 10,942,705. In other words, the population had doubled in twenty-one years. It was estimated that the population of Kenya, despite all the possible errors of underenumeration or overenumeration in both the 1948 and the 1962 censuses, has been increasing at a rate of between 2·8 to 3 per cent per annum. It seems clear that since 1948 the rate of increase of the population has been rising extremely fast.

The 1948 census showed a population of 4,960,000 in Uganda; by 1959 the figure had risen to 6,537,000, and by 1969 to 9,526,000. Uganda's population had increased at roughly the same rate as Kenya's, and the rate of increase appears to be rising. Uganda's population had almost doubled in twenty-one years. The figures for both countries are set out below.

TABLE 1.2

Total population of Kenya and Uganda

	Uganda	Kenya
1948	4,960,000	5,407,000
1959	6,537,000	–
1962	–	8,365,000
1969	9,526,000	10,942,000

(Figures corrected to nearest 1000)

If the rate of increase continues at the same pace (the if, of course is always highly problematical in demographic studies) then both Kenya and Uganda will have populations of about 30 millions by about 2009. This could occur, and if it does, it will be in the lifetime of most readers.

Conclusion

In the preceding three sections of this chapter we have examined what has happened to the population of Kenya and Uganda since 1890. Let us now try to answer the more interesting question posed at the end of the first section : how had the changes come about? The short answer is that the factors affecting population growth or decline had changed. First, by the 1930s the major causes of constraint of population growth in the early years of this century (unusually long periods of famine and drought, and some of the newly-introduced diseases) had been brought under control and the exceptionally vicious wars had come to an end. Secondly, factors which precipitate the increase of population have come to the fore. It is probable that death rates, in particular infant mortality rates, have been reduced. Such an assertion cannot be properly proved as we lack adequate statistics for the earlier periods, but from our knowledge of the behaviour of other populations in similar situations where the use of modern medical methods and improvements in living conditions have occurred, this would seem to be a reasonable assumption. Again, although it cannot be absolutely proved, it would seem that more women are surviving the years from 45 to 50, and thus are living right through their reproductive period and as a consequence producing more children. Another factor in the situation is that the tradition of sexual abstinence between married couples whilst a child is at the breast is not practised widely any more. As a result, a married woman may produce many more children, possibly as many as eighteen in her fertile years. Finally, most women seem to marry at about the age of eighteen, which is very young.

Are there any factors which might act as a constraint on future population increases? The age at which men marry may have a marginal effect on population growth rates. The age of marriage was, traditionally, determined by initiation, but this custom, like periodic sexual abstinence, is less widely practised now. Young people therefore have been freed from this constraint.

However other constraints, which affect the men particularly, have come to take its place. Economic constraints on the age of marriage have now come to have a greater significance than they had in the nineteenth century. The means for existence, land or jobs in towns, have now come into short supply in Kenya, while in Uganda jobs are also in short supply. As a consequence it is probable that the age of marriage for men is likely to rise as more young men are unable to find the means to look after wives and families until their middle or late twenties. It could be that as a result of this the child-bearing years of women will be reduced. This reasoning of course depends on the continuation of social sanctions against child-bearing outside marriage. There is some evidence which suggests that these sanctions are becoming less effective and that an increasing number of children are born outside wedlock. If this trend continues then the significance of economic restraints on the age at which men marry will be of limited importance.

Secondly there is some evidence that the provision of education has become a constraining factor on population growth. In some ways the means of obtaining modern education seems to be replacing land as a form of insurance against future uncertainties, and school fees have become a major form of investment for most families. As each member of the family passes from school to job, so a proportion of the resulting income is re-invested in the education of younger members of the family or kin group. Ability to pay school fees, therefore, may come to be a constraint on further births in the family. This has certainly been the case in Europe. As people realised that good education led to better jobs, they saw that it was worthwhile to concentrate the family's resources on a smaller number of children so that more could be spent on the education of each one. As a result, birth rates began to decline.

Finally the use of modern contraceptive methods could cause a rapid reduction of the birth rate. At present there appears to be a widespread aversion to modern contraceptive methods. Possibly this is partly because people are unwilling to limit births while infant mortality rates are high, and only a proportion of their children are likely to survive. Another likely reason for the lack of interest in contraception is that in most East African societies the children belong to the father while it is the mother was must operate most of the modern methods of contraception. If the mother is encouraged to do this, the father loses control over the reproductive ability of his wife; it is often the men who are most against these new methods of population control.

Much of the above argument is speculative, depending on the future interaction of many factors. Will the rate of population growth continue at 3 per cent per annum, or will it decline – or could it increase to an even higher rate? These are vitally important questions, but we will have to wait for the next census to find the answers.

Part Two

PRODUCTION

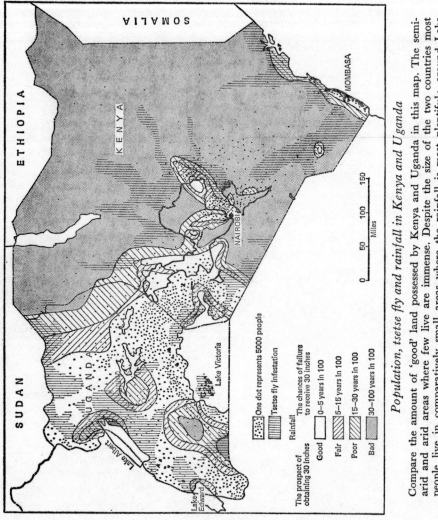

Population, tsetse fly and rainfall in Kenya and Uganda

Compare the amount of 'good' land possessed by Kenya and Uganda in this map. The semi-arid and arid areas where few live are immense. Despite the size of the two countries most people live in comparatively small areas where the rainfall is most plentiful: around Lake Victoria, just north of the lake and in Central Province, Kenya.

The following labels appear on the map:

SUDAN
ETHIOPIA
SOMALIA
KENYA
UGANDA
NAIROBI
MOMBASA
Lake Victoria
Lake Albert
Lake Edward

One dot represents 5000 people

Tsetse fly infestation

Rainfall
The chances of failure to receive 30 inches

The prospect of obtaining 30 inches

Good — 0–5 years in 100
Fair — 5–15 years in 100
Poor — 15–30 years in 100
Bad — 30–100 years in 100

0   50   100   150
Miles

2 Agricultural Change in Kenya and Uganda: A Comparison

We shall begin this chapter with an account of nineteenth-century land use and land tenurial practices. Land *use* covers the ways in which people farm their land, the techniques of digging the ground, the division of labour between men and women and the rotations of crops to ensure the continuing fertility of the land. Land *tenure* defines a person's rights in holding property. Land rights were usually directly related to an individual's connections by kin. The kinship system and the land holding system were closely connected, so that any man's or any woman's right to produce food from the soil was dependent on his relationships with other members of his particular community.

Nineteenth-century land use and land tenure

The three main factors which affected land use in the nineteenth century were (*a*) the abundance of land available, (*b*) the degree of fertility of the land and (*c*) the technology used to farm it. It is very important to note the absence of any land shortage throughout East Africa during this period. This meant that when their land was no longer sufficiently fertile people would move on to other places. The time spent by a group on one piece of land before moving on depended upon the inherent fertility of the soil and the rainfall in the area, which varied very widely. Land was therefore left fallow for varying periods.

The period over which one piece of land was cultivated seems to have ranged from between two and four years to near permanency in cases of exceptional fertility. In Uganda much of the land was used for three or four years and then left fallow for about eight years. In areas where the land was particularly fertile and the rainfall regular population densities may have reached 100 to 150 people, but generally they were considerably lower. Population densities clearly varied widely in nineteenth-century East Africa, although then, as now, high densities were directly related to rainfall.

The people were dependent on the distribution of rainfall as with one or two exceptions, there was no irrigation to increase productivity. The irrigation that did exist was in areas of land shortage, which was rare. Thus the location of good soils and rainfall distribution determined population density and the areas of settlement. Most settlement occurred in regions which received a regular rainfall of around 45 inches per annum. This includes the Highlands of Kenya, the fertile crescent of Uganda on the western shores of Lake Victoria, some sections east of the lake (Western Kenya) and parts of western and central Uganda. We find that in many regions of regular high annual rainfall, where the soil is rich, and in which there has been a long history of dense population, the banana is the staple crop.

The banana plant is perennial and reliably yields large quantities of fruit with little attention or manuring. One third of an acre was sufficient to support an adult. The Chagga of northern Tanzania, the Gishu of Mount Elgon, the Baganda of Uganda have each developed a culture based on banana growing. They have had little need for crop rotation and both in the past and in the present have been able to support large numbers of people without changing their techniques of agriculture.

Throughout East Africa there existed very many different agricultural practices. Old methods of land use from the nineteenth century and earlier were adapted to suit the environment. Agricultural systems were based on intimate knowledge of local rain and soil conditions and on familiarity with the characteristics of indigenous trees, grasses and plants. All this information had been handed down over generations and it is not surprising, therefore, to discover that it was the old men of a clan who would advise as to the rhythm of land use, the times of planting and picking, and who would decide when to move on to another area.

Because land was in principle easily available, it was used extensively and there were few pressures for technical innovation to extract more from the soil. People's rights to land were directly related to its availability, which again was linked to settlement patterns and kinship ties. A man would only become interested in his rights to cultivation once he was married. His wife would then also have a claim on a patch of the land tended by his mother. The man's mother, in her turn, had obtained her rights through marriage. If a woman had a number of sons it would not necessarily lead to a shortage of land as in most predominantly agricultural communities it was common for a man to clear a stretch of unclaimed land for his wife or wives. There was thus a continuous process of movement and splitting of families as young men moved down a ridge or along a plain to open up new areas and establish new households. A man's rights to land for cultivation also depended on his relationship to the founder of the group (who had received the land from *his* mother), or on his establishing his own claim to unused land. Alternatively a man could trade goats for land to give to his wife. A poor man, one without possession of land or goats, might obtain goats in exchange for some other commodity. For instance among the Kikuyu and Kamba the Magadi salt trade was regarded as a poor man's business. The goats obtained in exchange for salt could then be swapped for land in the usual way.

One of the few investigations into migration, settlement and land holdings was undertaken by Dr Muriuki who took the Kikuyu as the subject of his research. Dr Muriuki found that there was a tradition for individual pioneers to strike out on their own along the ridges. Anyone who cut down virgin forest could claim ownership of the land, *kuna*. Initially this land was used by the individual or by small groups of pioneers and the boundaries were extended over time as the population expanded. All persons directly related to the first pioneer or pioneers had more or less equal rights within this area, until another individual or group again decided to split off.

In the southern areas of Kikuyu land, migration and settlement traditions were similar in principle to those in other regions. The Kabete area was considered one of opportunity but a number of Athi, a hunter-gatherer people, had arrived here before the Kikuyu. Land transactions in this particular case, then, depended on Kikuyu and Athi friendship, peaceful settlement and intermarriage.

In the north, early claims depended upon extensive clearance of the forest as quickly as possible. A pioneer needed the assistance of others for this task and invariably, to obtain labourers, he needed stock. To obtain animals, sheep and goats, he had to enter into trade which was mainly with the Maasai in this period. This was the method followed by any ambitious man.

It is hard to ascertain whether the same principles of land rights by clearance, integration and, by implication, conquest, held for all peoples of East Africa. Certainly the Luo and the Logoli recognised ownership claims to newly-cleared land. Whisson has said of the Luo :

Friends and close relations would cultivate together in strips down the slope towards the stream . . . When a plot was exhausted, the group might move further up the valley along the ridge and dig another piece. In this way one woman might dig several strips in different places during her stay in one home, strips over which her sons alone would have rights of ownership, and her daughter-in-law of cultivation. As the group expanded, a part might hive off and go to build new homes, even further up the valley or elsewhere, leaving their old homes occupied by the old people.

In a situation of land surplus, the character of a clan member's rights to land were determined largely by the methods used to open up new tracts. In a real sense this system allocated land to clan members, either within existing farming areas or outside it. Among the centralised interlacustrine groups however the power of allocation of land and wealth was attached to political office. Political office was a result of the king's patronage (the Kabaka for Buganda, Omugabe for Ankole. Omukama for Toro and Bunyoro). In much the same way any man could attach himself as a *client* to a holder of political office or to a chief. The officer or chief acting as a patron would distribute the land rights which he had himself received from the king. In return his clients would fight on his behalf, provide him with labour, pay him tribute and generally support him politically. If clients became dissatisfied with their patron they could move on and find another. This flexible process did not apply to the Hutu of Rwanda, who were not permitted to leave their patron and were therefore bound tightly to him.

The means of obtaining new land clearly differed between centralised and acephalous communities, although there were smaller variations within each of the two types of societies. In centralised communities, the origin of clan rights to land stemmed in the majority of cases from the original grant of land given by the king. These allocations could be ten or so generations old, originating from the last royal grant to that family.

There was one great similarity between all groups, namely that every single individual could expect to have some right to occupation and use of land. A person's right stemmed either from his position as a member of a kinship group or from his entrepreneurial abilities. Only in the extreme circumstance of a total outcast might all land rights be lost, but even a man in such a position could attach himself to other people further away. By tradition everyone had a right to land.

Every large agricultural group had their rules governing (*a*) forms of ownership of land, which were normally associated with close kinship to the founder who first claimed the area for cultivation, (*b*) distribution of land to wives, sons and daughters and (*c*) distribution to friends and outsiders who wished to cultivate a plot for a limited period. These rules were very varied and it would be premature at this stage to try to find patterns common to all groups. Nonetheless there are certain widely-employed practices that can be picked out.

For example, land distribution *within* clans seems to have been subject to relatively equal division so that all sons could expect an equal share of part of their mothers' property.

Another common practice was to allow acquaintances to look after a piece of land for a while in return for a fee of goats or food. The plot could be redeemed by the clan elders by repayment of the original fee. The principles of equal division of inheritance and redeemability have become important in the twentieth century when land is in short supply.

The colonial intrusion

The impact of the colonisers on existing agricultural systems varied widely between and within territories. Essentially the colonising powers introduced two basic innovations to Kenya and Uganda,

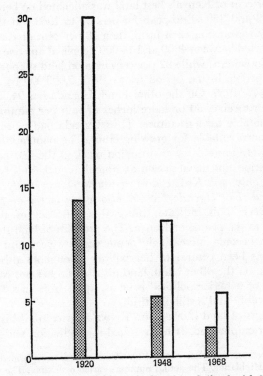

FIG. 2·1 *Comparisons of available agricultural land (land with 30" rain per annum) per head of the population, in acres.*

(*a*) cash crops and (*b*) new concepts of land tenure. Up to 1950 both these ideas had been introduced into limited geographical areas only, the so-called 'White Highlands' of Kenya and the Buganda and Eastern Provinces of Uganda. For the first fifty years or so of colonial rule the main economic changes and developments were confined to these areas. Developments therefore occurred in a limited enclave in both Kenya and Uganda.

Here the similarity between Kenya and Uganda ends. The advent of colonialism in East Africa and the establishment of the White Highlands in Kenya and the Buganda Agreement in Uganda had very different consequences on land use and tenurial practices in each territory. In Kenya 12,200 square miles or 5·5 per cent of the total land area was alienated. Of this land about 7560 square miles receives 30 inches of rainfall per year, making it suitable for crops rather than cattle ranching. But these figures can be misleading. Only 41,630 square miles in all of Kenya has over 30 inches of rainfall and is suitable for agricultural production, which means that 18 per cent of Kenya's best land was alienated on behalf of between 1000 and 3500 European farmers up to 1963.* If there were say four Europeans on each farm, then 18 per cent of Kenya's best land supported between 4000 and 14,000 people at any one time during the colonial era; while 82 per cent of good land supported about 2,000,000 people in the period up to 1940, 5,000,000 by 1948 and 10,000,000 by 1969. On the other hand, Uganda has 94,000 square miles which receives 30 or more inches of rain per annum, most of which is suitable for agriculture. Thus Uganda had twice as much land as Kenya suitable for growing crops. The populations of both countries were around the two million mark in the first part of the colonial period and have grown at roughly equal rates since then. *Thus not only did Kenya start out with considerably less high quality land than Uganda but she also lost a larger proportion to the colonisers.* This indicates the real significance of the White Highlands to the people of Kenya. The problem of land shortage in Kenya has become increasingly acute year by year and the land question has been central to her politics throughout this century. In Uganda, on the other hand, land distribution has not yet become a problem or a major political issue as, apart from in a few areas, good, cultivable land is still plentiful.

The effects of land shortage on Kenya's agricultural history cannot be over-emphasised. It has resulted in subdivision and fragmen-

* It is worth noting that about 100,000 or so squatters farmed alienated land in the Highlands. The actual numbers varied over time. The point here is that the squatters had no legal rights to this land and were pushed off during the 1940s and 1950s.

tation of holdings into smaller and smaller areas. It has created 'squatters', people who, pushed out of the traditional areas, have moved on to the big estates where they eke out a living by farming scraps of land to which they have no legal rights. It has led to periodic political crises of which the Mau Mau 'Emergency' has been the most intense so far. Every major report on Kenya since the mid-1920s up to the present has been concerned with these problems.

Yet Uganda has had no such difficulties and, therefore, despite the similarity in origin of the enclave development, Kenya and Uganda will be discussed separately in the following two chapters.

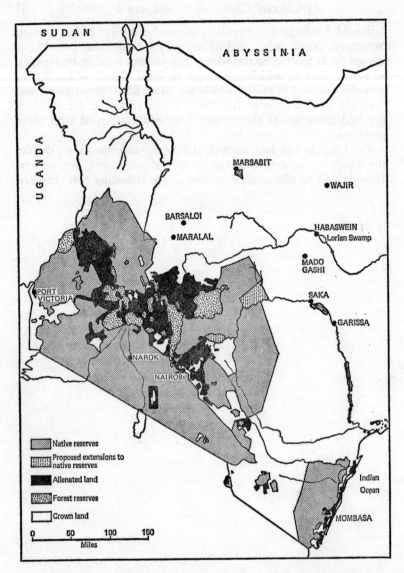

Map showing African Reserves and White Highlands in 1933

This map illustrates the boundaries between African and European reserved land at the time of the Carter Commission; it also shows how the Commission was proposing to solve the 'land problem' at this time by small extensions to the African Area. The map also shows the then Forest Reserves, which are now much depleted. As the demand for land and charcoal has grown in recent years so the forests have been cut back. This process would appear to reduce the rainfall in surrounding areas.

3 Agriculture in Kenya: Large- versus Small-Scale Farming

Large-scale farming and structural change

Before we embark on a chronological account of the changes and developments in Kenya's agriculture it would be helpful to look at the structural changes brought about by the setting up of large-scale agricultural estates by European settlers. The history of development or lack of development in the rural areas of Kenya has been largely determined by the imposition of this type of farming on the country. Did the kind of agriculture brought by the settlers lead to development? The following sections will show that after forty difficult years it brought about prosperity within the European-settled areas, but that it was directly responsible for (a) holding back agricultural development in other areas, (b) the political explosion in the 1950s, (c) creating the 'peasant capitalist' from the late 1950s and finally (d) the gross underdevelopment in the areas of the nomadic pastoralists.

First let us examine the reasons why this large-scale farming was able to succeed. Up to the mid-1950s the settlers' success was undoubtedly at the expense of the African farmers. A large proportion of the land and labour force, capital, administration, communications and marketing were directed by the colonial authorities with a favourable bias towards the settler section of production. The mechanics of this channeling of resources will be discussed in other chapters.

Initially and up to the mid-1950s the settler and peasant producers were in competition for the above resources. It was essentially a competition between a few large estates and very many small peasant plots to see which could produce the most cheaply. In principle the 'winner' would price the 'loser' out of the market. The first fifty years of colonial rule in Kenya was a period in which the new settlers struggled to dominate the peasantry politically in order to derive the greatest benefit from the country's resources. The settlers used the idea of racial superiority to justify their position of economic and political dominance. The consequences of this policy and the reactions of Kenyan farmers will be discussed in the following sections of this chapter.

The effects of settler agriculture on African traditions of land tenure and use will be examined now.

1. Land regulations

The first land regulation in Kenya which permitted Europeans to be issued with a twenty-one year, renewable land certificate was passed in 1897. Five years later in 1902 the first Crown Lands Ordinance allowed the Colonial authority to issue settlers with ninety-nine year leases on land which had been designated as Crown Land; in 1915 the length of such leases was extended to 999 years. The area which came to be known as the White Highlands had no legal demarcation until 1939 but in practice land in this area could not be purchased by non-Europeans. The Imperial authorities provided the settlers with constant verbal assurances of this.

The restriction of the indigenous peoples to 'Reserves' was not made law until 1926. Until then, African rights under Kenya's colonial law were defined by occupation, cultivation and grazing, so that only when land was left unused did it become Crown Land. The demarcation of 'Native Reserves' was strongly recommended in 1909 but little was done except in the Maasai areas. The land, to use the legal jargon of the time, was 'reserved for the use of the native tribes in the Crown' – the people of Kenya were tenants of the English Crown.

By 1939 all land in Kenya could be categorised as follows :

i. Native Reserves, where particular tribes has exclusive rights;
ii. The Highlands, protected and controlled by the Highlands Board for the exclusive use of Europeans;
iii. The Northern Frontier and Turkana district.

The 1939 statute was intended to be final. Within each area, land was supposed to be divided according to the tenurial customs of the group to which it had been allocated. Europeans could practise their system of freeholds and leaseholds, while the Africans could continue in their traditional ways.

Yet the marking out of distinct regions for Europeans and Africans undermined the foundation of the old systems in Kenya. This process has been well expressed by Dr Allan :

> One of the first effects of the division of Africa among the European administering and colonising powers was to solidify the population–land patterns which had previously been, to a con-

siderable extent, fluid. When a community increased until the numbers on the land it occupied exceeded the critical level for the system of land use, sections hived off and settled elsewhere, or the land area was increased by occupation of unclaimed tracts, or by peaceful agreement . . . or by aggressive expansion. Natural checks, warfare, and customs limiting fertility, probably restricted the general rate of population increase to a relatively low level and as communities waxed and waned there was a continuous rough and ready adjustment between population and land. The peace of the suzerain powers disrupted this mechanism of adjustment.*

2. *Effects of the regulations*

Despite the important implications of the Reserve boundaries, people continued to base their land use and tenurial practices on the old pattern, that is, until their land area became too small for their needs. It should be noted that land shortage can have different meanings to different people. In the sense used here, short supply means that an individual or clan became conscious that land was not available for expansion as it had been previously. The Reserve boundaries stopped all migratory movement which had occurred in pre-colonial Kenya and set up some new ones. For instance, the Kikuyu were halted in their southward movement, and because some of the earliest land alienation occurred on land to which they considered they had a right, they rapidly became fearful of the '*ahoi*'. The *ahoi* are people with traditional rights of occupation of land according to relationships of friendship rather than blood ties. The Kabete Kikuyu wanted to throw out their *ahoi* tenants once it was realised that land was in short supply, thus applying the traditional 'redemption' practices to the new situation. The southern section of the Kikuyu were the first of the agricultural peoples to experience in an acute form the impact of land alienation and of Reserve boundaries. Consequently, by 1914, the pressure for removal of the *ahoi*, the introduction of land sale and purchase for cash meant that the old system of land tenure came under direct attack from within traditional society.

The southern Kikuyu were the first of many groups of people to feel the effects of population growth and shortage of land. The old method of opening up new areas for cultivation had been stopped. In some parts of Kenya it was declared illegal to cut down forest or to move across a so-called tribal boundary. The amount of population growth varied widely from group to group but the common

* W. Allan, *The African Husbandman*, p. 335.

solution to the pressures of land shortage was to farm the existing
tracts more intensively. The period of crop and land rotation became shorter, plots were divided into smaller and smaller fragments
in an attempt to adhere to the traditions. As a result conflict over
rights intensified. This in turn led to the institutionalisation of the
concept of clan land. In the past the clan system of cultivation
rights had been a flexible one whereby land claims had been regulated by kinship ties and unused land could be taken over. But once
the harsh realities of boundary restrictions were experienced, competition for land rights petrified tradition. Young men could no
longer set out as pioneers to farm new acres and there was strife
within families over inheritance. The fact that a man's two sons
by different wives each had claim on part of his mother's land and
then a claim on some of both women's land via the father further
complicated matters.

Under these conditions of pressure the principle of redeemability
of land came to be used very frequently but in a distorted way. It
was used to displace those who were cultivating land they had
cleared for themselves and those who had purchased their plots
with goats. In Central Province some farmers had been trying to
obtain title deeds to land from the 1920s and there had been
attempts at consolidation since the 1930s. In order to consolidate
adjacent plots had first to be redeemed. A large tract of land thus
formed could then be sold for cash.

All over Kenya throughout the colonial period there emerged a
consciousness of the need to prevent the encroachment of the white
man. Awareness of the importance of an individual's particular
piece of land was more intense than ever before. As one Mtiva,
summing up the situation in 1935 for the Logoli, who had begun to
feel the cramp of land shortage by that time, explained :

> Long ago there were no clan lands in the sense of a continuous
> territory marked off by a boundary from the territories of neigh-
> bouring clans. Each clan consisted of a number of *amadala* (vil-
> lages occupied by one lineage or 'house') with their respective
> cultivation strips near them. People of any clan, so long as they
> were Logoli, could settle as near to those *amadala* as they pleased.
> Only when the land began to be filled with people, the clan
> elders began to set aside bush land to be used by their children.
> The lands thus marked off were called *skivala kyavayanga*, the
> land of the young . . . *

The safeguards of the traditional land-tenure system were severely
diminished under the colonial regime. Under the new system of

* G. Wagner, *The Bantu of Western Kenya,* vol. II, p 88.

Reserves the people's feelings of security were undermined by fear of alienation. This insecurity was exacerbated when those with superior claims to land as defined by the old tenurial system tried to assert their rights, forcing others to move off. By the early 1920s sections of the Akamba, Nandi, Kipsigis, Elgeyo and Abaluyha, as well as the Kikuyu, had begun to feel the pressures mounting.

1903–1940

1. European farming

i. 1903–14: Land speculation. By 1903 British Imperial authority had been established and the railway had been built, but the form that economic change would take was still not determined. Two possible schemes were suggested, either that the area should be developed by the peasants or that Indian, Jewish or European immigration should be encouraged. Both schemes seem to have been seriously considered.

The eventual success of white settlement occurred by default rather than by plan. Originally, it was the Governor, Sir Charles Eliot (governing from 1901 to 1905), and Lord Delamere who stimulated white settlement by their own personal drive. Eliot acted as an immigration agent and attempted to divert potential settlers for Australia and Canada towards Kenya. The colonial authorities in London were not happy at all with the enthusiasm shown by Eliot as he set out to encourage settlement by making available large grants of land. In 1905 he lost his governorship because of lack of support from the imperial London authorities. The big question was how much land should be made available to any individual settler and on what terms (length of lease, etc.). The London officials hoped to prevent land speculation such as had been experienced in other areas of white settlement, but failed to do so. In the first decade of this century there was a great deal of argument, between London on one side and the officials on the spot on the other. By 1915 it was the settlers who won all the points; large concessions of high-quality land on 999-year leases with little obligation to the colonial authorities to develop the land had been made.

By 1915, 8242 square miles of land had been alienated on behalf of about one thousand white settlers, but it was very unevenly divided; 20 per cent was held by five individuals or groups, Delamere, the two Coles, Grogan and the East African Syndicate. In other words, thirteen individuals or groups had control of 894,434 acres of land out of a total of 4,500,000 acres granted to settlers. Such excessive grants had been obtained by dummying in order to cheat the Imperial officials. Dummying meant simply applying for land grants in the name of wives, friends or others.

The consequence of allowing a small number of wealthy Englishmen to obtain enormous tracts of land was to encourage speculators rather than the small planter. The holders of these huge tracts held on to their acres for a while, then sold them off in small parcels. It was these capitalist speculators who obtained access to the Legislative and Executive Council and it was, therefore, this same group of men who were later responsible for the consistent political pressures to encourage white settlement in Kenya in order to bring in customers to purchase land. It was also these men who in the 1940s managed to persuade the colonial government to buy land from them and so make it available to a further influx of settlers.

The land speculators were able to gain substantially from settlers arriving during the pre-1914 period. Land values in the Rift Valley rose from 6d * an acre in 1908 to 240d or £1 an acre by 1914. At the turn of the year 1912, new settlers were forced to buy land from existing holders as there was nothing further available for alienation.

Delamere and Cole, with the backing of the Governor Girouard and in defiance of the London officials, were responsible for the tragedy of the Maasai moves in 1904 and 1910–11. This incident was one of the deceptions instigated by the settlers and colonial authority, which meant the opening up of the Rift Valley, the 'strategic key to the highlands', for the white settlers.

In short there was a firm division of Kenya into European regions and regions for the various ethnic groups, as occurred in South Africa.

ii. 1918–40: The establishment of export crops. The first period of colonial rule had not only seen the success of the settlers in obtaining land, but also their successful efforts to establish crops which could be exported. At first the settlers concentrated on products with which they were familiar, wheat, wool, meat and dairy products. But by 1914 it was apparent that these had failed as exportable commodities. On the other hand, sisal and coffee in Kenya and cotton in Uganda were much more successful and even by 1914 the export market for them was growing. Coffee had become the premier export to Europe. These crops would be the ones with which the settlers would establish a sound economy for themselves.

Immediately after the First World War a special scheme was

---

* British currency before decimalisation.

devised to attract new, 'ex-soldier settlers'. The scheme was a partial failure as many of the incoming farmers were allocated land that had not been surveyed and was either infertile or lacking in water. Nevertheless there was a steady stream of new settlers during the 1920s and by 1930 there were over two thousand white farmers in the Kenya Highlands.

With the exception of the years 1919 and 1920, the twenties were a time of prosperity for the white farmers. Prices of the major export products, coffee, sisal and maize, were rising. Yet despite the inflow of more settlers and the price increases, the problems of the small farmers, who made up the majority of the settlers, remained unsolved. By 1930 almost one thousand settlers, or half of the total number, were dependent on maize. In the 1930s when export prices dropped drastically most of these small-scale farmers incurred heavy debts to the banks.

The problems of the small and inefficient farms were the direct results of the speculation of earlier years. The vast majority of the two thousand or so white farmers were badly hit during the slump in world prices in the 1930s. Twenty per cent or about four hundred of these farmers gave up altogether and abandoned their farms. The entire structure of white farming very nearly collapsed during this period. But for aid amounting to nearly £1,000,000 which was pumped into white agriculture through the agencies of the colonial government, it is quite probable that white settlement would not have survived.

2. *African farming, 1903–40: Cash crops and land shortage*

It was precisely because the European farmers were in such straits that very nearly all the financial resources of the government went towards supporting them, rather than towards helping African farmers to develop export crops. Up to 1940, with only a few exceptions, government services and overseas loans were directed towards the settlers. These exceptional cases were as follows :

(a) The support given by Ainsworth, the Nyanza Provincial Commissioner, to peasant farming between 1908 (roughly) and 1914;
(b) colonial government support of African-directed extension services for a short period, 1920–3;
(c) similar support to that mentioned in (b) from 1931 to 1934;
(d) free distribution of maize seed in most agricultural areas;
(e) government support of cotton growing in selected areas.

Other than these there was virtually no support and certainly, by 1940, no concerted efforts to encourage the Kenyan peasantry to grow cash crops for export.

In practice the opposite occurred. There was persistent discrimination against Africans who tried to grow such cash crops. That African farmers were prevented from planting coffee is well known, but the same was true of pyrethrum. All producers had to obtain a licence to plant these two crops and the government simply refused to grant licences to African growers. There was considerable political controversy over the refusal of coffee licences and, therefore, in 1934 licences were offered to a very small number of growers in the Meru and Kisii areas. This had little effect as Africans were afraid that the Europeans would alienate their land if they planted coffee.

There was also little opportunity for Africans to grow sisal, tea, wheat or sugar. In these cases expensive machinery was required for processing or growing which could only be afforded by large companies. The only export crops to be grown in any quantity by African producers were cotton and wattle bark (used in tanning leather). Both these offered low cash returns and Europeans did not think them worth their while. Cotton was labour-intensive and fetched very low prices indeed. Even in the 1930s when prices rose, cotton production was not as popular in Kenya as it was in Uganda. Only wattle trees were grown in any quantity, mainly in Central Province, and many peasant producers amassed considerable wealth from this.

Up to 1940 colonial government policy towards African producers was based on the following principles :

(a) that there should be no opportunity for competition between African and European producers;
(b) that efforts should be made to increase food crops as an anti-famine measure and that crop surpluses could be sold on the domestic market;
(c) that demonstration plots should be set up to teach African farmers how to grow new crops;
(d) that seed produced by the demonstration plots should be given out free of charge to Africans.

The impact of these policies was slight and despite them many Africans were able to produce cash crops. The settler farms and the building of towns, particularly Nairobi, led to the growth of a domestic market for foodstuffs. Maize was the major crop with a demand from both settler farms and Nairobi. European vegetables such as beans and potatoes and also fruit were marketable.

Two important groups of people who found an outlet for their crops during the first forty years of colonial rule were the Machakos Kamba and the Kipsigis. Both had had a high proportion of their good land alienated and by the mid-1920s suffered from a shortage of pastoral land. However, in both cases, the land they had left was very good indeed. They responded to this situation by producing cash crops. The Machakos Kamba sold, for example, maize and chickens to Nairobi and the Kipsigis sold maize to the tea-growing district of Kericho. Meanwhile they sent their cattle to graze on land adjacent to European farms, thus becoming 'squatters'.

It was probably the shortage of land that stimulated this response and there appears to be a direct relationship between lack of pasture land and production of cash crops while sending cattle elsewhere to graze.

It is interesting that it was not until the middle of the 1920s that the Kamba and Kipsigis started growing cash crops for the domestic market. This was no doubt due to initial unwillingness to change their predominantly pastoral and very self-sufficient economies. The Gusii, Abaluyha and Kikuyu had responded much more rapidly to the opportunities offered by the internal market. They were producing crops for sale well before 1914. The Gusii even transported their crops to Homa Bay, via the lake, to Kisumu in order to find a market for them.

The efforts of the Gusii dwindled during the 1920s and 1930s because they received so little government help, but the Abaluyha and Kikuyu continued to produce very large quantities of maize and other crops for the domestic market. The exact quantities involved are impossible to estimate as there were no central controls of this market, but by 1936 South Kitosh alone was selling over 3000 tons of maize.

The government almost entirely ignored these developments, so the people themselves provided transport and traders to take the goods to the market places. Pack horses, donkeys and cart-owner associations and a large number of traders' groups sprang up everywhere. It is clear from the writing of contemporaries that there was a thriving peasant commercial activity based upon the internal market.

In north Nyanza and Central Province there is considerable evidence that there was land shortage, particularly pasture, and that people moved off to find land elsewhere. The Logoli from Maragoli took their herds into central Nyanza where pasture was still available. From the end of 1908 Kikuyu from all regions seem to have moved onto the European farms. Areas like Dagoretti, Limuru and Kiambu were most acutely affected by the European settlers, with alienation of 60,000 acres. Many of the *ahoi* were thus pushed out and they moved into areas adjoining white farms and into the Rift Valley.

c

3. Squatters

At this time the European farmers welcomed the movement of Kikuyu, Kamba and Kipsigis on to their farms. These people were looking for land and the European farmers were looking for cheap labour. Many white farmers, although they had land, lacked capital and could not afford to pay wages to European workers. Therefore, they permitted the migrants to settle on their land in exchange for labour.

In 1918 the colonial government attempted to regulate this arrangement between white farmers and displaced African peasants. The Africans were given the description of 'resident labourers', which in practice meant little, and a law was passed to the effect that a resident labourer had to work for a minimum of 180 days a year for an employer in exchange for a plot of land and a small wage.

The regulations were not very effective. Many white farmers with land to spare did not offer any cash payment at all to such labourers; instead the farmer often extracted a 'rent' from these people in the form of milk, manure or even animals.

The above situation was entirely unsatisfactory because there was no protection of squatter rights and because the squatters soon discovered that they had no security of tenure. What happened subsequently was that by 1922 or 1923 European cattle-owners began complaining that the squatters' animals were bringing tick-borne and other diseases into the white areas. This allegation was probably well founded. Therefore, white cattle-owners wanted to get rid of the squatters and their cattle, but the crop-growers wanted to retain their source of cheap labour. Argument between the two factions continued throughout the 1920s and into the 1930s when there was a decisive move to introduce mixed farming into the Highlands. In the mid-1930s some of the squatters were rounded up by the army and police and moved back into the Reserves. In 1939, a new Resident Labourers' Ordinance was passed empowering the army and police to do this whenever required. Unfortunately many, if not most, of the squatters had left their Reserves because they were overcrowded. When they were forcibly returned they found that because they had, in a way, left to clear 'new' land, they had, by custom, lost any rights they might have had to land in the 'old' territory. But by the late 1920s and early 1930s the extension of boundaries in the traditional sense had ceased to have any meaning. The setting up of Reserves had fixed the boundaries once and for all, and all groups had no option but to conform to colonial policy.

Exactly how many squatters were removed from European areas

in this period is hard to estimate. There had been roughly 100,000 squatters in the 1920s but by 1945 the number had doubled. There is no doubt that these forced movements created great consternation among all those involved, and it is likely that further research will prove that the backbone of the Mau Mau forest fighters came from amongst the displaced squatters. Up to the present this must remain uncertain.

4. *The political response*

Throughout the 1920s and 1930s the more wealthy and successful Kikuyu, Luo and Abaluyha demanded guaranteed land titles. All the African political organisations were persistent in their complaints about the insecurity of land tenure. In all public reports in which the people had the opportunity to voice their opinions, their feelings on this particular subject were strong. It was also quite clear from the numerous reports and inquiries initiated by the Government that it too was worried about the land situation. By far the most important of all reports and commissions of inquiry was the Land Commission of 1934. The resulting report with its four supplementary volumes of evidence took up five thousand pages of print. The Commission had been set up with the intention of solving the Kenya land problem for all time. The land claims and forms of tenure of all the 'tribes' of Kenya were investigated and the Commission was expected to estimate the land requirements of every tribe for the present and the foreseeable future. In other words both historical land rights and future land needs were investigated and various recommendations were made.

There were two fundamental contradictions inherent in the terms of reference of the Commission which doomed its recommendations to failure. First, the Commission approached African rights and requirements on a tribal basis. African 'tribes' in Kenya had never had any land rights as such but only members of a single clan could claim land as a group. Hence when the Commission recommended making limited extensions to the boundaries of Reserves, assigning each Reserve to a tribal unit, the people involved refused to accept the offer. Second, the Commission was asked to define the boundaries of the White Highlands in order to provide security for the Europeans. The Commission never called into question the division of territory by race and by tribe and it was this type of division that was the cause of many of the land problems. It is obvious, then, that the Commission could not possibly produce any satisfactory, lasting solutions.

1940–1960

1. European farming

i. 1940–45: Development. The Second World War created conditions favourable to modernisation of the settler agriculture in Kenya. Up to 1940 the settlers had farmed inefficiently in that they lacked the technology fully to utilise the land they had colonised. Only about a third of the potentially productive area occupied by white settlers was under cultivation of some kind by 1940. This inefficiency was mainly due to lack of cash or credit facilities, while the settlers' poor credit-worthiness was largely due to their vulnerability to oscillations in world prices. In summary, weaknesses in the settler farming system up to 1940 had been technical – lack of machinery; financial – short-term, high interest rate credits were all that were available to them: and commercial – they could have little control over world prices.

The coming of the Second World War provided the Europeans in Kenya with the means to mechanise their farming. The United States had provided Britain and her colonies with credit for the period of the war for essential wartime needs by the Land-Lease Agreement. The Kenya colonial government used the Agreement to increase her purchases of farm machinery tenfold, and mechanisation of European farming began in a serious fashion from 1941. By 1960 very few oxen were in use in the Highland fields as mechanised ploughing was now widespread.

As to finance, the colonial government took over the job of offering credit to farmers. Government credits were part of a general deal with white farmers. Production committees were set up in each district under the Board of Agriculture. The Board directed the committees as to the quantity and type of farm produce required as contribution to the war effort and the committees in turn directed the farmers as to how much of which crops to grow. The colonial government offered the necessary loans in order that their requirements could be fulfilled. Thus the commercial banks ceased to be important in the financing of European agriculture.

Finally, as discussed in detail in the chapter on marketing, the government offered white farmers fixed prices for bulk purchase of their crops. The farmers were, therefore, assured of both profits and sales. In short, under wartime conditions, the colonial government set about ensuring that the insecurities of large-scale farming were removed and that technical efficiency was vastly improved. The availability of capital, artificial fertilisers and mechanisation together with assured prices and markets prompted the rapid advances made by European agriculture in Kenya between 1945 and 1960.

This support for settler agriculture during the war prevented African agriculture from competing against the European in terms of efficiency. In a sense, any system of agriculture can be shown to be superior to another if the first system is highly privileged and receives financial and technical support, while the second is denied these benefits. This describes the Kenyan situation in 1945. European agriculture had received generous aid, while African agriculture had been denied even access to the markets in coffee, pyrethrum, stock and tea, and had received little or no financial or technical help in its permitted markets. Under these circumstances it was inevitable that sooner or later European agriculture would show itself to be superior.

ii. 1945–60: Growth. The years between 1945 and 1960 were times of rapid expansion for European agriculture. As after the 1914–18 war, so also after the 1939–45 war more white farmers were sought for settlement in the Kenya Highlands. An Agricultural Settlement Board was established in 1946 with a loan of £1½ million from London and was responsible for encouraging the new settlers. The Board even arranged special courses for the new farmers at Egerton College to teach them local agricultural conditions, etc. Nearly all the Crown land had already been sold to earlier settlers. The Settlement Board bought up the remainder and a great deal of the unused land on the large estates. Those land holders who had obtained enormous tracts of land in the pre-1914 period now sold their surplus acres to the Board. In this way government credits were used to pay for uncultivated land which had originally been purchased for speculation. The success of the Settlement Board can be gauged by the increase in the number of settler farmers from 1700 in 1938–9 to 3600 by 1960.

At the same time the wartime policies of market stabilisation, controlled prices, local production committees and government credits were continued into the post-war era. Every aspect of European farming came under strict central control and as a result both the quantity and the quality of produce rose steadily.

For example, between 1940 and 1960, the number of heads of cattle increased three hundred per cent, the number of sheep nearly doubled, while ox-drawn ploughs were replaced by tractors. The average yield of milk per cow per year increased from 214 to 238 gallons. The quantity of fertiliser used rose twenty-five times over. L. H. Brown has estimated that the Europeans spent something in the region of £46,000,000 in capital investment on the farms between 1945 and 1960. The money was spent on roads, dams, buildings, fencing, machinery and vehicles.

Yet despite these widespread improvements in technology and output, yields per acre of maize, wheat and barley hardly rose at all between the end of the war and 1960. Coffee was the one exception and yield per acre more than doubled. It seems that any increases in production during the period arose in the main from an increase in total area under cultivation, rather than from the greater productivity which one might have expected as a result of the improved farming methods.

TABLE 3.1

Increase in production on non-African farms

	1945	1959/60
		'000 tons
Wheat	54·0	126·7
Maize	76·3	95.6
Total grains	135·3	252·7
Sugar	8·2	33·5
Coffee	6·3	17·9
Sisal	31·7	60·7
Milk (millions of gallons) 1949–50)	19·7	57·6
Meat	33,114·0	130,800·0

Source: L. H. Brown, *Agricultural Change in Kenya 1945–1960* (Stanford University, 1968), p. 61.

2. *African farming*

Despite the concentration on the modernisation of European farming and the large sums of cash pumped into it, African agriculture was not entirely ignored. For the first time since colonisation, a coherent, long-term, planned policy of assistance was undertaken.

There were two important factors behind this. The first was that the White Highland farmers became efficient enough to withstand competition from peasant agriculture. The second factor was that the contradictions which had arisen from the attempts to establish white agriculture in the Highlands* forced the colonial government, in the mid-1950s, to alter their discriminatory strategy radically and support African peasants in competition with European large-scale farming.

* We refer here to land shortages, lack of government support and the gross discrimination over the growing of cash crops.

The circumstances leading to government support of African agriculture will now be examined.

The 1940s. By the end of the war in 1945, the land problem of the 1930s was still unsolved. Colonial officials saw the cause as being pressure of population and stock on the land with soil erosion as a result. The 1951 report on agricultural policy stated : 'Our first aim must be to prevent further deterioration of the land,' and 'Immediate and vigorous execution of projects for the conservation of the soil and the preservation of water supplies' had to be undertaken.*

In order to solve these problems a ten-year plan, known as the Worthington Plan, was drawn up in 1946. Over the ten years £11 million was to be spent on the agricultural sector for prevention of soil erosion and over half the sum was to be spent on African land under the African Land Development Programme, known as ALDEV.

European attitudes and prejudices of the 1940s actually determined to what use these funds were put. It might be noted that much of the hatred for colonialism stems from the type of arrogance which is expressed in the following quotation :

> The African in Kenya has not yet arrived at the level of education which enables him, of his own accord, to plan his agricultural economy successfully. He has little knowledge of farming practices . . . no means of gauging the effects of external factors on this economy. In his case, therefore, it is essential that his general farming policy shall, to a large extent, be dictated to him in the light of the experience and knowledge of officers of Government responsible for his welfare . . .†

Such attitudes were widely held among colonial officials after 1945 and implied that only Europeans were able to understand properly and, therefore, find a solution to African land problems. The money made available through ALDEV was spent in accordance with European convictions on what should be done to save African agriculture from further deterioration. The resulting policies were :

(*a*) African peasants must not be encouraged to become capitalists, i.e. to maximise their profits, for if they did they would use their land badly and further soil erosion would occur;

(*b*) subsistence agriculture should have priority over the growing of

* Quoted from A. Ruthenberg, *African Agricultural Production*, p. 6.
† L. H. Brown, op. cit.

cash crops, as in the 1939 period, and only surpluses should be sold;

(c) traditional forms of economic co-operation should be maintained.

These policies meant the denial of land to Africans as private property and prevented cultivation of the more valuable export crops, which were the basis of European land and crop development. The result of these directives was that government attempted 'planned' group farming, in chosen districts in Nyanza from 1948 to 1952. Tsetse fly infected land was cleared and further land was made available for settlement of Africans on the principles outlined in the 1934 Carter Commission. Lastly, existing farms were improved by terracing, planting of grass, setting up of grazing enclosures and building up of river banks against erosion.

The planned group farming schemes petered out within a couple of years. Such developmental ideas as the group farming schemes, whereby the existing, old social structures were adapted to new ends, seem to have failed because the initiative came from the colonial government, an alien and distrusted government. It is not surprising that they failed.

The settlement schemes were mainly on land which had been allocated to the African Reserves by the Carter Commission and 11,024 people were settled between 1939 and 1960 on thirteen different schemes. Both the economic returns from these projects and the numbers of people involved seem small in relation to the size of the population and the scale of the problems which were supposed to be solved.

Finally, the government attempted to introduce new methods of soil preservation. The administration attempted to persuade people to carry out soil conservation by terracing, for example, but persuasion failed. The upshot was that people were forced to work six days in every three months on communal schemes for soil conservation devised by local officials. Policemen stood behind agricultural instructors to oversee the terracing of hillsides. Such methods, as can well be imagined, created very great bitterness. While it can always be argued that compulsory terracing and soil conservation would ultimately benefit the people, the distrust of government was so great that several people in Ukambani threw themselves in front of tractors and, in Nyeri political activity was directed against any European initiative for conservation.

ii. The 1950s. There would seem little doubt that the factors mentioned in the last section were some of the factors behind the Emergency of 1952–4. By 1952 Agricultural Department field staff were amongst the most unpopular men in the country and it was clear that the Department's methods would have to be revised. In addition, although many government officers have since argued that forcible means of land improvement were justified by the results, the problem of landlessness or near landlessness still existed, in fact had scarcely begun to be solved.

In 1954 and 1955 two reports were responsible for fundamentally altering the direction of agricultural policy in Kenya. 'A plan to intensify the development of African agricultural policy in Kenya', known as the Swynnerton plan, was published in 1954, and the 'East Africa Royal Commission' was published in 1955. Swynnerton proposed that former government policy on African agriculture be turned on its head. He recommended that all high-quality African land, i.e. all of Central Province including Embu and Meru, all of Nyanza Province and Kericho, Nandi, Elgeyo and West Suk and the Taita Hills, be surveyed and enclosed. He argued that the policy of maintaining 'traditional' or tribal systems of land tenure be reversed and that all the thousands of fragmented holdings be consolidated and enclosed. He maintained that the new policy would allow 'progressive' farmers to obtain credit, previously denied to all Africans, and that title deeds would create security of tenure which would lead to investment and development. Further, he wanted African farmers to grow cash crops, to be given a major increase in technical assistance, and he wanted to open all marketing facilities to them.

The explanation given by Swynnerton for such a dramatic reversal of policy was simply that the African lands suffered from :

low standards of cultivation and income and . . . as a result of African customary land tenure and inheritance, from fragmentation whereby any one family may possess several, and in recorded instances up to 29 small or minute fields scattered at wide intervals . . . it is impossible . . . to develop sound farming rotations, to cart and apply manure, to establish and manage grass . . . or to tend crops in any satisfactory manner.

All these facts had been common knowledge for the previous twenty years at least but only in the circumstances of the Emergency, the failure of the ten-year-plan to solve the fundamental land problem and the economic strength of European agriculture could such a proposal be put forward and accepted.

The Royal Commission was even more wide-ranging in scope, and even more radical in its approach. The Swynnerton proposals were accepted in their entirety, but the Commission wanted to advance further and *remove all racial and political barriers which in any way inhibited the free movement of land, labour and capital.* The essence of the report was summarised in a dispatch by the Governor a year later.

. . . East Africa's natural resources are few and poor; that they are nevertheless capable of a vast expansion and that such an expansion could not fail to transform the whole region; that the key to this expansion lies in encouraging, by every possible means, a change in the agricultural areas from a subsistence economy to a modern cash exchange system; that in order to bring about this change every unnecessary restriction and safeguard must be lifted, and the rate of introduction of outside capital and skills must be increased; and, at the same time, that the best possible use must be made of the internal capabilities and resources of the local East African population.

These recommendations implied that all land barriers and the safeguards to sectional interests, i.e. the boundaries of tribal reserves and White Highlands, should be removed and that land throughout East Africa should be bought and sold in the normal way. The Commission claimed that they wanted to remove 'the idea of security based on a Reservations policy fostered over the years and for so long generally accepted and to replace it by the conception that greater security rests in the guaranteed recognition of private interests in land' (page 366–7).

These two recommendations with various modifications had both been put into practice by 1960 and led the way toward settlement between the outgoing colonial authority and the leaders of the newly independent country. Basically these policies have been followed to the present time.

The policy of consolidation was put into practice without delay and in Kikuyuland the Emergency provided the conditions for effecting measures which, while hailed by economists, had been widely resisted by the poorer sections of the community in many parts of the country who feared they would lose all rights to land for ever. Consolidation measures were forced through between 1954 and 1960 in the three Kikuyu districts of Central Province. The colonialists would reward those loyal to them by an offer of land – a disincentive against joining the recalcitrant groups. At the same time it was hoped that these measures would rapidly lead to the adoption of commercial agriculture in Kikuyuland and satisfy critics of colonialism in Europe who persisted in pointing out that nothing had yet been done to improve the lot of Africans in Kenya.

It was hoped that consolidation would provide a solution to the problem of the *ahoi,* as land ownership would now be strictly defined, and finally that a solid conservative peasantry would be formed in the countryside; a middle class whose main concern would be to maintain the *status quo.*

Because the malcontents were almost all locked up during the Emergency, the measures were pushed through extremely rapidly. The richer African farmers were at last able to consolidate their holdings and firmly reject any other claims to ownership of their land. Ever since land had been alienated at the beginning of the century conflicts over rights to land had been rife throughout Kikuyuland. The case of one Muhoya was a favourite example of the British in their propaganda for consolidation. Muhoya had been trying to consolidate his lands since 1945 against rival claims. He now wanted to start a dairy farm, which the government found very commendable and progressive. The Emergency provided the Muhoyas of Kenya with the opportunity to fulfil their ambitions.

1963–1970

1. Maintenance of large-scale farming
One might have expected that Kenya's political independence would have led to great changes in the White Highlands. One characteristic of the Highlands has certainly not changed – a few vast holdings taking up about 20 per cent of Kenya's best farmland still exist there, as the following table shows:

	1954	1960	1967	1970
Total number of holdings	3,163	3,609	2,745	3,175

Source: Statistical Abstracts, 1955–70

Division of the area into regions exclusive to one race was ended in 1960 by the colonial government. In the early period of independence it seemed as if these lands might be split up into smallholdings. Until 1967, the total number of large estates declined but since then more have been demarcated. Forty-five thousand African families had been resettled by 1970 through a number of schemes, the best known being the Million Acre Settlement Scheme. The 45,000 were allocated altogether 460,000 hectares. A further 1200 more prosperous Kenyans purchased another 460,000 hectares, approximately. Five per cent of the White Highlands was taken over by small-scale farmers, but most of the coffee, tea and sisal plantations and the cattle ranches remained intact. What had changed was the nationalities of the owners. Wealthy, indigenous

Kenyans, including several men well known in public life, bought farms from Europeans. The Land Bank which advanced loans in the 1930s to Europeans now lent money to the new farmers.

Once the decision was taken in 1960 to alter ownership patterns in the area, it was essential that the farmers whose land had been taken over did not try a scorched earth policy. An orderly transfer of farms was necessary for stability in the change-over of political power, and, therefore, loans and grants were made available by the British government for buying out European farmers.

It is interesting to note that it was the areas of highest productivity in the former White Highlands which were not touched by the resettlement schemes. The core of large-scale, mixed farming, the basis of the conflict over the distribution of economic resources, has been retained.

2. Consolidation and the land problem

The Emergency and the economic strength of the large-scale farms in the Highlands together with the earlier failures to solve the land problem led directly to land consolidation as the focus of new government policy. By 1962, roughly 300,000 holdings had been consolidated in the three main districts of Central Province and there were further farms enclosed in Kipsigis country. This amounted to about 2·4 million acres of consolidated land in all, leaving another 3·3 million acres of high-quality land still to be enclosed and registered.

Colonial government policy had taken a crucial about-turn. In principle, all agricultural land in Kenya could now be legally defined as private property, that is, it could be bought and sold, like any other commodity, by any member of the Kenya community. All the racial and tribal boundaries had been removed by 1960 and a free market in land had been created. Not only that; instead of keeping the African areas tied to the past by pretended preservation of African traditions, which really ensured a cheap labour supply to the white farms, African producers at last had the opportunity to grow cash crops.

This major policy change had been precipitated by the Emergency. It is also clear that the change led on further to the colonial government's offering political independence to the country. The barriers against African ownership of land in the White Highlands had been lifted and a substantial acreage had been transferred to Africans by 1960. In the handing over of political power both African and European interests had to be satisfied. The Million Acre Settlement Scheme fulfilled the African demand for land in the Highlands. Government compensation satisfied the demand of

European farmers that the government should buy them out at a fair price.

The British government provided the loans with which to purchase some settler farms. These loans were to be repaid by the Africans who took over.

The drastic changes in the colonial agricultural policy laid the foundation for a peaceful transfer of power. The government of independent Kenya has basically continued the same policies as those initiated after 1954 and 1955. The major objectives of land policy between 1955 and 1972 have been to :

  i. create political stability in the rural areas;

 ii. give land to the landless;

iii. stimulate the production of cash crops.

Whether this political stability has been achieved remains open to question. To assist the landless and encourage the production of cash crops have turned out to be contradictory policies. As government has tried to stimulate cash crops so, in general, the people attempted to maintain subsistence farming. The Swynnerton Plan has remained the chief policy document. Let us briefly examine the situation.

One of the aims in the consolidation of fragmented land holdings in Central Province was to register freeholds of not less than 7·5 acres which it was thought would be the minimum size farm on which cash-crop agriculture would be a viable proposition. Yet, in practice, 86 per cent of all holdings registered in Central Province were less than 7·5 acres. But perhaps of greater significance is the fact that as registration was completed, people once again subdivided their plots according to age-old custom. Certainly in Kiambu 20 per cent of all land holdings in 1970 were under one acre in size, 35 per cent were under two acres and 77 per cent under six acres.

It is probable that the size of a single farm unit has continued to diminish. In other words, most people have continued to regard giving land as the best way of supporting their kinsfolk, rather than as a form of investment. Under such circumstances, subsistence farming prevails over production for cash income as the major form of agriculture.

In general it seems that the granting of individual freeholds does not of itself prevent subdivision. In South Africa in 1894, for example, the Rhodes Glen Gray Act opened the way to land registration and individual ownership. Each Xhosa land-holder was given forty acres of registered land. But the Xhosa continued to subdivide their plots among clan members according to tradition. By the 1960s there were little or no cash crops being grown and subsistence farming prevailed. In South Africa, as in Kenya, the lack of security of occupations in towns led to a widespread need for maintenance of a rural base. For most people this meant the retention of pre-capitalist land distribution patterns and resulted in the undermining of the principles behind land consolidation.

Having said this, it must be made clear that there is a small group of farmers within Central Province who are becoming very wealthy. This group are those people who have been successful in both accumulating land and in farming crops primarily for marketing. For instance, in one coffee co-operative society in Kandara Division of Murang'a, 14 per cent of the members of the society collected 64 per cent of the payout in 1970–1. The significance of this comes with the realisation that only 25 per cent of the farmers in Murang'a were members of any coffee co-operative at all. Therefore the very great increase in the quantity of cash crops sold annually since the mid-fifties, that is, since African farmers were allowed to grow cash crops, must be due to the relatively small number of peasant farmers who have taken advantage of new opportunities. The remaining majority cultivate plots that are too small for growing anything other than subsistence crops.

In short there is developing a hierarchy of peasant farmers with a few rich men forming the core of a rural capitalist class. The precise characteristics of this class remain to be investigated.

What is also clear is that the land reforms of the 1950s which have been carried through into independence have not even begun to solve the land shortage problem for the great majority of poor peasants. As already mentioned, the number and size of the large farms has not dramatically altered since 1954. In Kiambu, one of the areas of greatest land pressure in colonial times, 90 per cent of all the farms cover only 36 per cent of the land area in the district, while 2 per cent of the farms make up over 50 per cent.

By maintaining the large farms, the government has opted for cash-crop production rather than an equitable distribution of land. Hence, as the available land diminishes and as the population expands it is unlikely that more people will turn to cash crops. Rather it can be foreseen that people will use land as a source of security.

While the above trends are probably true to a greater or lesser extent throughout Central Province, the area is in no way typical of the whole of Kenya. In much of Western Province, despite land pressure in many areas, people have, from 1955 to 1972, tended to resist government policies on consolidation.

Opposition seems to have been widespread during the late 1950s, when the Kikuyu areas were forcibly consolidated, and sprang from a deep distrust of the government's intentions. A second source of resistance has been the people with only a small amount of land. By tradition a man with a little land and a few cattle could graze his animals on the stalks of his neighbour's land after harvest. Such men can still beg for a small portion of land from a friend or rela-tive with a large plot. But as the fencing of land becomes common practice this becomes more difficult and the small, independent farmer can rely less and less on such informal help to eke out his livelihood.

Finally, in many areas, up to a third of the men are away from home at any one time, working in the towns. Under the old system they all have rights to some piece of land when they return. All such rights could be excluded under consolidation. Consolidation does not appear to many people, particularly the poorer people, to be in their immediate interests; and while government seems to see a direct relationship between cash crops and consolidation, it is quite probable that many people might find themselves without any land whatsoever.

Acute land shortage is becoming a problem in parts of Western Province as well. In 1970 in Maragoli location, an area which has experienced land shortages for at least forty years, 67 per cent of the adult men between twenty and sixty years of age worked outside the district. Ninety per cent of a sample of 139 had less than five acres of land in use (65 per cent had less than three acres). Maragoli is of course not typical of Western Province, but it is still indicative of the serious problems which are beginning to face the entire province in varying degrees.

What appears to have happened, therefore, since 1955 is that there has been a revolution in government policies on land and agriculture. The intention of the Swynnerton Plan and the 1954–5 Royal Commission was to solve the land problem once and for all. But unlike the 1934 Land Commission they presented the case for uniting commercial production and land reform *throughout Kenya*. Consolidation, high-priced cash crops, extension services, peasant credit facilities and co-operative marketing were intended to assist the small farmer in competition with the large-scale settler farms. There is no doubt that peasants rapidly responded to the oppor-tunities to grow the high-priced cash crops. For instance in 1955 they were producing 750,000 tons of coffee but in 1960 the amount had multiplied five times to 4,607,000. Yet the maintenance of the nineteenth-century forms of land distribution among clan members have been rigidly adhered to, whether or not the people were forced to consolidate their land. Even in areas of new settlements the more traditional forms of land distribution have remained. But consolidation has had its effects; in Central Province there is evidence of a new rural elite which is not in evidence elsewhere. However, the overall picture is far from clear, as people throughout Kenya still look to the land for their ultimate social security; as roughly 20 per cent of all wages earned in urban areas are sent back to kin in the rural areas; as population grows at 3 per cent; and as the balance between agricultural production for cash or subsistence has not yet found equilibrium, so, sooner or later, land will yet again be the dominant issue in Kenya's politics.

4 Agriculture in Uganda: Change without Development

Introduction

In comparison with Kenya, the history of land and agriculture in Uganda in the twentieth century has been less dramatic. The difference was due to two factors :

 (i) white settlement failed in Uganda;
(ii) there has always been at least twice as much high-quality land in Uganda as in Kenya.

As a result of these factors widespread land shortages in Uganda have not occurred (with the exception of a few areas like Kigezi and parts of West Nile District) and consequently the politics and economics of Uganda have not been dominated by the land question.

So far in the discussion of agriculture in this book the focus has been on land tenure and on the introduction of cash crops. In Kenya, land in the Highlands was made available for purchase or sale in cash transactions by the act of alienation. In Central Province, and to a lesser extent elsewhere in Kenya, population on the African Reserves increased, creating a land shortage. Farms were now fenced and bought and sold for money. As we have argued, while the old systems of land rights were abrogated by enclosure and registration, they still existed in practice alongside the new system. In the 1960s land in many parts of Kenya still maintained both its traditional value for *use* and its new exchange value for *accumulation*.

In Uganda forced changes in the rules of land tenure and population pressure have not occurred on anything like the same scale as in Kenya. Only Buganda experienced major changes in land tenure systems at the beginning of the colonial era.

Colonisation and structural change, 1900–1920

1. Land tenure

The colonial government in Uganda accepted, as did its counterpart in Kenya, that each 'tribal' group had its defined territory to
be kept exclusively for use by that one tribe. However, because the
Baganda allied with the British in the colonial wars at the end of
the nineteenth century, the boundaries of the Ganda 'tribal' land
were extended at the expense of Bunyoro, whose government had
opposed the British occupation. Also, as had been the case in Kenya,
'tribal' lands were to be held by the tribe in common except in
Buganda where a unique pattern of distribution was put into
effect.

The aid given to the British by the majority of the Ganda leaders
was of such great importance in establishing British occupation that
a treaty was drawn up between the two parties. The Buganda
Agreement of 1900 not only defined the political relationship between the British colonial government and the Buganda rulers but
also set out the way in which land was to be distributed, thus
ensuring that Britain's principal supporters in the area should benefit. Under the terms of the Agreement, 9003 square miles of land
(roughly half of what the British regarded as Ganda territory)
were to be allocated to the Kabaka and about a thousand chiefs
with freehold. This freehold land came to be known as *mailo* land,
a Luganda version of the English term, square miles. The remainder was to be regarded as British Crown Land, held in trust for the
Baganda, but to be alienated if the colonial government so wished.
The aim of this land distribution was first, to ensure that all the
leaders of Ganda society would have an incentive to support
British political domination and secondly, to ensure political stability
throughout Buganda. In practice, settlement was not as straightforward as it had appeared to be on paper. A major difficulty was
the determination of who exactly was entitled to land under the
terms of the Agreement. By 1907 there were 6000 claimants where
originally there had been 1000.

Two important consequences followed from the *mailo* distribution. The first was that Ganda landowners developed their
properties along capitalist farming lines. They were able to do so
because they were now assured of permanent ownership of their
land and could, if they wished, buy and sell land to other Baganda.
(A non-Muganda required permission from the Governor and from
the Lukiiko before he could purchase land in Buganda.) Ganda farmers were therefore able to grow an annual cash crop and to improve their holdings without fear of alienation or of redistribution

according to old traditions of land tenure. Thus they could participate more easily than any other group in East Africa in production
for the market, and take a share in the wealth generated by the
colonial, capitalist system.

Secondly the *mailo* system effectively disrupted the old relationships between the Kabaka, the chiefs and the ordinary people. Prior
to colonisation almost all land was the Kabaka's to give and was
distributed by him to chiefs for the duration of their office and then
distributed further by the chiefs to the common people. Now the dis-
tributing was done by the colonial government and the distribution
was permanent (apart from small estates which were to be assigned
to incumbent chiefs). This deprived the Ganda political hierarchy of
their powers of patronage : the new *mailo* landowners now owed
their political allegiance to the British colonial government. Similarly, the relationships between important members of Ganda
society or traditional chiefs and their tenants also underwent a
change. An exchange value could be assigned to land, and gradually
the patron-client relationship began to have less relevance while
freeing the common man from his obligations to his lord and taking
from him the protection which the old relationship had afforded.
These changes came about only very gradually. Until 1927 some of
the old obligations were maintained. For example, peasants were
still expected to act as labourers for their lords, while landlords
and chiefs used their authority over their peasantry to ensure that
the main crop they grew was cotton. Essentially the change was
from a patron-client relationship to a landlord-tenant one and laid
the foundations for the development of capitalist estates in the
mailo areas.

The leaders of the other large kingdoms of Uganda also demanded a similar arrangement of the British, both for the political
security it would provide and for the advantages accompanying
freehold tenure of land. The Toro Agreement of 1900 and the
Ankole Agreement of 1901 both established political relations with
Britain similar to those in the Buganda Agreement, but apart from
the allocation of estates to the ruling families the British took care
not to copy the system of land tenure they had instituted in Buganda. At the time Bunloro was regarded as a conquered territory
and thus, in this case, no treaty was made with the rulers. Eventually in 1933 a treaty was drawn up between the Omukama's
government and the British colonial government, but once again it
did not include distribution of land freeholds.

So except in Buganda, the traditions of land tenure remained
virtually unchanged. Unlike the situation in parts of Kenya, the
division of the land into 'tribal' units did not result in land short-

ages, except in limited areas, because there was, and still is, plenty of good land to go round.

2. *Introduction of cash crops*

More widespread in its effect upon the people of Uganda than the changes in land tenure was the introduction of cash crops, the production of which was well established by 1914. Again we can contrast Kenya and Uganda, this time in terms of their cash-crop production. Whilst in Kenya production of the major export cash crops was denied to Africans, in Uganda the African peasant producer was to become the backbone of the economy. The development of cash-crop production in Uganda grew initially from the demand for raw cotton supplies by British manufacturers. In 1902 the British Cotton Growers' Association (BCGA) was formed by the Lancashire Chamber of Commerce and Liverpool merchants in order to try and find new areas suitable for growing cotton in the British colonies, so that their dependency on supplies from the United States could be reduced. In Uganda the Association's agent was K. E. Borup, who was in charge of the Church Missionary Society's industrial missions. Borup obtained cotton seed from the BCGA and distributed it through the agency of the Uganda Company. The Uganda Company had been launched by T. F. V. Buxton, president of the Anti-slavery and Aborigine Protection Society, and his cousin F. A. Buxton, a British Member of Parliament. This company was to act as the outlet for the commercial activities of the industrial missions : it was, therefore, a business enterprise linking Christianity with commerce in the time-honoured manner of British philanthropists. The circumstances of the introduction of cotton into Uganda shows exceptionally clearly the links between industrial interests in Britain, the colonial government, the missions and the local population : the BCGA supplied cottonseed which was distributed through the Uganda Company to Ganda chiefs who were then ordered by the government to make sure it was planted by the peasants under their authority. The raw cotton was then to be exported back to the BCGA cotton manufacturers. Paradoxically, between 1920 and 1940, well over half the crop was sold to Bombay merchants. It is worth noticing that Britain was unable to direct all East African trade because of the Congo Basin Treaties of 1890 (see Chapter 12).

Within two years of initial distribution a small amount of seed cotton was being exported. Cotton growing was an immediate success in Buganda because the soil and climatic conditions were ideal for it. But perhaps more important in explaining the rapidity with which cotton was established as a cash crop was the forceful manner in which growing was encouraged. The Ganda chiefs were actually ordered by the administration to see that the cotton was planted and in addition the chiefs themselves were eager to adopt new ideas. As Christopher Wrigley explains of the chiefs :

> [They] were essentially revolutionaries who had achieved power by violent subversion of the established order, and they were inspired by a revolutionary dynamic which consisted of eager acceptance of things European . . .
> The Ganda leaders were clearly tough and ambitious politicians . . . The Christian Ganda to a large extent adopted the European view of the virtue of work . . . They saw to it that the experiments in cotton growing were brought to a successful fruition.

The chiefs were, therefore, prepared to use their authority and power to get the new crop going. It was very common for a chief to beat his drum to summon his people and then command them to dig the ground and plant the seeds, threatening punishment if they refused. The chiefs speeded up the initial introduction and acceptance of cotton growing in Buganda but as soon as the benefits of cotton growing were realised, many people grew the new crop without any further prompting. Like peasants anywhere, so long as there were no restrictions on their activities, the Baganda responded to new economic opportunities.

White settlement, 1900–1920

The alacrity with which Ganda peasants took up cash crop production was an important factor in the question of white settlement in Uganda. The key issue in the discussion of the advantages and disadvantages of white settlement was whether European planters would be more efficient than local peasant producers in establishing an agricultural export economy.

In the period up to 1914 the general colonialist opinion was that white settlement and economic development were synonymous. Plantation agriculture had played or was about to play a dominant role in the development of Kenya, German East Africa, Nyasaland, Rhodesia, South Africa, Malaya, Ceylon and Java. In West Africa peasant production had only just begun on a significant scale. With this background, therefore, it is not surprising that large-scale European-style agricultural enterprise was considered by most colonials as the best means for the development of export crops. Peasant producers, they argued, were inert and conservative in their attitudes and would not be able to grasp or exploit new economic opportunities.

As in Kenya in the early years of colonisation, there was no clear-cut government policy on development. However, in Uganda, unlike Kenya, it was relatively difficult for a prospective settler from Europe to obtain a sizeable grant of land. Alienation of over 1000 acres freehold was subject to special permission from the administration and leasehold of over 10,000 acres was forbidden.

A second constraint on prospective settlers was the limited availability of unclaimed land. Due to the confusion caused by the distribution of *mailo* land in Buganda the identity and extent of Crown land available for alienation was not clear for some years. A few settlers managed to buy land from *mailo* owners before restrictions were placed on sales to non-Baganda. In addition, Uganda had few areas comparable to the Highlands of Kenya, where the climate was so attractive to the early settlers. By 1914 there were only 140 or so white planters in Uganda, on 58,000 acres of land, of which 40 per cent was under crops.

The lack of a clear-cut policy on white settlement in Uganda led to considerable controversy among the administrators. As a consequence a committee, headed by Morris Carter, was set up in 1911 to consider land policy. The committee's objectives were to guarantee the indigenous people an adequate area of land and to define what land should be made available for large-scale plantation agriculture. Between 1911 and 1921 the Carter Commission published seven regional reports in which a strong argument was advanced for alienation of land by Europeans. The basis for the recommendations were :

   i. that land should be granted to 'tribes' under the jurisdiction of chiefs and not distributed to individuals as had been done in Buganda;
  ii. that each district of Uganda should have its Native Reserve, the extent of which would be calculated on the basis of four acres for every family of five people;
 iii. that the economic role of the African was as a subsistence farmer and wage labourer.

The Commission recommended that 80 per cent of the land of Bunyoro, Ankole, Busoga and Toro should be alienated. What Morris Carter, later to be appointed chairman of the 1934 Land Commission in Kenya, was in fact saying was that the principle of development in Uganda should follow the practice of Kenya and South Africa.

Up to 1920, in spite of the fact that in that year 80 per cent of

Uganda's exports were being produced by the peasant sector, it seemed as if the future of European settlement was assured. The coffee and rubber plantations were doing well and cocoa was expected to be equally successful. The supposition that white farming would be an important part of Uganda's economy in the future was reflected in the composition of the Development Commission of 1920; the majority of its members were settler planters. The Commission's report expressed the latter's feelings in very clear terms. It also appeared that Uganda had become a more attractive area for European settlement; between 1918 and 1920 the number of large estates rose to 220 and the total area of alienated land more than doubled from 58,000 to 126,000 acres (197 square miles).

However the Carter reports and the recommendations of the Development Commission were overtaken by events. In the slump which occurred in world prices in 1920–1, cotton prices dropped from the 1920 level of £160 per ton to £80 per ton or less in 1921 and rubber prices experienced an even greater proportionate fall. In addition the currency crisis (see Chapter 14) dealt the Uganda settlers a severe blow and the commercial banks ceased to provide them with credit. Under the onslaught European plantation agriculture collapsed and the prospects of large-scale white settlement in Uganda, which had seemed so bright, faded to nothing. By 1921 the acreage cultivated by white farms had been reduced from 35,000 acres to 24,000 acres and never properly recovered.

Settlers in Kenya had had to face similar problems in 1920–1, but after a slight setback they were able, as we have seen in Chapter 3, to recoup their losses and prosper. Why then did the European settlers in Uganda fail? To be successful they needed (a) a valuable commodity which, in spite of the cost of the 700-mile rail journey to the coast could still give a substantial profit and (b) generous government subsidies during periods of decline in world prices. Neither of these conditions was present in Uganda in 1920. If the planters had been able to grow a high grade commodity, arabica coffee for example, it might have been possible to fulfil the first condition. If they had had the support of influential figures in Britain – the wealthier Kenya settlers had the backing of several members of the British aristocracy – they might have been able to exert more influence on government policy at the metropolitan level. As it was, the Uganda settlers had few direct contacts at this level, and moreover, they were unable to show that they were, at that point in time, the dominant sector of the Uganda economy: they could only hope to be so in the future if the necessary help was forthcoming. The peasant producers, as we have seen, were responsible for the bulk of Uganda's agricultural exports and with their

lower overhead costs and standards of living they were better able
to withstand the crises. They responded to the decline in world
prices by doubling their output between 1919 and 1921 and then
more than doubling it again by 1925. It is not surprising therefore
that the colonial administration in Uganda completely switched its
allegiance from European to African enterprise. In contrast to their
counterparts in Uganda the Kenya settlers had all the advantages :
(*a*) they were producing a high-priced crop, namely, arabica coffee;
(*b*) they were closer to Mombasa and thus their transport costs were
lower, and in some cases, even subsidised; (*c*) they had government
and imperial support; (*d*) there were no peasant producers of an
export crop in competition with them.

Peasant agriculture, 1921–1940:
growth without development

1. South-central Uganda

From 1921 administrative support for peasant cash-crop production
became the order of the day. The Ugandan peasant had shown that
he could produce cash crops which provided sufficient return to
maintain a healthy balance of payments in the country. Throughout this period the majority of peasants living in the cash-crop
producing areas devoted most of their land to subsistence farming
with a small patch given over to the cultivation of cash crops. They
were issued with free seed, given advice on planting, growing and
weeding and they had a market where prices were controlled at
which to sell their crops (see Chapter 11). To increase production
the area under cultivation was extended but no technical innovations to raise the yields per acre were introduced. In fact yields
per acre of cotton, for example, hardly altered between 1921 and
1940. Once peasant cash-crop growing became accepted the paternalistic attitude adopted by the colonial government did little to
encourage initiative on the part of the growers. The government
was concerned with growth rather than development and the structure of peasant agriculture which existed in 1921 was deemed perfectly adequate for this. The freehold system of land ownership
instituted in parts of Buganda at the beginning of the century could
have laid the foundations for farming on a capitalist basis. That
this development did not materialise was the result of two factors.
First, few incentives were offered to Ganda producers to extend
their enterprises beyond the horizons of primary production;
secondly, in the late 1920s the relationship between landlord and
tenant in Buganda was amended in such a way as to limit the
activities of the nascent estate-owning farmers.

i. Lack of development. Once freehold land ownership was established in Buganda it would have been logical to set up a peasant land bank, to encourage farmers to process some of their primary products and to enter the marketing field. No such steps were taken. There was no land bank to provide credit, and processing and marketing remained in the hands of Asians and Europeans. An important reason for this lack of development was the attitude of the colonial government. The government was anxious to maintain social and political stability in the Protectorate and they feared the disruption that such developments might cause. The 'African' interest was interpreted as being concerned with primary production of foodstuffs and cash crops; African rights to such methods of production should be safeguarded and as a corollary, Africans should be protected from the dangers inherent in the wider aspects of capitalist production. Thus restrictions were placed on the processing and marketing sectors which at the same time attempted to protect the primary producer from exploitation and prohibited him from processing and marketing on his own behalf. In many quarters deep disappointment was felt at this lack of development. As one informant pointed out to Christopher Wrigley: 'You came here to teach us. You have been here for sixty years and we still do not know how to make so much as a box of matches.' In general the lack of development in the inter-war period turned the enthusiasm that the Baganda had felt for things European at the beginning of the century into apathy and inertia: the revolutionary class of the early 1900s had become the conservative establishment of the 1930s and 1940s. By 1940 conflict between religions had been subdued, few people could influence central political events in any way, there was plenty of land and enough to eat. Initiative to further development seems to have been severely limited.

ii. Changes in landlord–tenant relationships. In order to maintain a stable peasantry the government thought it necessary to provide total security of tenure for the individual peasant farmer. In Buganda before 1928 security for tenants of *mailo* land was limited by the remnants of the traditional relationship of patron and client. *Mailo* owners had been able to extract 'rent' from their tenants in the form of money, labour or tribute. The rents were probably not unduly heavy and if they were, peasant tenants were still able to find a less exacting landlord, just as in pre-colonial days they might have moved to another patron. However, peasant mobility was in itself a factor of instability which was probably compounded by the ability of landlords to remove their tenants if they wished. In addition the political position of the *mailo* owners had altered.

The colonial authority was now well established and had little need for the support of the major Ganda leaders, and the small peasant producer, rather than the relatively large landowner, was seen as being the essential unit in economic production. The Administration was thus able to argue that the *mailo* owners represented an oppressive element to the peasant; they extorted rents, controlled land-holding and made little direct contribution to the economy. With this as justification the Busulu and Nvujjo Law of 1927 was passed. Formerly Busulu was an annual tribute of about five shillings paid to the landlord and Nvujjo was a tithe on peasant production also paid to the landlord. These were now commuted into cash payments at ten and four shillings respectively for each acre under cotton. In return for these payments a peasant could not be removed from his plot by his landlord. At first these levies represented substantial amounts to the peasants; they were equal to a month's income or more. However, as the value of money fell and the amounts due as Busulu and Nvujjo remained unchanged, they gradually ceased to make up such a large proportion of a man's return on his crops. Therefore, subject only to the payment of Busulu and Nvujjo, every Muganda peasant, from 1927 onwards, in effect possessed the land he farmed. *Mailo* landowners were left with only very limited powers of control over their holdings. They could not, without great difficulty, remove their sitting tenants in order to turn their land into a single large estate. Their role was reduced to virtually that of rent collectors. But although the peasants were owners of their land in the sense that they could not be removed from it and that their land was heritable, it was not until the 1950s that the process of registration of land claims was begun. Without a title to his land the peasant was unable to ask a bank for loans to finance its development and so could make few substantial improvements. Neither the peasant tenants, therefore, nor the *mailo* owners were in a position to make radical changes in the techniques of production.

Legal rights to land in the remainder of the Protectorate had never been clearly defined. In the 1920s the administration offered Nyoro, Toro and Ankole peasants certificates of occupation but few people bothered to take them up; traditional customs provided sufficient security of tenure and besides not so much importance was attached to the growing of cash crops in these areas. In Busoga in 1922 it became legal for a peasant to pay his chief in cash instead of serving the required period as a labourer and by 1936 all labour service was abolished in the District.

Thus during the 1920s and 1930s the peasants of five major tribes in Uganda became, in effect, free peasant cultivators; in practice they were the 'owners' of small-holdings owing little or no allegiance to any overlord. Their land was rich and well enough watered to provide a reasonably certain subsistence plus a small cash income. This situation was the prescription both for political stability and a deeply conservative agrarian peasantry.

2. *The outlying districts*

While cash-crop production was expanding in the south, particularly in Buganda and Eastern Province, during the 1920s and 1930s, no such process was taking place in the outlying districts of the Protectorate – in the north-west and north-east. In these regions government policy placed emphasis not on the production of cash crops but on the provision of labour for the cash-crop producing areas of the south. The peasant cash-crop producers, the large sugar plantations and the government all required a large pool of unskilled labour and if their demands, particularly those of the latter two groups, were to be met without in any way disrupting cash-crop production in the south, labour had to be drawn from other areas. By 1925 it had become the policy of the administration to discourage, or at least not to support, the development of cash cropping in the outlying areas, so that if the people living there were in need of cash they would be forced to offer themselves as wage labourers. In theory wage labour could be an alternative means of acquiring wealth and could have resulted in the accumulation of as much wealth as in the cash-crop producing areas. In practice, however, the levels of wages were too low for there to be any chance of this happening. This division of Uganda into 'productive' and 'labour' regions was the origin of the regional differences in wealth which are illustrated in the figures on p. 71.

The relationship between the productive and labour regions of Uganda and that between settler agriculture and African farming in Kenya is in many ways parallel. Just as African farmers in Kenya were prevented from taking a share in export crop production, so farmers in the outlying districts of Uganda were discouraged from growing Uganda's major export commodities: cotton and coffee. In 1919–20, of the 162,000 acres under cotton in Uganda, 137,000 acres were in Buganda and Eastern Province; by 1928–9, 576,000 out of the 699,000 acres under cotton were again in these two areas. Admittedly the north and west were not highly suited to cotton or coffee production but although these areas might have been developed for cultivation of tobacco, groundnuts or sesame seeds, these crops never constituted more than 10 per cent of the value of Uganda's exports and so have made only a small contribution to

Uganda's overall wealth. Moreover, only a part of the total quantities produced have come from the outlying districts.

The result of these policies is illustrated by means of a few statistics:

Northern and Western Provinces

	% total cotton acreage
1919–20	15
1929–30	15
	% total cotton tonnage
1939–40	8
1949–50	14

By 1955–6 the Northern and Western Provinces had increased their proportion of cotton tonnage to 22 per cent of the total, but this was due to a relative decline in cotton production in Buganda in favour of production of coffee which fetched a higher price. Hence in 1959 the per capita income from cash crops in Buganda was 174 shillings per annum as against 60 shillings in Lango and Teso Districts, 28 shillings in West Nile District and 11 shillings in Ankole. As far as income from export crops was concerned, Buganda was twice as wealthy per head of population as any other single area. Income earned through wage labour was not sufficient to raise the total per capita income in the outlying districts to the Buganda level and therefore did not effect the overall imbalance in wealth.

3. Peasant response to economic opportunity

In the previous sections we have argued that the constraints on development of the Ugandan economy between 1920 and 1940 were for the most part due to government policies and, to a lesser extent, to the fact that growth could take place without significant development. Many writers have contended that lack of development in an agrarian peasant-based economy is due to the inertia and essentially conservative attitude of peasant farmers; reluctance to take advantage of new economic opportunities and to change their production patterns accordingly. However we have seen how, once cotton was recognised as an economically viable crop, Ganda peasants did not hesitate to seize the opportunity of growing it. Thereafter, the original methods of cotton, and later coffee, production remained unaltered with few technical innovations to increase yields per acre. Was this a reassertion of the characteristic inertia attributed to a peasant economy? We would argue that the peasantry was not given the chance to develop its economy further. Writers who believe in the inertia theory also suggest that peasants do not respond to changing levels of prices and, if they do, it is in an irrational manner. If we look at crop prices and compare them with output figures we can see that Ugandan export crop producers did respond to changing prices. Between 1929 and 1933 the price of cotton dropped by over 50 per cent and by 1937 the price was only three-quarters of what it had been eight years earlier. Yet the output of cotton had doubled in the years between 1929 and 1937. A similar story could be told for coffee prices and output. Prices (FOB Mombasa) declined from 86 shillings per hundredweight in 1929 to 32 shillings per hundredweight in 1937 but output multiplied by three times during this period. Ugandan peasant growers, therefore, *did* respond to declining prices by increasing their output. Was this a 'rational' response? Economists of the West usually regard decline in production as the most rational response to falling prices. Why, they argue, use up scarce resources to obtain a smaller return on the effort expanded? The settler farmers in Kenya, for instance reduced production in response to a drop in prices. The argument that the rational response to falling prices is to reduce output rests on the assumption that available resources can be used in other forms of production; in other words, that production can be diversified. This did not apply to the peasant producers of Uganda. They were unable to diversify production and therefore the only logical way in which they could react was to increase output. The peasant was conservative in so far as he was anxious to maintain the standard of living which he had achieved through selling crops in the years of high prices; as prices fell the best way for him to keep up his standard of living and to get the highest return on his inputs, of necessity limited, was to increase production. This made as much economic sense as the Kenya settlers' reduction of output. The Uganda peasants were also encouraged in this response by the administration, which was equally concerned that production should increase.

1945–1970: Attempts at agricultural transformation

As had occurred in Kenya (and elsewhere in the world) the conditions arising out of the Second World War prompted officials in Uganda to look more closely at their development policies and to introduce more comprehensive development plans in order to increase output per acre and per man. During the fifteen years after the war (up to 1960), the government in Uganda concerned itself with six main areas of agricultural production, aiming at increased production and transformation of the existing patterns of production. Government policy aimed at :

   i. expanding the production of existing cash crops;
  ii. diversifying production by introducing other crops;
 iii. stimulating the more efficient peasant farmers to greater efforts;
 iv. making tractor services available;
  v. instituting land registration;
 vi. encouraging large-scale farming.

1. Expansion of production of existing cash crops

Cotton was still the major cash crop in the 1940s and an extensive campaign was initiated to urge farmers to increase production. By the 1960s however, the quantity of cotton being exported was still below the quantity which had been exported in 1937–8. Cotton production had been curtailed during the war and output never regained its pre-war levels, despite the rise in prices between 1938 and 1945. One reason why production did not expand in response to better prices was that, compared to coffee prices, the rise in cotton prices was very small and Robusta coffee could be grown as an alternative to cotton in most areas. African peasants had been encouraged to grow Robusta coffee in Uganda from 1922. This type of coffee, although giving lower cash returns than Arabica coffee, was easier to grow, requiring less attention. Furthermore it could be grown at lower altitudes than Arabica, and was therefore better suited to conditions in Uganda. The administration had established coffee nurseries and had issued free seedlings to growers and Robusta coffee production was rapidly adopted in Buganda, which by 1940 was producing 80 per cent of Uganda's coffee crop. The remaining 20 per cent came from Bugishu, Ankole and Kigezi. After the war, coffee prices began to rise very quickly; between 1948 and 1955 they rose by over 300 per cent and coffee output, mainly in Bugandà, rose to match this. Even this rate of growth was in some respects disappointing. A large proportion of it occurred at the expense of cotton production and, given the increase in population and the availability of land, an even larger increase in output could reasonably have been expected. In addition, yields per acre remained constant. Methods of cultivation of cotton and coffee had remained unchanged since the inter-war years and subsistence crops still took precedence over cash crops for the peasant farmer.

2. Diversification of agricultural production

One way of improving the situation was to encourage the production of new crops. This policy was also an important part of the government's attempt in the post-war period to encourage agricul-

Geographical differences of wealth in Uganda

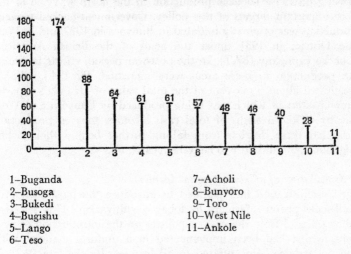

1–Buganda   7–Acholi
2–Busoga   8–Bunyoro
3–Bukedi   9–Toro
4–Bugishu   10–West Nile
5–Lango   11–Ankole
6–Teso

FIG. 4.1 *District differences of wealth, 1959, annual income per capita (shillings)*

Source: B. W. Langlands, 'On the Disposition of Economic Development in Uganda', EASSC paper, 1968

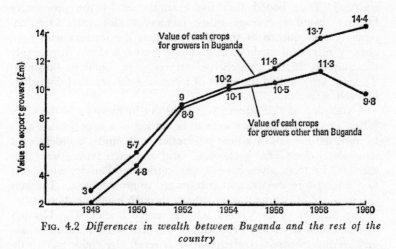

FIG. 4.2 *Differences in wealth between Buganda and the rest of the country*

Source: For statistics as above

Note: the growing disparities from 1956 even between Buganda and the rest of the country

tural production in the areas other than the cotton and coffee-growing districts. Tobacco production in the north was one of the more important targets of this policy. Government-backed tobacco production was originally initiated in Bunyoro in 1927 and in West Nile District in 1931 under the aegis of the British American Tobacco Company (BAT). In the post-war period, efforts to stimulate production in these areas were increased. By 1945, tobacco constituted about 6 per cent of the total value of Uganda's exports, three-quarters of which was being produced by Bunyoro and West Nile by 1956. In terms of total cash incomes, tobacco production prevented these districts from falling further behind their richer neighbours, but did little to help them catch up.

3. Stimulation of efficient peasant farmers
The administration had planned to introduce the most successful small-scale peasant farmers to tobacco cultivation. This selective policy differed from the cashier policies on the introduction of new crops, which had been implemented in a uniform manner, with seed and advice being offered to all farmers. By the late 1940s it was the opinion of the Agricultural Department that if they wished to bring about technical change, the most efficient way of doing it would be to concentrate on giving their assistance and advice to 'progressive' farmers who had already demonstrated their success with existing crops and would be the most likely to try out new methods. They hoped that the example set by the progressive farmers would encourage other farmers to innovate. One immediate consequence of this idea was that the farmers who were already successful made even greater progress and not surprisingly the majority of the progressive farmers were found in Buganda. Thus the scheme had the effect of increasing the regional disparities in levels of wealth.

A variation of this scheme was tried out in Bunyoro in the early fifties. Progressive farmers were to be settled in a depopulated area to form the nucleus of a new productive community. Bulldozers set to work to clear 8000 hectares of land and each farmer was allocated 8·2 hectares, given loans, expert agricultural advice and access to a tractor-hire service, and encouraged to grow tobacco. The aim was to transform agricultural methods through mechanisation rather in the manner of the Gezira scheme in the Sudan. The Uganda scheme failed abysmally. The soils of the area were found to be unsuitable for tobacco growing and as a result the yields were only half what had been expected and the farmers were unable to repay their loans. Quarrels resulted and the farmers packed up and left.

4. *Tractor services*

Another of the Agricultural Department's plans was to provide the peasant farmers with access to mechanisation. Tractor-drawn ploughs had been introduced as a part of the Bunyoro tobacco scheme, but the tractors were to be put to wider use. It was argued that manual labour was highly inefficient, scarce, and becoming increasingly expensive in most areas in Uganda and it would therefore be cheaper to use tractors. It was expected that mechanisation would lead to higher returns; ploughs drawn by tractors turned the soil more efficiently than the hoe, and much larger areas could be prepared for cultivation in this way.

The Agricultural Department set up tractor stations all over the country, but particularly in Buganda, and then hired them out with drivers to those farmers who wished to use these facilities. Up to 1963 the Department had about thirty to forty tractors in use on the scheme. After Uganda became independent the number was rapidly increased and by 1966–7 there were 870 tractors in service. The advantage of such a pool system was that an individual farmer could make use of a tractor without incurring the full expense of purchase, when, on a small farm, he would not want to use it continuously. But even so the Department found that the tractors were not in demand throughout the year. If they were used only for ploughing at the beginning of the planting seasons and left idle at other times charges to farmers would have to be relatively high to cover the cost of maintaining the machines, whereas if they were in constant use the rates could be reduced. Up to 1968 (the last year for which figures are available) the problem of covering costs was never overcome. Even in the scheme's most successful year (1963) the tractor hire service was operating at a loss of 13 shillings per hour or U£500,000 per year. Cotton growers also found the service too expensive. Even with a subsidy the return on the crop did not justify hiring the tractors.

5. *Land registration*

Another aspect of attempts by government to stimulate peasant farming was the registration of land-holdings and the granting of title deeds to individual farmers. In the Kikuyu areas of Kenya the granting of title deeds to farmers had been carried out hand in hand with the consolidation of scattered plots of land. The objective in Kenya had been twofold: to encourage a capitalist class of small-scale farmers who could grow any suitable cash crops, and to establish political stability after the Emergency. The registration of land among the Kikuyu was successful in the initial stages both because there was a real shortage of land and because the government took steps to enforce registration. When registration was introduced in Uganda in 1958 the same conditions were not present. The justification for registration in Uganda was that it would (a) provide land-holders with absolute security of tenure and (b) enable fragmented holdings to be consolidated into single tracts. Both security of tenure and consolidation were thought to be the prerequisites of modern cash crop farming. Security of tenure was necessary before a farmer would be willing to improve his land (by irrigation, application of fertilisers, long-term planning, etc.) and if his land were consolidated mechanical farming methods could be more efficiently used. Also, the farmer would no longer need to walk long distances from one small patch of land to another. If there were these advantages to recommend it why was registration not generally accepted?

First, in areas where there was sufficient land to go round the pressure to obtain a title to a particular plot was not acute – there was little competition for land and a farmer felt secure enough under the old system. Secondly, as we have seen, mechanisation was only of minor importance in peasant farming hence fragmentation was less of an inhibiting factor than might be supposed at first glance. In addition there were perfectly good, well-established reasons for keeping fragmented land holdings. Particularly in hilly country conditions could vary widely over a relatively small area and it was thought fairer to make sure that everyone had a share of both good and bad land. For example, a plot on a stony hillside where the soil was not very good and where watering was dependent on rainfall only would be compensated by a plot in a river valley where the soil was rich and where there was an assured water supply. Fragmentation on this basis had been practised in Lugbaraland for instance, for as long as anyone could remember. In 1966, 33 per cent of all land holdings in Bugishu, 58 per cent in Kigezi and 61 per cent in Acholi were divided into three or more fragments and many other groups had still retained their traditional system of fragmented land-holdings. In fact, fragmentation may not necessarily be indicative of land shortage, but rather only when land-holdings can no longer be distributed in such a way as to give a fair sample of plots in different ecological zones, could land shortage be said to exist. This condition of shortage was beginning to apply in parts of Lugbaraland in the 1950s; it had become impossible to give every woman her due plot in a fertile river valley. As a result, the traditional system of subsistence agriculture began to break down. In the parts of Lugbaraland where the problem was most acutely felt young men were going south in ever increasing numbers to find work as labourers, as the only alternative to farming for themselves. The population density of the Lugbaraland varied from area to area. In 1959, 240 people per square mile seems to have been the highest figure, according to the census. In Bugishu, too, the differences were apparent but here the mean level was much higher : some sub-counties supported as many as 1100 people to the square mile although the average was about 418 people per square mile. When such high densities were reached another and more serious aspect of fragmentation came into operation – the breaking up of land-holdings into smaller and smaller units in an attempt to comply with inheritance customs. Traditionally most societies assumed that everyone had a right to some land and that each one of a man's children was equally entitled to a share of the inheritances of the family. Where inherited land could be supplemented by clearing new areas for cultivation the traditional system worked well, but when there was no more undeveloped land, inheritance of already cleared land by itself was insufficient for a family's farming activities. In this situation competition for land would occur and it was in the interests of those who were in possession of land to resist the traditional pressures to break it up into still smaller segments to accommodate poorer kinsmen who might put forward claims of inheritance. This difference between interests of rich and poor meant that in areas of land shortage, such as Bugishu, attitudes to registration varied from the enthusiastic to the outrightly resentful. The well-to-do, well-educated, progressive farmers were in favour of title deeds because their already favourable position would be reinforced, while the poor were opposed to registration because they were very likely to lose whatever rights they still had and they stood no chance of being granted titles to plots in the most economically viable areas of farmland – these would go to the wealthy farmers.

6. Large-scale farming

The final measure taken by the administration in Uganda in its attempt to increase production in the years after the end of the Second World War is perhaps the most interesting of all. This was the experiment in development of surplus land by the government itself which began in the early fifties. Once again Bunyoro received most attention. In Bunyoro there were still large expanses of unused land. Even in 1964 less than 10 per cent of potential agricultural land in the district was under crops. This situation can probably be attributed to a number of factors. First, there had been widespread depopulation of Bunyoro during the wars of the 1890s and during the famines and epidemics of sleeping sickness which struck the area in the 1900s. Secondly, until the 1950s very little had been done to stimulate development in Bunyoro. Thirdly, the region was plagued with tsetse fly; in the early 1950s there was tsetse fly in 90 per cent of Bunyoro's land area. The government plan for Bunyoro was to establish large-scale, government-owned farms. An area of 1600 square kilometres was cleared and capital-intensive ranching schemes were introduced. By 1963 it was evident that the scheme had failed and the experiment was abandoned three years later. But although the large-scale scheme had failed the peasant farmer was able to take advantage of the elimination of the tsetse fly and start breeding cattle and producing milk for the local market, albeit on a small scale. Once again the peasant farmer, with his low overheads and flexibility, had proved that he had an advantage over the large-scale farmer.

7. Change

To what extent had these various attempts by the government achieved their objective of increasing output per acre and per man by the late 1960s? In 1961 the World Bank Commission in Uganda described 'most farmers as still essentially subsistence farmers with cash crops as a subsidiary activity'. The Commission, however, did note, as has been done before in the mid-fifties, that there existed a small number of very professional large-scale farmers but that there was no indication that this group was contributing substantially to Uganda's agricultural growth. The 1961 Commission stated, again as had been suggested ten years earlier, that there was a need for widespread changes in agricultural techniques.

Yet, while the World Bank's overall assessment of the situation was no doubt correct, there had, in fact, been some successful changes. In Bunyoro, for instance, where the attention of the Agricultural Department had concentrated, the area under crop cultivation had doubled between 1954 and 1968. Some new crops had been introduced and livestock production had increased by 600 per cent following the eradication of tsetse fly from a large area. But there had been many failures as well. Uganda was still largely dependent on only three or four cash crops and it is doubtful whether the efficiency of agricultural methods had been much improved.

One important development which took place was the growth of local markets for Uganda's produce. This was one area outside the purview of the Agricultural Department. The domestic markets had been slow to develop in comparison with Kenya. The domestic market in Kenya grew in response to the demand for foodstuffs from settler farmers, from the large labourer populations on the settlers' farms and from the town dwellers, particularly of Nairobi.

Moreover, there had developed in Kenya through its marketing boards a network for the distribution of products for the market. Such a system was lacking in Uganda. The demand for foodstuffs from the settler and urban populations in Uganda was not as great as in Kenya and hence the domestic market was limited. The sale of food products only gained in importance in the early fifties when the size of the population of Kampala increased considerably. Bananas, maize, meat, vegetables and locally produced beer all found a ready market in the urban areas. The exact volume and extent of the market is hard to gauge as precise studies are lacking. but it is probable that an underdeveloped system of internal distribution and a shortage of lorries for carrying foodstuffs over the long distances to the towns were major factors of constraint to the suppliers. The Baganda, living around Kampala, were able to benefit most from the growing market for foodstuffs, just as the Kikuyu living in the vicinity of Nairobi derived most profit from *its* markets. Again the system had been partial to the Baganda and the distribution of wealth had once more been in their favour.

If we look at Uganda as a whole over the last seventy years it seems that the stimulus towards agricultural development never developed as it did in Kenya. The widespread availability of fertile land and the relatively small scale of European settlement has meant that the stimulus for technical and structural change has been lacking in Uganda.

The 1966 Census Report showed that the average size of land-holdings was just over nine acres of which, on average, only four-and-a-half acres were being cultivated. A major work on agriculture in Uganda argued that 'it is conservatively estimated that there are five acres of good land available for every acre cultivated and that there is no scarcity of land for cultivation except near the bigger towns'.* It appears that there is plenty of room for population expansion before 'natural' pressures cause alterations in traditional land-holding practices. In other words, a peasantry with relative security of land-holding and a further supply of land yet uncultivated still exists in present-day Uganda.

Alteration of the existing pattern of low-productivity, extensive farming would necessitate the widespread employment of modern techniques, for instance the use of fertilisers, irrigation controls, mechanical cultivation, etc. Since the 1950s the colonial government and then the government of independent Uganda have been fully aware of the situation and have attempted to develop Uganda's agriculture on a technical base. Looking at achievement

---

* *Agriculture in Uganda*, ed. J. D. Jameson.

up to the present the success of these attempts can be judged as
limited.

It seems incongruous at first that Kenya with her larger settler
population and her limited land supply should have been more successful than Uganda in developing her agricultural potential, particularly when the struggles and sufferings of her peoples are borne
in mind. It may be argued from the export figures for agricultural
produce that Uganda was more successful than Kenya up to the
mid-sixties. However one must remember that it was only from the
late fifties that Kenya's peasants were allowed to participate in
the export market and since then Kenya's export trade and the total
value of her output have rapidly improved and overtaken those of
Uganda. Moreover Kenya seems to have been the more successful
of the two countries in introducing technical change.

The explanation of these apparent paradoxes would seem to be
that it was precisely because the people of Kenya have had to
struggle for their economic and political independence that the
changes discussed here have occurred. It would seem that availability of high-quality farming land is in fact the condition which
led to Uganda's lethargic response to agricultural innovation. The
incentive for change, to judge by the evidence of the post-war
period, does not come solely from the top administrative level,
rather the change must be one that is also actively desired by the
people. Perhaps as land resources decline in relation to population
growth, pressures for change in Uganda's economic and agricultural base will mount.

5 Nomadic Pastoralism: the Process of Impoverishment

Introduction

Few historical studies have been made of the nomadic pastoral peoples of East Africa and consequently we know little about their past, even in the nineteenth century. Such studies as have been made have concentrated on the broad sweep of the history of migration of pastoralists or on their recent political past and little attention has been paid to their economic or social histories. For information in these fields we have to turn to the work of anthropologists, but use of this source itself provides problems for the historian. Anthropologists, who are concerned with the economic and social aspects of the societies they are studying, tend to concentrate on the *current* structures and functions of social and economic institutions. As a result the view of life they present tends to be timeless and to give an impression that things have not altered, unless the studies are specifically concerned to examine change in the society. Existing studies of nomadic pastoralists in Eastern Africa give an impression of timelessness – that methods of production in the pre-colonial period have hardly altered and that in modern times change has passed these societies by.

Yet it would be most unusual to find any society in which no adjustments or modifications have occurred, and indeed, recently published linguistic studies begin to show us clues which suggest that nomadic pastoral societies, like other societies, did experience alterations in their modes of production in the pre-colonial period. As more detailed studies are made of the traditional period in these societies, we can expect to gain more information on such changes. More important for the purposes of this book, if we look closely at the information available on the economic history of nomadic pastoral societies in the nineteenth and twentieth centuries we can begin to see that the story is not simply one of societies which have 'fallen behind' in the process of change, or even of societies which have rejected change, but a story of a dramatic reversal of the fortunes of pastoralist societies.

In general we can say that the situation in which pastoralists were the predominant force in East Africa in the early part of the nineteenth century has been turned upside down so that today pastoralist societies are impoverished, dominated and underprivileged. In this chapter we will examine the main reasons for this reversal, but first let us look at the scale of the change which has occurred.

First, it would be true to say, in general, that even among settled agricultural peoples and in mixed agricultural and pastoral societies, the ownership and control of cattle and other livestock had a high economic and social value in the nineteenth century. To take an extreme example, the basis of the political power of the Bahima or the Tutsi classes in western Uganda, Burundi and Rwanda, was based on their ownership of cattle, rather than on any ethnic differences within the societies. In many predominantly agricultural societies, the Kikuyu for example, the acquisition and ownership of cattle was regarded as an important indication of wealth and prestige, and relationships with neighbouring pastoral peoples, the Maasai and Wakamba, were made in this context. Cattle-keeping peoples, therefore, were generally regarded as being wealthy and prestigious. Secondly, if we look at the relationships between pastoral and agricultural societies in the early part of the nineteenth century, we can see that this general underlying respect for pastoralists and their economic power was consolidated by their military power and control of territory. The predominantly pastoral peoples, like the Turkana, Somali, Karimojong and Maasai, had expanded their pastoral preserves over wide areas of East Africa. With their ease of mobility, their political cohesion and their general good health and strength, based on a high protein diet of milk, blood and meat, the nomadic pastoralists were militarily dominant over much of East Africa. In fact the economic geography of East Africa in the early to mid-nineteenth century has been described as a 'sea' of pastoralism, surrounding a few 'islands' of agricultural production. In terms therefore of social values, wealth, control of territory and political and military power, pastoral production and the pastoral way of life was predominant.

By the middle of the twentieth century this situation had been almost completely reversed. The pastoral way of life now no longer generates the same general feeling of respect and prestige; in fact nomadic pastoralists are often castigated as conservative and primitive peoples. Economically agricultural production, especially the production of cash crops for the international market, has come to be a major source of wealth; agricultural producers have gained social and political dominance in East African society, and nomadic pastoralists have been pushed out of many areas of high agricultural potential to make way for the new order. To adapt Soja's metaphor, the 'sea' of pastoralism, although still considerable, has retreated before the new 'land mass' of settled agricultural production.

Much of this reversal, as we argue in this chapter, is the result of external influences; the new economic and political forces of the twentieth century have favoured agricultural as against pastoral development. Yet some factors of change can be discerned at a slightly earlier stage in the nineteenth century. First, it seems that by the middle of the nineteenth century expanding pastoralist and expanding agricultural groups were impinging on each other's boundaries to a greater extent than before. In eastern Uganda, western and central Kenya, frontier situations were developing which sometimes led to conflict over land control, in which the agriculturalists sometimes won or were able to limit the pastoralists' advance. Secondly, groups in some pastoral societies (in Luo, Maasai and Iteso society, for example) began to change their modes of production from predominantly pastoral to predominantly agricultural pursuits when they found themselves in suitable areas with access to new production techniques. Thirdly, by the end of the nineteenth century, internal political and social disruptions in some pastoralist societies (especially the Maasai), together with the effect of the scourge of introduced disease in cattle and humans, were further weakening the military power of nomadic societies, a weakness which the settled agriculturalists were able to take advantage of. By the late nineteenth century these changes were still only incipient but with the establishment of colonial political and economic control the reversal of the fortunes of the nomadic pastoralists was to be consolidated.

The social ecology of nomadic pastoralism

The pastoralists
Who is a 'pastoralist' in East Africa? Dr Jacobs has distinguished between pure and semi-pastoralists, the pure type being those who rely entirely on livestock husbandry as their form of production while the semi-pastoralists indulge in agriculture and trade as well as herding. Dr Jacobs' distinction was made in 1962 and since then even his parent group, the Maasai, have been shown by Marris and Somerset * to supplement their stock-keeping by trade with agricultural people. It would seem more useful to argue that pastoralists are any group of people who subsist mainly or largely through stock-keeping.

* Peter Marris and Anthony Somerset, *African Businessmen* (International Publications Service, New York, 1971).

The geographical extent of pastoral country

Stock-owning is a common characteristic of nearly all rural peoples in East Africa. But the people who subsist mainly or largely through stock are found in the drier regions of the countryside.

In Kenya the area suited to pastoral production forms over 75 per cent of the total area (220,000 square miles). In Uganda the drier areas are considerably smaller, but are still some 6835 square miles. These are areas where livestock production provides the best form of land-use and where, given the existing level of technology, the areas where livestock keeping has been the only possible major form of production with which to sustain daily life.

We are thus concerned in this chapter with vast areas of land, where the relationships between animals and men have been largely determined by the limitations of the terrain. The physical environment in these dry regions has always limited the opportunities available for economic exploitation. In practice the regions vary widely in rainfall and have allowed some groups to be nearly sedentary pastoralists, while others have been forced to become nomadic to exist at all.

Varieties of nomadism

Three examples from Nandi, Maasai and Turkana will suffice to show the great variation which existed in the patterns of man/animal/nature relationships among pastoralists. On the one hand, the Nandi lived in country which had a rainfall varying from between 35 and 72 inches per year. This level of rainfall has been sufficient over the last thirty-five years to allow Nandi to move over from production which used to be predominantly pastoral into production which is predominantly agricultural. In the time when the Nandi were predominantly pastoral, stocks did not *have* to be moved during the dry season to find water and grazing. Cattle were moved about for reasons of security against disease and theft, so that each family divided up their cattle in different parts of the country. The Nandi in this respect are like all pastoral peoples; security concerns have played a major part in their treatment of the animals.*

By comparison the rainfall in the present area occupied by the

---

* The splitting of herds had a rationale beyond economic insurance. The strictures of productive relations were such that a man would often hide his wealth in order that others would not know how many cattle he owned when the time came to exchange animals for a bride or when an animal was needed for ceremonial reasons. A man who spread out his animals over a number of families would also have created widespread clientship relations with those people who herded his animals, which provided yet another reason for splitting the herd.

Maasai was generally far less than in Nandi. On the Mau escarpment it might average over 60 inches per annum, but elsewhere it only averaged over 30 inches per annum in the best areas and under 20 inches in others. The best rainfall areas might take crops but due to the high level of evaporation and the long dry season in all the areas, the area has been exploited through semi-nomadic pastoralism. Complete families and their herds are forced during the changing seasons to move in response to water and grazing shortages. Maasai settlement patterns are therefore strongly affected by seasonal variations in climate and the distribution of water.

Turkana country has an even lower rainfall than that of the Maasai. Over a twenty-year period Lodwar has averaged 6 inches per year, Lokitaung 12 inches and Kaputur 12 inches. Not only is the average rainfall lower, but the range or variation from year to year is unusually extreme. For instance Lodwar in one year had only 2 inches. The harshness of the environment of the Turkana is thus very considerable, and that life can continue at all is due to the great adaptability of human beings to the resources available.

The level of the rainfall in each of the areas briefly mentioned has not only affected the absolute numbers of animals that have been maintained in the area, but also the number of humans that have been sustained, and it has been a major determinant of the nomadic patterns which have always been forced upon the people. While the Nandi used to move stock about for reasons of social and political security, the Turkana were forced to move their animals in a complex system in order to survive at all. The Turkana have very considerable understanding (over very large areas of the countryside) of the rainfall patterns, the impermanence of water supplies, variations in soil fertility, the stock population an area will hold, existence of diseases and the distances it will be necessary to travel to find adequate new pastures. The Turkana, like all pastoral peoples, have always had a deep knowledge of these conditions of their environment.

Moreover, due to the very marginality of existence and the need to make the best use of their physical environment, the Turkana would split up their families into as many as five units for large parts of the year. The herds and flocks would be split into grazing and browsing stock, into milking and non-milking stock, while camels were often herded separately. Maasai on the other hand have not had the same need to split up their herds or flocks in this manner as their physical environment has been comparatively kinder and less extreme.

The range therefore of pastoral environments in East Africa has always been very wide indeed. Both the Karimojong and the Somali continue to live in harsh circumstances similar to the Turkana.

Variations in the man/animal nexus

Not only have the nomadic patterns varied widely with the environmental conditions but so has the actual balance of animals to man. The holdings of cattle, camels, sheep and goats per man in any one area show great variation. The Maasai for instance, according to recent estimates, have commonly had three or four times as many cattle as the Somali or Turkana, and correspondingly larger herds of sheep and goats. The Somali have in addition had camels, unlike the other tribes. It should be noted that it is probable that such differences vary not only within areas but also over time, as animals change hands through the bride price and other social mechanisms – not to mention famine. In the past, however, statistical information has been non-existent on such topics.

In line with these variations in *per capita* holdings is a variation in the extent to which the diet of any one people is dependent on meat, milk and blood. According to Dr Jacobs, the pastoral Maasai, who would appear to have the largest flocks and herds per head in East Africa, subsist almost entirely off their animals, while the Turkana not only exist off their stock and cultivate grains, but they also live off wild berries, nuts and fruits in the dry season. It would seem probable that environmental factors have played a considerable part in diet and flock and stock patterns, and go some way to explain the wide variation.

The harsh environment

Despite the variations mentioned above, all those communities in East Africa which have maintained some form of nomadic pastoralism up to the present day do seem to have one major factor in common : that is, the harsh character of the physical environment. The environment is harsh in two ways, physically and in terms of disease. All have severe limitations in terms of natural resources, which makes these environments marginal for existence. The rainfall is limited and as a result so is the natural vegetation. The probability of famine every few years is part of the character of the human physical opportunities. The peoples' nomadic patterns are forced upon them and can be understood in terms of geographical movements to areas where rain has led to suitable vegetation, a form of shifting pastoralism to maximise the gain from the meagre resources. As the soil becomes exhausted the only means of allowing it to recuperate is to leave it and move on.

The environment is harsh also in terms of disease. Redwater, east coast fever, rinderpest, pleuropneumonia and the tsetse fly have been major scourges of the animal population of most of the pastoral communities in the twentieth century. There is some evidence which suggests that these diseases have become common only fairly recently to East Africa, as a result of greater mobility and the opening up of the country by explorers. Redwater and east coast fever for instance, both tick-borne diseases, are said to have been imported through South Africa and Madagascar around the 1870s. Rinderpest is a virus which seems to have been introduced in Africa through North-East Africa around the 1840s; and pleuropneumonia, also a virus, infected African cattle from South Africa at about the same time. It is difficult to obtain accurate information on the origins in Africa of these diseases, but while some people argue that they have been spread through human migration, birds and wild animals, there also seems to be some evidence that animal disease has spread through the extension of commerce and transport and the consequent increased demand for meat, which are in turn consequences of the industrial revolution and the drawing of East Africa into the international economy of the nineteenth century.

The combination of drought and disease produces famine. During the nineteenth century widespread famine in pastoral areas occurred roughly every ten years : in 1868, 1878, 1888 and 1898. In the twentieth century famine occurred in 1903, 1908, 1918, 1928 and 1935, 1945, 1946, 1950, 1952, 1960 and 1968. The nineteenth-century famines seem to have been particularly severe. During the the last two famines of the nineteenth century we know that drought and disease, both animal and human, went hand in hand. The rinderpest epidemic of 1888–9 seems to have been the first outbreak of this disease in recorded history throughout *Eastern* Africa. In many areas the disease was accompanied in 1890 by drought, small pox, cholera, dysentry, typhus and bronchitis. Oddly enough historians have undertaken little research on famine. But two recent short accounts in the 1882–92 famine (one on Ethiopia and the other on Maasai) agree on its severity and the consequent misery and annihilation of herds and people. Clearly not all areas were equally affected, but all areas were effected at some point or another in severe conditions. Famine, it seems, can completely wipe out herds.

The very harshness of the environment has meant that the animals play a very vital role in pastoral economies in Eastern Africa. The need to obtain as large a number of animals as possible can only be understood against the background described below.

The value of stock

Animals have always been the pivot of the pastoralists' community values. To any pastoralist, his animals are the final insurance against the risk of famine. Security against death, which is often re-insured through dispersal of a man's herds at a number of different places, is of maximum importance. The animals provide pastoralists with the basic primary means of existence, the means of obtaining food, meat, milk and leather clothing. These are the *primary* values which stock-owning people take absolutely for granted.

But the pastoral peoples of East Africa are closely attached to their cattle and flocks for a variety of other secondary reasons. The animals provide a rational means (given the marginality of environment) of *storing wealth*. The object of all East African pastoralists has been to accumulate as many animals as they can possibly obtain. Animals provide a logical means of saving and accumulating wealth. Accumulation of animals has always been an economic necessity. However while some people in the nineteenth century accumulated enormous herds, few seem to have used their wealth to maintain their position through the generations. Most people seem to have redistributed their animals willingly enough, either through bride price and other social transactions or, in times of drought and famine, through exchange for food. A man who was considered to be generous during good years would find support and gifts after a famine so that he might rebuild his herd. The quality of men was measured by their generosity.

Intimately associated with accumulation of animals is the human relationships which accompany ownership. In a whole range of ways animals can be lent and exchanged and so bind people socially to each other. In the most extreme form in East Africa, in Burundi and Ruanda, cattle ownership among the Watutsi has in the past been the basis from which the Wahutu have been made a thoroughly dependent people. But in all pastoral groups animal ownership is the basis for a widespread social network of relationships. Thus the major object of cattle-rearing has been to obtain wealth and social status through accumulation, and so the socially ambitious turns his attention to his animals. The animals in a herd take on much more significance than mere utility; the future sus-tenance of the family is contained in the herds, they reflect a man's ambition in his community, they are in a real sense the measure of present and future values of the society.

Not only do the animals act as a measure of wealth, they provide the objects of exchange in social transactions. For instance in cases of law, of religious ritual, magic and at important events like mar-riage, birth and death, the use of the animals in sacrifice or in exchange expresses the importance of the social relationship. In all significant events the animals express the meaningfulness of the occasion, they bind people to each other, because the animals are considered important in themselves, and so lend importance to the occasion.

Finally, and perhaps not so surprisingly, the animals become the objects of warm personal affection. In many respects they are the repository of aesthetic values. Many clan songs and traditions surround the animals. In most pastoral societies each animal is closely associated with its owners. The herd is the chief object of interest among the people and it is protected by ritual observances.

In short the widespread secondary values of the herds predominate in people's consciousness. The cattle become objects of social ambition, rivalry and emotions; they are attributes of leadership and express meaning in social relations. People are passionately attached to their animals.

The deep meaning of flocks and stock in nomadic pastoral societies has been closely related to the character of the environment. Outsiders have many times over the last one hundred years noted this close attachment and berated the people for their 'sentimentality', particularly when they have refused to sell their animals for cash. But cash is not the same as cattle. Cash is impersonal, divisible, easily transferable and tends to alter in value over time. And while in principle it can buy the necessities of life, cash in the far-flung areas of East Africa has had very little use by comparison to animals, who not only maintain daily life but provide the final insurance against famine.

Growth and stagnation in the twentieth century

Law and order

In this section we shall examine what has happened to the peoples of the vast semi-arid areas of Kenya and Uganda during this century. We shall attempt to explain why the peoples have remained so poor right up to the present time.

The most important reason for the lack of change in these semi-arid areas is straightforward enough. Throughout the colonial period and up to 1970–1 the governments of both territories have been concerned primarily with the growth of agricultural crops, with the addition after 1945 of the development of overseas and locally owned secondary industries. (The chapters on agriculture, industry and exports in the twentieth century illustrate these dominating economic concerns of government.) It was therefore as a direct consequence of the agricultural and industrial direction of change that financial and administrative resources should be relatively denied to the nomadic pastoralists. At no time in either Kenya or Uganda, until very recently indeed, has there been a large-scale conscious policy to build up the stock-owning capacities of these areas.

Since the beginning of this century the predominant attitude of governments towards these areas has been to 'pacify' the semi-nomadic peoples and to maintain law and order. Initially the colonial powers found the Northern Frontier people the hardest to conquer, in particular the Somalis and Turkana who were themselves colonising territory. The Somalis had been slowly moving outwards till the middle of the sixteenth century when they had been defeated by the Ethiopians and Portugese. By the end of the nineteenth century the Somali were pushing southwards and had driven the Boran and Gabbra and Wardai Galla south of the River Tana. By 1902, when the British set up a military post at Darod, the Somali were seeking to dominate the area from Buna in the west through Wajir to the Tana river in the south-east. The initial British colonial policy in the area was to stop the Somali conquest, to divide the three groups' territories into grazing areas and so to control the entire area. The Wajir Boran were moved to Moyale District and some of the Wardai were moved to the south-west of the Garissa District to keep the peoples apart. The colonial policy was to separate the tribes and to impose definite boundaries between them. All the peoples in this area had a strong warrior tradition, an ability to move about rapidly in barren country and were able to obtain military support and arms from Ethiopia. The early British military expeditions found themselves faced by brave and intelligent forces who were able to maintain their resistance to pacification until the 1920s. The initial policy was simply to kill and disarm the men, burn their huts and seize the cattle, a straightforward policy of imposing 'law and order'. Having once established their military domination the British were concerned to stop the Somali advance and to establish firm boundaries between the grazing areas of different ethnic groups in an attempt to maintain peace between them. In 1934 a Special Districts Law Ordinance gave the Provincial Commissioner of the Northern Frontier District powers to define grazing and water boundaries in order to control human and stock movements in an attempt to avoid the armed combat which had taken place in the past.

The map on the opposite page illustrates what were called 'tribal grazing areas' east of Lake Rudolf. The Somali-Galla line was created by the 1934 Ordinance and constituted a grazing boundary between Galla and Somali, which neither were supposed to cross, in order to suppress local conflicts.

Throughout the entire colonial period Karamoja and the Northern Frontier areas were 'closed districts'. As in the initial period of conquest, the maintenance of law and order remained the major concern of the government officials. Raiding was considered to be

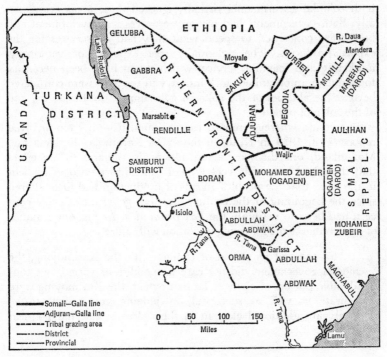

Northern Frontier District tribal grazing areas

This map illustrates the boundaries imposed on the northern nomadic peoples in Kenya which were intended to maintain law and order. In particular notice the Somali-Galla boundary.

the primary problem and as the British failed to understand the purpose of raiding, all they could do was to try and bottle nomadic people within boundaries. The best long-term hope, it was felt, for all these people was to settle them in agricultural pursuits, which would be administratively convenient. The white settlers feared competition from African herders and so were antagonistic to African livestock development. As a consequence the administration ignored the potential of cattle as a source of wealth, except in so far as the seizure of stock was regarded as an effective 'punishment' for misdemeanours and the basis on which levels of taxation were computed.

The entire Northern Province was considered essential to imperial Britain for strategic reasons. So the whole vast area was held through small scattered military and administration outposts whose job it was to maintain law and order and little else. Until the 1950s both colonial governments virtually ignored these areas economically. Both governments had meagre resources for development and both were concerned to spend what they had on services for the export producers. The potentially vast expenses of veterinary, marketing and scientific services which might have been necessary to stimulate an organised stock industry in the area were considered beyond the abilities of the colonial government until near the end of the colonial period.

As a result, wherever reports can be found from not too-involved reporters (in 1939 in Kitui, in the 1960s Karamoja, Turkana and Maasailand) one discovers again and again remarks to the effect that there had been only very limited expenditure on development in the area, that the peoples' means of production had little altered since the beginning of the century and that government's sole concern had been to maintain the *Pax Britannica*. As just one instance of these remarks the following quotation will suffice :

. . . for most of its period of contact with the Karimojong, the colonial government did not care to mobilise its varied and considerable powers of change. To that extent, the Karimojong were accurate as well as successful, in judging government to be merely an additional element in their already external political relation.

The altered ecological balance up to 1940

The diagram on the opposite page is a schematic illustration of the dynamics of the altered ecological balance in the semi-arid areas of Kenya and Uganda in the twentieth century. Ecology is simply the study of the relationship between man, animals and natural resources (land and water).

In the pre-colonial era the population of any given group was likely to have expanded. Certainly most nomadic groups of people were concerned to expand their herds of animals. And, as water supplies and grazing were limited there seems to have been a widespread tendency to divide up the resources according to (*a*) social accommodation with kin, and (*b*) force between alien groups.

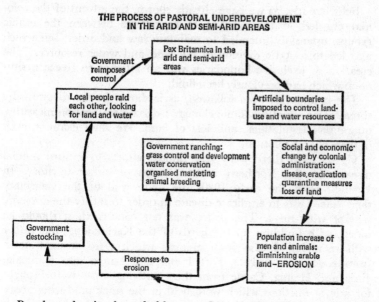

THE PROCESS OF PASTORAL UNDERDEVELOPMENT
IN THE ARID AND SEMI-ARID AREAS

Pax Britannica in the arid and semi-arid areas

Government reimposes control

Local people raid each other, looking for land and water

Artificial boundaries imposed to control land-use and water resources

Government ranching: grass control and development water conservation organised marketing animal breeding

Social and economic change by colonial administration: disease eradication quarantine measures loss of land

Government destocking

Responses to erosion

Population increase of men and animals: diminishing arable land – EROSION

People and animals probably moved hundreds of miles every year as cattle and camel owners migrated with their animals in response to the availability of water and grazing. Dr Chambers has described this pattern of movement as competition of nomadic opportunism . . .

> most able adaption to a harsh and unpredictable environment. Its flexibility, and the incentive it provides for vigorous exploitation of transient resources, make for more effective use of water and grazing than with a more rigid and more administrative system.

Thus it would seem that as the nomadic population expanded in the pre-colonial era the ecological balance was maintained by force. It is quite possible that behind the expansion of the Galla and then of the Somali people from the sixteenth century, there were expanding populations which had a major need for new pastures. These peoples had qualities of aggressive manliness and individual independence on the one hand, while on the other they had the political discipline to unite on a 'tribal-wide' basis. The environmental demands for herding had created peoples who were outstandingly tough and resilient. Certainly the peoples in the Northern Frontier who met the colonial invaders in the critical period of contact were able to maintain their independence until the 1920s, while their agricultural brethren had been unable to resist beyond 1905–8.

Subsequently, as we have already shown, the advent of the colonial era led to the erection of boundaries between the ethnic groups, ostensibly intended to maintain law and order, but which also led to a static division of the land and water resources. The creation of exclusive boundaries was an attempt to freeze a situation which had previously been fluid.

The boundaries were followed, as is shown in the diagram, by three major social economic changes: disease eradication measures, quarantine regulations, and loss of land. We shall examine each of these changes in turn.

Up to 1940 there were very limited efforts to control animal diseases in the Northern Frontier areas of either territory. In Uganda from the early 1920s the main goal of the veterinary department was to eradicate disease in order to satisfy the domestic market with meat. The policy was not concerned, it should be noted, with building up the herds of the Karimojong, but rather with removing disease from animals which were brought down from Karamoja, Ankole, Fort Portal and Lango into Kampala, Jinja and Hoima. Cattle from these outlying areas were brought for sale at auctions which were held in the stock-producing areas. Appointed and certificated buyers would then bring the animals for veterinary inspection and a permit was issued for movement out of the district. The animals were collected and walked along prescribed routes until they arrived at a quarantine boma where they would be inoculated and dipped against the various prevalent diseases. Finally they would be taken to slaughter at their destinations. There was little eradication of animal diseases in the pastoral areas themselves up to the period of the war, and consequently no opportunity to create a development and marketing policy. People would sell their beasts only when they had an absolute need for cash, for instance for taxes or in times of famine.

Equally in Kenya there were few disease eradication measures taken in the semi-arid areas up to 1940. In Uganda the veterinary department had had very limited financial resources and disease eradication had been beyond their means. In Kenya the situation was rather different, as it was not so much a lack of administrative resources but of the choice of priorities for expenditure. Here, we need to consider disease eradication and quarantine measures together.

Initially African cattle had provided the supply for European herds. Punitive expeditions during the period of conquest involved the confiscation of large numbers of cattle, which were then sold at private auctions to settlers. For instance in 1906, 11,000–12,000 head of Nandi cattle were sold in this manner.

As soon as Africans had provided the raw material for the European stock industry *great efforts were made to keep African and European animals apart*. The basic principles of stock development in Kenya were to support European ranching and to discourage African pastoralism. The policy of discouragement of African pastoralism was clearly spelled out by C. M. Dobbs, the Nyanza Provincial Commissioner, in 1914. At the time Dobbs was concerned with the lack of land available for Kipsigis.

> . . . it might seem as a gross piece of interference when we say that the native must be necessarily restricted in his pastoral tendencies. To such I distinctly state that the best interests of the natives are studied when they are restricted in such inclinations and are practically compelled to take to mixed agriculture. Among all African tribes excessive pastoral proclivities more or less influence nomadic or unsettled conditions in their life.

Belfield, the Governor, supported Dobb's contention strongly :

> I deprecate in the strongest possible way the suggestion that pernicious pastoral proclivities should be encouraged by the grant of any right for grazing purposes.
> My policy is to discourage these proclivities by every legitimate means, not only because they are productive of nomadic tendencies but because they inculcate in the minds of people a distaste for any settled industry.*

Nomadic pastoralism was administratively 'inconvenient', particularly as there was a constant 'law and order' problem. In practice there was no positive policy towards the people in the semi-arid areas. There was little understanding of the relationship between African and European stock-keeping and the dominant concern was simply to keep African and European stock apart so that the former did not infect the latter with disease.

The most important method used to keep the two sets of animals apart was to impose rigorous quarantine regulations on African pastoral areas, and then try to ensure that animals from a quarantine area did not move across the boundary. Rigorous measures characterised the Kenya Northern Frontier and all other pastoral areas in Kenya throughout this period. In order to understand this policy we need to examine the problems which the European ranching enterprise faced in relation to African stock-keepers.

While the pastoralists in the forest areas were denied access to markets through quarantine regulations, many of the pastoralists in

---

* The statements were repeated in the Kenya Land Commission, 1933–4.

the high rainfall areas lost their land to the European settlers and so were also denied access to the meat and milk market.

The Reserve boundaries provided the means to confiscate much of the land with the highest reliable rainfall and salt licks. The Maasai case is well known. They lost their best land : the Kapitir plains, Donyo Sabuk, the Central Rift Valley, the Mau, Laikipia and Uasin Gishu Plateaus. Not only was the area of land available to the Maasai reduced; what was left also had a lower and less reliable level of rainfall. The Maasai were forced to remain semi-nomadic pastoralists. Then to further compound Maasai problems of adaption to colonial economic conditions, their traditional form of selective breeding was denied them. 'Boran' bulls had always been selected with great care to produce animals adapted to dry conditions. The supply of such bulls came from Samburu and Somalia; with their fixed Reserve boundaries after 1912 and the European-settled lands forming a block to their north, the Maasai were completely cut off from new Boran stock.

The Nandi lost large areas of land too. In 1907 the Reserve was gazetted, in 1912 17 square miles was alienated from the Reserve and in 1919 another 130 square miles was taken for the soldier settlers; 60 square miles were returned in 1934.

The Kipsigis are said to have lost 800 square miles. They certainly had used land at Sotik, Buret, Londiani, Kedowa, Lumbwa and Fort Teran. Some of their lost land had been given to settlers, some to the Maasai and some was used by the Gusii. Not only had the Kipsigis lost so much land, but a large number of their salt licks had been taken also.

Both Nandi and Kipsigis were fortunate compared with many other pastoralists in the sense that the land left to them was well watered, and with the development of the tea plantations from the mid-1920s many pastoralists moved into cultivation of maize to provide *posho* for the tea workers. Many other Nandi and Kipsigis became squatters in order to find land for their cattle on the European land. They then provided cheap labour for the European. The Machakos Kamba had lost about half of the area they had once grazed. The Mau Hills, Donyo Sabuk and the Yatta plains had been lost although they were some of their most prized grazing lands.

The Tugen were another group which lost their best grazing land. Even the secretary of the Land Commission of 1934 argued that 'all good land, all the water, most of the grazing, was taken for European occupation; all barren, rocky, waterless land was left for the natives'.

Finally a section of the Samburu were moved in 1921 from the area they inhabited south of the Ewaso Nyiro river to Olormode, Lol Daikia hills; an area far less suitable for pastoral peoples. Many settled on the north bank of the river, which was infested with tsetse fly.

Very roughly, about 20 per cent of the settlers had gone in for herding and dairy farming. Many of these settlers had imported European bulls which were bred with local cows. It seems that the progeny of this crossing were more prone to the local diseases than indigenous stock as they lacked immunity. The settlers had an intense struggle to keep their animals free of disease and they attempted to keep their animals isolated from African herds. Thus they spent large sums of cash fencing their land and building dips. European cattle-owners spent a great deal of their time trying to remove African squatters' stock. It was vehemently argued that indigenous animals spread tick-borne and contagious diseases to European-owned animals. Thus fencing, dipping, removal of squatter stock and the quarantine regulations were defensive measures taken to preserve the European animals. The veterinary department co-operated wholeheartedly in these policy measures.

From the early 1920s every pastoral Reserve in the colony found itself in quarantine for one disease or the other. As a result it became illegal for African herdsmen to take their animals across a Reserve boundary for purposes of cash sales. The result of this policy was that the peoples of the Northern Frontier lost their old outlets for selling surplus animals.

In addition, the establishment of international boundaries affected the export of livestock. For instance the port at Kismayu, in the former British province of Jubaland, was ceded to Italy and so lost as a sales outlet for Kenyan pastoralists. Two other traditional outlets for the sale of animals from the North-Eastern Frontier were altered in character. One was at Lamu and the other was at Nyeri and Meru. For years before the colonial period stock was taken on the hoof to Lamu where it was transferred along the coast by dhow. Such a trade could have been developed as a major outlet for surplus animals, but no official encouragement was forthcoming, although by 1930 it seems the North-East Frontier beef had a major market at Zanzibar. During the colonial era severe difficulties were placed in the way of Kikuyu trade through the enforcement of stringent quarantine regulations at Isiolo. The Kikuyu goat and sheep trade did however continue clandestinely, often at night, when the animals were brought down to Meru and Nyeri in covered trucks. The quarantine restrictions and the lack of official encouragement to trade were therefore subsidiary but important elements in preventing the sale of surplus stock and fundamentally altering the ecological balance between man, animals and natural resources.

The tragedy of this situation can be vividly understood from part of a private letter written in 1932 by a European stock-owning member of the Carter Commission :

> I had not realised before that this province [the Northern Frontier] is bigger than the whole east of Kenya put together. It is hot and badly watered but it produces the best native cattle and sheep that I have seen in Kenya. It was surprising to put it mildly, to motor as we did through mile after mile of country which seemed nothing but rock bare earth, thorn trees all about . . . and then came to Uasa Nyiro, a real good river and find a herd 7500–600 head of real good native cattle in splendid conditions. Some of bullocks were really big and fat and as fat as some of our fattest Queen. The sheep are really good for native sheep and give most excellent mutton. The numbers of both are immense, probably well over 500,000 head of cattle and more sheep to say nothing of large herds of camels. There is a good market for the sheep mainly to the Kikuyu, but the cattle are as if shut in a tin box made of quarantine regulations. The abuse of the Veterinary Department by officials one meets up here exceeds anything that F.J. [Frank Joyce] and I can produce at our hottest . . . It does seem wrong that a country like the NFD with all the possibilities it holds as a great stock area should be completely held up by Quarantine Regulation. If it was developed by boreholes and better watering facilities it should be a most valuable asset to Kenya but . . . ? It is rather depressing to sense the feeling of hostility there is in really all the officials one meets and distrust towards the settlers in this part of the world. A great deal of it is due to these Quarantine Regulations which they look on as being forced on Government by Settlers . . .

This letter illustrates not only the missed opportunity for development of the Kenya stock industry, but also the feelings of frustration held by veterinary department officials in carrying out a policy which was concerned solely to support ranching. Quarantine regulations not only kept African stock off the domestic market but also reduced the supply of meat, so keeping prices high for European producers. An official memorandum in 1937 clarified the situation.

> For many years the pastoral native reserves have been in perpetual veterinary quarantine. This has been caused partly by the presence of disease but largely by economic considerations.

The expenditure at any time of comparatively small sums of money on veterinary services for these areas would have enabled them rapidly to be liberated from quarantine with disastrous effect upon the price of stock and stock products within the Colony.

Africans were even restricted from buying or selling cattle at official auctions in order to stop the price dropping too far and to protect European sales. The restrictions on African pastoral development in Kenya can only be understood in relation to the positive emphasis that was placed on European stock development. African pastoralists in Kenya were sacrificed on the altar of white settlement. In the longer run the very success of the Kenya Meat Commission and the Creameries Co-operative (both of which developed originally from the production of the large farms) was due to the pauperisation of the peoples of the pastoral areas.

Erosion, land shortage and overstocking
By the 1930s the semi-arid areas of Kenya and Uganda had begun to be seriously eroded, although there was no indication of erosion in Uganda until the 1950s. As the population of men and beasts grew, and as the people could not compete militarily for land and water resources, the land became over-used. In many areas due to the pressure of the animal population the grass never had time to recover from one season to the next. Thus when the rains came the crucial topsoil would be washed away as there were no plants left to hold it in place. The ethnic boundaries and the quarantine restrictions held the animals inside the Reserves, while the lack of positive marketing arrangements did not allow a reduction of the numbers of beast in a controlled fashion. By the mid 1930s even the colonial authorities had realised that it was necessary to open the pastoral areas of Kenya and Uganda to a market which could sustain a regular off-take of animals. The problem was where could a market be found which would not reduce the prices of European stock sales, and which would not come into contact with European herds.

By the 1930s the increasing population of people and animals had begun seriously to press against the static natural resources. Malthus had argued in 1803 that worldwide population would inevitably increase faster than the production of food. In most parts of the world technical change has kept food production increasing as fast as population, but in relation to the semi-arid areas of Kenya and Uganda, Malthus' predictions appeared to be ominously correct.

At one time pastoralists would fire an area, which would kill bush and unwanted ticks while leaving the grass roots intact. In the 1930s many district officers with experience in pastoral areas discussed the fact that once the grass had grown as high as men, but that by the 1930s the land had become covered with unpalatable bush and the grass rarely grew to more than a few inches high. The availablity of succulent grass in Kenya had declined and people had ceased to burn the undergrowth : not only was the pasturage poor, but the ticks were uncontrolled.

The pastoral problem was clearly acute, but what could be done depended on who defined the problem. Was it one of erosion, of overstocking or of land shortage?

The question was confused by the different attitudes and values placed on stock by Africans and Europeans. The African pastoralists' pre-colonial attitude to cattle has already been outlined at some length. There was no rational reason for pastoralists to alter their existing attitudes. They still wanted as many animals as possible, not simply for purposes of status, but because everyone knew that famines were part of the climatic cycle. The creation of Reserve boundaries had done nothing to alter this stark reality; there had been little alteration in pastoral technology, in water or disease control for instance, and the new restrictions had made the traditional insurances against the environment almost impossible to operate.

African pastoralists were not wedded to their traditional way of life in the twentieth century out of misplaced sentiment but because of the hard realities of their situation. In the past, raiding other people's cattle had been part of the system. All people who practised the art of moving cattle according to the season also practised the art of obtaining as many cattle as possible. The basis of nomadism had been maintained in the capitalist era and so it followed that raiding would too. It was not surprising therefore that pastoralists did not see that they were overstocked, but only that they were denied green pastures elsewhere.

The European attitude towards African nomadic pastoralists was a compound of self-interest and mythology, based on the culture-bound assumption that animals could only be valued as exchangeable property. It was widely believed that nomadic ways of life were inferior and should be stopped and that agriculture should be introduced instead. In the short term they believed that it was quite useless allocating extra land in overstocked areas since this would only encourage further animal accumulation. The problem, as it was widely understood by Europeans, was the pastoralists' irrational attitude towards stock accumulation. They argued that the only way to deal with the problem was to destock the herds drastically at frequent intervals, by either finding a market for people to sell their animals or simply to shoot the animals, until the people's irrationality ceased and they would destock of their own accord. The Europeans' view of African pastoralists was that 'native economics are makeshift, unorganised and primitive opportunist rather than based on rational constant and socially observed principles'.

This view held far greater currency than that of one acute observer who noted that the pastoralists'

> economic system is one which is rational within its own tradition . . . efficient on its own level and in harmony with the society of which it has traditionally formed an integral and closely knit part.

Clearly there was no compromise solution between these two viewpoints. And for a while the majority European view prevailed. The problem was understood in terms of 'overstocking'.

Overstocking is only a relative term. It is concerned with the relationship between the number of animals and the shortage of grass in a given territory with an unchanging technology. Overstocking has nothing to do with the numbers of people who require a given number of animals to remain alive. The Europeans concerned figured that if the number of people and animals increased then it was likely that the number of animals would reduce the vegetation and browsing in the rainy seasons to such an extent that there would be insufficient fodder available for the animals during the dry season. The results would be, first an increase in the likelihood of famine, and secondly that the top soil would be washed away during the rainy season as there would not remain sufficient cover to hold it together. The people, they argued, were destroying their own lands through wilful neglect.

There was widespread evidence for the development of soil erosion in the pastoral areas of Kenya by the late 1930s. Published and unpublished reports illustrated the problem; the following are just a few extracts from these reports which showed the extent of the impoverishment of the nomadic pastoral areas in Kenya in the late 1930s.

> The Kamasia, Elgeyo, Marakwet, East Suk, West Suk and Njemps reserves may be considered to be amongst the agricultural slums of Kenya colony . . . these areas have been little touched by the activities of the technical department of Government.

The semi-arid grassland has become the fixed abode of the great native tribes, the Maasai, the Kamba, . . . the Samburu, the Meru and the Embu. The continuous pressure wrought by their grazing animals on what was once a rich and palatable pasture-land, has now almost completely destroyed the original cover and given rise to unpalatable herbs, water-robbing thorn thickets, serious erosion and famine.

From the point of view of man the conditions of the Kamba reserve is deplorable . . . the mainly uninhabited and uninhabit-able [area] is encroaching steadily and aggravating a pressure problem which is already dangerously acute.

. . . when I first knew Nandi in 1921, the greater part of the reserve from Kapsabet northwards was good agricultural stock country with grass growing to a height of 3 feet and over. Today a great change for the worse is noticeable, and the grass produces no more than 2 or 3 inches of herbage which cannot nourish the stock it has to carry; all the stock I have seen recently in the reserve were in a half-starved condition.

The evidence showed conclusively that the pastoral areas of Kenya were becoming impoverished. The European response to this situation was to cull the cattle by force or else to arrange the forced sale of the animals.

From the late 1920s and throughout the 1930s the interconnected problems of erosion and overstocking were hotly debated by the veterinary section of the colonial administration. A meat canning factory was suggested at the beginning of the 1930s; it was arranged that it would be supplied on government guarantee with a minimum number of animals every year at a fixed price. The factory would create a market for the pastoral peoples to sell their animals, thus destocking could be enforced and the European stock industry would be protected as the price offered by the factory for the beasts would be well below the price demanded by European stock-owners.

From the middle of the 1930s stock routes were planned from the main stock-holding areas of the country: they were planned so that the animals could be brought down from the Samburu, Kajiado, Narok and Kitui areas to supply the factory at Athi River. The planned routes were organised so that the cattle avoided the European areas and thus could not infect the European beast on the way.

The factory was owned by Liebigs, a Rhodesian, private, profit-making concern. It was invited by the colonial government to set up its business at Athi River, where the Kamba and Maasai stock routes connected. The factory cost £120,000 and required a minimum of 40,000 head of cattle per year to break even. This minimum requirement was guaranteed by government and so the administration set about organising themselves in order to provide the animals. They decided to create public auctions in the reserves where Liebigs would offer a fixed price. But this idea had to be dismissed because it was realised that Nairobi butchers would be able to buy at a price just above that offered by Liebigs, bring the meat back to the Nairobi market and so undercut the prices paid for European meat. The European stock-owners, who were organised in an association, were keen to see that the African animals were taken by force in one way or the other in order that the meat taken by Liebigs would not compete in the market-place with their own.

Liebigs began buying operations from the latter half of 1937 'without any success at all', as the prices they offered were very low. The highest price they offered was 15 shillings for a full-grown animal, while they were offering 2 or 3 shillings for a goat or sheep. The prices outside the Liebig market at this time were in the region of 60 to 100 shillings for a bullock down to 10 shillings for a goat. Liebig had clearly hoped to take full advantage of the semi-monopoly they had been offered by the colonial government. The first strategy to obtain the African animals had failed.

By the end of 1937 the administration decided to brand the poorest cattle in the Machakos region, confiscate the branded animals and to sell them compulsorily at public auctions. In this manner they thought they could obtain the requisite number of animals at the price which Liebigs said was profitable. Hence they developed two prices for meat, one for European cows and another, much lower one, for African animals.

On 25 January 1938, the Governor gave the go-ahead for the forcible confiscation of animals. By July of that year 20,000 had been obtained. But the Europeans acted without any comprehension of the situation among Kamba stock-owners and in some cases took up to 80 per cent of an individual's herd. These draconian measures which led directly to the well-known Akamba political protest when some of the people marched on Government House and the whole matter was brought up in the British Parliament. This incident severely embarrassed the Kenya colonial government, as one of the guiding principles of colonial government was to maintain freedom from interference by the imperial power in day-to-day affairs. As a result the compulsory culling of Akamba stock was stopped in August 1938.

The original question of overstocking remained; so far as Kenya's colonial government was concerned the above incident was a temporary setback; Liebigs was their answer to the pastoral problem and so in November 1938 they were preparing to reinstate compulsion. Liebigs were also in favour of compulsion. By May 1939 branding and culling in the Samburu and Kamasia areas had begun again but on a smaller scale to the earlier Akamba culling. The whole pastoral question was, however, shelved with the outbreak of the Second World War.

Attempts at pastoral development since 1945

The Akamba incident exemplifies the difference between African and European attitudes to nomadic pastoralists. But the colonial governments could not ignore the pastoral problem after 1945, as the land was deteriorating rapidly everywhere. Also, as we saw in both chapters on agriculture, colonial attitudes towards change in the African areas altered considerably after 1945. Money was made available for a range of schemes and projects in both territories.

In northern Uganda rough animal censuses showed that the number of beasts had increased from 47,000 in 1919 to 93,000 in 1948, and to 132,000 by 1959. This was an increase of nearly 300 per cent in forty years. Part of the increase was due to extensive vaccination programmes against contagious bovine pleuro-pneumonia which were carried out in the late 1940s and early 1950s, and by the 1960s the FAO had developed an anti-rinderpest vaccine. In the three years between 1964 and 1966, 760,000 cattle in Uganda alone were innoculated against the latter disease. These were the only stock health measures in northern Uganda which had ever been carried out in the area.

During these years nothing was done to improve the quality of the pasture land in Karamoja. There was no effort made to introduce the new species of hardy grasses nor any attempt to introduce range management or principles of rational grazing. In fact the area of grazing available to the Karimojong was reduced as areas were ceded to Teso and Sebei districts, while the Kenya Suk people were allowed into the Karimojong areas. By Independence the Karimojong had been forced into a smaller area than they had commanded 60 years previously despite their increased population.

It was reported that by 1963 there was a deep resentment of government 'among the people in Karamoja district'. Not only had there been little effort at economic development, but it was widely believed that the government took large profits out of the existing trade, and continuous exhortation of the people to settle down into agriculture was an attitude which was hardly likely to win respect. There was a saying by 1963, 'the government eats our cattle'.

Cattle development did take place in parts of Uganda after 1945 but not in the north. Efforts were made to introduce new feeding techniques and grazing enclosures in the areas around Kampala. The Kampala area was chosen for pastoral development because the administration argued that the Baganda were more responsive to change, thus money and effort expended on them were more than in peripheral areas. Such an argument was no doubt correct, as the Buganda province was close to the centre of administration. This area was also well watered. But by denying support to the north, regional economic differences were likely to be exacerbated over time. Secondly, Uganda on the whole found herself short of beef; by 1960 she was importing high-quality beef and £1 million worth of dairy products from Kenya. If Uganda had the potential for pastoral development this situation was hard to justify.

Moreover, and more seriously, in Karamoja there was evidence by the late 1950s and early 1960s that 'overstocking' and erosion had begun to occur at an alarming rate. It was argued that the edible vegetation was diminishing and was replaced by parasitic vegetation, which was inedible. It seemed that the dry season pasture was diminishing so that the stock-carrying capacity of the land was reduced. Thorn bush cover was replacing grass and bare open surfaces were leading to massive gully erosion. It was even suggested by some authorities that desert conditions were being created from which there could be no return. While technical experts, as usual, disagreed on the extent of the problem, the fact of diminishing pastures appears to have been incontrovertible.

The first act of the new independent government was to demonstrate an interest in the area. The government agreed that the Karimojong needed to be 'modernised'. Once more, however, it seemed that nobody considered attempting to make them into better herdsmen : cattle again were ignored and agriculture was supported by the new administration. To the Karimojong very little must have seemed to have altered. Admittedly, 108 new dams were built, but they did not last long as they were built of earth.

The people of the area still await an integrated policy covering all the forces of production which include marketing and disease eradication, land rotation and water development. Yet it ought to be added that even when all the forces of material production have been altered by the outside forces of government, we should not expect the nomadic pastoralists to stop accumulating animals. It seems that it will be most unlikely that they will begin to market their animals under such altered economic conditions. The nomadic pastoralist has had a long experience of drought and famine over the last eighty or ninety years, so we can expect that the social relations of pastoral production (which are concerned primarily with the accumulation of stock) are unlikely to respond to changes in material conditions until it can be shown that these conditions have in fact altered and that they are not being advised by some official who, in their opinion, is an outsider who will soon go away. The existing basic problems of land shortage and erosion have occurred in a situation of increasing numbers of people and animals and are by themselves only the initial problems to be solved.

In Kenya the situation overall was very different, in that considerable economic and administrative resources had been invested in the high potential areas, i.e. areas receiving over 20–30 inches of rainfall of which roughly 90 per cent were held by Europeans. Initially, the major pastoral developments had been concentrated solely in the White Highlands through the Kenya Co-operative Creameries and the Kenya Meat Commission. After Independence in 1963 the knowledge and expertise of these monopoly institutions was extended to small-scale farmers in many areas of the countryside. As a result the high quality side of the meat and dairy market has developed rapidly until today when there is a large surplus of high-quality meat and milk for export.

But efforts to develop the lower quality side of the market from the semi-arid areas were not so successful. The semi-arid areas included 73,000 square miles which received between 10 and 20 inches of rain annually, and 60,000 square miles with less than 10 inches, virtually useless semi-desert. Out of this total of 133,000 square miles only 14,000 square miles had received any attention from grazing schemes by 1960. It should be added that this figure implies that 14,000 more square miles had received some attention by 1945 and is of course no small achievement. The goals of the grazing schemes were to heal the existing damage to the land, to prevent further erosion and finally to increase the carrying capacity of the land.

The grazing schemes were located in the areas which were very badly damaged. They all also happened to be concentrated in the smaller districts, such as West Pokot, Baringo, Elgeyo Marakwet and Samburu, and so the large areas of the Northern Frontier tended to be ignored. Between 1945 and 1960 820,000 shillings (£54,700) per annum was spent on the ranching schemes in all. The European and African veterinary staff more than doubled, while veterinary department expenditure trebled between 1946 and 1952.

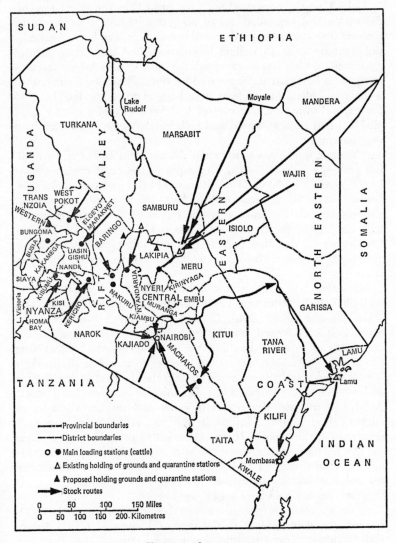

Kenya stock movement

Here we see the direction of stock movement and routes which have been
developed since 1945. It is not by chance that the poorest areas of Kenya
export their main food commodity to the richer agricultural areas. (This
is explained in the text.) Even Swynnerton realised that one of the colonial
administration's greatest functions was to control stock numbers, disease
and the denudation of the land in this vast area.

E

As in Uganda, compared with the pre-1940s, the effort towards disease control expanded out of all recognition as it began to be realised that European cattle could not be kept free from disease by isolation. By 1955 13 million inoculations had been given against rinderpest, which again excepted the north. Also bovine pleuro-pneumonia had nearly disappeared by 1960. The tsetse fly remained a major problem, but at least it had begun to be tackled. In 1945 the expenditure on tsetse control had been virtually nil, by 1952 £67,000 had been allocated and reclamation of tsetse-infected land was under way.

A further important eradication development is worth mentioning although it has affected all people in the rural areas : that is locust control. A plague of locusts could in the past cause a famine. Locusts were an international problem as they did not respect national boundaries. Since 1945 the red locust has been eradicated with the help of the International Desert Locust Control. The Control discovered that they bred from the Arabian peninsula and was able to destroy them before they spread and devastated grass and crops.

Marketing was also developed over these years. Between 1945 and 1960 stock routes began to be organised between the semi-arid areas and the urban areas, Central and Nyanza Provinces. The routes had to be fenced, grazing grounds created and water supplies and cattle dips built. In 1952 the African Livestock Marketing Organisation (ALMO) was set up, in order to stimulate the marketing of animals from these areas, to help the destocking programme and to help the Kenya Meat Commission obtain cheap stock. ALMO went into the northern areas and set up abattoirs at Archer's Post and at Marigat in Baringo. ALMO was run on a non-profit making basis. It was intended to provide market-places for the northern cattle keepers and to encourage traders to come up from the south. ALMO itself then provided a minimum price for animals sold in an attempt to stop traders working in combination which would have kept prices low.

As we see there were some considerable efforts made in the 1950s towards the development in the semi-arid areas of Kenya before Independence. There is little doubt that many of the European participants were genuinely concerned in their efforts. But the understanding of the problem and the intentions of the administrators left much to be desired. The attitude of slight contempt for the pastoral peoples' way of living, which was so prevalent before 1940 had not altered very much by Independence. For instance the outgoing colonial Ministry of Agriculture wanted to show just how much the British had done for Kenya. They produced a glossy

publication* in which they argued that the land of the pastoral and
semi-pastoral peoples

> . . . is owned by the tribe and grazing is free for all. As a result
> of this system coupled with such factors as the control of stock
> diseases and the curbing of lawlessness introduced by the British
> Administration much of this land was badly overgrazed 16 years
> ago.

The point that the Ministry ignored was that much of the land
remained overgrazed and that most of the grazing schemes were
failures. Even the above-mentioned book noted that less than 25
per cent of the area under grazing schemes had been improved,
and the actual figure was lower. By 1962 only 10 per cent of the
schemes were operational. The explanations for these failures were
individually complicated, but overall the aim had been negative
rather than positive; it had been to preserve an area from further
erosion, rather than to fully develop the resources of that area.
Thus the rehabilitation of the land took precedence over improved
animal husbandry and large-scale ranching, i.e. integrating development of the various factors of land, water, grass, animals and man.
As a result the compulsory reduction of the numbers of stock was
usually the first step taken by the administrators of these schemes.
Not surprisingly, these measures met fierce opposition by the
people, as they had done in the 1930s, for exactly the same reasons.
After the disastrous drought and floods of 1960–1 the rotational
schemes went into abeyance as once again the pastoralists were
reinforced in their wisdom in the accumulation of animals and the
stupidity of the government officials.

Conclusion

As a result, we find that the semi pastoral areas of Kenya and
Uganda are grossly underdeveloped in the 1960s and people still
continue to grope for an economic solution to these vast but thinly
populated areas. In North-Eastern Kenya the water controls and
arbitrary boundaries established by the British have broken down.
With the breakdown of local and international boundaries came
the Shifta problem, as many Somali tried to push the international
boundary westwards by force. The Kenya Army dealt severely with
the people, killing men and animals with little discrimination and
hardly bringing the economic solution any nearer. In a report on

* *African Land Development in Kenya*, Ministry of Agriculture, Nairobi
(1962) p. 7.

the Turkana it was argued that 'Turkana is in a dangerously over-populated condition . . . The district is severely overgrazed which causes a dangerous deterioration of the natural resources.' It was also quite clear that the Turkana's attitude to stock-keeping had remained unchanged, as had the precariousness of their existence. A real effort was being made among the Maasai who, it may be remembered, did not have such a hostile environment to combat as the peoples of the north. Here the people were being persuaded to take up wheat-growing in the Narok area, or to establish privately-owned group farms at Kaputei. This latter scheme too had failed, as during a local famine the people in the scheme had allowed their neighbours to use grazing. As the people argued, 'when famine comes to us we too want to use our neighbours' grazing'.

The major failure to bring the nomadic pastoralists into the capitalist system can be seen in relation to the question of raiding. Raiding had been at the heart of the problem of administration from the beginning of colonisation. In the Karamoja district raiding had been slight in the late 1920s and 1930s. But the number of raids appeared to be increasing slowly in the 1940s and more rapidly in the 1950s. In 1950 74 cattle-raids had been reported to the police; by 1960 it had risen to 410 per annum. As the pressure on the grazing area increased in the Karamoja, Suk and Turkana areas, so each group turned towards their neighbours to find new land and bitter fighting resulted. In the 1960s the new governments reacted exactly like their predecessors in many of these areas. A special police force was set up in both territories and there is plenty of evidence that they acted brutally, seizing cattle and killing people. In one incident it was reported that a special Uganda force seized 47,000 head of cattle and 65,000 goats and sheep 'plus the loss of many lives during the operation'. The Turkana remain desperately ungoverned people who live more or less permanently at or below the margins of existence.

By 1969, 20 per cent of the Turkana had migrated to find work as herders in Samburu and Isiolo. Only 450 Turkana were in the main cities. They, like the Karimojong, have become grossly under-privileged to the extent that they have lost their independence as herders. The new government attitude towards nomadic peoples had not fundamentally altered; they wanted to settle the people and introduce agriculture, a typically foreign viewpoint based on different assumptions and ideals to those of the people whom they were supposed to help.

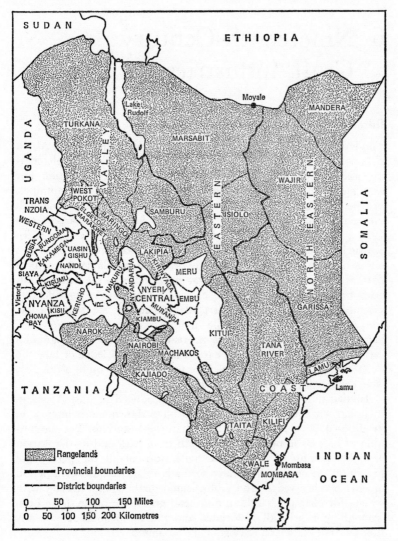

Kenya rangelands

This map illustrates the enormous area in Kenya which is suitable only for keeping cattle. The carrying capacity for animals varies within the area; in the most arid parts the potential for existence is almost nil.

6 Nineteenth-Century Craft Industries

Introduction

The industry in hand-made goods in nineteenth-century East Africa is important because such goods were vital to society, supplementing and complementing agricultural and pastoral activities. For example, iron hoes were used by all agricultural communities. Weapons, such as iron spears, were also important. The people with the more skilful blacksmiths, who could forge the sharpest and longest-lasting swords, had a distinct advantage over people without such craftsmen. Salt was another essential commodity produced on a small scale. A great deal of salt was available from local natural sources, for example salt was extracted from the water of salt lakes or dug from the shores. Salt was traded over considerable distances but supplies were irregular especially for those people who did not have a suitable natural source of salt in their neighbourhood. As a substitute a great deal of salt was manufactured from plants, leaves and earths. But our knowledge of how the extraction processes, of which there were probably quite a number, were carried out is still very limited.

Textiles and clothes were also being produced in East Africa in the nineteenth century. But tourists have shown more interest in 'traditional' East African clothing than the historians. Yet the tanning of hides, the production of cloth from bark and its decoration and the making of ornaments to be worn about the person are highly skilled crafts which have virtually disappeared over a period of only seventy years. The sophisticated methods and artistry with which, for example, clothing and head gear were made, have been ignored by nearly all historians, and sadly the abilities of many thousands of craftsmen have gone unrecognised.

Because of the lack of data we can only provide a sketch of iron, salt and textile production in nineteenth-century East Africa. Other goods were also manufactured, including pottery, basket work, house construction, boat building, the making of fish traps and weaving and also silver working at the coast, but so little information is available that we are unable to give an adequate description of these industries. The brief descriptions of the making of agricultural implements, weapons, clothing and ornaments have all been adapted from *Tribal Crafts of Uganda,* by Margaret Trowell and K. Wachsman. They illustrate the variety of iron goods that were manufactured in Uganda before 1900.

The iron industry

In order to understand the nature of the iron industry we need, first of all, to describe the essential processes of iron manufacture. The iron ore used was found only in a few specific places. In some areas it was found in rough stone, in others it was found in the sands and rocks of river beds and in yet others it was found as particles in the earth. In all cases the sediment could be washed or sieved away leaving the ore.

The second stage was the smelting process. The ore was placed in specially constructed clay furnaces in which the heat source was charcoal and into which air was blown by means of bellows as a form of temperature regulation. After anything from half an hour to two or three hours, depending on the skill of the smelters, the red-hot iron became molten, the waste material evaporated in gaseous form and the slag (solid waste) could be separated. This process may seem simple but it took both time and a great deal of skill. The smelted iron had to be made malleable (capable of being hammered) so that it could be forged by a smith. In order to make the iron malleable to the correct degree the smelting process had to be just right. If the charcoal was of the right quality and the air draught was sufficient and well-directed to bring the furnace to the correct temperature, the carbon formed would combine with the iron in the correct proportion to produce the properly malleable metal. Considerable quantities of iron ore and charcoal were needed to produce only a small amount of usable metal. Often one smelting, which involved all the work described above, would produce only enough metal for a simple hoe. Iron goods were therefore highly valued. When East Africa was colonised by European nations the import of relatively cheap iron goods from the West began. The blast furnaces fell into disuse releasing many men from the laborious task of smelting. The smiths could now obtain all the material they needed from discarded cars and other sources of scrap metal.

The design of the blast furnaces appears to have varied considerably not only between areas but also within particular localities. Some of the taller furnaces were up to ten feet in height and as they were fed from the top, a ladder was needed to fill them. Dr

Sutton in Tanzania has argued that the size of the furnace was determined by the type of ore that was to be smelted. In areas where the ore contained small quantities of iron, a large amount had to be smelted down to produce a worthwhile quantity of iron and so large furnaces were used. In some areas both tall and small furnaces were used in conjunction. In these areas it was necessary to carry out the smelting process twice in order to produce iron of a suitable quality for forging.

Once the molten metal had solidified and cooled it was ready for forging. The smith would place the piece of iron on a bed of red-hot charcoal in a small furnace in which the temperature was again regulated with a pair of bellows. When the iron was soft enough he would remove it from the fire with a pair of tongs. He would then cut the iron with a special knife. Next, with a large hammer weighing about eight pounds, he would hammer out the rough shape of the article he was making. The iron would be replaced in the furnace a number of times during shaping in order to keep it sufficiently soft for hammering. Finally, the smith would shape the article into its final form with a three-pound hammer. The heavy hammer created the crude outline of the tool and the lighter hammer was used to add the finishing touches.

The heat of the furnaces was regulated by bellows which could be either of two types. One type consisted of a single piece of wood covered with soft goat skin and then worked up and down to create the blast of air. These are known as bowl bellows and appear to have been much more common than the second type, bag bellows. Bag bellows consisted of a whole goat skin attached to a wooden frame which was worked up and down to produce the blasts of air. Operating either type of bellows was an art in itself. Bag bellows are known to have been used in different parts of Tanzania but, as far as the authors know, they were not found in Kenya or Uganda. There were several variations of the two types used in different areas.

The smith used a number of special tools. He needed a pair of tongs with which to remove the heated iron from the furnace. For hammering the iron he used a large flat stone as an anvil and he needed one hammer approximately eight pounds in weight and another of about three pounds, themselves made of iron, with which to beat the hot metal into shape. The hammer was the smith's specially treasured tool – the symbol of his trade. While the smiths still working at their ancient craft will be content to use imported tongs, they invariable prefer their locally made hammer which has probably been handed down to them over generations, to any other of foreign manufacture.

The smiths' work was very important to all societies of East Africa. The reason for this is easily understood when one considers the range of tools and weapons the smiths could make. The following is a list of some of the more common articles made.

1. Small knives for harvesting millet and knives for kitchen use.
2. Large knives for cutting trees and hewing wood.
3. Tools for canoe manufacture.
4. Hoes – many different types were manufactured in Uganda.
5. Sickles.
6. The metal parts of spears and walking sticks.
7. Axe-heads.
8. Arrow-heads.
9. Chisels for cutting wood.
10. Coiled ornaments worn about the ankles and wrists.
11. Needles used in basket weaving.
12. Bells which were hung round the necks of domestic animals.
13. Wire.
14. Fine chains for decoration of the person.

This list is not an exhaustive one by any means. Some groups of people produced particular articles which were not available elsewhere, e.g. the chains made by the Akamba. The services of the smiths were essential to both agricultural and pastoral peoples.

The apprenticeship and status of smiths

It will be apparent from the above outline of the technology of the iron industry that smelting and forging required special skills which had to be learnt. These skills were acquired by young men through apprenticeship and very often the skills were passed on from father to son. But although iron-working was the exclusive preserve of particular clans, it was often the case that only some of the young men of a clan would learn to become smiths or smelters. It was very common to find young men paying a fee of goats to a master smith in order to obtain entry into the trade.

Part of the reason why smiths and smelters usually made no attempt at keeping their industry an exclusive one seems to be that they were, in fact, often looked down upon and young men would leave the iron industry in order to take up agriculture as the more favourable occupation. It is an over simplification to suggest that all iron-workers had a low status in their societies; in many cases they commanded an attitude of fear or one of respect. Also, their industry was associated with religion and magic for the smiths and smelters fashioned iron from sand or rock into useful objects for the community. While people knew very well how the operations of iron production were carried out, nobody understood the chemical processes involved. It was natural therefore that magical properties should be assigned to the process of iron production. A whole range of mores, prescriptions and taboos surrounded the people who worked in the iron industry. In some societies a smith was not permitted to marry a farmer's daughter unless he gave up his work to become a farmer himself. In other cases smiths were exempt from taking part in battle and so were described as being like the women. It is probable that a poor man's son might become a smith in order to accumulate enough goats and animals which he would then use to buy a plot of land of his own. Or he might become a smelter for the same reason. The social standing of the groups or clans associated with the iron industry varied widely from one place to another. Although smelting and iron forging were activities which were essential to all communities in East Africa – hoes for agriculture and spears for warfare were indispensable items in nearly every area – it was quite common to find that smelters and smiths were regarded as inferior people.

It would seem probable that as the political organisation of communities developed and changed over time, rulers began to employ specialised craftsmen. In such a suitation the talents of such men received wide recognition and their status rose accordingly. Thus we find that the royal households employed craftsmen whose work would enhance the positions of their masters. Such men rose to privileged positions in their communities, unlike their counterparts in acephalous societies.

The following description is taken from an article by Margaret Trowell written in 1941.

All royal craftsmen in Buganda were given gifts of land and were exempt from paying taxes or labour duties. They were a protected minority. Trowell's article deals only with smiths, drum-makers and potters, although it is probable that bark cloth makers, house builders and canoe makers were among the royal craftsmen, all of whom had equal privileges and were closely attached to the Kabaka's household. The smiths especially were extremely skilled men and their work was highly specialised, as the following quotation illustrates :

> The leader of the royal craftsmen and often his second in command holds a hereditary position and comes from one particular clan, although the workmen under him may be of any clan. But among the smiths many of the clans seem to have their own closed groups where all the workmen will be of one clan and

where only a certain type of work is done. Thus the *Nvubu* clan have always been makers of the royal shields and the bracelets, anklets and other ornaments for the Kings' wives; while the *Ente* clan make the weapons and agricultural implements.

The geographical distribution of the iron industry

The manufacture of iron goods took place in many parts of East Africa during the nineteenth century, although our knowledge of the exact distribution of the industry is still incomplete. It is probable that most people will know about local blacksmiths who worked in their own area, but no proper surveys have as yet been carried out. The following account should give readers some idea of how widespread the iron industry was and how many peoples manufactured articles from iron.

The Akamba of the region that is now part of Kenya were skilled iron-workers. They obtained their ore by panning in streams. Their smiths produced a variety of iron products, including chains for decoration of the person; which were famous from the Coast to Lake Victoria. The Kikuyu also seem to have made wide use of articles made of iron. Routledge, in 1910, mentioned spears, swords, arrow-heads, adzes, knives, tweezers (used for extracting hair from men's chins), branding irons, digging knives, cattle bells, personal ornaments, tools, wire and so on. Their iron deposits were found in the sand of a particular area which Routledge does not name. The sand was dug by women and children as a part-time occupation. It was then sieved many times before the iron ore was ready for smelting. Iron forging was still being practised in southern Mbeere in Meru District in 1972 although very little is known of the history of the industry in this particular area. The Gusii made hoes, axes, spears and arrow-heads, which they traded in Luo-land. The Nyangoto iron works in the Sironga Valley were famous throughout the area for the decorative iron jewellery made there. Apparently the Akamba smiths were not necessarily found only among the members of particular clans. On the other hand the Gusii smiths were the richest people in their area : they were few in number and monopolised the trade which indicates that they had been able to limit the teaching of their professional skills to selected people only. Of course it is possible that the Akamba, Meru and Kikuyu iron-workers also organised themselves into exclusive groups and controlled entry into their profession thus governing the exchange value of the goods they manufactured, but at present we do not know whether this was in fact the case.

The iron industry was also widespread in what is now Tanzania.

Among the North Pare peoples, the Shana clan of smiths had complete control of apprenticeship. In other areas iron-working was not the preserve of one particular clan, and outsiders were not barred from learning the craft although there was a tendency for fathers to teach their skills to sons. A considerable amount of historical research has been done in Tanzania and already historians in Tanzania are arguing that 'there was a basic uniformity in [technical] principles and methods of iron working through Tanzania; but at the same time there is or has been considerable variation in detail in the furnaces, in forging instruments and in the iron that was produced'. Sutton's work in particular indicates that the techniques of iron manufacture had reached similar stages throughout the area, although the actual methods employed in production and finishing varied.

Iron-working in areas of Uganda seems to have reached the most sophisticated level in East Africa. In Kakara, in the north-west of the West Nile district, there was a unique, specialist clan of blacksmiths, Nyangila. All the peoples in the locality, the Kakwa and some of the Northern Lugbara obtained their ironware from the Nyangila clan. In another area, Kigezi, at the turn of the century, there were about one hundred blacksmiths working in one village, Mushunga, all apparently members of the same clan. Little is known about this group but it would seem that they developed a technique that was was quite unusual. Many other groups in Uganda were involved in iron-working and forging.

The Palwo worked part time as blacksmiths and part time as subsistence farmers until the demand for their hoes became so great that they became full-time smiths trading iron implements for food. In the nineteenth century the Palwo had organised themselves, as had the Gusii in Kenya, into an exclusive group which regulated exchange rates and governed recruitment into their profession. The Palwo blacksmiths provide an excellent example of division of labour. They had a unique skill and because of increasing demand for the goods they manufactured, they began specialising solely in the production of these goods.

Perhaps the most highly developed of the iron-workers' skills were to be found among the Banyoro, as the following quotation illustrates.

From ancient times in the history of the country the Banyoro have had a knowledge of iron work, having for many generations supplied many of the surrounding Bantu tribes with iron. . . . The people . . . had their furnaces and men who made iron smelting their life work, as far back as their legends carry them. The iron ore is dug from the hills where it is abundant; though at times the smelters follow a vein of good ore some distance under the ground, in many instances it is found lying on the surface or only two feet deep. It is smelted and passed on in the rough to the smiths who work it into spears, hoes, knives, bells, bracelets . . . The men who quarry the ore smelt it. They are a distinct class from the smiths and rarely work iron after smelting it; and conversely smiths rarely smelt it. Iron smelters generally work in companies. They first prepare their charcoal by felling and burning the special kind of trees until the amount of charcoal required is obtained. The fires which have been made to char the wood are extinguished by covering them with green boughs and grass and heaping earth on the top. . . . When the amount of ore required has been dug, the workers dig a pit two or three feet deep and two feet in diameter which they fill with dry reeds. Round the mouth of the pit the ground is beaten hard and a dome of clay built over it, leaving a small hole in the centre to serve as a chimney. Holes are made round the dome for the nozzles of the bellows and the iron is put into the pit in layers with charcoal between them, and the fires are now lighted. More charcoal and iron ore are added as required and the blast furnace is left going until the amount of iron stone to be dealt with has been smelted, when the pit is broken open, covered with green boughs and grass and left to cool. . . . The smelted iron is cut into pieces large enough to make a spear or a hoe and the smith purchases the pieces with goats, vegetables, food or cowry shells.

The growth and decline of the iron industry

The iron industry was widely distributed through the settlements and villages of East Africa, some areas specialising in making bracelets and ornaments, others in making chains and so on. We have no idea how many smelters and smiths there used to be working in East Africa at any one time and how many are now to be found working in the same way. An excellent piece of work done by a student on the subject of the Samia iron industry shows how their numbers declined between 1900 and 1972.

The numbers of smiths in Samia

Year	1900	1914	1972
Number	82	30	4

As the nineteenth century progressed the Samia ironsmiths experienced a growing demand for their products from a growing number of people in the Lake Victoria region. The demand was principally for hoes because hoes could be exchanged for other goods. With the expansion of Arab trade throughout East Africa in the 1880s, the demand for hoes as a 'medium of exchange' had grown enormously. The Arabs were trading cloth and other goods in exchange for valuable ivory. Ivory and cloth to sell to the Arabs could be obtained in exchange for hoes and iron goods and therefore ironware was in great demand.

The experience of the Samia smiths was probably similar to that of many other groups of smiths throughout East Africa. The Nyamwezi smiths, for example, would almost certainly have benefited from the increase in demand and exchange value of their products. Probably their industry would also have experienced the same decline as the Samia iron industry and for similar reasons but so little data is available that it is hard to make any generalisations at this stage.

It is probable that in the year 1900 the iron industry in East Africa reached its peak. The advent of colonisation brought decline to the industry but it cannot necessarily be assumed that in all cases the decline was as rapid as in Samia. Iron smelting was no longer essential in East Africa because, as already mentioned, the iron could now be more easily obtained from sources of scrap metal. In Samia the Kakamega gold rush of 1931 gave the people another good reason to give up smelting. The Samia smelters became frightened that the Europeans would discover the Samia location of iron deposits as they had done in Kakamega and invade their territory. In 1937 it was reported that in Madi in north-west Uganda, which also had had a thriving iron industry in the nineteenth century, scrap iron was being used by the smiths instead of locally smelted iron.

The number of smiths was also rapidly decreasing. In Samia the incoming Indian merchants were selling imported hoes at a cheaper price than was asked for the locally made ones and the imported hoes lasted just as long. No local industry could withstand such competition without technical innovation, which was unlikely to be introduced in the circumstances that prevailed at the time. The smiths in Samia continued to make only those agricultural implements which were not being imported. In the 1930s the Madi smiths were making hoes of the traditional type only for their symbolic significance in marriage dowries, and spear harpoons for hunting hippo. Margaret Trowell reported from Buganda in 1940 that 'most of the highly skilled craftsmen are old men – the last of their kind'. The young men were finding better remuneration in other work. The income of smiths working in East Africa today is pitifully small and it is probable that there will be no one to take their place. The industry will have died completely unless conscious efforts at revival are made by governments. Most imported iron and steel goods are cheaper, lighter and more efficient and the age-old iron industry of East Africa could never withstand such competition.

The salt industry

The production of salt was another industry of considerable importance which was widespread throughout East Africa. Salt is an essential part of the diet for both humans and animals, so that people who do not have a natural supply close at hand must manufacture it or obtain it from elsewhere. There are a number of salt lakes in East Africa including Magadi in Kenya, Katwe and Kasenyi in Uganda and Balangida, Eyasi and Uvinza in Tanzania. The salt from these lakes was either cut out in blocks from deposits on the shores or the salt water was boiled to evaporate off the water and leave the salt. These lakes could provide large quantities of high-purity salt. Caravans would travel long distances to obtain and sell the salt. The salt trade in the area of each of the lakes mentioned has an interesting history which will be dealt with in a separate chapter.

Other methods of obtaining salt were by extraction from the soil or by burning suitable leaves. In the case of saline deposits in the soil the salt rises to the surface by capillary action. The quality and quantity of the salt which could be obtained by these last two methods was generally not high compared to lake salt, except for the saline earth deposits of Kibero on Lake Albert and around Kisingiri which yielded better-quality salt than the lakes. Salt from these two particular sources was said to be quite exceptional and there was very great demand for it. It is unfortunate that we know so little about the techniques of salt extraction, although from the authors' own inquiries there is little doubt that the industry was widespread.

The quotation which follows refers to Kisingiri District in South Nyanza, Kenya, where salt obtained from saline earth was traded over a wide area even across Lake Victoria to Buganda, because of its exceptional quality mentioned above.

The soil of a large part of this district is impregnated with salt and the natives dig this up and put it into earthenware pots. A small hole is knocked in the bottom of the pot, and water is poured in at the top. The water, filtrating through, comes out quite clean. It is then caught in other vessels and boiled, till by the process of evaporation the salt is left behind.*

This method of salt extraction was still in limited use in 1973. The surface of the soil is scraped and the soil processed in the manner described by Dobbs. Before it is sold the salt is packed into conical shaped lumps and wrapped in dried banana leaves.

The method employed to obtain salt from the leaves of plants known to have a high salt content was as follows. The leaves would be burned to ashes and the ashes added to water. The mixture would be filtered as with the saline soil solution and the filtrate would then be boiled to evaporate the liquid and leave the salt crystals. Banana leaves or stems seem to have been fairly widely used for this purpose.

The manufacture of clothing

The history of the manufacture of clothing in East Africa seems to have been only superficially investigated by historians. Not only has the import of cheap cloth made in Europe killed the old skills and trade of tanned leather and bark cloth, it has also deadened the historians' interest. All peoples of East Africa used to tan hides for clothing and the Banyoro, Baganda, Banyankole, Batoro and Basoga were skilled in the production of bark cloth. Bark cloth was made from the bark of a species of fig tree, *Mbugu*, which was softened by beating until it became thin and fairly supple.

The tanning of hides and the beating of bark for cloth were highly skilled operations. The Banyoro seem to have been masters of the art of tanning while the Baganda and Basoga were renowned for their beautiful bark cloth. The following extract describes how carefully clothing was made.

> The people are skilful tanners and make dresses of skins that equal cloth in softness. The tiumbe are mantles formed by joining goatskins, tanned, prepared and sown with such care as to present the seams well covered with hair, they also make these garments with ox hides, which they render soft and light, to serve the poorer classes. The working of such stuffs requires patient labour; and it is executed with the greatest skill by means of repeated rasping on the back of the skins, which are previously moistened and stretched by means of wooden pegs on the ground . . . The traditional dress, however, that is still used by the

* C. M. Dobbs, 'The Kisingiri and Gwasi Districts of South Kavirondo, Nyanza Province, *Journal of the East Africa and Uganda Natural History Society* (Aug 1914) pp. 129–30.

greater number of people . . . is made of the bark of the Mbugu
. . . The most beautiful and the softest . . . comes from Buganda
and Busoga . . . the strongest is made at Monyara in the district
of Monli. Special artists attend to the manufacture, the production of which . . . is a source of constant if not very great profit.*

The above passage illustrates the very considerable skills of the
craftsmen involved who must have played an integral part in East
African societies in pre-colonial Africa. At one time bark cloth was
traded between the major lacustrine kingdoms, even as far as what
is now Tanzania. But in 1902 Harry Johnstone noted that skin and
bark cloth clothes had 'long since passed out of fashion anywhere
on the shore of the Victoria Nyansa' and had been replaced by
imported calico. Judging from old photographs it seems that skin
clothes were worn for many more years before all peoples of East
Africa took to wearing imported calicoes; the poorer the area the
longer traditional wear persisted. Nevertheless the clothes production industry was one of the first major East African industries to
collapse under the competition from Europe and Japan. The cheap
textiles from Europe were to be found in every part of East Africa
by 1945.

Conclusion

It is indeed strange that we know a great deal more about iron
production in East Africa thousands of years ago from the findings
of archaeologists than we know about iron production in the nineteenth century. We know even less about the recent history of salt
production and research on the history of tanning processes and
textile and bark cloth production is woefully inadequate.†

The reason for this relative lack of interest in industry in East
Africa in the nineteenth century may be because people are more
fascinated by the European industrial revolutions and with the kind
of goods produced in the West. Yet there are many important
reasons why we need to know more about the men and women who
produced essential, non-agricultural goods in nineteenth-century
East Africa. First, we need to make a closer study of the range of
East African science and technology in the pre-colonial era. The
people of East Africa were fully capable of adapting their natural
environment to their needs – what we need to know is how they

* Major G. Casati, *Ten Years in Equatoria* (London, 1891) p. 54.

† Tanzanian historians have collected a great deal more material on nineteenth-century industrial production than historians working in Kenya and
Uganda.

did it, what kind of technology they used. It must certainly not be assumed that the knowledge which had been gathered and passed down from generation to generation was somehow primitive or worthless. It would be a great pity to ignore the knowledge which has been built up over so many centuries because it is assumed that modern know-how is in some way superior. We need to understand the history of technical knowledge in East Africa, so that young people in the future can continue to appreciate the abilities of their ancestors and so that the knowledge handed down over the ages should not be forgotten.

7 Industrialisation in the Twentieth Century

The basis of the wealth of the western capitalist world and Soviet Russia, wealth which has been created over the last hundred and fifty years, has been the rapid growth of manufacturing industry (which for convenience we can call 'industrialisation'). All societies, however simple their technology, manufacture some goods which include clothes and tools for production and defence. During the last two hundred years or so we have learnt how to manufacture not only the old things which people have always wanted, like clothes, on a vast scale, but also new things like motor cars and aeroplanes, which our forefathers never even dreamt about. We have learnt how to produce all these things by understanding our material environment. Men have always understood their environment to some extent; those aspects which they could not explain in material terms, they explained in terms of the working of supernatural powers. But it has only been since the time of a *scientific* understanding of the material environment that man has been able to *consciously* manipulate it in order to produce the goods he wanted. The difference between an historical understanding of the physical environment and a scientific understanding is as follows. In the former case, knowledge, understanding and explanation of how things work is passed on from father to son and from mother to daughter. New knowledge and explanations percolate into the society from time to time, so that change tends to be slow and gradual. Thus man's ability to exploit the physical environment tends to follow one generation after another. But since the sixteenth century in Europe there has grown up a scientific understanding of the world we all live in : by this we mean a sustained and methodical observation and experiment with the elements of the environment. Such observations and experiments are intentional and conscious, concerned with understanding how the elements of the world work in order that, through such understanding, we can manipulate the world in our own interests. Over the last three-and-a-half centuries people in the western part of the world have developed scientific understanding in order to produce more and more goods, good for consumption and goods for destruction. The non-western world has willy-nilly been drawn into the orbit of the economies of scientific production, because it possesses the raw materials which are needed for this process. It is because the western powers were first in harnessing scientific understanding to production and manufacture that they have been able to dominate the rest of the world. In most countries of the West industrial manufacture has become so important that less than 10 per cent of the people live and work in agricultural production, in contrast to East Africa where over 90 per cent of the people remain at work on small farms. Thus we can see from such simple statistics that the process of industrialisation in the West has been a revolutionary process; it has involved major structural change in the society; the techniques of production and transport have become unrecognisable in comparison with the pre-scientific and pre-industrial era; and finally there has been a major shift of people out of agriculture and off the land, into the towns.

It should be clear that at the heart of this process has been technological change, by which we mean that scientific knowledge has been consciously applied to the various processes of production. As a result change has ceased to be slow and periodic as in the pre-scientific and pre-industrial era; instead change has now become built into all our societies and become part of the expectation of daily living. We dealt with the characteristics of change rather more fully in the introduction to this book, where we pointed out that as we learn more and more about our environment through scientific observation, so we can apply the new knowledge in technical change. But what is more important at the moment is, where does all this scientific knowledge come from and who controls it? This is an important question as those people or institutions who own and control scientific knowledge can utilise it for the production of goods in their own interests and in order to increase their power.

It should be obvious to everybody today that, as the western world began the contemporary process of scientific change, so today it has continued to operate a near monopoly of that knowledge. In the western capitalist countries the technology of production has been developed through company organisation. (A company is simply an organisation where two or more people have come together with their cash – capital – and have been recognised as a company for a specific purpose of production or distribution.) Initially many of these companies produced goods such as shoes and clothes for the domestic market in Europe; after some years they expanded, and as they produced more than they could sell in their own countries they began to export the surplus abroad.

Over the last one hundred years western capitalist industrial companies have expanded at a fantastic rate in three ways. First, the more successful companies bought out the less successful, secondly they developed their technology so that they could use more machines which would increase the output of each worker per machine, and finally they began setting up new companies for manufacturing in different countries. Thus by 1970, the giant companies like Unilever have manufacturing plants in nearly all non-communist countries of the world, which includes, of course, the territories of the Third World. These companies control their own technology and still have their headquarters in the western countries. Here we are only concerned with this process in East Africa where we shall find that these international companies have set up branches to manufacture products locally. The question we must keep in mind for the rest of this chapter is this: can the presence of these branch companies of international giants lead locally to the same massive transformation of societies and economies as occurred earlier in the western world?

An historical outline, 1939–1963

By 1939 Kenya was producing her own beer, cigarettes, soap, cement, and canned fruit and vegetables. Although, in total, Kenya's industrial growth had been very small, she was already ahead of Uganda and Tanzania. Kenya's industrial growth had occurred under the protection of tariff barriers. After the 1922 reports of the Customs Tariff Committee and the Economic and Finance Committee, the colonial government had given positive protection to the infant manufacturing industries from which the European agricultural interests would benefit. At the same time the imperial government strongly resisted most industrial developments in her colonies which would have provided competition for its own manufacturers. For instance by 1939 only 2 per cent of the cash from the 1929 Colonial Development Fund (the earliest aid fund, formulated to stimulate the economic development of the colonies) had been directed towards secondary industry. Another example is given by the Japanese match manufacturing firm that was unable to set up a match factory in East Africa in 1928 because match companies in Britain objected. Likewise, the rope, twine and net makers in Britain complained about the manufacture of binder twine in Tanganyika in 1934. The Tanganyikan factory was closed in 1936. In general industrialisation was not favoured by colonial government because it would mean loss of revenue from import duties. It was therefore common for colonial governments to manipulate railway rates and taxes in order to discourage new industries. On the other hand the European settlers in Kenya wanted to encourage new industrial development. Over this issue the colonial government and the settler interest were opposed.

European investors and financiers were not interested in encouraging industrial development in Africa at this time. Their main concern was with the exploitation of mineral and food resources and with government-supported investment infrastructure (railways and roads, etc.) For example, the finance for the Uganda railway and its branch lines was raised privately in London with government guarantee on loans, and all the lines and rolling stock were imported from Britain. As a result there were few technical and financial benefits from the investment to Kenya and as the payment of the interest on the loans was channelled back to Britain there could be little reinvestment of any kind in the colony.

Up to 1940 imperial policy had been straightforward : it was against the development of industries in the colonies; the colonies provided a captive market for goods and capital. After 1940 this remarkably conservative approach to colonial economies changed and economic development on a number of different levels, particularly in industry, began to be encouraged.

One of the reasons for this change in attitude was that during the Second World War the Europeans living in East Africa were unable to obtain goods they had earlier imported by sea from Britain. All ships were in danger of attack during the war so that only essential war supplies were sent to East Africa from Europe. In response to this state of affairs, the Kenya Industrial Management Board was set up in Nairobi in 1940/1. The Board was intended to encourage the local manufacture of some goods formerly imported from Europe in order to save having them shipped. The plant and equipment of this Board was bought up after 1945 by East African Industries Ltd. This company was financed by the British government and by Unilever, one of the world's largest international manufacturing complexes. Initially East African Industries produced Sunlight, Lifebuoy and Lux Soaps, Omo washing-powder and Kimbo and Blue Band margarines.

The war was the stimulus behind major alteration in colonial policy on East Africa. Throughout East Africa the small, wealthy communities, mainly the European and Asian colonists, had found themselves short of goods which they had been used to having. The only alternative to importing such goods was to manufacture them locally. Therefore, for the duration of the war manufacturing industries were encouraged by the colonial authorities.

After the war these policies were continued. There were three basic reasons for this. First, the war had led to the rise of gigantic international firms. Unilever (East African Industries) was one such firm. It was necessary for firms like Unilever to decide whether to produce goods in Britain or Europe for export to East Africa, as had been the case before the war, or to set up new factories in East Africa itself to produce the same goods. For many firms the choice was a difficult one, but nevertheless, since 1945* many factories have been established in Nairobi manufacturing products for the East African market. It seems that one of the reasons for this has been the level of wages in Britain, which are at least 400 per cent higher than in East Africa. Hence firms like Unilever concluded that it was cheaper to use East African labour. A second reason for the continuation of policies adopted during the war was the coming to power of the Labour Party in Britain in 1945. The Labour Party, with its socialist leanings, was anxious to encourage the growth of new industries in British colonies. It instituted special investment banks like the Commonwealth Development Corporation, whose aim it was to provide government-backed cash loans to private firms like Unilever. In this way it was hoped to encourage and subsidise the giant international firms.

Between 1945 and 1963 a new industrial base of light industry was established in East Africa. These industries manufactured goods that had previously been imported. Some of the industries and their products are given in the following list :

Cement

1933   First factory in Nairobi
1952   Bamburi Portland Cement
1953   Second factory in Uganda
1958   Athi River cement factory

Beer

1922   Kenya Breweries
1935   Tanganyika Breweries
1944   City Breweries
1951   Kenya Breweries taken over by Allsopps
1951   Uganda Breweries

Biscuits

1946   House of Manji set up as a bakery
1953   House of Manji begin to produce biscuits
1956   Mukisa Biscuits (associated with the Diamond Jubilee Trust and Wright Biscuits, Britain)

* See Chapter 12.

Gas

1946   East African Oxygen and Acetylene Co. sets up a factory in Nairobi. This company is part of the British Oxygen Co.

Metal Cans

1948   The Metal Box Co. sets up a factory at Thika

Pharmaceuticals

1942   Kenya Overseas Ltd begins as a trading company
1947   Kenya Overseas Ltd becomes a producing company

Shoes

1935   Bata begins export of shoes to East Africa
1940   Bata build a tannery and shoe factory in Limuru

This list is by no means complete, but it does illustrate how new industries began springing up in the 1940s and that, despite their names, most of these firms were supported or run by international outfits. For example The Portland Cement Co., Allsopps Breweries, Jubilee Trust and Wright Biscuits, The Metal Box Co., British Oxygen and Bata were and still are part of multi-million pound firms operating on a world-wide scale. The East African companies are just small sections of their operations.

The negative attitudes to new industries prevalent in the 1920s and 1930s among both imperial and colonial government officials had entirely disappeared by 1945. By then, the colonial governments of both Kenya and Uganda placed considerable emphasis on policies designed to attract and encourage large firms to set up subsidiaries in their territories. For instance the Governor of Uganda in 1952 argued strongly for the need for the 'establishment of heavy and secondary industries'. As there were no sources of cheap coal or oil available to East Africa, the Owen Falls Dam was planned to provide hydro-electric power for the region and bring about industrial growth. The drawing up of plans for the territory and the preparations to exploit and develop copper, cobalt and iron deposits in the area are clear indications of the change of attitude.

In Kenya the general encouragement of industrial development also began at this point. By 1947 the Annual Report for the colony noted that there were already 'many processing plants established' for coffee, jam, pyrethrum and other products. It also mentioned that there were promising possibilities for secondary industries such as those producing bricks, tiles, and glass which could be sold on the domestic market. Overseas industrial investments continued to flow into the country throughout the forties and fifties. By 1946,

280 private companies were incorporated in Kenya, valued at £40 million, which was well over double the number and value in Uganda and Tanganyika put together. Over the next twelve years another 3380 private companies were established, valued at £120 million, as against 2650 companies valued at £81 million in the other two countries combined. While many of the new companies were privately owned by Europeans and Asians living in East Africa (two-thirds of these companies were owned by Europeans and one-third by Asians) many were branches of companies of international industrial complexes.

Exactly what proportion of these industries were foreign owned is difficult to say, particularly as it was from 1945 that developments in small-scale, backyard industries began to appear. Furniture works, small bottling plants, production of carvings for tourists and so on grew up rapidly after 1945. There has been almost no research undertaken in this field. Banks, government and academic institutions have, since 1945, virtually ignored these spontaneous developments, yet small-scale enterprise can be found in every town in East Africa.

Governments until quite recently ignored the development of small-scale industrial enterprise, as they were mainly concerned with the encouragement of overseas industrial manufacturing firms in East Africa rather than small-scale local producers. Overseas companies who produced goods under licence in East Africa were not at first offered any tariff protection against outside competition but they were free to export all the profits they made, which seems to have been sufficient encouragement for them at the time. Even by 1955, when it was estimated that the value of output of foreign manufacturing firms in Kenya was 12 per cent and in Uganda 5 per cent of the total monetary production, there were few incentives such as tariff protection designed to support foreign enterprise.

Colonial government policy gradually grew to encourage these industrial changes positively. Between 1922 and 1945 a few infant industries had been protected by the 1922 tariff structure. After 1945 other encouragements to industry included a system of industrial licensing and, in addition, land in urban areas was made available for the construction of industrial projects. From 1954 financial assistance was provided by the Industrial Development Corporation from government loans.

The industrial policies

Obstacles in the way of massive industrialisation have always been considerable in East Africa. There is a lack of cheap sources of power; up to the mid-fifties there was a shortage of both skilled and unskilled labour and the market for consumer goods is relatively small even when the separate East African territories are considered as a whole. The market is small primarily because the cash income of the majority of the people remains low as the income distribution is highly skewed and any industry that has developed has tended to supply the wealthier classes. Furthermore, the distances over which goods must be transported are great and so transport costs are high. Also, the western world has set up tariff barriers against finished goods from the Third World War in order to protect its own producers from imports that might be marketed more cheaply. Finally, the problem of mobilising savings for industrial investment from the local population has never been considered on any scale as the people have generally been too poor. Instead, Kenya has depended mainly on growth through industries set up as branches of international firms.

The obstacles in the way of local or even foreign-based industrialisation for Uganda has been even more dramatic than for Kenya and it is instructive to see how Uganda has attempted to cope. The colonial government in Uganda became anxious to industrialise the country in the late forties. By the early fifties it was realised that foreign industry would not naturally flock to Uganda unless investors were given considerable incentives to do so. The government, therefore, undertook first to provide massive supplies of electric power from the Owen Falls Dam, to be built across the Nile, secondly to set up a development corporation which would sponsor industrial projects, especially those of overseas firms, in partnership with existing local, private firms. Thus some of the risks to investors would be eliminated and local know-how would be made available. Finally the government undertook to set up an industrial estate with suitable services which was to be sited at Jinja.

Construction of the Owen Falls Dam was begun in 1948 and completed in 1954. It was to provide a cheap power source as the basis for industrial expansion. Planners and local businessmen expected something like an East African Detroit to grow up around the dam. But although there was an initial growth of industry, Jinja was not transformed in the following ten years into the expected industrial metropolis because there had been a failure to attract additional foreign industry and to create a permanent labour force. Not until 1964 did the Uganda Electricity Board make any profit. The Board was then dependent on a textile mill, a copper smelting works, a cement factory and on Kenya as its main customers. The area around the dam did not become the leading sector for growth of the Uganda economy as had been hoped when the dam was built.

Even the cement factory was built by the colonial government of Uganda because local or foreign enterprise refused to put up the cash.

Uganda is a landlocked country, 800 miles from the sea, with an indigenous population nearly as poor as that of Kenya. Uganda had hardly any secondary industry by 1945 and had failed to attract it even after providing a massive source of electric power. The colonial government's answer to the reluctance of private capitalists and the slow rate of private investment was to force the mobilisation of savings from the export-crop-producing peasantry and to create the Uganda Development Corporation (UDC).

The Uganda peasantry's export production of coffee and cotton was taxed by the simple expedient of directing all their export produce through a single channel, a marketing board. The board collected all the export earnings which were then taxed. By 1952, £20 million had been paid over to the government to finance its expenditure. Roughly another £20 million went towards government revenue between 1952 and 1958. Out of taxes collected by this means, the UDC obtained its funds, which in 1952 amounted to £5 million. Moreover, this £5 million was interest-free and no dividends were payable on it. Not only that, the UDC has always has the unique advantage of being able to plough black its profits directly. The Corporation may be described as a form of state capitalism and it has acted rather like a holding company of an international firm. The UDC, from its inception, proceeded to invest its resources in a wide range of undertakings which, by the middle of the sixties, included processing industries, secondary industries, mining, finance, property and tourism. It had been designed to assist in Uganda's industrialisation, almost to take the place of foreign private investors. The Corporation now owns cement, textile, metal, chemical, fertiliser, and distilling companies, some of which it owns outright and others in conjunction with overseas interests.

The UDC was able to attract foreign finance by providing adequate security for overseas firms. This was only one strategy used by the Uganda government. The other strategy was a straightforward and traditional attempt to attract foreign private enterprise by itself. To this end an industrial charter was published by the government of independent Uganda in the early sixties in order to provide for the security of investors, the remittance of profits and the repatriation of capital.

The governments of independent Kenya and Uganda have in many respects continued with the industrialisation strategies used by their colonial predecessors. The counterparts of the UDC in Kenya are the Industrial and Commercial Development Corporation (ICDC) and the Development Finance Company of Kenya (DFCK), a body particularly concerned with the provision of a secure framework to attact overseas finances. But the Kenyan bodies have both been operating on a smaller scale than the UDC in Uganda. By 1966 the UDC had assets with a book value of £21 million and a turnover of £22 million, while the DFCK's investment was only £2 million by 1966. This is because Kenya has been able to attract foreign branch industry more easily than Uganda. Kenya has had a great deal more 'success' in her industrial policy than Uganda and as a consequence the government of Kenya has been able to concentrate more of her government resources on infrastructural growth (roads and other government services) and has played a much smaller role and been less involved in the industrial growth itself. The success of Kenya's industrial policies can be judged from United Nations statistics. Figures for gross domestic product have been available since 1954. In that year Uganda's manufacturing sector contributed U£9 million to the GDP of U£128 million; by 1958 the figure for the manufacturing sector was just over U£10 million which decreased to U£6·2 million in 1962. (The period from the late fifties to the early sixties was one of economic uncertainty throughout East Africa, being the period leading up to independence, and there was a flight of capital from the area during this time.) By 1968 the manufacturing sector only contributed £13·2 million to the GDP. Compare these figures with those given for Kenya for similar years: K£14 million in 1954, K£20 million in 1958, K£23 million in 1962 and K£49 million by 1968. The value of Kenya's manufacturing sector was over 50 per cent greater than Uganda's in 1954 and 350 per cent greater in 1968. The rate of growth of Kenya's manufacturing sector was of the same order of magnitude.

Why should this situation have arisen? If one goes back to the beginning of the twentieth century, it was Uganda which was the territory expected to be the second Japan. But the emphasis shifted to Kenya, especially to Nairobi which has become both the commercial and industrial centre of the entire region of East Africa. Not only is the geographical location favourable in relation to Mombasa but the large number of Europeans living in the country during the colonial era provided the demand for consumer goods and so made Kenya and Nairobi the pinpoint of capital investment in industry. Even before 1939, as has been mentioned, Kenya had attracted more industries than the other two territories put together. Its larger, wealthier population has continued to attract investment by foreign companies manufacturing consumer goods from the 1940s right through to the present. Despite the problems involved, the possibility of the successful operation of the East African common market with Nairobi as its industrial centre has made this city even more attractive to overseas investors.

Industrial growth through foreign capital

Despite Kenya's relative 'success' in comparison with the industrial performance of Uganda, neither territory has begun to achieve the type of growth which will lead towards an industrial society, that is a society that is dominated by industrial production and urbanisation. First of all therefore let us show clearly what we mean when we argue that industry has failed so far in its major task in directing society towards massive change and growth.

In 1953 the East African Royal Commission estimated that the contribution of manufacturing activity to the monetary economy was in the region of 12 per cent of the total and that manufacturing industries employed 10 per cent of all the people in paid employment. In 1961 the proportions were unchanged, although the monetary value of manufacturing had increased from K£4·5 million to K£10 million. The figures before 1954 were estimates arrived at before National Income statistics became part of the economic scene. During the period from 1954 to 1963 the manufacturing sector as a whole continued to grow at the rate of 8·47 per cent per annum, but in the National Accounts of 1964, manufacturing and repairs contributed only 10.47 per cent to the total gross domestic product. Since 1964 manufacturing has continued to grow marginally faster than the economy as a whole, but by 1970 it made up only 11 per cent of the GDP. Moreover, although the total value of manufacturing output had grown annually since 1950, the number of people employed in this sector has not shown the same increase. Between 1950 and 1962 the percentage of Africans employed in the manufacturing sector dropped from 9 to 8 per cent of the total number. This decrease was common to both the other two East African territories up to 1962.

In terms of numbers, 36,000 people were employed in 1950 and only 38,000 in 1962. Admittedly, 1962 was a year of economic depression as far as Kenya and East Africa in general were concerned. Between 1963 and 1970 the number of people employed in manufacturing and repairing industries increased to 61,000. Yet the steady increase in the numbers employed since 1963 is misleading. In fact the statistics show that between 1968 and 1970, in most industries, the number of people employed was either static or falling. Four industries, the textile, electrical machinery, railway equipment and road-vehicle repair industries, together employed

11,500 more people. These four industries *alone* were responsible for the increase in the total employment figure.

The critical point is that manufacturing has not at any time since 1945 provided the dynamic which is essential if independent and self-sustained growth is to occur in Kenya. At the most, the growth in the manufacturing industries has only kept pace with other forms of production. The question is why? Why has overseas investment failed to lay the foundation of massive development. Why do foreign firms not invest in those sectors of the economy, for instance in the heavy engineering or chemical industries, which will lead to sustained growth?

The first important explanation concerns the *type* of production which foreign companies have been willing to set up. Before 1939 the character of the industry that had been introduced was based on the processing of agricultural produce like coffee, tea and sisal for the export market and on the manufacture of agricultural products for the European domestic market – bread, bacon, cheese and so on. Since that time there has been a considerable expansion of manufacture of this type. As Ann Seidman has argued :

> A major share of industrial output consists of first-stage processing of agricultural products, largely for export, while the rest tend to be dominated by production of luxuries and semi-luxury items for limited high-income groups, including last-stage assembly and/or processing of imported materials and parts.

Since the mid-fifties there has been considerable growth in the industries manufacturing goods that used to be imported.

All the major industrial sectors, including the food processing industries, the industries producing beverages, tobacco, textiles and chemicals, the industries processing wool and those processing metal, have been concerned with the local market. Even if one takes the chemical industries as being the most likely to fall outside the general pattern, the goods produced by them (they include matches, pharmaceuticals, fertilisers, glass, soap, wattle bark extract, paint, pyrethrum, cement and petroleum) have still been largely sold for domestic consumption. Nearly all foreign investment in industry has been concentrated on light manufacturing industries, consumer industries and on processing industries. What is missing is the development of any form of capital goods industry such as the machine tools industry. The capital goods industry not only makes the machines for the other industries and so stimulates further production – called forward linkages – but should also stimulate technical knowledge, the use of local raw materials and transport – called backward linkages.

But although it is arguable that processing and consumer-based industries *might*, at least in principle, be able to provide the stimulus for rapid industrial growth, it does seem that unless such industries are indigenously based and not partially or fully foreign owned, then it is unlikely – many would argue impossible – for this massive process to begin. The reasoning behind this argument is as follows.

Branch industrial companies, whether or not they are owned in part by indigenous capital, are most likely to want to :

i. export some or all of their profits so that part of the surplus created by the project ceases to be available for further production;

ii import the technology to be used in the new company from the parent company in Europe or the United States. In this way the parent company makes a profit on the sale. As a result there is little thought given to whether the technology is suitable, there is little learning undertaken as the knowledge in the development of the technology comes from the parent company, and it is usual for a 'patent' to be taken out so that there is no pay-off for East Africa in technical knowledge at all;

iii. import the raw material from another subsidiary of the parent company if the material is not locally available;

iv. provide most of the top management and the methods of company organisation.

The extent to which any or all of these events take place varies from one branch industry to another. Each of these four factors taken by themselves will limit further growth, but taken together there seems to be an absolute loss of wealth. Firestone Tyres seems to be a particularly bad example of all these four factors operating and in addition the company has, as of 1973, a monopoly of the tyre market in Kenya resulting in rising prices and falling quality of all types of tyres. The actual cases of losses of revenue are probably rare, but the lack of impetus for rapid growth is crucial. In extreme cases the raw materials used, the technology introduced and the management brought in are all foreign, and only the unskilled labour is indigenous.

The consequences, which result from the existing patterns of foreign-based industrial development, are first, an exacerbation in the inequalities between the rich and the poor. Because these industries employ relatively few people and because they are likely to lead to no major developments for further growth, only a few local managers and workers receive any direct benefit. Thus one consequence is the growth of wealth for a few while the mass of people remain in poverty. The second consequence or characteristic of dependence on private, overseas capital with which we shall concern ourselves here is the increasing concentration of industry in terms of amalgamation, location and technology, which factors are all closely linked.

Industrial growth can occur through the amalgamation of firms which are involved in the same or similar processes of production. This is called horizontal integration. Sometimes firms with processes which are complementary may amalgamate; for instance, private oil companies own the drilling rig, the pipe lines, the ships and the refineries. This is called vertical integration. In Kenya there would seem to be a strong tendency in favour of horizontal integration and the marketing boards have gone furthest in this direction by their monopolistic policies. The introduction of licensing and the availability of international capital in the second half of the 1950s created similar tendencies in the manufacturing industries, although it must be mentioned that data on the subject is scanty. One indication of this trend comes from Uganda where in 1964 only 44 out of a total of 322 establishments employed 61 per cent of the urban labour force. In Kenya the number of establishments in the metal goods industry decreased from 71 in 1957 to 48 in 1963, while the gross value of output nearly doubled. The increasing concentration in this industry was partly due to the more successful firms taking over the less competitive ones and to the ability of the former to introduce more capital-intensive technology. This same process also occurred among the car sales firms such as the Cooper Motor Corporation which owns Wilken manufacturing, telecommunications and avaiation companies. This holding corporation was reported to be increasingly involved in local manufacture. Similarly the amalgamation of two branches of separate international firms, Cadbury and Schweppes, is another indication of the general trend.

Though there is not a great deal of evidence to confirm this, it is unlikely that major problems for Kenya will result from these types of amalgamations, simply because the directorships in many Kenyan industries co-operate with one another where amalgamation is thought likely to be profitable. The introduction of expensive machinery in such companies has made horizontal and vertical integration the most probable direction that industry in Kenya will take.

Developments in capital-intensive technology have been much more closely researched than developments in industrial amalgamations. Research into capital-intensive technology and industrial change has been undertaken because the failure of industry to supply a sufficient number of new jobs was disturbing. It is strange that a comparatively low wage level in a country should not lead to labour-intensive industry.

Capital-intensive technology is part of the new relationship between man and the techniques of production. With the advancement of science in the twentieth century many processes of production can be mechanised. In some cases the number of men needed to look after the machines can be cut to a mere handful. In the early stages of industrialisation in the West, in the nineteenth century, large numbers of comparatively unskilled men were employed in addition to a few semi-skilled and skilled men and supervisors. But in the second half of the twentieth century the complexity of technology has led to a smaller demand for labour, and a demand for labour of a different kind – higher level, specialist manpower, for example, production and maintenance engineers, accountants, and so on. Only a few semi-skilled labourers need to be employed.

One very important advantage which developing capital-intensive technology can give to industrialists is seen in the case of East African Breweries, a highly capital-intensive industry. The *East African Standard* of 8 August 1967 reported the managing director of the Breweries as saying that if five breweries each produced 20,000 crates of beer a month, no profit whatsoever would be made. But one large brewery would progressively increase its profit the more it sold. The reason for this is that once certain types of machines are set up, production on a large scale has to take place if the plant is to be profitable. It is perfectly possible that given less sophisticated machinery regional bottling plants might have been created but given the import of highly sophisticated beer-manufacturing plant from the parent company, such a policy was not economically viable in the short run. Subsequent decisions to establish regional plants depend in part on the rise in demand for beer and in part on non-economic considerations.

A reply to this argument can be given in terms of conditions prevailing in Kenya, the fact that highly skilled manpower is scarce and that the market is comparatively small. Thus it would seem that a very large financial outlay of millions of pounds would hardly be justified whereas the use of labour-intensive techniques in a country of comparatively low wages and with an unemployment problem would be far more logical. But this has not been the case. Since the early fifties and probably before, the manufacturing sector has been increasing its output at a rate of 7–8 per cent per annum, while the rate of increase in the number of people employed in this sector has been in the region of 1–2 per cent per annum. There is a clear implication here that machinery has been replacing men. Another example can be taken from Uganda where

F

in 1964 only 15 per cent of the total costs of the manufacturing industry was made up in salaries. In the sugar and tobacco and the metal and engineering industries the total costs in salaries was 13·6 and 9·6 per cent respectively, while the value added for each employee was 26,520 shillings and 36,530 shillings respectively, which is indicative of very intensive use of capital.

Why has this occurred? A number of explanations have been put forward, all of which go some way towards explaining the apparent paradox of capital-intensive industry in an economy of low wages and unemployment. First, the taxation system encourages capital-intensive industry through investment allowances, tax reductions and rebates on the initial costs of machinery. Secondly, many firms have European managers whose experience and knowledge is of capital-intensive techniques. Thirdly, and against popular belief, international firms are not short of finance, unlike their small-scale counterparts in East Africa. They are able to finance their developments either from accumulated funds from within their own international organisation, that is from abroad, or they are able to raise credit from the local branches of international banks because they are able to offer excellent security. For instance, one researcher has noted that in one month in 1963, 3·5 per cent of all loans made by the commercial banks accounted for 82 per cent of the value of all the loans of that month, and that all these loans were of over £100,000.

These three reasons are insufficient in themselves to explain the undoubted movement towards capital-intensive industries. We have little doubt that, if firms could earn larger profits by using cheap labour they would certainly do so despite tax advantages, the previous experience of managements and the availability of capital. It would seem probable that the managements of large international companies have decided that, under Kenyan conditions, it is easier and more profitable to employ a few highly skilled and semi-skilled men than to employ a large number of unskilled people.

Up to 1954 there was an almost constant labour shortage in Kenya. A part explanation of this state of affairs was given by the Carpenter Report of 1954. Low wages and poor conditions have been the basis of short-term migratory labour from the early twentieth century. The setting up of branches of large-scale, overseas firms, from the mid-1950s, with their long-term planning, their intention to exploit market opportunities and their ability to pay higher wages, led to the stabilising of a substantial section of the labour force.

Between 1950 and 1970 salaries in most African countries rose more rapidly than output. In Kenya between 1961 and 1970 the earnings of Kenyans employed in commerce and in manufacturing industries rose by 300 per cent and it was in the medium and higher grades that the rise was sharpest. As Alice Amsden has argued, in the late 1950s the large firms were the first to back Kenyanisation policies through the Federation of Kenya Employers; they also encouraged the growth of 'responsible' trade unions and systematic collective bargaining for higher wages.

These moves were no doubt prompted by the realisation that low-paid, short-term, migratory labour was expensive in the long run. Such labour was unskilled and output per man tended to be very low. Yet it has been convincingly argued that although the higher wage levels now common in Kenya are still much lower than those of Europe, there is still lower productivity in Kenyan industries than in comparable industries in Europe and that lower productivity is much more important than wage rate differentials in determining the forms of technology utilised. The firms set up in Kenya were anxious to increase their profits as quickly as possible in order that they could recover capital outlays in a short time in a politically insecure environment. Such firms concluded that it was preferable to utilise their finances for equipment and for training a relatively small but skilled force than for longer term projects of training large numbers of people at a lower level. Therefore the movement towards capital-intensive industry has not been so much a reflection of progress, as a reflection of the social poverty of the environment. These developments do nothing to change the situation.

Finally, let us deal with the localisation of industry. The reasons for this are simple : population and industries have a tendency to move towards major urban centres. In Kenya, Nairobi and Mombasa are the great population and industrial centres of the country. Before 1939 many processing industries were located all over the country, but the growth of secondary industry has meant that the populations of the major towns have been growing at a considerably faster rate than the population of the country as a whole.

Manufacturing industries tend to locate themselves either close to their sources of raw material, if the sources are local ones, or close to the point of entry or their market if raw material is imported. It was to be expected therefore that many industries which import raw materials for the manufacture of intermediate and consumer goods should locate themselves either in Mombasa or in Nairobi. Industries with their sources of raw material within Kenya include the soda-ash, pyrethrum, cement and wattle-bark extract industries.

The processing plants of these industries are located close to the raw material supply. On the other hand the fertiliser industry with its main market in the Highlands of Kenya, which uses imported nitrates, phosphates and potassium, has located its factories close to its market, at Nakuru. Firms seem to choose Mombasa as the location of their factories if the cost of transporting the imported material would be higher than the cost of transporting the final product. However the market of the capital cities is the major attraction for manufacturers. Nairobi and Kampala, for instance, which have a supply of electricity, water and technical and administrative services such as shops, banks, etc., and where there is an infrastructure of communications – telephones, railways and airports – provide favourable conditions for industry not found elsewhere. In Uganda 294 out of a total of 332 manufacturing concerns are concentrated in Buganda and Eastern Region. Nairobi was, by 1950, the one centre in East Africa with over 100,000 people, 10,000 of whom worked in industry. Ten years later Nairobi was still by far the largest urban centre in East Africa with over 20,000 of its population working in industry. If one includes Nairobi's satellite towns such as Thika, it will not be long before Kiambu will be drawn into the city as well.

Over the last twenty years the most significant industrial growth has occurred in and around the following towns: Kampala, Jinja, Nairobi, Mombasa and Dar-es–Salaam. These are the areas of East Africa with the highest population and purchasing power. The concentration of industrial growth in Kenya in particular can be shown by building statistics. In 1966, of the 1157 new non-residential private buildings put up in Kenya, 1129 were in Nairobi and Mombasa; in 1970, of a total of 4587, 4452 were in the two major cities.

Therefore, as long as the growth of the manufacturing industry in consumer and intermediate goods (what are called import substitution industries) is dependent on foreign, private investment, the pattern of capital-intensive, localised industry is likely to continue. Not only will the big cities grow even larger at an even faster pace but there will also be a continuation of the concentration on industrial and commercial development in these cities and the resulting gross imbalance in wealth between urban and rural areas will persist. The concentration of industry will become more intense not simply because of the introduction of overseas capital, but because the branches of foreign firms wish to maximise profits as rapidly as possible. They will, therefore, continue to use their considerable financial resources to introduce the most up-to-date technology.

This process means that smaller plants will find competition greater and will be taken over, and the process of amalgamation will continue.

Conclusion

The processes of colonisation in both Kenya and Uganda seems to have castrated the old indigenous industries without having created the basis for growth of new technologies. Unlike European industrialisation, where the process of growth and development became an integrated and cumulative process (the growth of engineering in one field like iron production led to the steam engine and so on), the process of industrialisation in East Africa has been very different. Here, as we have argued, the process has originated out of the growth of western industrialisation rather than out of a process of indigenous savings and knowledge. We have argued that as a result we cannot discern the beginnings of an industrial revolution, or the creation of the basis for sustained and rapid growth. It is worth adding that the urban areas in both countries have been growing over the last twenty years at double the rate of the population as a whole, but this is not an indication of the economic revolution we have been looking for. Rather it is the consequence of the imbalance in the growth of resources between the town and countryside, and especially of the impoverishment of a large section of the rural peasantry who flock into the towns looking for something better. We have argued that the form the new industries have taken may lead to a growth in the country as a whole, although in Uganda even this form of growth has been weak, but that it will lead to greater and greater regional differences as well as greater differences between the fortunate few and the great majority of the people. The process of industrialisation which we have described for Kenya and Uganda has often been called growth without development, that is an increase in money incomes but little of that integrated process which we have emphasised as so important for the development of the total system.

Part Three

EXCHANGE
AND DISTRIBUTION

8 African Trade in the Nineteenth and Twentieth Centuries

In this chapter we shall be looking at the patterns of trade which have been predominantly controlled by Africans in the nineteenth and twentieth centuries. In reality, we cannot isolate African trade patterns from others in either century; African and Arab trade patterns overlapped and intertwined in the nineteenth, while in the twentieth African, Asian and European trade patterns were divided on a racial basis, until just before political Independence. Incoming foreigners have therefore stimulated, as well as severely limited, African trade in both centuries. But for purposes of historical analysis, it is useful to look at the African dominated patterns of trade alone for the following reasons.

First, in the nineteenth century African trade pre-dated the development of Arab trade in the interior of East Africa, and to a large extent the incoming Arabs relied on the trade routes established by the local traders. Secondly, in the nineteenth century much of African trade had a different purpose and dynamic to that of Arab or European trade; for instance, in some areas one of the dominating concerns of African trade was to overcome famine. It was therefore irregular and sporadic. Nineteenth-century trade, as elsewhere, was a means for accumulating wealth, but the difference was that the old forms of accumulation of wealth, mainly cattle and foodstuffs, could not lead to the massive economic and technical changes which have occurred through accumulation of wealth in the twentieth century. In the nineteenth century there were major limits placed on innovations and productive reinvestment by the character of the technology.

While trade and the accumulation of wealth in nineteenth-century East Africa were closely associated, they could not lead to the conscious application of knowledge to production (as has occurred in the twentieth century) in order to increase output. It will be useful, therefore, to examine a little further how changes in technology did occur and what relationship they had in trade and the accumulation of wealth.

Pre-colonial East African economies have often been described as 'subsistence economies', which meant that the people produced foodstuffs and goods only for their own consumption, with no intention of producing a surplus for exchange with other peoples' goods. Each economy or even each household was supposed to be self-sufficient. This chapter will show that the term 'subsistence' cannot usefully be applied to East African economies in this strict sense as all communities were exchanging some of their goods for those of other peoples.

Changes in technology were comparatively slow. Iron hoes began to replace wooden digging sticks through trade, and the influence of the technology of the hunters and gatherers was being replaced by the technology of the agriculturalists. But those changes were on a different level to the changes in technology in industrialised societies. The extent to which a producer could manipulate his environment placed limits on his productivity, and thus on the extent of the surplus which he could use for trade and the accumulation of wealth. But some surpluses were created in every community, and small-scale trade was widespread.

Trade was one way of accumulating wealth; look for example at the lacustrine kingdoms of Uganda where governments were concerned to control trade and market-places so that the state could reap some benefit from the trade. In acephalous societies too, trading was an important source of wealth; Kikuyu traders, for example, exchanged foodstuffs for Maasai livestock which could then be used for exchange in rights to land.

The purposes of accumulation in the nineteenth century were of a different character to those in the twentieth century. In East Africa in the nineteenth century people accumulated sheep, goats, cattle and grains. These surpluses were then often redistributed for consumption. In a situation of slow technical change this was very practical and rational behaviour; it was a social investment, maintaining and expanding social relationships and, in a situation where famine and disease were likely to occur, it acted as an insurance against the future. People who had succeeded in accumulating animals and grain stocks were expected to be generous and redistribute some of their surplus to friends, neighbours and relations. In societies with centralised political systems, the government too redistributed taxes and tributes as a political investment which ensured support from, and control over, people. Where and when it was possible to invest surpluses in technical innovations, this was done, for example in Buganda in the late nineteenth century missionaries who had such technical skills as reading, writing and mechanical knowledge were paid for their services by the Kabaka from the proceeds of taxation.

In general, therefore, we can say trade could not have led to *rapid* technical change in the nineteenth century, although it was important for comparatively slow dispersion of technical goods over wide areas. Trade was concerned largely with social accumulation within the confines of existing technical knowledge. On the other hand, trade in the twentieth century, while also concerned with accumulation, has resulted in more rapid technical change which in its turn has led to sustained economic growth.

Accumulation through trade in the twentieth century has led to higher and higher levels of consumption – levels which were unthinkable in nineteenth-century East Africa. What we see is that the changed character of trade has gone side by side with a changed form of accumulation which in turn has led to new means of technology – all in a circular process.

Thus we can conclude that the extent of surplus goods in a community limits both the ability of the community to trade and the form that accumulation is likely to take, and so determines the limits to which a community can expand. It follows that the character of trade reflects the characteristics of the economy, and this is a good reason for treating African trade as a separate topic.

The characteristics of East African nineteenth-century trade

There are two initial problems in analysing the characteristics of African trade. The first is concerned with the simplistic idea that there were two types of trade, long-distance and short-distance. The second is the idea that there were either 'market-orientated' or 'subsistence-orientated' economies. Both ideas are most misleading.

Let us start with the idea of long-distance and short-distance trade. Some goods like iron and salt did travel long distances, but very often the good were taken and traded from point A to point B, a relatively short distance, and then taken further on by another trader to point C. Is that long or short-distance trade? Clearly, it is both. The important point is that 'long' or 'short' are comparative terms, a matter of opinion, and tell us nothing about the character of the economics involved. They do not help us to understand the trade of the pre-colonial era.

Secondly, it has been argued that there was a general absence of markets in East Africa before the coming of the Europeans. By this it was meant that there was a lack of demand for goods which were not produced from the work of individual families and kin groups. As there was little or no exchange there was no need for markets.

This is the view of some western scholars who have argued that there were two types of pre-industrial economies. The first were those in which the people were dependent on production for sale as their main means of livelihood, communities where commercial production was more important than subsistence production. In such situations they argue that the price mechanism allocated factor resources among producers – the market was the central mechanism of the society. The second type were the subsistence societies, where markets only operated peripherally and so trade played a limited role in economic activity. The scholars who have commented in this way have tended to be economists or economic anthropologists and have lifted the market concept straight from western industrial experience. As is so often the case, we must examine the pre-capitalist, pre-colonial societies closely before blindly using ideas and concepts which have been derived from a different experience.

We have categorised three major forms of trade in nineteenth-century East Africa. First, there was village or local trade between contiguous people who lived under different ecological conditions and so specialised in certain forms of production. Much of this form of trade was symbiotic in nature, in that the exchange occurred between groups of people who had a basically different mode of production, trade that is between agriculturalists and pastoralists. Secondly, there was trade within the centralised kingdoms of Uganda. Because the market-places were protected by a central authority, trade became a more regular and a more organised affair than in the previous case. Finally, we are dealing with international trade in the sense that exchange of special commodities was taking place between alien communities, over long distances, in expectation of profit. This categorisation of types of trade is not exclusive but it does help to explain the forms of economies concerned.

First, let us take local trade. As with so much of this work we lack sufficient examples. But in one study in Nyeri, Kenya, it was found that agricultural production was more suitable in some areas and soils, less in others. In the Mathera and southern parts of the Tetu areas of Nyeri for instance, the rainfall was heavy and consistent and there were rich volcanic soils. The peoples of other areas came to Mathera for their foodstuffs, particularly in times of drought. On the other hand, in Mukurweini and parts of the Othaya area of Nyeri, the rains and soils were less suitable for agriculture, so here the people specialised in iron-working, basketry and pottery. There was a third area in the Tetu areas where the people lived close to the Maasai and were able to accumulate live-stock – in particular goats – in exchange for foodstuffs. As a result of these local specialisations in Nyeri, there developed a horizontal form of exchange between the people in the different regions. Each region developed its own specialised form of market-places. In Mukurweini they sold iron tools, pottery, baskets and string bags; people from Mathera would come there with foodstuffs for exchange. The people from Tetu would exchange their sheep, goats and skins for foodstuffs and iron goods, which they would then take to the Maasai to exchange for more animals. Nyeri thus provides us with a good example of an area where due to varying local conditions people had tended to specialise and produce surpluses for others in surrounding areas.

Under the local type of trade situation, we can include exchange between peoples with basically contrasting forms of production. Here of course, we are referring to agricultural and pastoral people. Nowhere in East Africa do we find people relying solely on agriculture without any animals, and equally, nowhere do we find pure pastoralism; yet each area concentrated on food or animals, and each traded with the other.

Trade between predominantly agricultural and pastoral peoples provided a natural bond. Agricultural peoples lacked meat and milk, while pastoral peoples in times of drought became dependent on grains and other foodstuffs. For instance, in the nineteenth century the Gusii, an agricultural people who occupied the south-west of the cool fertile section of the Highlands, traded with their neighbours the Nilotic Luo, who lived in low country which favoured extensive pastoralism. During droughts the Luo depended heavily on the Gusii for grain. Certain Gusii blacksmiths were adept at making iron instruments, which they exported. Other articles of export were leopard and baboon skins, which were all exchanged for cattle, pots and poisons which the Gusii used on spears for hunting.

A similar economic symbiosis can be found between the southern and northern Kikuyu and the various sections of the Maasai community. The local trade between these two agricultural and pastoral groups has been written up by Peter Marris and Anthony Somerset. In this case, the nineteenth-century trade between the two groups was slightly different to those of the Gusii and Luo as the problems of access to each other were more complex. But in basics the trade was between two groups of peoples with complementary economies. The Kikuyu in the main imported sheep and goats from the Maasai and exported flour, honey, ochre and tobacco, goods which were not available in Maasai country. This form of trade was similar to 'local trade', in so far as peoples living relatively close to each other specialised their mode of production according to the ecological conditions. There were differences of culture and economy so that people tended to make special relationship based upon blood brotherhood and intermarriage to ensure confidence on both sides. But these were only differences of degree.

The third type of trading situation is between the centralised kingdoms, which has recently been outlined in an interesting paper by Professor Uzoigwe. In the royal kingdoms he has argued that by the nineteenth century the clan and kinship relations were not the sole basis of village and economic organisation; that the societies were more specialised and technically advanced than the acephalous communities in Kenya; and that market-places were widespread and functioned daily. As with local trade, and symbiotic trade, specialisation of production in the Bunyoro-Kitara kingdom was carried on according to geographical and ecological opportunity. For instance, those people who lived near the Budongo forest specialised in coffee production, those in Buddu country in bark cloth production, those in Bugahya in millet, while the Abaluma cattle-keepers herded their stock on the grasslands. The Kinyoro economy was characterised by specialisation in a range of occupations – iron production, salt, mining, fishing and elephant-hunting for ivory in the nineteenth century. Bunyoro's pre-colonial economy was diversified in terms of production, which explains the widespread number of market-places within the kingdom.

Bunyoro had the local village types of markets we have already described in Nyeri. There were also royal markets established under the patronage of the *Omukama*, the ruling clan. People came to such a market from all over the kingdom. There were also 'frontier' markets, which were situated at strategic sites along the transport network. These markets came under the authority of the Omukama. And finally, there were the international markets at Katwe and Kibiro which specialised in wholesale trade for long-distance traders.

The range of markets under the control of the Bunyoro-Kitara kingdom was sufficient to place trade in the areas in a different category to the trade in the acephalous communities of Kenya in the nineteenth century. The Omukama were concerned to control and exploit the markets under their control for political ends. Abakama collected tax from these markets from *abakoya*, tax collectors, throughout the empire as a form of royal revenue. The royal household controlled the export trade by giving a group an exclusive royal prerogative. No one except the Omukama was allowed to buy guns from the Arabs and only a privileged group was allowed to hunt for ivory.

The extent of trade within Bunyoro was reflected by the people from outside who came to purchase Bunyoro goods. The Alur,

Acholi, Langi, Iteso, Kumam, Basoga, Baganda, Banyankole and Congolese peoples used to come to buy the many goods, so bringing diverse peoples together within the royal kingdom. It is not unreasonable to expect a similar situation to have arisen among and between the other royal kingdoms of the area, although we must await further research.

The last form of trade we want to deal with here is international trade. Here again, we lack sufficient research on the subject and the long-distance international trade we do know about became part of and integrated into the Arab ivory and slave trade of the second half of the nineteenth century. The purely indigenous international trade was limited to salt and iron goods. The explanation for this was that deposits of high or special quality salt were in short supply and so the demand was widespread; with iron it was not necessarily the short supply of raw iron deposits, but the limits of special skill which led to high-quality iron goods being traded over long distances.

Here we want briefly to examine the character of the international salt trade from Lake Katwe and Kasenyi in south-western Uganda and the international iron trade from Samia in north-western Kenya. The salt trade seems to have originated at the end of the seventeenth century when people would travel to the lakes to collect salt in exchange for iron goods or food. During the eighteenth century markets began to develop on the shores of Lake Edward and Lake George, two lakes in close proximity to the salt source. Salt markets began to spring up at a number of points along the shore which allowed people from further afield to come and collect the salt. During the nineteenth century the hinterland of the salt trade developed further and further afield to north-western Tanzania, Buganda, Ankole, Rwanda, Bunyoro, Toro and eastern and central Zaïre. Trade routes became established and relations between the peoples along the way formally instituted, so that food, safety and shelter for the traders was available. It is not clear whether a specialised class of salt traders developed, or whether the salt was carried by a range of different people along the routes. In the case of the Magadi salt trade in central Kenya (Magadi salt was of much lower quality than that from Lake Katwe), the salt would pass from hand to hand. People from northern Kiambu or northern Machakos would take about a week to travel to collect it and return home. Traders from Muranga or Kitui would then come and buy it and return to their home area. The salt would thus pass from hand to hand over a hundred-mile stretch of land.

The Samia iron trade, like the Katwe salt trade, originated as a local trade. People would either come to buy from the ironsmiths or the smiths would carry their finished products to neighbouring clans. The longer distance trade originated with the development of friendly relations with people from the Kadimo Bay area. Men from this area would travel by canoe to Samia to exchange fish for hoes; they would then take the hoes south again by canoe to Kaksingiri. The trade also developed with local groups who travelled with hoes from Samia in a large armed band. Over time as they made friends along the way, they visited Teso, Bukhayo, Ugenya, Bunyore and Maragoli. The further such groups would go, the higher the exchange they received for the hoes. The trade was probably at its height by 1900, as the incoming Arabs had increased the demand for iron implements. Stock or hoes could be exchanged for elephant tusks which could be exchanged for goods from the coast.

A more general form of foreign trade was undertaken by the Akamba peoples. The Akamba traders have interested a number of scholars who have asked why they enlarged their hunting activities and began travelling all the way to the coast and back over difficult terrain. The Akamba foreign trade probably began well before the large demand for ivory in the nineteenth century. It seems that during the second half of the eighteenth century population outgrew the available resources of the area. With the increase of food shortage entire villages began to pioneer homesteads in uninhabited areas, especially in the Kitui region. As Kitui was less fertile, standards of living dropped and people began looking to local trade to supplement local resources in Kitui. By the beginning of the the nineteenth century Kitui Akamba had penetrated Kikuyu, Embu, Mwimbe and the Taita Hills. As the small trading expeditions became known, they became prone to ambushes. As a result, young warriors began to participate in the trade in order to create greater security. As the caravans increased in size, they also began to travel longer and longer distances. By the early nineteenth century, large well-armed parties of Akamba traders had reached the coast and were participating in the coastal ivory trade.

Problems for traders

Trade in the nineteenth century was a dangerous affair and the further a man travelled the more dangerous it became. Wild animals – snakes, lions and buffalo – were common over great areas of East Africa. Secondly, a man bent on trade had to carry goods for exchange on the way and goods had to be brought on the return journey. He was therefore always prey to robbers and thieves. Therefore people would travel in armed caravans of usually ten or more people for protection on the journey and particular attention would be paid to making good relationships with those who lived along the route. When the traveller had arrived at his destination there was the problem of physical control and protection for the buyers and sellers at the market-place. Market-places unless they were kept under strict order were likely to be rowdy and often became out of control. Order at the market-place was a major problem in nineteenth-century East Africa. Let us look at each of these problems in turn.

First there was that of organising a caravan. The social composition of caravans varied; among Kikuyu on the Magadi salt trade, members of the caravan were the poor people who needed to obtain land and wives. The Machakos Kamba, on the other hand, organised themselves into armed bands of young warriors who hunted as well as collected salt. Caravans were organised, therefore, on two principles (*a*) according to the expected dangers along the route and (*b*) according to organisation of traders. If the route was known to be dangerous, caravans would consist of young armed men, who might also be specialised traders, or as in the case of the Kikuyu Magadi salt trade it was the poor men who travelled together.

It can be seen that it was most important to reduce the hazards of any journey as far as possible. This meant that relations of trust and confidence had to be built up over time between the peoples encountered on the journey and the peoples with whom trade relations were established. The first common problem to overcome along the journey was the language. The caravan trader would become familiar with the language of his hosts. The Kikuyu caravan leaders who traded with the Maasai would speak Maasai. All traders found that they were accommodated more easily if they spoke the local language.

A second method of regulating the relationships of trade was through intermarriage. In most accounts of local African trade one discovers that trust and hospitality in foreign territory would be achieved by a local girl marrying one of the trade leaders. Kikuyu girls married Maasai and Samia iron traders married girls along their route. Lasting friendships would be established in this manner and customary differences of eating and other habits reduced. Such means of creating strong bonds of intimate security were common among traders who ventured outside their home clan area.

Another method, which seems to have been common at many levels of African trade, was the creation of bonds through blood brotherhood. For instance, in Lango District, Uganda, Baluli and Palwo peoples formed links through relatives and blood brotherhood with the Langi people across the Nile. These social bonds provided the conditions for the development of trust and so pre-pared the way for commercial relations across the river. A second example can be taken from the salt trade of north-western Uganda. Wars were endemic in this area, caused in part by the struggle to control the lucrative salt trade. Traders would travel armed in groups of up to thirty or so; they bonded themselves to com-munities through which they travelled by blood brotherhood. The traders would stay and eat with the people with whom they had made these relationships and they would expect that each would protect the other.

Trade itself was a dangerous business unless there were socially accepted patterns of behaviour. If people could not agree on what both parties considered a *fair* rate of exchange, trade could end in violence. Moreover, both parties to trade always suspected that their opposite member would try and cheat, particularly as there were no standard measures of weight or length or cash as exchange. It was normal therefore for traders to create the bonds of blood brotherhood with buyers. The Bunyoro friendships created by traders of blood brotherhoods have been described as follows :

> The two parties made incision in their respective stomachs, smeared the coffee berries with each other's blood, and then ate each other's coffee berries. After this short ceremony it was be-lieved that an enduring brotherly relationship had been estab-lished. It was irrevocable.*

Blood brotherhood relationships were considered at least as strong as clan relationships.

Market control and power

But problems of control were far more complex than the problem of the relationship between trader and buyer. There were essen-tially two types of problem. The first, concerning control over the market, meant obtaining political power in the geographical area where the goods were supplied. Goods like salt could therefore be taxed. Those who had political power over the market-places could tax the traders. The second and related problem was control over law and order *within* a market-place. As we shall see the problem of law and order was comparatively simple within markets in the royal kingdoms but complicated in the acephalous societies.

First, there is the question of the political control over markets. There is no doubt that around the lake there was always a close

*Uzoigwe, 'Precolonial Markets in Bunyoro-Kitara', pp. 448–9.

relationship between invasions and economic resources. This relationship can be clearly understood from the emergence of Mirambo, a Nyamwezi chief who sought to dominate the important trade routes between Tabora and Ujiji in the 1860s and 1870s. Mirambo was particularly interested in capturing the Uvinza salt trade and brine springs. Not until 1884, when he died, did Mirambo and his soldiers cease to be a threat in the area.

The conquest and wars of Mirambo are just one example of how warfare and economic factors coincided at the end of the nineteenth century.

Secondly, there was the question of control *within* market places. In the centralised kingdom the problem was relatively simple due to the hierarchies of political power in the kingdom. The Bunyoro Kitara kingdom used agents, who also acted as tax collectors (*abakoya*) in charge of markets throughout the kingdom. The *abakoya* were rich as they would take a portion of the dues before handing them over to the local *saza* chief, who would take their share before handing the remainder over to the Omukama.

Control of market-places was a far more difficult task among the acephalous communities as there was no central body to lay down rules by which trade should be transacted. The following quotation is taken from an old informant of Dr Wagner who did his research on northern Nyanza in the 1930s. It gives a vivid illustration of the problems involved.

How markets began in the country of the Logoli

Perhaps some people will think that formerly there were no markets, but we can believe that they were there indeed, though we shall find the markets of long ago to have been different from those of today. The first market in the tribe of the Logoli was started by a man of the Dindi clan who was called Dindi, together with his helper who was called Masava. These [two] people established [lit. built] a market to the north of Kisumu where one enters the country of South Maragoli, in a valley called after another man who lived nearby and whose name was Angoya. So they came to call it the market of Angoya. The people of many different tribes assembled there. I shall tell their names : The Logoli, the Isuxa, the Nandi, the Nyole, the Luo [Avavo], and the Idaxo. All these tribes liked very much to meet at this market.

As we all know, the Logoli from the days of their forefather had a better knowledge of tilling the soil than the Luo, but they knew more about getting rich in cattle than the Logoli did. And in those years everybody who wished to obtain [lit. find] anything he liked could go to that market. It was located between the country of the Logoli and that of the Luo.

The Logoli offered to the Luo different kinds of grain, such as sorghum and eleusine, as well as bananas, chickens, potatoes, tail-feathers and baskets which were made [lit. woven] by the Nyole and the Logoli and many other things besides. And the things which the Luo offered [lit. pleased with] to the Logoli were these : *Fish* which they caught in the Lake of Kisumu [the Kavirondo Gulf] and *cattle* of which they had plenty and *pots* : The over-seers of Angoya's market collected [dues] of all the things which were brought there to be sold. If they had not collected a share of these things there would have been nothing else to pay. When they established this market they did so on account of the dues. After a while the overseers of this market began to get tired and they no longer performed their work with strength [energy]. Then there was another man in the Dindi clan, an influential man whose name was Udzwanga, son of Ndwehe. He was a man who grew up to become powerful and clever indeed.

'Then he took this market into his hands, and he also had his helpers to work under him. Udzwanga, son of Ndwehe, was 'a man of a man' who was not to be treated with disrespect. Among all the tribes I have enumerated in this story, if there was anyone who tried to challenge his authority, such a person must be beaten by the overseers of Udzwanga, son of Ndwehe, and if that man had brought his grain to the market it would be taken away from him by force. Once a famine broke out in the Luo country, and they had no place where they could get any grain.

Then they were told : On Angoya's market they want to barter the cattle for grain, and so the Luo began to bring their cattle to Angoya's market. In those days they were bartering a heifer-calf for a basketful of the ekihinda type while one tail-feather would be bartered for a bullock.

Udzwanga, son of Ndwehe, in his dealings with all those tribes had no market dues collected from the Dindi, but only from the other tribes [or clans]. If the people took grain to the market he would collect grain from them [as market due], but from those who did not bring grain – like the Luo – he could not collect grain but fish, and the fish that Udzwanga took from the Luo he would give to the Logoli, especially to the Dindi; and he would unrelent-ingly drive the sellers [lit. the owners of the fish] off the market if they stirred up trouble amongst one another. The Logoli and the Luo, and perhaps the others, too, would want to know how much grain or food he was collecting from the others. When a man brought grain to the market, Udzwanga, son of

Ndwehe, would collect from him one basketful [of the enavodo type]; but if he was a man whom he does not like he would collect two.

This market was moved [to other places] many times, but the people did not like the work of Udzwanga to be taken over by another man as long as he was still there. Once when the market was flourishing [lit. helpful to the people], a certain man called Musoma Mudindi was killed there. Then all the people of the market began to hunt one another; hostility broke out among them and they wanted to fight one another, but thanks to the arbitrator [*eligaya liavandu*] they became reconciled again. The market, however, did not remain there for another day or a week, but it broke up indeed. Then Udzwanga, together with the people of his 'house' [*navanda venyumba yeye*, i.e. the people of his lineage], began to leave his clan [*oluhia*] to move to a village called Ideleli.

There Udzwanga soon started another market. It was in his hands together with his tribe and all the other tribes which bought on this market. Then they were also anxious to frequent this second market, and Udzwanga counted the market dues as was his trade. Then all the tribes that used to go to Angoya's market began to come to the market of Ideleli. Later, when they saw that it was not very good there, they moved that market to a third place near Makanval [located] between Vihiga and Vindizi. But there, too, it was little better. But when the Logoli saw that the market was theirs only [?], Udzwanga told them, 'you must watch this market well, because now I am an old man and I have no strength left'. When he said that he knew that he was going to die, all the clans [or tribes] saw that the work he had done had been very great, and they were very sad because they saw that they could not find a man of strength [or power] who could run [lit. watch] their markets as well as Udzwanga, son of Ndwehe, had run his market. He had stood on his own [*vasingira ku wiwe*] without another person above him, and since the time of his death they did not forget him. Many people named their children by the name of Udzwanga, son of Ndwehe. From his grandsons down to the grandsons of the Christians we can still find one whose names is Johannes Udzwange.

After Udzwanga, son of Ndwehe, had died, the Logoli themselves took over this market and moved it to another valley. When you come from Kisumu and you go towards the north as far as mile 24, there is a place called Lunyerere. There were the Swahili who cleared the bush land [*ekisaka*] or [*tilled*] the new fields. This market was in the hands of a chief who was called

Kivagi and who lived to the north-east of it. He gave permission to the Moslems to be the butchers in that market; then he put there a few other overseers, but they did not have the same authority [lit. power] as Chief Udzwanga, son of Ndwehe, had had over his market.

Their power was small only and their collectors took the things [dues] with fear, and all the things which were taken from the people were taken to Chief Kivagi and later Kivagi would divide them among his collectors.

When he gave permission to the Moslems to be the butchers of the cattle there was no other person who could slaughter a cow; if another person were to have done so the Moslems could not have bought of that meat. And the owners of cattle too, did not want other men to slaughter their cattle. If they let another man do so who was not a Moslem, the owners of the cattle would not make any profit.

Many different things were taken to that market: withies for weaving baskets, string made of papyrus [*vikunyi*] and of the bark of the elikambi tree, ripe bananas which were brought there to help the hungry people [i.e. for consumption on the spot], fifty bananas could be bought for two evinusu [half coins], sweet potatoes [lit. potatoes of the black people], three of them selling for two evinusu, baskets woven by experts for winnowing grain which could be bought for fifty cents each; handles made of the omuhaya tree, milking jugs, mortars for pounding cassava [*mihogo*] and other things, and grain bins.

About the Mbale market: This market was called after a man who lived in the country of another chief called Odana. It is twenty-three miles to the north of Kisumu at the place where the Logoli meet [i.e. at the border between North Maragoli and South Maragoli]. It is not located in a valley, but on a plateau. This market which took the place of Lunyere was started by a man called Chief Mnubi. He put a collector there whose name is Imbira. He is a lame man whose tongue is sticking out and his arms are crippled, so that he cannot till the soil. He watches the market well indeed. The following tribes are trading on the Mbale market: The Nandi bring tobacco to sell; the Luo bring fish and pots; the Idaxo bring groundnuts and sesame; the Logoli bring grain, bananas, string of the elikambi tree, quails, handles, milking jugs, mortars, and quail cages; the Nyole bring grain and quails. When all these things are brought to the market, the collector of market dues must collect a few things from everyone. They do not have a house [i.e. a market hall] but they sell the things out in the open. On a single day between fifteen and twenty cows are slaughtered, and eight o'clock [i.e. 2 p.m.] all the meat is finished. The butcher of the cattle is called Nasolo bin Kihalangua, he is a Dindi. He gets 50 cents for slaughtering one cow. The people crowd each other very much to buy the cooked blood of the cow. When it was started in 1931 the Mbale market was with little strength only, but there were many dukas [i.e. shops selling imported goods]. In these days you can see many people there on Saturdays, but not on the other days of the week.

African trade in the twentieth century

This last paragraph was clearly concerned with the Mbale market in the first years of the twentieth century. African trade did not suddenly stop with the advent of the colonialist – in fact it expanded; people could begin to move around the countryside without fear of being violated. The patterns of trade altered considerably. First, there was a central governing authority which had the political and administrative power to regulate trade in all its manifestations. Secondly, the growth of railway and motor transport revolutionised the communication problem from one area to another. Finally, the major direction of trade altered; exchange had previously been between local communities, or occasional long-distance trade involving a very small number of articles; with the advent of the colonial system agricultural products were grown and exported regularly, while imported cheap consumer goods became generally available.

We deal with all these changing facets of trade in other chapters. What is important here is that the colonial economy *increased the opportunities for trade on an enormous scale* and the question we now need to answer is to what extent were Africans able or allowed to take advantage of these new opportunities in trade?

Up to 1900 or so, the main area of trading had been around the lake among all three present-day territories. The densely populated area of the lacustrine kingdoms and the relatively well watered areas on the east side of the lake probably constituted the major area of *local* African trade, while the western area of the lake contributed the major sources for exports at the coast and the major market for imports from abroad. As we show in the following chapter, Zanzibar was the focal point of trade for the whole of the eastern African coast in the nineteenth century.

With the coming of the Europeans, these commodities of trade and the direction of trade altered. Mombasa, and to a lesser extent Dar-es-Salaam, took over the international trading role of Zanzibar, while Nairobi and the Kenya Highlands and to a lesser extent

Kampala and the Buganda hinterland took over as the source of exports and the main market for imports. The participation of Africans in this trade was of a very limited nature.

Given time and encouragement, there seems no particular reason to doubt that local peoples could not have learned the tricks of the new areas of trade. But time and encouragement were not to be made available. Indian traders had been trading along the coast for many years and had become established as the money-lenders for the caravans and the exporters to India from Zanzibar from around the 1840s and 1850s. Then with the growth of the railway from 1896–7 Indian traders followed the railway line inland and established *dukas* at Voi, Kibwezi and Machakos. With these traders came the use of rupees, and the regular import of western consumer goods.

Indian traders also followed the early military expeditions and established their *dukas* at the new military posts, which subsequently became Fort Hall, Nyeri, Embu, Kisii and so on. Then, because the Indians were so quick to take up the opportunities for trade offered by the incoming colonialists, indigenous African traders who had had less experience in this field were unable to grasp the new opportunities. As a consequence, the earliest British colonial reports in Uganda argued that as the local people showed little ability in the field of trade, British Indian immigration should be encouraged. It is not in the least surprising, therefore, to find that Indian *dukas* rapidly spread out throughout Kenya and Uganda, wherever the British established a military outpost, which later became an administrative centre.

Nearly all the earlier colonial reports in both territories deprecate the lack of interest by Africans in the export-import trade and ignore the growth of local domestic trading. Yet there is little doubt that this latter form of trading expanded considerably. Interviews with the old successful African traders in Kampala and other towns in 1970 indicated that at the beginning of the century they had grasped the new opportunities by buying small quantities of goods from their fellow Africans and selling them to the Asian *dukas*. After some years, when they had saved sufficient cash they had set up their own *dukas* on the outskirts of the main trading centres.

It seems very probable, although here again we lack sufficient evidence to be certain, that the old methods of trading by hawking a commodity from one home to another had been expanded in the colonial era. By the 1930s in Kenya, when the colonial authorities began to take active interest in the domestic market, we find that there are many thousands of local men involved in trading in a small way. Large numbers of people (we have no idea of exactly how many) were involved in buying in the rural areas and selling to Asians; while others were setting up tiny shops in and around the trading centre.

It would be very surprising if these economic enterprises had suddenly begun in the 1930s when the colonial authorities began to take an interest. It would seem far more likely that African trading enterprise was a continuation of the methods of exchange in the pre-colonial period. The problem for Africans by the 1930s was that they had very little opportunity to expand into the import-export trade as it was already controlled by Europeans and Asians.

In Kenya, as we suspect in Uganda too, African enterprise in the 1930s was considerable. There were donkey owners who took produce from the outlying districts and brought it into the trading centres. There were others who had organised themselves into chambers of commerce and who were taking on contracts and agitating for greater freedom of opportunity. For instance, in Western Kenya the Kisumu Native Chamber of Commerce (KNCC, founded in 1927) was forwarding milk by rail to the Lumbwa Co-operative Creameries. The KNCC also gave evidence to the 1934 land commission. There were other similar forms of organisation in central and western Kenya, and most probably elsewhere.

From the beginning of the century market-places had been institutionalised under colonial laws. Village markets, trading centres and townships were established under new urban laws. The village markets often existed before the colonial era and were places where mainly local and some imported goods were exchanged. The townships and trading centres were established from the very beginning of colonial rule as centres of colonial administration. Initially, local trading activity was encouraged and the earliest District Officers were instructed to encourage trade. Part of this encouragement consisted in inviting Indian traders to take up plots in order to establish *dukas*.

By the 1930s African traders were also attempting to compete with the Indian traders, but by then their earlier lack of experience had been compounded by time. Furthermore, African traders had had no means to obtain credit, while their Indian counterparts were able to use ninety-day credits from Indian wholesalers, and also they were able to draw on the credit of their castes.

Despite these limitations, by the 1930s there were many thousands of small-scale African traders; they brought goods to markets and to wholesalers from outlying areas. But as we show in the chapter on marketing which follows, the colonial government began to step in actively to control and limit indigenous trade enterprise from the mid-1930s. The complex patterns of licensing traders at all levels began at this time. The government's purpose was clear: Where the European marketing boards thought there was profit to be made in the African domestic and export trades the numbers of traders were to be controlled by the issue of trade licences. The system of trade licensing was designed specifically to limit competition between traders and has provided the administrations, then and now, with the power of economic patronage. Since the 1930s trade licensing has grown up in both territories although in Kenya it has covered a wider range of goods than in Uganda. During the colonial period, licensing traders led to patronage along racial lines, thus further limiting African opportunities of benefiting from the colonial economy.

As a result of these problems, Africans continued to find difficulties in access to the rewards of trade in the 1940s and 1950s. As agitation in both territories grew during these years Europeans began to encourage Africans in the field of trade, only to find out that historically the lesser privileged local people would need special privilege to catch up. It began to be realised that the Indians had successfully monopolised the more profitable aspects of exchange both in the field of exports and imports and in local trade. For instance, in the early fifties it was discovered in one study that the average trader through Nyansa had a market of only 178 people for his trade. The pressure to enter trade, as a potential profitable venture, was so great that large numbers of people had entered with the resultant limited opportunities.

With the advent of Independence in 1962–3 this basic situation of large numbers of very small-scale African traders, with a preponderence of Asian traders in the towns in both territories, was unaltered. As a consequence the last ten years have seen considerable political pressures building up, aimed at removing the Asian shopkeeper and replacing him with a Kenyan or Ugandan. In 1972 when General Amin removed the Asian communities *en bloc* in Uganda, the move was met with joy from all sections of the local community in both territories. At last it was felt that the longstanding frustrations of the colonial era were being swept away at a stroke. While the process in Kenya was less abrupt, these is no doubt that the Asian traders are being removed rapidly. As a consequence we can expect a new class to arise in the very near future; although in the past the middlemen traders were disliked for assumed profiteering, they could be castigated as foreigners. Future middlemen traders may find that they too are disliked for the same reasons – except that they will be seen as a class rather than as a race.

9 Nineteenth-Century Arab Trade: the Growth of a Commercial Empire

Introduction

The expansion of Arab caravans and Arab personnel into the interior of East Africa throughout the nineteenth century was in a sense the first stage of imperialism which was to transform the face of Africa in the twentieth century. Nineteenth-century Arab trade did not produce such radical changes as the European imperial trade which followed. The technology of transport was still based on human muscle power, the main export goods were ivory and human beings which were exchanged for cloth and a few iron goods. The Arabs were concerned almost exclusively with the export-import trade. Unlike the Europeans they did not have the physical means to set up central government controls in any part of Eastern Africa. Yet, despite this lack of innovation, by the 1880s there were very few areas that had not been influenced by the Arabs' activities in one way or another.

This vast expansion of Arab trade and influence throughout the area would not have been possible at all if there had been no political stability along the East African coast and particularly at Zanzibar. Political stability is nearly always a condition of economic growth. The political stability at the coast stemmed from British support of the Omani Sultans, first at Muscat and Oman in the early nineteenth century, and then from the 1840s at Zanzibar. It is worth while, therefore, first of all to examine British intentions in the Indian Ocean in the nineteenth century, as British strategy provides the background to the Arab expansion in East Africa during the nineteenth century.

Background to Arab expansion

British imperial policy in the Indian Ocean in the nineteenth century
Palmerston was the major architect of British foreign policy in the middle of the nineteenth century. One of his primary concerns was

to expand British trade over the entire world : Africa, India, China and Latin America. His policy on slave trade was clear; he argued that it must first be driven out from any place before legitimate commerce and civilisation could be firmly established. Palmerston was less concerned with the humanitarian angle of the slave trade than he was anxious that the products of Britain's industrial revolution should find markets in the world at large. For him, the ending of the slave trade was a necessary step along the way to achieving his wider aim.

During the first half of the nineteenth century, as Britain expanded her economic interests in Asia, and particularly in India, Palmerston's concern was with excluding French and Russian influence from the area. The route to India through the Mediterranean, Egypt and the Red Sea was being threatened. In 1815, by her seizure of Mauritius, the Cape and Ceylon (Sri Lanka), Britain appeared to have secured the route to India. At that time she appeared to be in a very strong strategic position in the Indian Ocean. However, by the late 1830s both Russia and France were menacing Britain's overland route to India through Turkey, Egypt and the Ottoman Empire.

Palmerston's response to these threats was an attempt to create a line of defence along the entire eastern seaboard of Africa. He attempted to stabilise the North Indian Ocean and the Eastern Africa coast in order to preserve Britain's trading interests by a policy formulated between 1838 and 1841. In order to carry out this policy the Imam of Muscat was to play the leading role in stabilising and protecting the Indian Ocean on Britain's behalf. The British intention was to protect the Imam's authority against all petty chiefs in Arabia and along the African coast. Thus there would be a single, central, Arabic authority over the entire region, virtually dependent on the British. As Cogan, Palmerston's adviser, argued :

There is no doubt that the Imam's military means is to us quite insignificant; but his alliance politically speaking is of real importance to our government. It would be through his agency that we might exclude from an extensive line of Sea Coasts of Africa and Arabia the formation of settlements by European States, now anxiously sought for by the French; and which must ultimately neutralise any permanent control of the East Coast of Africa north of the Portuguese settlements to the mouth of the Red Sea and of Arabia from Aden to the banks of the Euphrates.*

* PRO. FO 84/425 Cogan to Forbes, 28/10/1842 (quoted by R. J. Gavin).

Palmerston implemented all of Cogan's strategic ideas. Gradually the entire area was centralised under the authority of the Imam of Muscat in the interest of British–Asian trade. Moreover, under the British political umbrella, the Omani Arabs became instrumental in the opening up of East African trade to British goods, imported by the Europeans.

Arab imperial expansion in East Africa, 1750–1820
It would be entirely wrong to assume that the Arabs were mere passive pawns in the hands of British strategists. The Arabs from Muscat had begun their expansion along the East African coast long before the British attempted to obtain control in the Indian Ocean in the nineteenth century. Omani influence had reached Kilwa and Mozambique by the middle of the eighteenth century. The Arabs could help meet the French demand, on the increase at this time, for slaves for her Indian Ocean island colonies. Slaves exported from East Africa were now required to make up the deficiency in the New World slave markets. Thus during the 1770s and 1780s the price of slaves at Kilwa doubled as the East Africa slave trade expanded in response to increased demand. By 1800 Kilwa had come under the political control of the Omanis and Zanzibar had already become the entrepôt for the slave trade. By the turn of the century the Omanis were already beginning to dominate the East African coast in terms of ocean transport, finance and commercial organisation.

By 1800, therefore, Zanzibar was the centre of a complicated web of Omani trading and political relationships. Imports from India and Arabia were channelled through Zanzibar to the East African ports under Omani suzerainity, while the exports of ivory and slaves tended to centre on Zanzibar before re-exportation to India, Arabia and the Indian Ocean islands. Yet no straightforward political relationship ever existed between the coastal towns and Zanzibar. Military conquest of a coastal town involved the establishment of an accommodation system whereby local rulers collected taxes from traders and a fixed sum was regularly sent to Zanzibar.

Between 1800 and 1820 the character of the Arab-dominated trade of East Africa altered. First, the ivory trade with India collapsed because of Mozambique's imposition of heavy taxes on it. The main ivory supply had until then come from Mozambique. As a result the supply pattern began to change, the ivory now coming from the more northerly ports. Secondly, the demand for ivory in Britain and the United States had risen steadily from the 1820s to the end of the century. In 1825 the price for one frasilia (36 lb) of ivory had been 21 rupees; thereafter it rose steadily to reach 60 rupees per frasilia in 1875. Thirdly, the prices of cotton cloth, brass wire and muskets, imported to East Africa from Europe, had either remained stable or had declined. Thus the prices obtained for exports were rising while those of imports were stable or declining. This then is the dynamic of the trade expansion in the nineteenth century. The fourth factor in altering the character of East African trade was a marked decline in the demand for slaves for the French Indian Ocean colonies and the southern states of the USA. In fact, by 1825 ivory had become a more valuable export commodity than slaves and remained so throughout the century. For these reasons, therefore, the rulers of Muscat and Oman had been able to establish their own independent, commercial interests on the east coast of Africa.

We now return to the role of British imperialism in the light of Arab expansion. Here we have two expanding, imperialist societies, each with different forms of technology and each having, in the end, different economic and political goals in the Indian Ocean and along the East African coast. Just as the Omanis had attempted to come to a political accommodation with the rulers of the weaker city states, so too did the British attempt to come to terms with the Omanis at Zanzibar.

Here we can best refer the interested reader to the works of M. V. Jackson, C. S. Nicholls and R. Coupland, or to works of lesser scholarship but of considerable interest such as that by R. N. Lyne. Each of these authors deals, in his own way, with the political and economic relationships between the British and Omanis at Zanzibar. The British gradually tightened their hold over Zanzibari rulers, until, at the death of Said in 1854, they felt themselves sufficiently powerful to control the succession. Henceforth the political independence of the Omani Empire in East Africa declined. Finally, at the end of the century, the British decided that they had no further use for a client state on Zanzibar and annexed the island. Yet despite its increasing political subservience the Omani trade empire in the interior of East Africa continued to expand until the 1880s. The reason for this was that the Omani sultans had succeeded in establishing political stability at the coast, which was supported by the British who saw this stability and the maintenance of the Omani trade empire to be in their interests.

The Arab export economy

The coastal enclave
Precise knowledge of the economic developments along the East African coast is still limited. Until recently all knowledge was based

on the accounts of travellers and missionaries who concerned themselves with the issues of slavery; or, in the late 1880s and 1890s, with the economic opportunities for European enterprise. Much detailed work remains to be done on the development of the Arab plantation economy of the nineteenth century.

From the outset of Omani occupation of Zanzibar, in the mid-1820s, Sayyid Said encouraged Arab estate ownership and the planting of cloves, a spice first brought to Zanzibar in 1818. Said himself established his own large estates on the island. By the early 1830s he had devoted a great part of his land to clove growing and forced other estate owners to do likewise by imposing the penalty of land confiscation if they failed to comply. Between 1834 and 1856 he was able to alienate large tracts of land on Zanzibar and Pemba Islands. Extensive areas of forest were brought under plantation cultivation. Probably local landowners were evicted from their holdings and pushed into the interior of the islands. The economic basis for the changes now taking place on Zanzibar and Pemba was the great demand for cloves on the international market. Before Said's control had come to the area Pemba's economy had been based on the export of rice and millet to Zanzibar. Now it was based on the export of cloves to international markets. Said also encouraged Arab settlement and plantation development in the regions of Mombasa, Malindi and Lamu. Under Islamic law, as in African practice, occupation and cultivation of a tract of land carried with it rights of ownership which lapsed if the land was abandoned. Much of the land in the vicinity of these towns was uncultivated and therefore Said directed that it be given to his followers.

Malindi in 1846 was said to have been virtually deserted, but after 1854 the town and its outskirts were being rapidly transformed into a thriving centre of commerce. The surrounding areas up to ten miles inland were swiftly being put under cultivation, supplying Arabia and Persia, as well as the rest of the coast, with grain. Likewise Lamu seems to have enjoyed a period of great prosperity under Said's economic domination. By 1865 Lamu's economy was entirely based on its exports of grain to Arabia, the Persian Gulf and India and on export of ivory to India, Europe and America.

At Lamu, and probably elsewhere too, Arab landowners were businessmen involved in the export markets. Their tendency was, therefore, to live in the town rather than on their plantations. This led to the growth of thriving coastal towns.

Much of the coast north of Mombasa was under cultivation for the first time in two hundred years. The clove-exporting centres,

Zanzibar and Pemba, needed an agricultural hinterland and plantations developed all the way along the coast from Mombasa and Malindi. Also Arab and Swahili trade with the Mijikenda people give the hill-dwellers economic links with the coast. However most of the land south of Mombasa remained under subsistence agriculture.

Land availablity was no problem and as farming technology was limited to the use of knives and axes, capital investment was relatively unimportant. The crucial factor in terms of land use was labour. The amount of land under cultivation could only be increased if the size of the labour force were increased. Thus any surplus capital was used to finance caravans travelling to the interior which would bring back slaves to work the plantations. Said would lend cash to his Arab kinsmen for the purchase of slaves. Other credit-worthy landowners would borrow from Indian money-lenders in order to buy slaves.

It is useful in the understanding of the Arab Empire in East Africa to think of it as a powerful middle rung of an economic ladder; European industrial production and shipping at one end, production and trade in East Africa at the other and Said in the middle. Said was anxious to control economic intercourse between Europe, Arabia, India and America on one hand and East Africa on the other. In the demand for goods from overseas lay the basis of economic growth. He therefore not only encouraged and stimulated production for export along the coast but also provided the conditions conducive to international trade. Indian money-lenders, conducting their business in politically stable Zanzibar, were the economic backbone of the caravan expeditions. The caravans, in their turn, brought back ivory for export. So inland trade was expanded by the penetration into the interior by Arabs and Africans. In fact, Said had the means by which to create a territorial or political empire; in this he was encouraged by Kirk, the British adviser on Zanzibar.

The caravan trade

The large scale expansion of Arab caravan trading did not start until the early 1830s. Until then the Mijikenda and Akamba had been the most important caravan traders on the routes from Mombasa. Annual fairs at which ivory, cattle and iron goods changed hands were held along or near the coast. Of these the Jumvu fair was the most important. But from the early 1830s there was a major expansion of Arab caravan routes into the interior. During the nineteenth century the goods taken by these caravans into and out of the interior were carried on the backs and heads of porters as the only means of conveyance then available.

However the financial organisation of the caravan trade was sophisticated. First, the initial finance had to be obtained. Until around 1800 Arab traders had organised and financed the trade themselves. But as the trade expanded northwards and trade with India grew, Indian money-lenders replaced the Arabs as the class which provided finance and imported goods to caravan traders. The Arabs had become the plantation owners and concentrated on the caravan trade.

By 1840 Indian money-lenders were firmly established in Zanzibar. They would lend money or advance goods on credit to a trader on the security of his expected profits. They would be repaid when the trader returned to the coast with his ivory and slaves. A high rate of interest would be charged on the loan reflecting the level of risk involved; there was always the possibility that a caravan would fail to return and the money-lender would make a complete loss. During the nineteenth century the primary concern of the caravans was to bring ivory down to the coast. Slaves were a secondary commodity. The accompanying maps show the vast area covered by the trade routes, stretching from Lake Nyasa to the eastern regions of Zaïre and far north to Mogadishu and beyond. The routes can be divided into three groupings: the southern routes from the ports opposite Zanzibar Island down to Kilwa, the more northerly routes from Mombasa and Lamu and the routes which stretched from Lamu along the Somali coastline. These are, of course, arbitrary divisions but help us to understand some important differences in the trade patterns involved.

The southern routes used the coastal ports close to Zanzibar: Tanga, Pangani, Banga, Bagamoyo, Sadani and Mboamaji, the take-off points for the Arab caravans of the 1830s. For many years Kilwa had been the major slave port. The Yao peoples provided the caravans with slaves for the Kilwa market from where most slaves were sent to Zanzibar for further distribution. From the Zanzibar ports caravans set out to Moshi, Arusha and across central Tanzania to Tabora (Unyanyembe). Tabora became an area focus of the ivory trade during the nineteenth century. From here, caravans turned south or continued west to Ujiji and north to the inter-lacustrine kingdoms.

The routes centred on Mombasa and Lamu were in the 1840s, 1850s and part of the 1860s dominated by Akamba and Mijikenda caravan traders, although from the late 1840s the coastal Swahili and newly arrived Omanis had begun to break the monopoly of the local traders. By the late 1850s the Akamba and Mijikenda long-distance ivory caravans had begun to decline and after the 1860s ceased to be of major consequence. The reasons for the success of

G

the Arabs in ousting the local people from the caravan trade are still rather uncertain. It is likely, though, that a combination of coastal Swahili competition, attacks by the Kikuyu, Mbeere and Embu peoples and the destruction of elephants in Kitui all contributed to the decline of Akamba and Mijikenda ivory trading. From the 1860s to the 1890s these northerly routes were dominated by Arab caravans from the coast.

The third group of caravan traders were the Mijertain Somalis who travelled along the coast between Kismayu and the mouth of the Tana river. North of Lamu trade was entirely in the hands of Somalis. Unfortunately less is known about Somali trade than about that in other areas. The coast trade was linked to the town of Lugh, 400 miles up the Juba river. Lugh was apparently a central point for the trade in ivory and slaves moving in one direction and cloth, wire and iron in the other. The Somali's caravan routes extended across all of southern Ethiopia and northern Kenya as far as Lake Rudolf. In the first half of the nineteenth century these traders were of the Wardai Galla people but in the 1860s they were defeated by the Gabra Somali who dominated the caravan trade until the end of the century.

The most northern of the three groups of caravan-route patterns always seems to have been controlled by local peoples while the middle northern routes were wrested from the Akamba during the century and along the southern routes there was continuous struggle between Arabs and locals for control over and benefit from the caravan trade. These struggles resulted in numerous raids and wars fought along the western and southern parts of Lake Victoria during the second half of the nineteenth century.

The Baganda attempted to control Arab trade in a number of ways. They welcomed the Arabs in their own capital but stopped them entering the adjoining kingdom of Bunyoro. As the Bunyoro were their enemies they hoped to restrict the sale of weapons to their own government. It was not until the 1870s that the Arabs managed to circumvent the Baganda by opening up a new route to the centre of the Bunyoro kingdom.

Clearly the Baganda were, for a large part of the century, struggling for control of the trade routes. There is no doubt, for instance, that Mutesa was particularly keen to trade directly with Zanzibar. The Baganda, being expert canoemen, were able to monopolise the water route around the lake to the ports of Kageyi and Mwanza at the southern end of the lake. The struggles of the Baganda were only equalled by those of Mirambo who wanted to keep control of the Unyanyembe-Karagwe route.

Not all local peoples reacted in the same way. Although the Arab

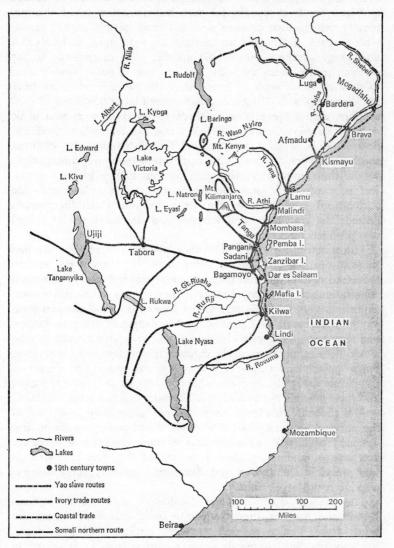

African and Arab trade routes in nineteenth-century East Africa

traders' main interest was to obtain ivory for which they would exchange the goods they had brought from the coast, they needed to barter for food supplies for their travels. They would also buy local products such as hoes and salt from people in one region which, again, they would use to trade for food from the locals at a later stage of their journey. So another type of response to the caravan traders from the coast was to increase production of local foods and goods such as hoes. Some of the caravans may have numbered up to 2000 men and so required large quantities of food supplies. Along the middle northern routes there were said to be only three points between the coast and the lake where food was obtainable; Kibwezi, Machakos and Kikuyu (Ngong). By 1900 the southern Kikuyu had built up a tradition of trade and commerce to supply the caravans. So, though again our knowledge on the subject is scanty, it is probable that the caravans helped stimulate agricultural production in the areas through which their routes passed; the traders needed supplies and the local people gained new products from Europe.

The nineteenth-century caravan expeditions were thus the first stage in opening up Eastern Africa to the products of the western industrial revolutions and they also were the first step in European penetration of the area. Indian money-lenders in Zanzibar were exporting ivory to India and to the United States. European companies were based in Zanzibar for the export of ivory to Europe and they imported goods which were sold to Indian merchants who would then supply them to the caravan traders for their expeditions. So, in principle, a three-tier system was operating. The European companies dealt with import and export, the Indians dealt in export and finance while Arabs and African undertook the actual trade.

It is probable that most Arabs did not make large profits out of the caravans although there were no doubt some exceptions, like Tippu Tib. The Arab traders had to cover the costs of porterage and rations, and repay interest on capital they had borrowed. It was probably the Indian and European exporters and financiers who made the large profits.

The Indian and European companies imported cloth from Britain and America, dyed cloth from India, silks from Muscat and beads from Venice as well as wire, muskets and gunpowder. Roughly one-third of goods either exported from or imported to Zanzibar were sent to or came from Europe and America. Forty to fifty per cent of Zanzibar's trade was with the East African coast. Zanzibar was acting as an emporium for a large part of East African trade. While some of this trade was the result of production and consumption on the coast – what proportion is not known – a considerable amount of trade was carried on with the interior. It is this trade with the interior, particularly in ivory, which must now be examined.

Exports

Ivory

The most important factor behind Arab economic expansion in Eastern Africa during the nineteenth century was the increase in the demand for ivory. Up to the 1820s the main demand had come from India, but from 1820 there was rapid growth in the demand from Europe and the United States. As a result the price of ivory had increased threefold within sixty years. This steady increase was the influence behind the Arab caravan penetration of the entire area.

The demand for ivory led Arab, Swahili and African caravans to cover vast areas of East Africa in their search for herds of elephant. The last two areas to be penetrated by traders from the coast were Bunyoro and northern Kenya although a little trade had already occurred between Bunyoro and the Khartoum traders from the north. Bunyoro was kept isolated by the vigilance of the Baganda until 1877. As the area was exploited for only a short period the elephant population in the region of Murchison Falls remained very large. The Maasai's reputation for ferocity – warranted or unwarranted – kept northern Kenya in isolation. Not until the early 1880s did Arabs and Europeans begin to exploit the elephants around Lake Rudolf. By the 1890s every part of East Africa seems to have been penetrated by tusk dealers. Throughout the century East Africa was the world's leading supplier of ivory, the steady rise in prices providing a strong incentive to traders. East African ivory is soft and ideal for carving; it was also cheaper than that from South-East Asia. It was sought after throughout Europe and North America where it was manufactured into billiard balls, dice for gambling, piano keys, jewellery, and many other luxury articles. Vast numbers of elephants were probably destroyed and certainly, during the century, herds of elephant seem to have either retreated or been annihilated as the search for ivory continued. It is also possible that the reasons for caravan movement further into the interior was that the local peoples raised their prices and the traders moved on looking for cheaper ivory. This will be clarified by further research. Nevertheless, such great quantities of ivory were available that, as late as the 1890s, the Europeans considered that the export of tusks might well pay for the Mombasa–Kisumu railway.

The tempo of economic activity in many parts of East Africa was altered by the ivory trade. Very many East Africans became involved in the trade as hunters, traders or both, while many others seem to have been affected by growing demand for locally-made goods. In exchange for ivory the Arabs traded imported cloth, guns, beads, cups, plates and other luxury consumer products. Thus from the 1830s cheap mass-produced consumer goods reached Africa. East Africa was indirectly feeling the effects of Europe's industrial revolution. The European firearms introduced via the Arabs in Zanzibar were not the result of new industry. Guns that were considered obsolete in Europe could still be put to use in Africa. According to the estimate of one author, between 1885 and 1892 alone the number of such out-of-date guns reaching East Africa was in the region of one million individual weapons. The Brussels Act of 1892 attempted to control this import of arms, for the European Powers feared that they would be used to equip peoples they intended to conquer.

The demand for all these consumer goods provided the stimulus for the participation of very many people in trade. Older forms of production and trade were also stimulated. Caravans required food which had to be purchased along the way; hoes and other iron products not easily obtained in the area were often exchanged for provisions. For instance the Nyamwesi bought ivory in exchange for their own locally-produced goods.

The salt trade was stimulated by the ivory trade. Salt, like iron, was a scarce commodity and was used as a form of currency, if necessary used to buy ivory.

African specialisation and the Arab trade
The ivory trade created the conditions for *specialisation, widening the division of labour in East Africa*. People who were already highly skilled in hunting various kinds of animals turned their attention to killing elephants. Many Palwo in northern Bunyoro abandoned agriculture entirely in order to hunt elephants and soon became an elite class of specialists, concerned only with securing ivory for foreign traders. The Palwo ivory hunters, the *aligo*, created a local monopoly in order to control recruitment into the occupation, organisation of large-scale hunting and the exchange of ivory. The *aligo* formed a new class in Palwo society.

The Akamba provide another example of hunting specialisation, a change amply documented by John Lamphear.* The Akamba

* J. Lamphear, 'The Kamba and the Northern Mrima Coast', *Precolonial African Trade in East and Central Africa*, ed. R. Gray and D. Birmingham (OUP, 1970).

organised themselves quite differently from the Palwo, utilising their existing *utui* (groups of homesteads on hilltops) as the basic units in hunting and trading. They travelled widely in search of ivory, hunting in the forests as far to the north as the Tana river and westward as far as the Mount Kenya area. They also spread southwards into the north-east of present-day Tanzania.

These examples show how the development of trade could affect local systems of production, by encouraging specialisation. The development of elephant hunting as a specialised occupation is the most obvious and, at the moment, the best documented of economic developments in Kenya and Uganda arising from the ivory trade. In the case of the Kamba it is clear that specialisation began before the expansion of the Arab coast-based caravan trade. The role of the Arab caravan trade was to intensify such developments, by increasing the opportunities for trade which African traders and producers were eager to grasp.

Slaves and slavery

A discussion on slaves and slavery arouses strong emotions. We tend immediately to think of slavery in the Americas or the picture as drawn by white missionaries of black slaves yoked by their necks, tramping down to the coast. Yet today we must be careful of the meaning of the word and institution 'slavery'. Caution is necessary because the European invaders of East Africa used the issue of slavery to justify their conquest and rule of the area. The following quotation is just one of many, written as late as 1961, which illustrates the 'anti–slavery ideology of colonisation'.

> The abolition of slavery (in East Africa) was achieved by the super-human efforts of many men. First the explorer-missionaries, such as Livingstone . . . Then there were the people of England who, through their elected representatives in Parliament and successive committees, influenced British policy abroad, so that British Consuls from Cape to Cairo . . . urged, exhorted, threatened and cajoled the rulers of the territories to whom they were accredited, to end the slave trade. Then there were the men of action, directly responsible for its suppression . . . There were sailors such as Captain Sullivan who wrote, 'Africa has to be civilised . . .'*

These briefly are the sentiments with which Englishmen gave moral justification to Britain's conquest of East Africa and which were used throughout the colonial period. We must therefore look closely at the issues involved in slavery.

* P. Collister, *The Last Days of Slavery*, p. viii.

A slave can be defined as someone who (*a*) is in a servile position in a society, (*b*) is not a member of any group in that society, kin or otherwise and (*c*) has usually ended up in a servile situation by being captured or by being seized from his home by the host society.

The manner in which a society treats a slave varies very widely according to its history and social and economic organisation. In societies such as those of pre-colonial East Africa, when status was based primarily, but not wholly, on kinship, a person captured in war could rapidly intermarry and be incorporated within the kin-based community. In Arab societies slavery had been an accepted institution for many hundreds of years. Slaves would be expected to take on the religion of their masters. Female slaves became concu-bines and their children were the legal responsibility of the master. For the Muslim the Koran clearly laid down the rights and duties of master and slave. Although to be a slave in an Islamic society may not have been exactly pleasant, the slave was at least regarded as a person, with recognised rights as well as duties. On the con-trary, in the western capitalist system the slave was simply a unit of production; a pair of hands to be used on the huge plantations of the West Indies or the southern States of North America. Hence the character of slavery in Buganda, on the East African coast or in the West Indies should be examined in relation to the existing economic system.

East African 'slavery'

In order to understand slavery in East Africa we must understand in *principle* the conditions which gave rise to it. Slavery is a form of obtaining labour; in the extreme case the slave is the property of his owner who has the right over his life and death.

In East Africa Arabs and Africans used labour which could be called slave labour. They had developed plantations along the coast and in some areas of settlement along the trade routes. Cash was available which might have been used to pay plantation workers. However it seems that there was a shortage of men for this type of employment. The use of slaves to work the plantations allowed the landowners to use their money instead to bring in foreign goods and to finance caravans. Similarly the Baganda and Akamba used some slave labour. They lacked a sufficiently large labour force and the purchase of slaves also left them free for other economic activities such as trading or porterage.

The growth of slavery in nineteenth-century East Africa should be looked at in the context of the expansion of economic activity inland, the key to which was the expansion of the ivory trade. The ivory trade had created (*a*) new demands for luxury goods and (*b*) developments in occupational specialisation, such as hunting, trading, iron-working and in salt production. All these activities, together with farming, were labour-intensive and the need for a larger labour force led to the demand for slaves to work inland. The coastal plantation export trade was again dependent on manual labour and if expansion was to occur more manual labourers would be needed.

In Europe the critical factor of production in short supply was land – in Eastern Africa the factor in short supply seems to have been people. As Gray and Birmingham have argued, the key to production and prosperity was control over people. Men and women who were captured in warfare could be either incorporated into local society or sold to a caravan in return for cloth, guns, liquor or tobacco. It was a direct choice between acquiring another producer or acquiring exotic goods. Many cases seem to have occurred where Africans sold Africans as slaves to either African or Arab traders. Often local communities acted as the middlemen, as illustrated in the examples which follow.

Slaves and caravan porters
The interlacustrine kingdoms were apparently not very interested in the slave trade. Rwanda, Burundi and Ankole ruling groups already had as labourers clients or serfs and these serfs were a too-highly valued part of the local economies to be sold. Only Bunyoro and Buganda indulged in a little slave trading for export but even then they were prepared to keep most of the men and women acquired in their own areas. Slaves were captured during raids on weaker neighbours living around and across the lake and exchanged for goods brought by the incoming Arab caravans. The Waswahili seem to have had most interest in taking female slaves who could be incorporated within the Arab social setting as will be described later. Whether the slave trade led to a drain of people from the area is doubtful, but must be investigated more fully. At present most accounts indicate that raids from Bunyoro or Buganda on the other groups were primarily in order to capture cattle and for political reasons, not for the sole purpose of seizing slaves. However, there is some indication that towards the end of the century, ivory and slave hunting were becoming a combined operation. It is known that by the 1890s the Wanyamwezi were purchasing slaves from the Baganda but detailed information on these activities remains very sketchy. The Arabs who had settled at Tabora and Ujiji were probably the main buyers, requiring slaves as bodyguards, to cultivate their land and as servants. In the 1870s and 1880s the Arabs also used slaves as ivory hunters, arming them with imported guns. It is

difficult to know whether or not slaves were used extensively in this way, but, if so, it would indicate that their living conditions were probably not very harsh.

Sale of slaves to Arabs by Africans was not a simple one-way transaction. In some cases Arabs also sold slaves to Africans. Those Africans who imported slaves into their communities incorporated them into their social structures. For instance the Akamba and Mijikenda were buying male and female slaves from the coast by the early 1850s. In the 1880s the Sultan prohibited the trading of slaves along the coast and the Arab and Swahili traders began to look for new markets inland. The Kamba and Nyika people soon became their best customers. The Kamba, despite their talent as traders and like nearly all inland 'Kenyan' peoples, do not appear to have captured and sold slaves themselves. It was common that women and children were taken during cattle raids, but these were probably rapidly absorbed into the Kamba community, a pattern frequently found in East African society. Such behaviour once again emphasises our earlier point on kinship absorption and reinforces Gray and Birmingham's opinion concerning the shortage of people and therefore of labour in the area, so that to have control of people was of primary importance.

The Palwo were another group who used slave labour. They, however, organised their own raids to capture slaves who were then distributed to the wealthy and powerful men of their community. Provided a slave behaved in a satisfactory manner he was permitted to participate in all community activities, much as any Palwo-born man, and he could marry a Palwo girl. Nevertheless he remained subservient to his master, working for him and dependent on him. But he could attain wealth and status in Palwo society. This indicates the vast difference between the role, status and expectation of slaves in societies such as the Palwo and slaves in the West Indies or in the southern United States.

Once again, as with so many other aspects of East Africa in the nineteenth century, proof of theory is difficult. But just as the concept of slavery in this part of the world differed from that in Europe, so conditions of slavery on the East African coast differed from conditions inland.

From this account it should be clear that the demand for slaves was not simply a consequence of the need for labour on the coastal plantations or a result of the export trade, as the accounts of nineteenth-century missionaries would have us believe. A further myth propagated by the missionaries of the period is that the porters who carried the ivory to the coast were slaves, manacled and chained. Until the final phase of the 1880s there is little evidence that the latter ever occurred. Thirty or forty years before 1870 a considerable proportion of the slaves brought down from the interior seem to have been women and children. For most of the century the large Arab caravan expeditions in search of ivory hired professional porters either at the coast or inland. Commonly the load borne by one porter weighed 50 lbs, which would have been far too heavy for a maltreated slave to carry for any distance. The missionaries' tales of wretched slaves struggling with impossibly heavy burdens and being beaten or tortured by their Arab masters are still to be found in local history books. My interviews with men who witnessed Arab caravan expeditions bring the truth of these stories into question. My research, though limited, indicates that Livingstone and others may just possibly have grossly exaggerated their accounts, so concerned were they to persuade the British government to lay claim to East Africa in order that they might extend their evangelical work.

Further studies in the areas concerned will tell us how far the explorer-missionaries were merely disseminating propaganda for their own reasons.

One fact over which there can be little doubt is that the numbers of slaves reported to have arrived at Kilwa and Zanzibar have been exaggerated. Dr Sheriff, after taking a great deal of evidence into consideration, argues in a recently published thesis that :

i. between 1800 and 1825 most western-based reports were exaggerated and that it is likely that a total of 3000 to 3500 slaves were passing through these ports annually;

ii. due to the increasing demand from the coastal plantations the annual numbers rose in the 1840s to around 13,000 per year;

iii. in the 1860s and 1870s the picture has again been grossly exaggerated even in works like *Zamani*, and Dr Alper's pamphlet on the subject. It has been assumed that roughly 180,000 slaves started out for the coast in these years and 60,000 reached there.

From records of customs Dr Sheriff estimates that over the years 1862 to 1866, between 17,000 and 22,000 slaves were being exported from Kilwa every year and rather less than 20,000 were being imported into Zanzibar, where roughly half were sold and the other half were sent on to Pemba, Mombasa and Lamu. The slave dhows travelled along the coast, into the Red Sea, through the Persian Gulf and around the coast to India, and even as far as Calcutta. The groups thus scattered are only now being investigated. Although it is extremely useful to know where they were taken it must be borne in mind that the story of slavery in East Africa is exaggerated. This does not mean that slavery is to be condoned but that further thorough and unbiased research should be undertaken on the subject.

The end of the Arab economy

Lack of capital, shortage of people and limited technology meant that slave labour was a necessary precondition for the development of the nineteenth-century Arab coastal plantations. The slaves for the plantations came in the main via the Yao traders to Kilwa and Zanzibar, the principal slave markets. They were then transported to other coastal towns and resold to the plantation owners or sent on to Arabia. The slave gangs of the West Indies or the Southern States of America were not found here. The slaves seem to have been comparatively well treated and many came to hold positions of considerable authority and were skilled in their work. In fact, their situation seems to have been rather better than that of the forced labourers used during the first two decades of the twentieth century, and quite superior to that of the Carrier Corps of the 1914–18 war.

An excellent paper by F. Cooper gives a clear account of the background to Arab slave trade on the coast of East Africa. Mr Cooper points out that slavery was taken for granted in Islamic society. Islamic law laid down an elaborate code governing relations between masters and their slaves. Another important point made by Mr Cooper is that slaves could fairly easily run away as they worked unsupervised. That few took this opportunity or that there are no records of slaves murdering their masters is significant. Another distinguishing factor of slavery on the East African coast in the nineteenth century is that, unlike their counterparts in the American southern states, the Arab plantation owners did not run their estates along fully capitalist lines. Certainly they wanted a good profit from their land but they had no urge to extract the absolute maximum. Therefore they had no need to drive their labour force as hard as southern states plantation owners did their slaves.

Slaves at the coast were trained and employed in various skills such as dhow building and crewing, masonry and wood carving. A number acquired professional skills, and could earn an independent living.

Several travellers had documented this but in the furore of western expansionism at the end of the nineteenth century such knowledge was anathema to the ideology of colonisation, colonisation which was to uproot slavery. For instance W. Fitzgerald,

surveying the economic opportunities along the coast, noted that
the slaves

> . . . did not really [have the utter miserable and wretched life]
> that most English people imagine . . . On all shambas . . . each
> slave is entitled . . . during the dry season to two free days during
> each week . . . Each slave is allowed an allotment for his own cul-
> tivation . . . No owner has the right to enter a slave's house.

Nor could the owner touch any of the livestock which might be
owned by the slave. Fitzgerald's observations were probably fairly
accurate. When the debate over abolition of slavery was taking
place in the 1890s, a number of British officials, not wishing to see
the Arab economy completely destroyed overnight, made similar
comments. If Fitzgerald was correct then slavery was an enviable
state when compared to labour conditions in the colonial period.
But the situation must be carefully assessed and the necessary research is yet to be undertaken.

Ultimately the Arab plantation economy was destroyed by the
abolition of slavery. The first effective efforts to suppress the export
of slaves resulted from the recommendations of the Frere Commission of 1872. The slave markets were closed and the export of
slaves forbidden, although the treaty of 1873 did not outlaw the
procurement of slaves and their transportation by land, nor did it
prohibit their use at the coast. A second proclamation in 1876
attempted to stop the trade by land but remained unfulfilled until
the Imperial British East Africa Company provided the physical
means of putting the decree into effect. The arrival of the Company
enabled the law to be enforced. In 1890, under British direction,
Sayyid Ali, Sultan of Zanzibar, prohibited all sale or exchange of
slaves, ordered the markets to be closed and ordered all slaves to
buy their freedom. But the prohibition was not strictly enforced
until the period 1895–8 when the British began to consolidate their
rule. A few slaves continued to be smuggled into Zanzibar in small
boats and by little-known routes but the numbers involved were
very small indeed.

Production from the plantations along the coast was slowly
strangled by this cutting off of the labour supply between 1897 and
1907. The British East Africa Company's enforcement of the 1876
treaties was having its effect. The caravan trade faltered once the
slave-owners could not hire out labour to caravans; the final death
blow was dealt by the railway. The ivory trade declined and the
new Indian *dukawallahs* set up trading posts and ousted the Arab
merchants. It was the policy of the Foreign Office in London to
stop all plantation cultivation, although its administrators on the

spot were more pragmatic and saw the economic advantages to be gained in maintaining the plantations. When the Colonial Office assumed responsibility for the area, however, they called for a full report (1907) and consequently slavery was made illegal in Zanzibar. Some of the ex-slaves remained in the employment of their former masters, some found work on the building of the railway and others obtained their own plots of land. The final blow to the plantations was the alienation of Arab-owned lands in 1908. It has been estimated that by this time 172 square miles of land once under cultivation had reverted to bush.

The British colonisers had both deliberately and by default killed the most flourishing and dynamic part of the East African economy when they might have boosted it by bringing in paid workers. Instead they utterly destroyed Arab commerce on the coast. Not only had they crushed the plantation economy but also the whole imperial economic and political system which had been founded on it.

The Arabs had begun to sell their land as early as the 1890s for fear of confiscation. Some of this property was sold to Indians to whom it had been mortgaged. Thereafter European planters took over the estates and a new imperial economic system and an even more powerful ruling elite were about to be introduced into the area.

10 Foreign Trade in the Twentieth Century

Introduction

In the previous two chapters we have dealt with two types of trade of the nineteenth century, the patterns of internal African trade and external Arab–African trade. The chapter on the latter has illustrated the mechanics of the trade which initially opened East Africa to the goods of an industrialising Europe. The Arab incursions into Eastern Africa were, in a sense, the first stage in economic integration of the area with Europe. The second stage of this economic integration came with colonisation. The introduction of crops for export – cotton, coffee, sisal, tea, pyrethrum and a few others – provided the means of earning foreign exchange, mainly sterling. With this cash East African communities began to import a wide range of goods manufactured in Europe, such as motor cars, whisky and fertilisers.

Before we examine the growth of export trade and the different characteristics of trade in the two economies, it will be useful to show how colonisation was an important part of the greater purposes of European imperialism in the nineteenth and twentieth centuries.

Colonisation of East Africa and the export economy

European imperialism replaced Arab imperialism in Eastern Africa in the late 1880s. There is a growing literature on nineteenth-century European imperialism as a whole, but little detailed work to date on East Africa in particular. Why did Britain, Germany and Italy invade *Eastern Africa* in the last fifteen years of the nineteenth century? The general debate on imperialism has become stale as historians argue in circles about the motives of the intruders. Were the motives of late nineteenth-century imperialists mainly political or were they economic? For our purposes it is useful to distinguish between the object of *acquiring an empire* in the nineteenth century and the short-term objectives of *conquest* of Africa and Asia in the 1880s. There is little debate by historians over the object of amassing an empire. The purpose of the British Empire in the nineteenth century, at its largest and most powerful at that time, was to integrate the economies of the world into the British economy. In the case of India, for instance, economic integration was preceded by conquest and colonisation. Once India had been colonised she had to be defended against other European powers – France wanted India for herself. Consequently, Britain employed her great military and sea power in the Indian Ocean, particularly at the Cape, Zanzibar and Oman, in order to ensure strategic dominance over the Ocean and secure India against attack.

In other instances, conquest and colonisation were unnecessary as Britain could attain her objectives through informal imperial relations rather than formal defeat. Argentina and Egypt are two such territories. In both cases Britain was able to get what she wanted without conquest: (*a*) food and raw materials, (*b*) free access to foreign markets and (*c*) free entry of private capital and the free return of profits. In the nineteenth century, expansion of the British Empire involved the setting up of relationships, deemed to be in her interests, with other territories. Thus to gain free access to the Indian subcontinent conquest was necessary, but in territories where local rulers could be persuaded, bullied or bought to concede access to incoming British goods, conquest was thought expensive and unnecessary. In the nineteenth century European capitalism and imperialism grew simultaneously. The actual form of the links between the British Empire and other territories varied enormously, but so long as no other major power challenged British naval and military supremacy, they were very often a matter for negotiation and diplomacy between the British government and the government of the weaker party. Conquest and colonisation was only one of several means to British economic ends. The British government could and did reject direct colonisation in many instances as being impractical, for example in Mombasa in 1823 and Zanzibar in 1877. In both cases it was felt that colonisation would require an extension of her military and economic presence with little additional economic return.

Britain's imperial supremacy was first challenged in the late 1870s by the French and the Germans. From the 1870s these two European powers had begun to catch up with Britain's industrialisation. But Britain had, as first-comer, integrated much of the world's economy with her own.

Up to the early 1870s there had been general amicability in the economic relations of the major European powers. Britain had taken the lead in a general move towards free trade (trade between a group of nations without duties or tariffs on imported goods and capital). However, during the early 1870s there was a general slump in world prices and the European powers began a policy of economic nationalism which involved putting tariffs on each other's goods as each country attempted to limit or stop the importation of foreign goods. The intention was to create monopolies in the domestic markets for national, capitalist concerns, and it can be understood in terms of economic nationalism.

Following from these developments a logical next step was that the newest, expanding European powers should try to control the supply of raw materials and their export markets. Economic nationalism naturally looked outwards to imperialism. But, as already mentioned, Britain had been first in the field. Hence, it is from the late 1870s and early 1880s that the international struggle for overseas territory began. Moreover, it is not surprising to find that it was the newest European industrial powers, France, Germany, Belgium and Italy who took the lead in grasping colonies for themselves, while Britain, already established as a colonial power, was the last to add new territory to her empire.

If the conflicts of the European powers are examined around the late 1870s and 1880s it is found that national prestige, diplomacy and power politics all play a major role. So far as the British were concerned, the immediate objectives of *conquest* included the defence of India, the protection of the Suez Canal and the establishment of economic control over Southern Africa – which included much of Eastern Africa too. The strategy was to bring an area under British influence before a rival European power could do the same, and claim the land and the potential mineral and other resources. In this explosion of conquest and in the rivalry between the European powers much of the original object, namely that of acquiring an empire, was lost for the time being. But by the end of the century imperialist statesmen were reasserting the principles of colonisation in statements like the following :

We know from experience the wonderful productiveness of Ceylon and can thus draw fairly correct conclusions as to what may be expected from the East African coast belt from an agricultural point of view.*

In short, we can contend that by 1870 Britain's concern was to hold, defend, consolidate and enhance all the formal and informal relationships around the world which she had already established.

* A. Whyte, 'Recent Travels along the Sea Coast Belt of the British East Africa Protectorate', *Africa*, no. 3 (1903) col. 1534, quoted in R. D. Wolff, 'The Economics of Colonialism: Britain Chooses Crops for Kenya', Historical Association. Conference of Kenya (1972).

This pattern of relationships was broken down by the competitive struggle of the industrialising states of Europe. As this happened, Britain's answer of the 1880s was an empire founded on conquest.

The goals of British colonialism in East Africa, once the scramble had died down and the European powers had temporarily come to an agreement over the distribution of the African territories among themselves, were as follows :

  i. to make the colony pay for itself;
 ii. to obtain a high return on capital invested;
iii. to produce commodities for import into Britain thus reducing or removing dependency on non-British colonial sources.

Much of the literature on East African colonialism has emphasised the necessity of making the colony pay for itself. It is also maintained that, although the railway was built for strategic and political reasons, in addition it happened to provide an invaluable amenity for development of export markets. It is argued that the colonial governments, missionaries and settlers together undertook experiments in farming which resulted in the economic self-sufficiency of each territory. But this is not the whole story. The imperial authorities in London and the colonial authorities in East Africa were concerned equally with producing crops which maximised returns on capital and which would reduce the vulnerability of the British economy to changes in world prices and availability of foodstuffs, and with extraction of raw materials formerly imported from areas not within the sphere of British influence. This important point can be illustrated by the examples of coffee and cotton.

In the 1870s and 1880s Britain imported coffee from Ceylon and India, both part of the British Empire at this time. In the 1880s the coffee plants in Ceylon were stricken with leaf disease which virtually destroyed the entire crop for years thereafter. Britain had, therefore, to import coffee from Brazil, the world's largest producer of coffee, in order to supply her customers. The coffee was sold through the United States which controlled most of Brazil's coffee exports. During the 1890s prices of raw coffee sold via the United States rose rapidly. The rise was largely because the United States had sole control over distribution of coffee and so could control its price. The British government of 1900 was disturbed by these developments, as Britain had been making a sizeable profit by re-exporting Ceylonese coffee to European consumers. This source of revenue was lost when high-priced coffee had to be imported from Brazil. The British Board of Trade quickly became interested in developing coffee growing in the Empire so that they could have some control over its price. Between 1905 and 1907 the Department of Agriculture in Kenya sent a series of coffee samples back to Britain and began the systematic encouragement of coffee production among settlers. In 1908 only £235 worth of coffee was exported from Kenya, but by 1914 the value of settler coffee production for export had risen to £18,502.

The importance of control over cotton-growing areas was of the same order. The textile industry was of prime importance in the growth of British industry during the nineteenth century. For most of the century Britain was dependent on the raw cotton supplied from the United States. In the 1860s a cotton famine led textile producers in Lancashire to turn to Egypt and India for supplies. But dependency on America remained. In 1901–3 there was another cotton crisis. In 1902 British textile producers set up the British Cotton Growing Association with government support. The Association's explicit purpose was to foster cotton growing in suitable parts of the British Empire in order to reduce their dependency on the United States. By 1914 roughly fourteen colonial territories which had not previously produced cotton were selling the raw fibre to Britain.

By 1904 the Association was reporting on the prospects for cotton growing in Uganda. Over the next few years they donated two gins and 1000 pounds of cotton seed to the protectorate to be distributed by the colonial authority. In the ten years that followed officials of the Association took a personal interest in the cultivation of cotton throughout East Africa.

A similar story could be told about all the other crops introduced into East Africa on a large scale – sisal, flax, wheat, rubber, maize, etc. Especially, Britain was concerned that the territories of her empire should produce the crops she required either for industry, as food for her people, or for re-export. From around 1900 she began to use the empire as a way of controlling the production of these crops, reducing her reliance on her capitalist competitors. This meant that rival territories could not 'unreasonably' raise the price of a crop to thwart British interests.

Britain had, therefore, to discover which crops would be best grown in which areas. Research stations were established by the agricultural and veterinary departments in order to investigate the suitability of conditions in East Africa for the required crops. The Botanical Gardens were established in Entebbe in 1898, and soon after government experimental farms for testing cocoa, sisal and coffee were set up in different parts of the country. The Entebbe Botanical Gardens established connections with the Kew Botanical Gardens in London. Also mineral samples were sent for examination to the Imperial Institute in London. Experiments on the effects of varieties of crop diseases and on methods of cultivation were undertaken and the acceptability of different strains to the British market was tested through the London connection.

Thus, the foundations of the economy of the colonial era were laid. The integration of East Africa into the British economy had begun. It was not a simple exploitation, extracting all the profits possible, as is sometimes asserted; but British traders and producers certainly wanted to make money and take it home. What is much more important is the *structure of economic dependency* that was set up by the process outlined above.

East Africans were offered certain crops for cultivation which grew well in the climate and soils of the area and which were needed in Britain. In return they bought finished goods, including textiles, bicycles and whisky, manufactured by the newly revolutionised industries of Britain. This is the origin of the export market in primary products and the root cause of the under-development in Eastern Africa. The growth of this export trade will now be followed.

Colonial growth and economic dependency

Up to 1940 very little effort was made by the colonial governments in both Kenya and Uganda to develop the African agricultural or pastoral resources for *internal* trade. Far more effort was directed towards stimulating *agricultural* production for export in both territories. As a result the economic backbone of development in both communities was the money obtained from the sale of primary commodities for export. Possibly from 50 per cent to 70 per cent of all economic activity, up to 1940, which resulted in the sale of goods for cash, came either from exports or from imports. This meant that the wages paid to labourers, the income of the settlers and the taxes levied by the colonial governments were mainly from that one source. What is more, as a considerable proportion of the income obtained from exports was used to bring in imports such as matches, cloth and whisky, there was no large local demand for the goods of the domestic producers.*

After 1940 East Africa's extreme reliance on export trade was relieved a little with the growth of industrial import substitution and of peasant production for local urban markets. It has been

---

* This situation, typical of colonised territories, is called a 'low multiplier effect – economic activity in one field does not lead to economic activity in another in the same country, but in fact generates economic activity, in this case, in the colonising country.

estimated that between 1950 and 1963 East Africa as a whole was still dependent on exports to the extent of 35 per cent of the monetary gross domestic product. This dependency on export crops did not change with independence. The new African governments found themselves unable to make a sudden cut in their source of economic expansion. The patterns of international trade, created in the colonial era, were maintained. All economists would accept that the growth of the East African economies is still greatly dependent on the cash earned from the export of cash crops. That is to say, the world market situation (i.e. the demand in Europe, the United States and Japan) for the primary produce of East Africa is still the determinant of any growth experienced by the East African economies.

To depend on foreign markets is one thing, but to produce only a very few crops and be dependent on them alone is another. Each country of East Africa has been producing a very narrow range of goods for export, Uganda more so than Kenya. Up to 1939, 75 to 90 per cent of Uganda's annual exports was cotton. Coffee was a minor export item up to 1938–9, when it made up less than 10 per cent of total exports. The value of coffee rose rapidly after 1945; by 1955 the values of cotton and coffee were almost equal and by 1968 coffee exports earned two-and-a-half times as much as cotton. Together they constituted 75 per cent of the total value of Uganda's exports.

Kenya has not concentrated on only one or two crops in the same way. The following table illustrates the Kenyan situation in selected years.

TABLE 10.1

Kenyan export products as percentages of total exports

	Coffee	Sisal	Tea	Maize	Hide/Skin
1914	4	—	—	8	33
1925	30	20	—	15	12
1935	31	14	7	6	6
1955	35	8	11	7	5
1965	30	8	15	—	4

Because East Africa was dependent on foreign markets for a limited variety of crops, the prices offered for these crops became of vital importance.

We can learn a great deal from the graph showing the price variations of a few of East Africa's export commodities, which illustrates price changes in Uganda coffee and cotton and in Kenya sisal. An important point to notice is that the price changes of the three commodities vary in the same direction over time. During the period between 1910 or 1911 and 1919 prices rose, but a more rapid increase took place in 1919 and 1920. The prices for cotton fell throughout the 1920s. During the twenties great efforts were made in Kenya to introduce cotton in south and northern Nyanza and along the coast but they were unsuccessful mainly because of

FIG. 10.1   *Prices of coffee and cotton exported from Uganda and of sisal from Kenya (at prices FOB)*

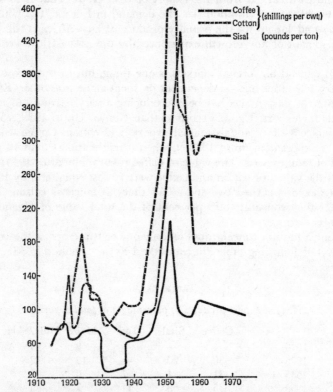

This graph illustrates the cyclical pattern of economic deveopment which was first discussed in the introduction. Although all prices have not moved exactly together the trends are clear enough. There was a sharp rise and fall immediately after the 1914–18 war, a steady rise during the mid-1920s, a dramatic fall in 1929 and a slight recovery in the mid-1930s. From the early 1940s to 1952–4 prices rose dramatically, followed by an equally dramatic fall until the early 1960s when they seem to have stabilised to some extent. These trends have followed world movements of prices and can be explained by world conditions of supply and demand. The differences in the movements of individual commodities has depended on the supply and demand which has existed at particular times.

the poor price offered to the growers. In Uganda the output of cotton fluctuated between 1960 bales in 1934 to 12,900 bales in 1929–30. Output of cotton was not expanded further as prices were low or declining.

However, after the sharp drop in world prices for coffee and sisal in 1920 (actually, all prices fell during this period) there was a recovery. Coffee prices in Uganda and Kenya, as is shown in Fig. 10.1, rose rapidly during the 1920s and many growers in Kenya benefited from the boom years 1922–3 to 1928–9. This was a time of prosperity and output of all produce for export was considerably increased.

But in 1929, prices of all products fell dramatically, as illustrated by the three products shown on the graph. They fell below the prices offered for the same commodities in any other years of the twentieth century. This was part of the general depression when prices throughout the world dropped very fast indeed. By 1936, as the graph shows, the prices of manufactured goods began to recover but the prices of primary products continued to fall. The graph shows the rather dramatic fall in coffee prices.

The slump of 1929 originated in the United States and via her trade affected the rest of the world. Economies like those of Kenya and Uganda suffered severe blows, more particularly because, by 1937, when Europe and the United States were already recovering, Kenya and Uganda's export prices remained depressed.

All the events described above illustrate the extent of East Africa's dependency on world markets.

Between 1940 and 1942 prices suddenly rose and continued to do so until 1952–4 when an equally sudden fall occurred in the late 1950s. During the years 1939 to 1952 the value of both Kenya's and Uganda's exports had risen remarkably quickly, Kenya's increasing by 77 per cent and Uganda's by nearly 120 per cent. In the thirteen years before 1939 the value of each country's exports had barely doubled; but in the thirteen years after 1952 the value of Kenya's exports grew by 150 per cent whereas Uganda's only increased by 50 per cent. These figures again illustrate the importance of export prices to the growth of the East African economy.

We need to examine why international prices fluctuated so much over the years considered. Up to the early 1960s, international prices were primarily affected by the supply and demand of a particular commodity. The marketability of a product from the Third World countries was subject to the demand in industrial countries. Kenya and Uganda were not in a position to affect world supplies of commodities like cotton, coffee, sisal or tea, because in world-wide terms they produced only a very small proportion of the total. For example, between 1952 and 1968 Kenya produced only between 0·2 and 0·7 per cent of the total world coffee output, and Uganda 1·9 to 5·0 per cent. Over the same period Uganda's contribution to the world's cotton supplies increased from 0·6 to 0·7 per cent. Thus, in world terms, both countries were marginal suppliers; they were unable to influence the changes in price of any of these commodities by adjusting the flow of their produce.

All African producer countries were in a similar weak position and up to the 1960s there was little attempt at the international level to control supplies. The unsteady prices have made export production extremely hazardous for East Africa. In response to this insecurity centralised marketing arrangements have grown up in both Kenya and Uganda (see Chapter 11, on marketing) in an attempt to protect growers against the changes in demand and in prices on the international market.

The pattern of world demand for primary produce has altered radically during the twentieth century, as is suggested by the graph. Demand rose during the 1914–18 war and producers responded by increasing their output. Once the war was over there was an economic crisis throughout Europe and prices fell accordingly. Most, but not all, prices rose again as production in Europe and the United States picked up during the 1920s. Then after 1929 came the years of the depression. The cause of this slump is still a matter for argument among economists. Certainly there was over-production, particularly in industry in the United States. The international system of finance had not been stabilised since 1914. In East Africa prices began to rise in 1939 and climbed steadily. In the 1940s even greater demand resulted from the Second World War. The war in Korea kept up demand for a further period. After the Korean war demand diminished as might be expected and prices of primary products fell very rapidly, as the graph shows. However, agricultural producers, particularly of coffee or sisal, cannot suddenly cut back on output in adjustment to smaller markets. Consequently there was a flood of primary products on the world market in the second half of the 1950s and again prices fell rapidly (see Fig. 10.1).

The price fall of the 1950s can be attributed simply to oversupply as a result of the fall-off in demand after the end of the Korean war. But it is not unreasonable to ask why prices did not pick up again at the end of the 1950s; the European and US economies were expanding and the Vietnamese war should, according to past experiences, have led to further increase in demand. This did not happen – it seems that prices have tended to decline, and it may be taken that demand patterns in industrialised countries for primary produce have altered permanently.

First, it seems that, although the western countries become wealthier, the demand for food products has not increased in direct relation to wealth. 'The desire for food is limited by the narrow capacity of the human stomach.' This straightforward economic fact was recognised two hundred years ago. As income levels rise in western countries a smaller proportion is spent on food. Also the demand for coffee and tea has been limited more by the stabilising of population levels than any other factor.

Secondly, as the technologies of the western world develop, synthetic products have, in many cases, replaced natural raw materials. For instance the manufacture of nylon and its derivatives has drastically reduced the demand for cotton and sisal. Industrialised countries have been able to produce the synthetics for themselves and have therefore tended to reduce the import of foreign raw materials. These trends are not likely to be reversed. Sisal has been particularly hard hit and exports from Kenya between 1964 and 1970 dropped steadily from 67,000 tons to 44,000 tons.

Thirdly there has been a growth of protection policies among the European countries. Many European countries have set up tariff barriers and placed quantity restrictions on some imports from less-developed countries. One of the outcomes of such policies is that East African countries have attempted to find ways of exporting their primary produce to Europe, bypassing the restrictions. For instance, they have applied to become associate members of the European Economic Community. This type of reaction could result in the independent countries of East Africa voluntarily tying their economies to those of their former colonisers.

There is little doubt that the limitations of the human stomach, the development of synthetic fibres and the protection policies have seriously reduced demand for the products of East Africa. What is even more important is that in these circumstances it is unlikely that East African countries will be able to substitute a product of nature that will provide them with sufficient income to lead to rapid growth. In many respects it is one of the paradoxes of international capitalism, that, having set East Africa up as a source of foodstuffs and raw materials, the demand for her products has subsequently declined. The tragedy for East Africa is that when countries are trying to increase production, using all the resources they possibly can, the world markets cease to provide the necessary stimuli.

There have been attempts to stop international raw material prices declining. As a result of the price falls of the 1950s and the apparently permanent nature of the reduction in world demand for primary products, there has been a major attempt in the 1960s by the producers, the Third World countries, and the consumers, the industrialised countries, to control the supply flows. For instance, the International Coffee Agreement attempts to regulate the quantity of coffee that may be exported each year. Signatories of the agreement try to control the number of trees planted annually and hence determine the amount of coffee produced.

The most that these type of agreements can do is to stop the rapid price decline because in doing so they must inhibit the producer and therefore make it even less likely that East African countries will be able to induce rapid economic growth through the export of primary commodities. It is true that in the nineteenth century Canada, Australia and New Zealand saw rapid economic growth through the export of primary produce, but in the 1960s, what with the reductions in world trade for such goods, the expansion of these types of export products will not achieve the same for Africa.

The historical role of exports in development

So far we have argued that the colonial and post-colonial export trade has not only played a vital role in the growth of East African economies but has also made them dependent on the West. Now, if we compare the export statistics of Kenya with those of Uganda the following surprising picture emerges.

TABLE 10.2

Total value of Kenya's and Uganda's exports at five-yearly intervals, 1908–68 (£m)

	Kenya	Uganda
1908	150	140
1910	190	212
1915	314	507
1920	1,178	1,828
1925	2,724	5,097
1930	3,422	2,188
1935	2,978	3,631
1940	4,176	3,956
1945	—	—
1950	17,200	28,700
1955	25,700	41,900
1960	35,200	42,600
1965	47,100	63,900
(1968	57,800	66,300)

The first somewhat unexpected fact is that in every year with the exception of 1930 and 1940 Uganda exported goods amounting to a higher value than those exported by Kenya. Despite many economic advantages and the much greater government support given to the agricultural schemes of the white settlers, Kenya was not able to produce as large a quantity of goods for export as were the Ugandan peasant farmers. A second point to notice is that up to 1925 the Ugandans were increasing the value of output much more rapidly than the Kenyans. While both territories reduced their output during the Depression, Uganda recovered more swiftly. Between 1940 and 1950 Uganda again was more able to respond readily to the war and post-war price rises than Kenya. Thereafter, between 1950 and 1965 both territories expanded their exports at roughly the same rate. Only in the last five to eight years has the value of Kenya's exports grown very rapidly and begun to catch up with Uganda's. This demonstrates that the peasant agricultural development has, in general, proved more successful than development instigated by colonising settlers, from the point of view of the value of exports.

Kenya's comparatively poor export performance is unexpected in view of the fact that Kenya has undergone swifter economic growth throughout the period considered. An examination of the visible trade balance of each of the two countries is also of interest.

Visible trade balances,
Kenya and Uganda, 1923–70 (£m)

	Kenya	Uganda	
1923	−1·3	+1·2	
1925	−2·9	+2·4	
1930	−1·6	+6·5	
1935	−1·9	+1·9	
1939	−0·5	+2·0	
1950	−13·2	+23·0	
1955	−43·5	+7·0	
1960	−23·1	+14·0	
1965	−19·2	+16·5	
1970	−48·1	+18·2	(1968)

Note:
1. Before 1923 the two countries were considered as one territory in the calculation of the export figures.
2. From 1950 inter-territorial trade is taken into consideration. Kenya's deficits in visible trade would be much higher without this.

Again, it is surprising that Kenya has been able to maintain a permanent visible trade deficit since the beginning of the century. But this is before her *invisible* trade is considered. A viable economy could not have existed if more cash were flowing out of the country than coming in. Kenya has always been able to balance her accounts through the inflow of private and public finance. Simply because Kenya has been a country of European settlers with a comparatively large European population, British nationals and others have been given the confidence to invest in Kenya.

We shall examine the inflow of European capital into Kenya in a little more detail in order to show just how Kenya has had the advantage over Uganda despite her poor visible export figures. Firstly, let us consider tourism, earnings on Mombasa harbour and re-exports, all of which have earned foreign currency for Kenya. Both Kenya and Uganda have always had *potential* attractions for tourists but Kenya, with the assistance of European expertise, has been able to provide the amenities necessary to encourage tourism – unlike Uganda. Kenya has always earned foreign exchange through the facilities provided at Mombasa harbour. Foreign firms have set up headquarters in Nairobi particularly and have imported goods from Europe and these companies have been another source of foreign exchange.* Between 1923 and 1939 Kenya increased her foreign currency earnings from these three sources by 33 per cent to 50 per cent as compared to her income from other sources. Kenya has benefited more than Uganda from the import of private and public capital. Settlers and firms who came to Kenya in large numbers† brought in a regular supply of foreign currency. Secondly, it must be remembered that the government provided extensive services to settlers during the colonial period and therefore there has always been a comparatively large inflow of public capital. These inflows of capital have fluctuated depending on confidence in Kenya abroad. During the 1920s they nearly equalled the foreign exchange earned by exports; during the 1930s they decline to almost nil. The inflow of foreign exchange from invisible earnings has allowed Kenya to maintain an annual deficit on her visible trade balance over the last sixty to seventy years.

This difference in the income sources of the two countries has had far-reaching effects. Uganda has never been very successful in encouraging an inflow of foreign capital and has, in the main, had to finance her development from surpluses on her visible trade

* See Chapters 7 and 13.
† See Chapter 1.

account.* Kenya, on the other hand, has been able to finance development mainly from the inflows of foreign capital. Admittedly Uganda has not had to repay large loans with interest whereas Kenya has had to repay foreign debts which has often been a major burden. However the total sum of foreign cash to spare for development has always been very much larger in Kenya than in Uganda, which relies on export earnings alone. Kenya's and Uganda's sources of foreign currency will now be examined further.

First of all, if we look at the values of imports from the two territories between 1923 and 1970 we find the following:

TABLE 10.3

Value of imports entering Kenya and Uganda, 1923–70 (£m)

	Kenya	Uganda	
1923	2·9	1.2	
1925	5·6	2·7	
1930	5·0	1·6	
1935	4·8	1·7	
1939	4·6	1·9	
1945	—	—	
1950	30·5	24·2	
1955	69·2	33·9	
1960	65·1	26·0	
1965	89·1	40·8	
1970	142·0	43·8	(1968)

Only during the 1950s did Uganda's imports begin to approach half the quantity of Kenya's and in most years Uganda's imports bill was less than a third of Kenya's. While a proportion of all imports would consist of luxury items which are not necessary for development purposes in a pure sense (large motor cars, whisky and so on), a very large proportion would be machinery, fertilisers, building materials and other goods not made locally and required for development. In this sense, therefore, the quantity of imports reflects the level of growth in a community. The problem which arises when growth and development are paid for by loans, is that, sooner or later, the annual interest payments from old loans overlap the annual inflow of new loans. This happened in Kenya in 1930 when a third of the national budget was being used up in repaying interest on loans. Thus the 1930s were particularly un-

* See Chapter 7 and Chapter 11, particularly the sections which deal with the way in which the Uganda colonial government used their cotton and coffee marketing boards to tax peasant earnings and so accumulate cash for reinvestment in industrial and service projects such as roads and schools.

stable economically for Kenya, but the country was rescued by price rises in the 1940s. Instability, due to balance of trade deficits, remains as a major problem for the government today.

Conclusion

Knowledge of foreign trade in East Africa in the twentieth century is essential if one is to understand why the economies of African countries have remained so relatively far behind those of Europe. The patterns of trade in East Africa also help explain why there has grown up in both Kenya and Uganda a small elite who have amassed considerable wealth while the majority of people have remained in poverty.

Why, then, is this so? Part of the answer lies in the fact that most of Western Europe and North America began the process of industrialisation about one hundred years before East Africa was thrown into the world of capitalist economies.

Another reason is that when colonisation did begin, the level of economic productivity and technology was less advanced than European productivity and technology in 1750 or 1800. These two reasons go some way in explaining the unevenness in the economic development of different parts of the world. But because different peoples have started at different levels of technology and at different points in time there is no absolute reason why they have not been able to catch up. Both the Soviet Union and Japan started their industrialisation comparatively late and both have shown that to catch up economically has not been an unrealistic dream in this century. What requires explanation is why the economic gap between Europe and East Africa has been maintained or, as some people believe, even widened.

A study of the history of East Africa's export trade will give part of the answer to this problem, as it was through the mechanics of trade that the region was integrated into the world economy. As described in the introduction, the economies of East Africa were connected to those of the rest of the world via the supply of crops in demand in Europe, particularly in the countries of the colonisers. In other words, colonisation created a division of labour on an international scale – the industries of the West and the subsistence economies of Africa. One opinion on what gave rise to this situation stems from western scholarship and is the theory of comparative advantage. Every country is endowed with a different set of land, labour and capital resources. In order to utilise these in the most efficient way possible, each country should specialise in those areas of production where it has a special advantage over other countries. For example, because the Americans have a very large number of people highly trained in sophisticated engineering it would be logical if they were to specialise in the further development of advanced technology. The United States would then, according to the theory, be able to maximise income and exchange its own specialist goods for those produced by another country. This principle of specialisation taken on an international scale means that the first countries to industrialise have the better ability to produce manufactured goods and they should therefore exchange these for the primary produce of agriculturally-based countries, such as East Africa. But practice is quite different to such theory.

East African territory was not colonised according to the above theory of comparative advantage. As had been argued, primary products like tea, coffee, cotton and sisal were not grown in East Africa by the colonial powers with a view to increasing the wealth of the area but rather for their own benefit. One of the reasons for the integration of East Africa into the system of capitalist economies lies in the search by colonising powers for sources of cheap raw materials. As a consequence of colonisation and the lines on which export trade developed, each East African country has been made economically dependent for her growth on the demand for her crops in Europe. It is relevant to summarise the causes of this economic dependency, as follows :

i. the demand for East African agricultural produce in western countries;
ii. the small range of crops which were introduced into East Africa;
iii. the price given for these crops, in the main determined in Europe;
iv. the small proportion of total world output produced by each territory, which, therefore, cannot by itself affect world supplies;
r. the fluctuations in prices on the world market.

It has already been described in this chapter how Kenya has been more successful than Uganda in encouraging a flow of capital into the country. She has therefore been able to sustain a greater import level which, in turn, has stimulated greater overall development. But in this century both Kenya and Uganda have been in a similar position in that both their economies are based on the export of primary produce. Neither can expect to import foreign capital if they do not maintain a healthy, expanding export trade. For instance, in the 1930s Kenya's import of private funds was cut off because the value of her primary produce declined. It is therefore essential for Kenya to encourage international confidence in her economy. The economies of Kenya and Uganda are firmly bound to the economies of Western Europe and, as we have discussed, the decline in demand for East Africa's produce does not bode well for future economic growth and stability.

Another question posed in this chapter was why have a few people been able to attain a high standard of living, by European standards, while the vast majority remained poor? The growth of a wealthy class can again be explained in terms of the system of foreign trade. All wealth that has been accumulated in Eastern Africa in the twentieth century has come from foreign trade. Among those people in Kenya who were well placed to benefit from trade during the colonial era were the European settlers, suppliers of services to the settlers (e.g. hotel owners), owners of export-import firms and administrators. In the period after independence those who have reaped the benefits of foreign trade have been the citizens who took over these positions. In Uganda, those who became wealthy during the colonial period include a few chiefs, the displaced Buganda aristocracy, the foreign owners of export-import firms and the administrators and again, the citizens who have taken over these positions since independence. In both countries all these people were strategically placed, either as producers or traders, to gain most from foreign trade.

11 Marketing and Distribution

What is marketing and why is it important for the process of production? Marketing is the vital link which connects the producer to the consumer. This link is of crucial importance in all economies because without a marketing mechanism, the producer's surplus crops rot in the field. In economies which are strongly orientated towards external trade as is the case of East Africa, it is the marketing mechanism which connects the producer to the world market, and which, as will be shown in this chapter, supports the producer against world price fluctuations dealt with in the previous chapter.

The mechanisms of marketing can include collecting the product, processing it, acting as wholesalers, and financing or providing credit to the producer. It is a complex but very important process, particularly in East Africa.

Many products, like tea, coffee, sisal and cotton, need a degree of processing from their raw state before they can be transported to the next stage of their journey. In some cases the processor is separate from the producer, as with cotton ginning, but often the large producer undertakes the processing also, as with coffee and usually tea (although smallholder tea and coffee producers use co-operatives for their processing). From the producer the goods go to a central point, which may be the premises of a wholesaler or financier or exporter whose job is to arrange for the goods to be sorted, graded and distributed to the manufacturer; often the link is provided by foreign firms established abroad and sometimes nowadays in East Africa, which for instance produce cloth from cotton or twine from sisal or which package, grade, finance and ship goods like tea or coffee. Then the goods are sold to traders in different parts of the world, including East Africa, from whose hands we, the people, again come into contact with the product. There are then many stages of marketing; the goods must travel from the producer to the manufacturer and back again to the consumer. We shall concentrate here mainly on the first movement from the producer to the manufacturer (except in cases like maize where no manufacturer is involved).

Clearly marketing is complex, and each product has a different system through which it is sold, processed, marketed and finally consumed. It would be tedious to analyse the mechanics of the marketing of each product grown in East Africa, and so we hope to pinpoint some of the general trends. From the East African producers' point of view the efficiency of the marketing mechanism is vital, as this is the factor which determines the price he receives.

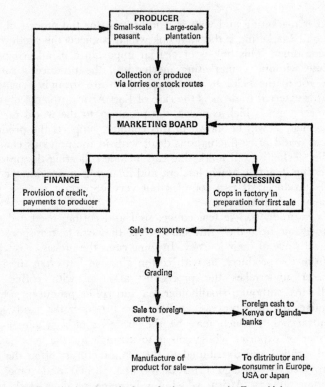

Fig. 11·1 *A typical marketing process in East Africa*

The history of marketing in East Africa is a history of a movement towards centralisation and monopoly of sales of crops. The apparent insecurity of both domestic and foreign markets has been partially circumvented through the development of marketing boards, which attempt, with government support, to offer producers secure and stable prices. This movement away from competitive producers and traders and towards bureaucratic organised marketing can be traced back to the early years of the twentieth century. Today the movement to monopoly marketing is more rapid than ever before. This chapter will trace these developments.

The organisation of export marketing until 1930

In Kenya the Europeans dominated the export scene of this period. The principle of marketing was that it should be left to each farmer to make his own arrangements. The wealthy farms often sold direct to London, receiving payment many months after the initial sale, but the majority needed cash immediately. The smaller European producers would take their crops to Nairobi and sell to a merchant. As the number of merchants was small, they often operated a price ring by agreement, thus offering a uniform fixed price which the small white farmers could not influence. A similar situation operated in Uganda, where the comparatively small peasant cotton-producer took his crop to the Asian traders. In both cases the producers were dependent on a small number of traders to buy their crops and in both cases producers, white European, black Ugandan, felt most strongly that they were being cheated.

It is not surprising that both sets of producers should feel this, as most producers the world over feel that middlemen take an undue profit. In the most developed capitalist enterprises, for instance Unilever, the producer and middlemen become part of the same giant enterprise. But in less developed capitalist situations as in the 1920s in East Africa the two functions of production and marketing were distinct. Inevitably both producer and marketer wanted high profits and so their interests were not congruent. If one assumes there are such things as 'a just price' and 'just profit', then one might argue that objectively 'cheating' occurred, but if one accepts that all capitalists great or small will attempt to make as large profits as possible, the idea of cheating is highly subjective and not open to proof or disproof.

In Uganda up to the early 1920s cotton-buying centres were few and far between and peasants had to walk up to fifty miles to the market trading post, which then made them very dependent on the prices offered by the cotton buyer. Up to the early 1920s there were no fixed weights or prices and producers believed that the weighing scales would be fixed against them, or that a lesser weight would be written on the slip of paper taken to the accountant. Peasants retaliated by bribing the man who weighed the cotton, by wetting the crop to increase its weight or even by putting stones in the bag covered by cotton.

African and European traders strongly disliked this early marketing system. In the early 1920s in Uganda cart transport *(kasimbye obwala)* became common, cotton buyers established themselves at the nearest *duka*, and a group of African intermediary traders between the Asian buyer and the producer emerged – all of which reduced the long distance people walked to the market, but not the feeling of resentment at being cheated.

In Kenya a system of selling produce to a merchant bank developed rapidly in the 1920s. The system was broadly that certain merchant banks with headquarters in London would offer a producer a short-term loan of say 6 to 9 months on condition that the bank bought the whole crop, shipped it to London and sold it on the London market. The merchant banks specialised in trading in certain lines: Messrs Dalgety and Co. came to East Africa in 1922 and handled sisal and coffee, Milligan and Co. began estate agencies in 1912, moved into coffee financing and merchanting and were bought out by Gilliat and Co., a London bank, in 1922. Jardine Matheson and Arbuthnot Latham dealt in sisal and Mitchell Cotts in coffee. There were a number of other merchant banks operating this system.

Beginnings of organised marketing in the 1920s

The development of organised and centralised marketing occurred concurrently in both Kenya and Uganda. This may seem at first sight surprising to readers who understand the different thrust of the export economies of the two territories. It is possible that the movement towards centralisation occurred by chance or coincidence, but this is a doubtful argument. Both territories as a whole suffered from the insecurity of wild fluctuations in overseas prices; both colonial governments were dependent for their revenue on exports.

The crucial point to note was that support against these price fluctuations was given by the colonial governments to those groups with political influence, the white settlers in Kenya, and the white-owned ginneries in Uganda. Throughout East Africa in the twentieth century access to political influence has been of great value to those sections of the economy able to gain from it. The story of centralised marketing was as follows.

In Kenya during the 1920s, the marketing system outlined above continued in practice, but a number of stresses and changes began to appear. The European producers felt that they needed to control all production and marketing in such a way that they either monopolised the growing of valuable crops like coffee, or that they controlled the selling mechanisms so that they (a) received the highest possible price for their produce and (b) regulated the market so that Africans did not have access to it.

There was no problem in the control of production or the marketing of sisal or tea, as in the 1920s these were plantation crops and were out of reach of peasant farmers. But maize or stock-rearing were potentials for African production. Maize in particular was important, because in 1922 the Bowring Committee recommended a rapid growth in maize production. The Committee's report in 1922 was the outcome of three years of insecurity and low prices for the settlers. Between 1919 and 1922 the rupee (the standard East African currency) was revalued into shillings, which in practice led to a considerable loss of cash for the settlers; the post-war famine in 1919 and drastic post-war fall in export prices in 1920 together hit the settlers very hard. The Bowring Committee report was concerned with the economic recovery of the settlers; the objective was to find means to re-establish the colony's export trade. They recommended a massive expansion of maize production in both African and European areas plus a specially low railway-rate to be charged on maize exports.

Acreage under maize increased annually on European estates from 31,000 acres in 1921 to 234,000 acres in 1930, an increase of just under 800 per cent in nine years. European export maize production increased over this period from 165,000 bags in 1921 to 1,859,000 bags in 1930, an increase of over 1800 per cent. But despite these large increases in total output, output per acre was static at around five to eight bags, varying according to the season. Maize was technically a simple crop to grow and by 1929 over 50 per cent of all settlers were operating as maize growers in the colony. In addition it seems that for the majority of these maize growers it was either the sole or the major crop that they produced. The success of the maize industry during the 1920s became essential for the stability of European settlement in Kenya.

It is not surprising therefore that the Kenya Farmers Association arose out of the financial needs of European maize producers. It seems that European export maize marketing began in 1912–13 in the Nakuru district because, as Mrs Huxley has put it, 'Africans had taken to growing maize with surprising enthusiasm and the local markets were glutted'. In other words Europeans had to find and monopolise the high-priced markets. In 1919, therefore, the British East African Farmers Association was registered. It changed its name in 1923 to the Kenya Farmers Association. Its purpose at this time was to buy and deal in cereal crops. The Association therefore began to organise members' crops for grading, which then enabled the Association to negotiate forward bulk export sales for each grade. Thus by the early 1920s bulk export sales had been arranged for European maize producers in Kenya, providing them with the institutional means of excluding African maize from the higher-priced export markets.

The KFA did not cover all European maize growers in the early 1920s. A separate maize marketing co-operative developed among the Uasin Gishu Plateau farmers at the same time, 1922–3. Within four years the two associations had amalgamated under the Kenya Farmers Association. The KFA was then in a position to represent all the European maize growers in negotiations with the railways, government and exporters. The bargaining position of individual farmers was potentially enormously enhanced and they could henceforth be represented in regard to maize legislation. The European maize growers could speak as one body, while many thousands of African growers were entirely unrepresented.

Export control in the 1920s was one aspect of the mechanism whereby Europeans monopolised marketing. The other aspect concerned production. With the exception of 1922 and 1923, Africans in Kenya were not encouraged to develop maize for export. Again and again in the 1920s colonial government papers stressed what they called the 'dual policy' which in practice meant encouraging African subsistence crops. The position was well stated by the influential 1929 Agricultural Commission :

> It is desirable to encourage food crops of which the surplus can be sold; rather than inedible crops, though the latter may yield a higher cash return. The yield of crops in Kenya is subject to droughts; hence to avoid risks of famine it is undesirable that the native should devote too much land to crops that cannot be eaten.

Under the policy no attempt was made to standardise or grade African crops for export, hence African maize was restricted to the lower priced domestic market. Moreover, as the quotation illustrates, this idea was the germ of a maize famine policy, a policy which was to be developed in following decades.

Developments in Uganda marketing moved even further towards centralisation than in Kenya during the 1920s. In Uganda the problem was naturally different if only because 70 to 80 per cent of all exports consisted of a single crop, produced mainly by peasants. Cotton required processing before export and the problem of co-operation among tens of thousands of peasants was inevitably greater than among a few hundred estate owners. Thus although there was widespread conflict between the primary traders, and although the conflict was the basis of the African movement in the 1940s, the movement towards monopoly trading in the 1920s occurred at the level of processing.

Cotton had to be ginned. Ginning separates cotton into two parts, seed and lint, which is necessary before it can be exported. The first facilities for ginning were created by the Uganda Company in 1904; thereafter until 1916 most of the nineteen new ginneries that were established were owned by British firms. Between 1916 and 1925, 136 new ginneries developed making a total of 155, 100 of which were Indian owned.

These rapid developments in cotton processing had not gone uncontrolled by government. In 1907 small hand gins, which had earlier been distributed to Africans by government, were withdrawn as it was argued that the quality of hard-ginned cotton was inferior. From this period on government enforced restricted entry into buying and ginning through licensing both parties. Africans were thereafter precluded from the cotton industry as itinerant buyers or as processors. Between 1910 and 1913 cotton buying in Eastern Province became restricted to central government marketing places in order to facilitate inspections. Upcountry ginneries were given a monopoly of cotton buyers within a five-mile radius in order to encourage them in certain outlying areas.

The rapid growth in the number of ginneries after 1916 led to considerable competition and high prices being offered to peasants for their cotton. The British-owned ginneries complained to the colonial government about 'reckless competition among middlemen' for the cotton crop and urged government to limit competition. The British firms were economically badly placed against Asian or African competition due to the high salaries demanded by British operatives. But politically these firms were well placed, as they had political representation in London and Kampala. In 1921 for instance the Uganda Company had taken the matter up with the Colonial Office in London. The major British companies corresponded together while under their pressure the colonial government set up a Cotton Control Board to control new ginnery licences and to advise on markets. The Control Board stopped issuing any new licences in 1927 and by providing the high-cost British ginneries within the five-mile rule, gave them a measure of protection. It was the pressure of the high-cost British ginneries to establish monopoly control over buying and to regulate the whole cotton industry that led to the first major Cotton Commission in 1929.

The 1929 Cotton Commission entirely ignored the demands of Africans, (a) for competitive buying (which would probably have led to higher prices for peasants), (b) to learn about market conditions and (c) for the right to build gins. The Commission's basic findings that all ginners should combine in one association was clearly in the interest of the high-cost firms. They argued (i) that a high degree of quality was desirable so that elimination of competitive peasant buying would stop scrambles at the place of purchase and enable purchases to be graded; (ii) that abuses and adulteration arose from militant competition; (iii) that transport for producers could be rationalised; (iv) that overcapitalisation on ginning should be eliminated by closing down redundant ginneries and prohibiting new gins.

The Commission argued that the cotton area in Uganda be divided into zones and each ginnery be given a quota of cotton for the season. Controlled quantity buying allowed prices paid to the grower to be fixed centrally by the Director of Agriculture. The 1929 Commission wanted the maintenance of privately-owned firms under a government-controlled monopoly of cotton buying and ginning. Hence with elimination of competitive prices to producers the high-cost British ginning firms could be supported through the controlled price system.

The 1929 Commission provided the basic blueprint not only for cotton marketing in Uganda, but directly for the smaller-scale cotton marketing in Kenya and for coffee marketing in Uganda.

Local competitive enterprise and the previously alleged overpayments to cotton producers was to be ended. Prices had to be fixed and the only people for many years able to assess prices accurately were the ginners themselves. Costs – the use of buyers, profits expected, hours of work, costs of transport to pick up producers and costs to Mombasa, etc. – varied from ginnery to ginnery. The African peasants were represented over prices to be paid to them by European government officials, while the ginners were able to present their own case. The consequence was very high prices paid to ginners for ginning. A few comparable prices in the 1930s were as follows :

Costs in shillings per 400 lb bale of cotton (ex-ginnery) in the late 1930s

India	10·00
Egypt	12·00–14·00
Cyprus	26·00
Uganda	40·00–55·00

The ginning monopoly in Uganda was to ensure the maintenance of European business against the threat of Asian enterprise and against the economic interest of the Uganda grower.

The challenge of the depression years, 1930–1939

Developments in marketing in Kenya during the 1930s were directed at the same type of goals (essentially price controls) as had been outlined by the 1929 Uganda Cotton Commission, although the groups destined to benefit were not the same. Essentially European producers, threatened out of existence by the depression of the early 1930s, struggled to perfect their marketing organisation in order to ensure high controlled prices. The movement towards monopoly selling of European produce, of price controlled buying and of attempts to control the prices in the whole local market continued apace. The movement was neither simple nor straightforward, monopoly involved government legislation and there was no simple conspiracy of European administrators and settler producers; it was a struggle all along the line.

Between 1930 and 1935 the prices of all export crops in East Africa fell drastically. Maize fell from 12 to 3 shillings a bag, wheat from 19 to 6 shillings, while coffee, sisal and cotton also fell in price but to a lesser extent.

In Kenya the colonial government, despite a growing burden of repayments of interest on the public debt, reacted immediately to maintain the settler farmers in existence. Immediate financial aid was available through the 1930 Agricultural Advance Ordinance. The surpluses of income over expenditure which the government had slowly accumulated in the 1920s (just over £700,000) were used to pay off farmers' mortgages and debts. After 1934 this role was taken over by the Land Bank. The Bank was initiated in 1930; between 1930 and 1938 it borrowed £1 million from London and re-lent it to farmers. Roughly one-third or over £300,000 was used to take over private mortgages to buy out creditors. Thirdly the KFA was able to borrow cash from commercial banks and lend to maize farmers. Finally the government instituted mortgage relief legislation between 1936 and 1938 in order to stop borrowers taking over farms in payment for unpaid interest.

During the 1930s the colonial government of Kenya used every possible means at its disposal to maintain European white farming in existence. The most important long-term measures were the centralisation of marketing but it was Uganda's cotton marketing system which led the way. The price of cotton dropped at least as much as maize : from 86 shillings per 100 lbs FOB Mombasa in 1928 to 23 shillings by 1938; yet output had doubled. Despite the lack of any threat to government stability from a fall-off in revenue, the colonial government implemented the major recommendation of the 1929 Cotton Commission in the Cotton Zone Ordinance of 1933. The country was divided into 14 zones. The existing ginners divided up each zone among themselves through individual agreement and allocated a percentage of the crop in the zone to each ginnery. The government, in agreement with the ginners, set up minimum prices. Trading centres were scheduled by government, trading licences issued, and itinerant African traders disallowed.

Thus the competition between gins for the cotton crop and the movement of prices according to supply and demand was finally ended. 'Commerce' and 'agriculture' were thus legally separated, the cotton industry was to be regulated as far as possible by government dictate, but profits remained in private hands. This system of controlled marketing and prices to growers has lasted to the present day.

The Uganda government followed cotton marketing and processing controls with coffee controls. Coffee was the other major export crop in Uganda. From 1932, all coffee had to be passed through licensed curing works. Only seven such works were licensed. Coffee buying from the peasant was also monopolised, through licensing the traders at government-recognised markets; in some cases government established minimum prices. By the mid 1930s all African-grown coffee sales were controlled in this manner.

Centralisation of all the marketing mechanisms for all African crops was carried through under the Native Produce Marketing Ordinance. The activities of the small-scale Asian shopkeeper, who had previously been the main trading agent for peasant growers, were severely curtailed. Under this law the government gave itself the right to limit traders in any African-produced commodities to individuals or firms chosen by itself. The restrictions provided the means for further control of production and prices and thus provided the supports for high-priced European traders to continue in profitable business.

In Kenya the situation was more complex as the colonial government had to provide the supports for the European *producers* to stay in profitable business. The financial supports for white farmers already mentioned constituted short-term measures to help most of them survive the depression. It was natural therefore that the marketing organisation developed during the 1920s should be further and rapidly developed during the 1930s.

Maize farmers were some of the hardest hit by the depression and they reacted by reinforcing their marketing mechanisms in order to obtain the highest possible price. In December 1930 at the annual maize conference the European maize producers argued that 'maize should be regarded as an industry of a permanent character . . . further it is one which a large percentage of farmers rely for their livelihood [sic].' The colonial government, then and until Independence, agreed. It was a matter of working out marketing details.

The European maize interests in 1930 asked for a guaranteed price of 6·50 shillings per bag, and for two years £143,000 was paid out to these growers in maize subsidies. By 1933 the KFA realised that the maize producers could not be permanently subsidised from the country's surplus revenue and as world prices still remained too low for European producers, the KFA began to press the administration to introduce legislation to compel all maize sales to be channelled through one source so that the domestic price of maize could be controlled by dictate and raised above the export price. The KFA wanted to monopolise all sales of maize which involved the buying of African-grown maize. The internal market had been monopolised by African growers. African producers could produce more cheaply than Europeans because they did not have the overhead costs of plantations and they were willing to accept lower profits. Europeans felt this was destructive competition.

In 1938 the international price for maize was still only just above 6·00 shillings a bag, and although the acreage of maize harvested on European farms had fallen to 234,000 acres in 1930 (below the acreage of 1924), maize was still thought of as a principal European-grown crop. In order to stimulate maize production the European farmers needed to have access to the domestic market where the price could be adjusted without reference to the international price. The domestic price of maize, therefore, now became of primary importance to the European maize producers and they attempted to raise it, at the same time seeking to involve African producers in sharing the low international price.

The KFA's argument to obtain these ends was that *all* growers should share the low export prices and that a 'national' effort was therefore necessary to achieve these ends. The Association put forward a detailed scheme in 1933 for the compulsory pooling of *all* maize.

By 1935 the Economic Development Committee Report, a major report concerned with finding means to help the economy recover from the depression, supported the idea of a compulsory maize pool and an attempt was made in 1936 to put it into effect. The 1936 Maize Bill was justified with the following arguments :

i. only maize surplus to Kenya's requirements should be exported;
ii. the burden of exporting should be divided among all 'classes';
iii. controls to maintain a high stable internal maize price were necessary because 'at present the internal price of maize is depressed periodically by the native throwing a large amount of maize on the market at one time'.

There was no evidence to support this last assertion.

But not all European growers were maize growers; many were maize consumers, in particular the sisal, tea and coffee plantation owners who needed cheap maize in the form of *posho* for their labour. They objected strongly to the 1936 Maize Bill and the idea was dropped for the time being.

Despite these objections the Kenya Farmers Association was able to go into the African Reserves from 1935 and buy African maize. They were able to do this quite legally. The explanation for this was as follows :

Up to the early 1930s African produce for export had been virtually ignored. But with the depression the value of European export produce declined drastically from £3·4 million in 1929 to £1·9 million. It was decided to bring African produce on to the export market in order to increase export sales. The decision to stimulate African production was taken up at the 1934 Mwanza conference. It was decided that exclusive licences would be offered to traders who would set up inspection centres for weighing and grading produce : wattle, maize, cotton, hides, cashew nuts and dairy produce. The aim was to standardise quality and prevent adulteration, short weight, etc. Standardisation was a major condition required for export. In 1935, as in Uganda, a Native Produce Ordinance was passed with these aims. It was also thought that the KFA would be one of the large exclusive traders. As in Uganda, part of the scheme was to offer European traders privileged trading positions in order to oust the Asians and Africans from an area where they had the monopoly.

The explanations given by the Europeans for this measure sounded reasonable enough on the face of it, but the vociferous attack by the Asians in the Legislative Council (the transcript of the debate over this bill took one hundred pages of print) indicated that there were other factors behind the African Marketing Ordinance. The Asians feared that the measure would eliminate both themselves and the African itinerant trader. Under this onslaught the anti-Asian prejudices could not be expressed publicly in Kenya but J. A. Stockdale, the agricultural adviser in the Colonial Office, argued :

> We do not wish East Africans to accept the Indian standard. It is well known that the general run of Indian produce is the most heavily adulterated in the world and that India accepts in its markets excessive adulteration without complaint.

The discouragement of African trade was part of the same marketing policy. The government and white farmers portrayed African traders as agents of Indian business; moreover it was argued that they should be producers not traders. Trade licensing successfully limited African enterprise. African traders were widely regarded in the administration as the unemployed and mostly the unemployable . . . As they emerge from the mission school their main ambition appears to be the achieving of a competency by means of petty cheating . . . This finds expression in the incredible number of middlemen – traders who are found on almost every reserve road trading on a miserable capital, but persuading the native producer . . . to dispose of his produce at a figure much below the market prices. It further finds expression in the shops . . . butcheries and 'hotels' which have sprung up like mushrooms and owe their existence to that misguided patriotism which is the last refuge of the scoundrel.

Such opinions were widespread among the administration both in Kenya and Uganda; while illustrating the widespread ability of Africans to grasp economic opportunity, they provided the ideological justification for the centralisation of marketing African produce in European hands, as well as illustrating the remarkable distrust of the process of capitalism among white officials. The bill became law in 1936.

By 1938 the process towards limiting competition and controlling prices and centralised marketing was well under way for many crops. The crops monopolised by European producers, like coffee, tea and sisal in Kenya, were the exceptions. The Kenya Farmers Association was acting as the government agent in the handling of wheat and as the agent for the marketing boards of pyrethrum and passion fruit (both exclusively in European growers' hands). The KFA was also buying maize in the African reserves at government-agreed minimum prices. Cotton in all three East African territories was highly controlled, so too were wattle bark, tobacco and cashew nuts in Kenya and Uganda. In all cases prices to be charged were under the control of the Director of Agriculture. The scene was set for further extension of these principles of control.

1940–1945: Bulk buying and selling

The wartime emergency, like the depression of the 1930s, rapidly extended the areas of marketing control and monopoly throughout East Africa. The war provided the conditions through which the economic relations between colonists and colonised were rationalised for the first time. This meant that British government departments became the sole importers of food and raw materials. Competitive trading was abrogated, and monopoly state trading instituted through bulk buying agreements. Buying was co-ordinated through the Colonial Office in London. Bulk orders in advance ensured (*a*) that supplies were forthcoming, (b) that Britain chose the commodities she required, (c) that they were received unprocessed. Sisal, tea, coffee, cotton and sugar were all obtained through these means.

Bulk buying began in 1942. Prices were based on estimates provided by producers on average costs of production. The system ensured that the commodity had a stable market at a profitable price to growers and the contracts, usually over a five-year period, provided an insurance against declines in the free market price.

Thus the British government provided bulk orders and the East African Central Government provided the mechanics for bulk selling. The war was an emergency, just as the 1930s was an emergency for the European Kenya producers. During emergencies there has been a tendency, historically speaking, for capitalist organisations to rationalise production and distribution in order to increase output and cut costs. During the war the bulk buying and selling operation was designed to bring Britain's economic interests into line with East African producer interests. In effect this meant producing the quantity of goods required by Britain and her allies during the war at a price which supported and encouraged the producers. The entire competitive element was removed so that producer resources and shipping and railway transport could be used in the most productive manner.

Thus in East Africa the private commercial concerns left in the field of marketing by 1938 became irrelevant and were replaced by statutory centralised marketing organisations with monopoly power over quality and prices. Bulk buying and bulk selling went hand in hand. Each crop in East Africa was centralised and sold in bulk, separate agreements were made with sugar, sisal, coffee, cotton, maize and tea. The Kenya Farmers Association for instance became firmly established as a parastatal organisation during the war.

The Association acted as an agent to the Maize and Produce Control, i.e. as an agent of government; yet the organisation remained the European producers' marketing organisation. European producers and government thus became irrevocably tied together through the marketing organisation and the KFA began to handle government credit finance to farmers, acting through the Land Bank and the private commercial banks; it undertook to collect, order and sell the farmers' produce while at the same time recommending to government prices which should be paid for produce. The KFA thus acted on behalf of both government and producers, although the former had to pay the latter.

Perhaps the most far-reaching economic measure of the war was that government became responsible for paying minimum prices for the first time. This provided European farmers with a genuine measure of economic security. Production orders were given to European farmers and the crop was then government property. The government offered fixed prices and a minimum return in case of crop failure. As Huxley noted in relation to fixed prices :

> This all-important principle came in quietly . . . as a product of winning the war, and upon it rests the whole edifice of postwar prosperity in the Kenya Highlands. A buffer has been installed between the individual farmer's efforts, and the unpredictable and sometimes crushing behaviour of the rest of the world.

Government-controlled prices were in one way or another to become the core of post-war marketing in East Africa. The prerequisite for controlled export and domestic prices was a central marketing mechanism for each crop, so that all produce was sent through a single channel. The marketing mechanism was also used in Kenya to provide European producers with short-term credits to bolster their production.

In Uganda, as in the rest of East Africa, prices of exports under the bulk-buying scheme rose rapidly. The value of exports and government revenue very nearly doubled between 1940 and 1945. Cotton and coffee export marketing was centralised under government-organised 'Exporters' Groups' (firms with interest in Uganda coffee and cotton). After the war these groups became the Lint Marketing Board and Coffee Marketing Board respectively. Through the centralised organisations government obtained control over prices paid to growers and channelled off the cash 'surplus' to the 'needs' of peasants. In 1940 the cotton-growing peasant received only 50 per cent of the export price of his crop; in 1942–3 he received only 28 per cent of the export value and by 1945 he received 38 per cent. The money prices received by Ugandan peasants during the war for their cotton in a period of rapidly rising prices were still below the prices received in the free market in the 1920s. In Uganda a precedent had been set, centralised marketing was to be used to tax the low-income peasant, while the foreign-owned ginners and exporters worked on generous margins of profits.

The peasant in Uganda was badly off during these years; not only was his cash income static, but the import prices of cloth, for example, had increased five times and adult men had to pay a poll tax of between 8 to 21 shillings. A man's real income was thus declining.

In Kenya centralised marketing worked in the opposite manner to increase prices paid to European farmers. European farmers were paid the full price obtained through the bulk-buying agreement. The critical event for the European maize producers was the Maize Shortage Commission of Inquiry Report of 1943. A severe food shortage in 1942–3 led to the Commission's appointment. The findings of the report were critical as they provided the basis of future maize policy until the late 1960s. The important points were as follows:

1. European-grown maize was indispensable to provide for the food needs of the colony.
2. The colony should be self-sufficient in maize.
3. Exportable surpluses should be kept to a minimum.
4. Fixed prices should be announced *before* the planting season.
5. The Commission approved the differential fixed price of 9·00 shillings per bag for European-grown maize and 4·90 shillings per bag for African-grown maize.

As a consequence European maize producers obtained a monopoly of the Kenyan market at secured prices well above world market prices throughout the 1940s and 1950s. The white farmers and administration argued that African producers could not be trusted to provide sufficient maize for the demand of the colony, although there was not a shred of evidence to justify these assertions. The Europeans were provided with an economic sinecure, at the expense of all consumers who were forced to pay high prices for a locally produced staple commodity.

In Uganda there were comparatively few European farmers. The Africans' staple food crops were left to peasant producers on the free market.

The post-war years of established marketing

Between 1945 and 1954 world prices of East Africa's export commodities continued to rise. Between 1940 and 1945 the bulk value of cotton exports had nearly doubled from £3·7m to £7·0m, and coffee export had increased in value from £0·48m to £1·16m. The bulk prices of cotton continued to rise from 16·88 pence per lb in 1947 to 47·62 pence per lb in 1952. All export prices rose in roughly similar amounts, yet the colonies did not disband organised and centralised marketing to take advantage of the situation. One reason for this was that after the war Britain maintained her bulk-buying policy with her colonies. Commodities on the world market remained scarce and Britain wanted to conserve her trading currencies of dollars and sterling. Britain's interest was therefore to continue to monopolise the production of her colonies. Also, the

Labour government (1945–51) argued that bulk buying gave the colony an assured market. Thus bulk buying was in the economic interest of both parties – or so the economic rationalisation went.

The Uganda colonial government found a satisfactory set of arguments to maintain bulk selling. The Uganda government revenue had increased rapidly during the war through peasant production taxes. They argued that there was a lack of consumer goods on the world market immediately after 1945; thus by holding down prices to the producer, they were controlling inflation. If producers received the full price they would only plant more cotton and coffee which would only increase the price of imports as there was a shortage on world markets. Moreover, they argued that by taxing the peasants they would hold a reserve fund which could be paid to producers when export prices fell. Thus bulk buying and selling was continued between imperial and colonial governments after the war.

In practice, coffee producers probably did not gain as much as they would have if a free market had prevailed; the spot prices for coffee on the New York auctions were consistently higher than the agreed bulk prices, despite the renegotiation of the contract in 1949. Bulk prices were as first around £130 a ton for Robusta while free market prices were £175–£190 a ton. In 1953 the agreement came to an end – that is, one year before world prices began their steady decline; Uganda coffee was sold thereafter through a single channel, the Uganda Coffee Marketing Board.

On the other hand, cotton producers did rather better in that the bulk prices were consistently above the US spot prices until the agreement ran out in the early 1950s. Part of the explanation of the ready agreement of the colonial governments to participate in bulk buying and selling after 1945 was that the experience of the war and the recollection of the 1930s had convinced many people of the great advantages of organised and centralised selling; producer incomes were stabilised, boards could influence the volume and distribution of purchasing power and government income could be stabilised. The basis of the present-day bureaucratic rigidified and inflexible marketing organisation was laid down by 1950. Each organised pressure group could use the system to its advantage.

The above are only some of the marketing and control boards which have been set up to control production and distribution. Other crops with centralised boards or centralised marketing mechanisms included sugar (with a committee in the Ministry of Agriculture), cotton, pyrethrum and sisal. Similarly, the marketing of meat has come under the control of the Kenya Meat Commission. Since 1945 the trend has been clearly towards organised controlled processing and marketing of an increasing number of products throughout East Africa. By 1960 all export and most domestic crops had their board of control in Kenya, while in Uganda only export crops were centrally controlled. The centralisation of marketing and processing included both the amalgamation of existing boards and an increase in the functions of the marketing board. After 1963 the process was accelerated. Sessional paper no. 10 in Kenya argued that the growth of marketing boards had been 'haphazard', there tended to be 'duplication' and 'confusion in policy' and therefore rationalisation of the existing policy would promote 'socialist policies'. The Minister of Agriculture, Mr McKenzie, acted on this policy. The outstanding examples of marketing rationalisation between 1966 and 1968 were the amalgamation of the two coffee boards, the two pyrethrum boards and the two maize boards – thus creating a unitary and centralised marketing organisation for these crops. Equally in Uganda although there were only two boards by 1966, the Committee of Enquiry into the cotton industry of that year proposed amalgamating the Lint Marketing Board and the Coffee Marketing Board to bring all agricultural crops under a single organisation.

The growth and development of the centralisation of marketing in the 1940s occurred in a situation of rising prices for reasons already dealt with. Prices continued to rise until 1953–4, but since then prices of nearly all commodities in Third World countries have declined steadily. The simple explanation for this decline is that world demand for the products has not increased as fast as the increase in the supply of goods. The second reason is the increase in synthetic fibres developed and produced in the rich countries; nylon for instance is a substitute for cotton and sisal. Finally tariffs have protected the agricultural sectors of the developed countries, in particular the countries of the European Economic Community which has a self-sufficient agricultural policy and tends to import only tropical commodities. The marketing boards have thus since 1954 been operating in conditions of declining world prices; and have been a vital protective mechanism to producers. This vital factor goes some way towards an explanation of the centralisation movement.

A second reason involves an understanding of the overall purpose of these boards. It was not by chance that in Kenya by 1966 there were seventeen marketing boards against only two in Uganda. The Kenya boards, with the exception of cotton, have always been a mechanism for the economic protection of the large producers (up to 1963, the European producers) against movements in world prices, while in Uganda the boards have been concerned to protect the processors and exporters. In both territories, it is those groups with political influence which have helped to form the characteristics of particular boards.

The primary aim of protection of large Kenya producers was well expressed in 1949 by a committee on the Development of Agricultural Marketing :

> We should also perhaps make it plain from the outset that . . . we regard the interests of the agricultural producer as our primary concern, and where there is a conflict with other interests our preference tends to remain with the producer. At the same time we believe in the long run the general interests of the Commercial Community will be benefited by a policy based on this preference . . .

Historically the formation of the commodity boards has been directly connected with European agriculture. High-cost production of commodities like wheat, dairy and maize products sold on the domestic market, have been developed since 1923 behind tariff barriers and, since 1942, with the addition of high guaranteed prices (higher than world prices). These producers have had heavy overhead costs due to (*a*) running large enterprises and (*b*) the high standard of living of the producers. These high costs have in effect been subsidised through the marketing boards by the rest of the community.

The marketing boards have not been able to guarantee prices in the same manner for the export crops like coffee, tea, sisal and pyrethrum. In the case of tea and sisal the boards have not even had a monopoly on buying producers' goods. The explanation here is that tea and sisal have always until recent years been primarily plantation crops. Tea for instance has been grown mainly by large-scale vertically-integrated oligopolies which grow, process, ship, package and sell the commodity to the consumer. The East African tea companies for instance tend to sell the tea to their parent companies in Europe and have no need for monopoly marketing organisation – they are already in this position. The coffee and pyrethrum boards on the other hand can try to obtain the most favourable prices for growers on world markets through specialised selling. Both products have had centralised and monopoly selling since the war. Both boards are involved in licensing growers, giving technical advice and processing and grading crops before marketing in order to obtain the best prices. But unlike the domestic marketing boards, they cannot even try to guarantee producers a profit through the manipulation of prices; in the end world prices prevail.

A third factor which is part of the explanation of the growth of horizontal concentration of marketing power is that of duplication of functions and inefficiency towards consumers. This latter factor applies particularly to those boards concerned with domestically consumed products. As already noted, the policy of marketing boards has been towards the protection of growers' interests rather than that of the consumers. The gross inefficiency which has been the result can be most clearly seen from a short analysis of the problem of maize marketing. Since 1945 there have been six reports of Commissions of Enquiry into maize marketing: in 1946, 1952 (2), 1961, 1963 and 1965,* which in itself indicates the ongoing problems.

Since the 1943 maize shortage, self-sufficiency has been the pivot of Kenya's maize policy. It has been argued that as maize is very bulky it is expensive to import, especially if the maize comes from the United States, while losses are made if it is exported at the FOB Mombasa price. As a result, when there has been a glut on the domestic market and maize has been exported, the maize board makes a loss because it guarantees prices which have been higher than the export price. It should be noted however that the loss is recouped through sales on the domestic market. Yet when there has been a local shortage due to famine conditions and maize is imported the Maize Board again makes a loss, as the price it pays for the imported maize has been higher than the guaranteed domestic price. And due to the variability of climate conditions in Kenya, maize shortages and surpluses have been common.

The maize 'problem' centres around the guaranteed prices which are directly related to marketing policy. Maize control from the board's inception in the early 1940s worked through the KFA which was concerned to guarantee settler farm prices, the backbone of settler agriculture. As a consequence African-produced maize until the middle of 1960s received a price only a little over half of the European-produced maize. One author quotes 32·50 shillings against 17·50 to 22·50 shillings in 1963. In the same year the consumer price was between 42·00 and 48·00 shillings or over 20·00 shillings higher than the guaranteed African price. Not surprisingly, very little African-produced maize has been channelled through the Board; estimates vary between 5 and 10 per cent, and the rest of the African crop has been sold 'illegally' on the free market. Yet the Board's figures throughout the post-war period show that roughly 50 per cent of the crop which it sells is produced by the smallholder African. Hence something in the region of 80–90 per cent of

* A seventh commission of enquiry was completed in 1973.

the total crop of maize has not gone through the Maize Marketing Board mechanism at all.

Thus the consequences of centralised maize marketing since 1943 have been first, that official maize prices have tended to be higher than they would be if there had been a free market in maize. Secondly, inefficient large-scale producers have been successfully supported against competition from small-scale peasant producers. Thirdly, peasant producers' maize products have been kept off the organised market. And finally maize exports have been curtailed because the high domestic controlled price leads to losses to the Marketing Board.

The problem has been over-rigid control, high prices, regular shortages and surpluses and smuggling, all of which can be directly related to the price support which the Marketing Board has given to European producers.

Part of the maize problem, like the problems of all the Kenya boards, has been that there has been no control over the costs of the marketing boards, which as a monopoly organisation have had no competition to keep down costs. There have been no criteria by which the efficiency of the boards can be judged except that the difference between the costs to the producer and sales to the consumer seem very high indeed. Moreover, in a community where a shortage of skilled and educated manpower is critical it is worth considering whether the setting up of monopoly marketing organisations, which protect the politically conscious interests, is the best use to which skilled labour can be put.

The contradictions associated with maize marketing in Kenya have been particulary intense, as very nearly the entire community are maize consumers. The case vividly illustrates the problem thrown up when one section of the community, the large-scale producer, has been protected against another section, the consumers – a major goal of all the marketing boards in Kenya associated with locally-consumed goods.

In fact *all* the Kenya marketing boards, with the marked exception of the cotton board which is significantly a peasant crop, have attempted to maximise returns to growers. In Uganda on the other hand the centralised boards have been used to maximise returns to government, processors and traders, rather than to the peasant producers. The marketing boards have been used to maximise the interests of those people who have wielded political influence, just as in Kenya.

As already noted the Uganda government began to use its marketing control, i.e. its monopoly control over the disposal of the peasant export crop, between 1940 and 1945 to extract taxes from the sale of the crop and to ensure profitability to the high-cost ginners and exporters. The Uganda government had discovered a cheap and easy method of taxation which was collected at source and in bulk. In 1938 only 8 per cent of government revenue came from export taxes but this proportion rose to 16 per cent in 1945, and to 52 per cent in 1952. Meanwhile the laborious and expensive method of direct poll-tax collection became of considerably less importance to revenue, dropping from 31 per cent of the total in 1938 to 2 per cent in 1955–6.

The overall result of limiting farmers' incomes was to limit the pace of export crop expansion and to hold down local economic initiative. Surplus cash could have been used for purposes of accumulation. Altogether cotton growers between 1945 and 1960 were deprived of 32 per cent of their income by taxation; 18 per cent as contribution to government development funds and 12 per cent in price assistance funds; altogether 62 per cent or £83·6 million was levied on cotton incomes. Likewise 26·5 per cent or £35·3 million in total, was levied on coffee growers between the same dates. In total £118·8 million was taken from peasant producers between 1945 and 1960.

The explanation given by government for this high-handed and arbitrary action was that it would avoid import inflation, stop growers increasing output (which would, they arrogantly argued, mean that less food crops would be grown) and finally it would provide price assistance funds for periods when export prices fell. In practice guaranteed prices had been paid to peasant growers between 1939 and 1947 by a public body and again between 1947 and 1963. The price was announced at planting time each season, which was seven months before buying commenced. The boards were only able to do this because of the price assistance funds which accumulated cash in the period up to 1953. After 1953 government decided to give the grower something approaching a market price. Meanwhile the government continued to transfer considerable sums from the accumulated balances of the marketing boards to the revenue of the Protectorate government. While on the surface the policy of the Uganda government does appear quite arbitrary, yet it can be argued that government can better spend the surplus finance. For instance, as is shown in Chapter 7, the colonial government initiated industrialisation in Uganda through the Uganda Development Corporation. Moreover, the taxes from the peasant producers have been spent on education, roads and other such services. In the end it is probable that an 'efficient' government could probably use the funds for better and more rapid development than the peasants. But it is hard to be exact on such a question.

The price fixing was undertaken by a price fixing committee made up of the major interests concerned (with the exception of the growers). In 1963 under the independent government, price fixing was changed and became the responsibility of the Ministry of Agriculture. In 1961 the funds stood at £135 million for cotton and £6·5 million for coffee. The new government appears to have very rapidly used up these funds by paying high prices to peasant producers in the election years. Certainly international prices had been declining in coffee and cotton since 1954–5. And growers have had their price levels maintained since then. While the export taxes and the costs of marketing had remained at around 15 to 18 per cent respectively of the total costs, the proportion of the total paid to growers rose from 41 per cent in 1948 to 65 per cent in 1957. The Price Assistance Fund was utilised to maintain producers' prices until 1966–7 by which time it was £2 million in debt, and so producers' prices thereafter dropped drastically and the fund was wound up. After 1962–3 the price assistance funds were used to satisfy the peasants' aspirations which had been raised by Independence. The Ugandan peasants had suddenly become of political significance, and as with the Kenya settlers it was not possible to withhold surplus funds from groups with political influence.

In summary therefore how can we view these marketing developments in East Africa? As has been stressed throughout this account, the movement towards centralised monopoly marketing has been a great success for politically influential interests. Monopoly control of production, distribution and prices (the actual balance depending on the crop concerned) has been a driving force since the early 1920s. On the other hand the restrictions imposed and the lack of dynamism within the production system have been most marked. Let us deal with the latter point first.

Growth within any system of production where there are large numbers of producers depends on the producer reaction to the price movements. In principle and throughout in practice African and European producers have been very conscious of price movements, and should therefore have altered their crops according to expected prices. The effect of marketing policies in East Africa has been to support or maintain growth in existing crops rather than to lead toward experiment and technical innovation. Colonial governments in particular have been more concerned to obtain secure revenues, right the way through the colonial period, than to develop a dynamic system of agriculture; individual African enterprise was rarely supported in any economic field and the desire for political stability, based on paternalistic attitudes, held administrators in a rigid grip. Security and efficiency rather than 'development' and 'dynamism' have been the basic motivation of colonial government. Why should this have been the case?

There have been three basic reasons : (a) the pressures of vested interests, (b) the experience of development based on the fluctuations of international prices, especially in the 1920s and 1930s, and (c) the social dispositions of the administrations themselves. (a) and (b) have already been dealt with in the text; (c) involves an understanding of the anti-capitalism of the administration.

The administrators in East Africa came from a homogenous educational and social background, which has now been well documented. They were mainly British middle class with a public-school education, often from Oxford or Cambridge. Their ethos was that of the traditional, aristocratic, British ruling class. This traditionality was based on the 'habit of authority' of public service and on a concept of the society as an integrated organic community. Change was part of evolution which was gradual and which did not upset the stability of the social order. There was a strong distrust of economic individualism from among the lower orders and a strong preference for political, social and economic hierarchy and authority. There was therefore a continuous emphasis for the preservational of the 'traditional' African society. They saw themselves as impartial men, guided by 'fair play' and a 'sense of justice', whose job was to protect the lower orders from themselves which was emphasised in concepts of 'trusteeship', 'civilising', and so on.

They were also anti-intellectual, which was expressed in terms of strong preference for amateurs over professionals and for pragmatic empiricism over theories and abstract ideas. Events were therefore dealt with on the basis of 'common sense' and by men with 'practical experience'. Hence the access offered to vested interest to influence policy and the lack of technical experts to advise them on such matters as pricing policy.

Up to 1939 the colonial administrator was in a second heaven. No industrial development to speak of had been started, there was merely a traditional rural society to oversee. But after 1945, with pressure from the imperial government to institute development, administrators became overtly concerned with the problem of maintaining the integrity of tribal society. One aspect of these changes was the growth and development of the marketing boards, which provided the basis in Kenya for the strengthening of the settlers and the maintenance in Uganda of peasant coffee and cotton, both the core of the export economy. The marketing boards therefore provided the hierarchal mechanism to stage-manage growth and to ensure that any change was gradual.

Conclusion

The economics of imperialism is the historical process whereby a small number of countries, who have managed to obtain a technological lead, strive to maintain and increase the technical gap between themselves and the rest of the world. It is a process whereby the gap between the wealth of the European states increases in relation to the large numbers of comparatively poor states; a process which in Africa begins with the colonial situation. This process of differentiation between the technology and wealth of the rich and poor societies occurs not only as a relationship *between* states, but also *within* the states of the Third World. Over time, the gap between a small number of rich and the large number of poor is reproduced within the local community. The mechanics of this process are in considerable part contained within the process of marketing.

Up to the period of Independence, the European *export* producers strove to protect themselves from the insecurity of fluctuating prices. In particular, during the slump of the 1930s there was a concerted effort to bring the mechanics of export marketing under a monopoly in order to increase bargaining power. Likewise as domestic prices slumped in line with export prices, European producers attempted to monopolise the domestic market in order to raise domestic prices above those prevalent on the world market. Maize was the critical produce. In Uganda, where the producers were peasants, the process towards centralised marketing was similar to Kenya's, but the purpose was different. In this case it was the middlemen – the European and Asian processors and exporters – who were concerned to maintain high profit margins, directly against the interests of the peasant producers. Moreover, the problem of attracting European private capital in a territory far in distance from European markets and lacking a large local European population was temporarily overcome through mobilising local capital by further taxation of the peasant producers.

In both territories, the marginality of producers in relation to world trade has led over a fifty-year period to an increasing bureaucratisation of the process of marketing. The need for high stable prices and profit for those producers and traders with political influence at the centre has been fulfilled by marketing boards. It is significant that in Kenya trade in the staple food, maize, has developed a rigid and highly centralised character, while in Uganda trade in local staples has developed with a free market. Not surprisingly it is the large farm producers who have benefited most from this situation.

The rise of the corporate centralised structure in a community predominantly made up of small-scale peasant producers is a reflection not so much of progress as of the disequilibrium between rich and poor. The rich have been able over the years to protect themselves to a considerable extent from the mechanics of the free market. The ever-increasing character of marketing rationalisation indicates the growing sway of marketing controls over all producers. The mechanics of marketing in East Africa have developed at the expense of the small-scale, often subsistence, producer and on behalf of the large-scale producer and trader. The latter group have, as a consequence, been able to enjoy an enormously high living standard.

12 East Africa and Economic Federation: the East African Common Market

Introduction

Why have so many people considered it desirable to federate the countries of East Africa? The idea of creating a larger economic and political unit from the existing separate sovereign countries of East Africa has a history of almost one hundred years. Let us first examine the financial reasons which make the larger political and economic units desirable before we turn to the history of the East African federation itself.

In 1776 Adam Smith in his celebrated work 'An Inquiry into the Nature and Causes of the Wealth of Nations' contended that the size of the market will always provide the ultimate check upon economic development. The size of the market is determined by two factors : (a) the number of people to whom a producer can sell his goods and (b) the wealth of these people. Adam Smith's argument runs as follows : if there is a *large* number of people in a community who are wealthy, they create a considerable *demand* for goods and services. This is called a *large market*. In such a society a producer is likely to invest money in order to increase his production and so sell more and make bigger profits. Thus large markets are associated with the re-investment of profits. The American and European markets are larger than the African market because of the greater wealth of the people. In principle, therefore, it should be more advantageous for Africans to sell their goods to America and Europe instead of on domestic markets. However the foreign markets are tightly controlled, often by tariff barriers, in order to limit the import of finished goods manufactured in Africa. So experience has proved that to have a rapidly expanding economy it is necessary to have a large home-based or domestic market. A large and wealthy population at home provides a relatively constant demand for agricultural and industrial goods. But this is precisely what is lacking in East African countries which have neither large nor wealthy populations. Hence there is no strong purchasing power within any of the separate East African territories and, therefore, the stimulus towards industrial expansion is weak. By itself each country has too weak a purchasing power to support modern industrial plants, but put together their purchasing power is multiplied roughly by three and the countries become more attractive to investors. Thus it is argued that if a federation or common market of East African territories were formed it would bring benefit all round and economic development would be accelerated. Private investors would be far more likely to start up new projects in a federation than in one separate territory.

Formation of a common market implies that the sovereign states involved join themselves in some form of economic union. It implies economic co-operation at an agreed level. At the lowest level a *free trade area* would be created which means that each state would allow produce from the other states to be brought in free of any import restrictions; but each country would maintain its own restrictions against imports from countries outside the free trade area. At the next level countries involved in the free trade agreement would decide on a common tariff policy and so create a *customs union*. At the third level a *common market* would be formed which would mean the unrestricted movement of finance, capital and labour between countries belonging to the *common market*, besides the existing common internal trade and tariffs. Agreement at this third stage would allow a subject of one country to be employed in any of the other common market countries and permit him to buy property there if he possessed the necessary means. There would be a free flow of goods, capital and labour. At the fourth level an *economic union* would be formed to bring the economic policies of the countries concerned into line, i.e. there would be a common system of taxation, common budgetary policies and so on. Finally, political, as well as economic unity could be envisaged with a single central government to formulate and implement policy. Thus any move towards any of the levels of economic integration between states has very strong political implications. It is also possible for all these stages to happen at the same time, particularly if integration is brought about by force. In the case of East Africa the approach to economic integration has so far always been through agreement between the countries concerned. Up to 1931 the problem was primarily a political one; the colonial authorities wanted to set up a political organisation with wide-ranging powers over and above the authority of the separate colonial governments. Since that time efforts have concentrated on forming a central body with less authority than the government of each independent state.

The most powerful argument that can be put forward on behalf of an East African economic union would be based on Adam Smith's original theory on the importance of the size of the market for development, but would expand it so as to relate it to contemporary international economic conditions. In any examination of nineteenth-century economic history of the developed countries the importance of annually expanding international markets, in particular for Europe, Australia, Canada and Japan, cannot be stressed too much. The fact that these countries were able to find external markets for their products (very often by expanding economic relationships by acquiring colonies) meant that foreign trade became their *vehicle of growth*. Producers in these countries were able to expand production much more rapidly than if they had had to rely on the demand for their products from domestic markets alone. In short, these countries expanded their markets by opening up the world to their trade. This historical fact has led some economists to argue that economic development in Third World countries should also depend on the expansion of their international trade. It is true that colonised territories had their economic growth instigated by international trade, but it has not acted as the engine of growth nor has it led to widespread industrialisation as it did in Europe.

As we have already argued, the colonial societies were economically dependent on their metropolitan centre. The colonising country used the East African economies for its own needs through control of production and trade.

While it is correct to say that international trade has not led to widespread industrialisation in East Africa, the dynamic element in the *growth* of East African economies may still be attributed to export trade. The gross domestic product has increased directly with the value of exports. This dependency on exports overseas has become one of the major factors behind the need for an East African common market. It is by this means that the extent of East Africa's economic dependency on European trade could be reduced.

The need for a reduction in economic dependency on foreign export trade has recently grown more acute, as we saw in Chapter 10, where we showed that since the middle fifties there had been a slowing down in the growth of demand in industrialised countries for the goods of the Third World countries. As a result the trade *between* the nations of the developed industrial world since then has been increasing faster than that between these nations and the Third World. Because trade among the developed nations makes up an increasingly large proportion of total world trade the percentage of world trade left to the Third World has decreased. The Third

World's share of world exports has dropped from 25 to 19 per cent between 1960 and 1968.

A second reason why East Africa badly needs to develop a local market for its produce is given by the character of its international trade, as mentioned in Chapter 10. East Africa's exports to the developed world consist mostly of primary products or very partially processed products, while she imports mainly the finished products of the western world's industries. As Europe continues to develop economically and to improve the technical efficiency of her agricultural production, *the Third World's share of total world exports of primary produce has been declining over the last twenty years.* This decline is only one of the problems of East Africa's export specialisation; there is also the problem of industrialisation. It will be remembered that initially one of the main reasons for the colonisation of Africa was that she could produce crops that were required in Europe. This aspect of the economic relationship between Europe and East Africa has not altered. The startling fact of which one should be aware is that there are very few markets open to goods produced by industry in East Africa. The entry of most finished products which would compete with manufactured goods made in Europe or the United States is restricted by means of tariff or quota barriers, while the entry of partially or non-processed goods, and especially raw materials, is not controlled in any way. East Africa has therefore continued to specialise in the export of raw materials. Thus the development of trade *between* East African territories has provided one vitally important outlet from the international 'bottleneck'.

But simply to develop inter-territorial trade is not sufficient. Although trade has been the basis of a common East African market, the alternative goal is that the larger protected market which has been created should provide an economic base for the formulation of industrial policies. In their early stages new East African industries are not likely to be as efficient as the longer-established industries in the countries with which they would have to compete. They may therefore require some sort of protection from foreign competition until they have gained such experience as would put them on more equal terms. As the following account will show, the policies intended to encourage industrialisation have run into considerable difficulties because (a) many of the industries which have benefited from the expanded market are branches of international companies and (b) there has been a strong tendency for these industries to cluster around Nairobi, Kenya, to which Uganda and Tanzania have objected on political grounds.

Many people feel that some form of economic integration is vital for economic development; the expansion of the East African economy has became a *sine qua non* for growth with development. We shall now turn to the history of the East African federation in order to examine the problems faced and the progress made by the economic integration.

The first attempt at forming a federation

The first attempt to create an economic unit in East Africa controlled by a single central government occurred in 1876–7.* In 1876 King Leopold III of Belgium called an International Geographical Conference at Brussels. He invited a number of representatives from Britain including Sir William Mackinnon, who eleven years later was to head the Imperial British East Africa Company. The conference was intended to draw up the plans for an international organisation which would open up a block of land stretching from Zanzibar westwards to the mouth of the Congo river. There would be established 'a continual line of communication between the eastern and western coasts of the continent'. The Englishmen present at the Conference, representing private interests, gave wholehearted approval to these proposals and the Association Internationale Africaine (AIA) was set up. It was a grandiose, imperial notion, which if it had succeeded, would have created a larger union of Central, East and West African territories than ever conceived before or since.

The Englishmen most involved in Leopold's plan, Mackinnon, Kirk and Hutton, were themselves imperialists with a grand vision. Mackinnon and Hutton, already wealthy men, had direct economic interest in the venture. Mackinnon was the partner in the Mackinnon and Mackenzie Trading Company and the chairman of the British India Steam Navigation Company and these companies both stood to gain considerable profit from the enterprise. J. H. Hutton owned a firm, based in Manchester, which exported goods to West Africa and in 1877 he was appointed director of the Manchester Chamber of Commerce. Neither of the two men's business interests had any real need for such imperial adventures, but all the same the success of such an enterprise would benefit their companies enormously. Both Mackinnon and Hutton, in common with many other individual imperialists, believed that the Congo offered an immense and very lucrative potential market. John Kirk was the British Consul at Zanzibar from 1873. He is better remembered for his concern to abolish slavery at Zanzibar. But the abolition of slavery

* See R. Anstey, *Britain and the Congo in the Nineteenth Century* (OUP, 1962) ch. 4, for a full account of this.

and the ideas behind nineteenth-century European expansion in East Africa were closely linked, the former providing the justification for the latter. Kirk's primary aim was to open up East and Central Africa to British economic influence, although it is not clear whether or not he personally had anything to gain. But the British government steadfastly refused to annex any territory until the late 1880s, and meanwhile Leopold's schemes of 1877 gave Kirk a chance to achieve his ambitions. But he, like all the others with interests in the AIA, was to be disappointed. The reason for the failure to open up the region to British enterprise, although it might have proved extremely profitable, was that no attempts had been made to obtain the support of the British government in the first place. This first try at creating one huge state stretching from East to West Africa, a single political unit spanning the continent, was characterised by the involvement of groups with specific economic interests, who believed they had much to gain from the venture. Later efforts to create large geographical units were also characterised by similar interest-groups, again believing that there were large profits to be had.

The second attempt

By the turn of the century there was no doubt that the imperial visions and ambitions of King Leopold and those associated with him had come to nothing. During the next thirty-odd years there were two major interest-groups concerned with creating a single economic and political unit of the various East African territories : (*a*) a group of architects of imperialist policies whose formative experience had been the South African federation and (*b*) the European settlers in Kenya.

British East Africa, Uganda and German East Africa had been created with some feeling for the national and historical unity of the area. At both the Berlin Conference of 1884 and the Brussels Conference of 1890 the prevailing opinion was that territorial boundaries should not restrict free trade. What came to be known as the Congo Basin Treaties were passed, laying down the rule that there should be uniform trading policies in the region. In particular it was agreed that there should be no discrimination by one country against the imports of another and that a maximum tariff of not more than 10 per cent could be imposed on imports. The 'no discrimination' clause meant, for example, that cheap Japanese cloth could enter East Africa in the 1920s and 1930s to the benefit of all consumers. Thus, from the beginning of the era of colonisation in East Africa there existed external tariff arrangements common

to the entire region. The more far-sighted of the imperialist poli-
ticians set about the creation of political unity in the area.

Between 1899 and 1914 a number of suggestions were made concerning a possible union of territories in the area. Sir Harry Johnston in 1899 and Sir Charles Eliot in 1905 made some specific
recommendations on the subject of imperial government but the
British Government did not take them up. Then in 1917 a customs
union was established between British East Africa and Uganda
which involved free movement of all goods between the two countries and a common tariff policy. The second move towards the
formation of an East African federation came in the terms of the
mandate over German East Africa given to Britain in 1919. Germany, after losing the Great War, was deprived of her colonies
which were placed under the authority of the newly-formed League
of Nations. Britain then acquired Tanganyika as a mandated territory. Her legal responsibilities included one laid out in a special
clause as follows :

> The Mandatory power shall be authorised to constitute the
> territory into a customs, fiscal and administrative union or feder-
> ation with the adjacent territories under his own sovereignty or
> control . . .

In other words the architects of the mandate were looking forward
to or planning for a union of territories in East Africa. The latter
clause had been added by Leopold Amery, then the Under-
Secretary of State for the Colonies. Amery had not included this
clause merely as a whim or by chance; he, like others before him,
had a grand imperial vision of a single colonial edifice under a
single, central governing power. Amery was an architect of
imperialism and part of his building project was to be an East
African federation. Inserting the above clause in the mandate was
essential to his plan. By 1919 Britain had gained control of the whole
of East and Central Africa from the Turkana in the north to the
Zambezi in the south, which in total covered a region of about one
million square miles, almost the size of India, but with a comparatively tiny population of approximately twelve million people,
whereas India had 300 million people. Amery regarded the whole
area as a potentially rich and undeveloped estate. If it were
governed by a single authority it could mean that the entire region
might be developed to further British colonial interests. Amery had
included in the mandate the clause which provided the legal basis
for unification with the particular intention of avoiding any international objection to his plan.

Amery's ideas stemmed from his South African experience and it is useful to examine this experience briefly in order to demonstrate the continuity of the ideas involved and the persistence of men like Amery.* Alfred Milner had, in the period 1901–10, envisioned a South African federation. Milner's goals had been seen as follows:

> . . . the ultimate end is a self-governing white community, supported by well treated and justly governed black labour from Cape Town to Zambesi. There must be one flag, the Union Jack, but under it equality of races and languages . . . I think, though, all South Africa should be one Dominion with a common government dealing with Customs, Railway and Defence, perhaps also with a Native Policy . . .

Milner's aim was an economic and political union in Southern Africa to be achieved almost at one stroke. To this end he recruited a group of young and brilliant British civil servants which later came to be nicknamed 'Milner's Kindergarten'. The members of the 'Kindergarten' had a common social and educational background. They had all attended public school and one of two Oxford colleges, New College or All Souls, and had similar interests in imperial affairs. The two members of the group who were later to play vital roles in the controversy over 'Closer Union' for East Africa, were Leopold Amery, by the time of the controversy Secretary of State for the Colonies, and Edward Grigg, Governor of Kenya from 1925 to 1930, whom Amery intended to have appointed as the first governor-general of the region.

After 1910, when unification of South Africa had been successfully concluded, Milner's young men turned their attention to the unification of the entire British Empire in Africa. They wanted to create an 'organic imperial union'. Many members of the 'kindergarten' reached the very senior positions in imperial and colonial affairs and through their office they intended to bring about imperial, political union. Imperial union was to be achieved by means of the establishment of a British imperial government, which would be constitutionally responsible to the white electors who lived within the Empire. The 'Kindergarten' was in effect a committee consisting of Milner's closest disciples, bent on establishing a programme for imperial unity.

In effect, therefore, the East African Closer Union idea which surfaced between 1923 and 1931 was part of a much wider movement which had originated in South Africa under Milner's guidance. Federation of British territories was just one aspect of a great

* The following account has been adapted from W. Nimcock, *Milner's Young Men: the 'Kindergarten' in Edwardian Imperial Affairs* (Duke University Press, 1968).

imperial plan which between 1910 and 1960 had found concrete expression in Central Africa, East Africa, the West Indies and Malay states and finally in the formation of the British Commonwealth of Nations. In each case the belief in the ability for self-government of Europeans living in each of the proposed federations was all-important. The whole of the British Empire was to be administered under the guidance of Milner's 'Kindergarten' and based on the concept of an 'organic imperial union'. East Africa, according to this plan, was closely connected with the South African federation – Leopold Amery and Edward Grigg, who had made the South African federation a reality, were among the men involved in formulating the plans for East Africa. Both men have provided us with an insight into their purposes in their respective autobiographies. Referring to the time when he was Secretary of State for the Colonies, Amery wrote of his aims :

A project that I had very much at heart was to bring about a greater measure of administrative and political unity in Eastern and Central Africa. As a first step I arrived at unifying the three East African territories of Uganda, Kenya and Tanganyika, which form a natural unity for development purposes divided by fairly arbitrary historical boundaries . . . The task of bringing this about was obviously one for someone with a broader political outlook than that of the ordinary colonial administrator. Sir Robert Coryndon, the Governor of Kenya had many of the qualities required – but his death early in 1925 left a vacancy which I decided to fill from outside the service. Sir Edward Grigg [Lord Altringham] had an exceptionally wide knowledge of Imperial affairs . . .*

Grigg was more explicit in his autobiography. He argued :

The forces which drove von Lettow Vorbeck [the German military commander] out of German East Africa were white South Africans assisted by Rhodesia and Kenya volunteers . . .

so that

argument for closer union was simple enough. It derived *in primis* from the fact that German East Africa conquered by a South African general at very considerable sacrifice, would no longer be a barrier to the Rhodes-Milner concept of a British Dominion stretching from Rhodesia to Kenya.†

* L. S. Amery, *My Political Life*, vol. II, 1914–1929 (London: Hutchinson, 1953).

† Lord Altringham, *Kenya's Opportunity* (Faber & Faber, 1955).

Here was a clear statement of the British purpose in fighting in the East African campaign – it was part of the grand purpose of unifying an empire stretching from the Cape to Cairo. Grigg then gives his economic rationale of the need for federation :

> It could never raise production and revenue or attain a higher standard of living without some considerable development of communications, more particularly of forts and railways; and it was obviously desirable that these should be on a comprehensive and co-operative plan. All three territories would moreover need a large variety of common services from external relations and defence to posts, customs, research, human and animal health etc.

No one who has since the 1930s argued for common economic services in East Africa would have disagreed with Grigg. Grigg, like Amery and Milner, had integrated his political and economic visions of what he saw as the future East and Central Africa.

We have laid considerable stress on the political *background* to the Closer Union debate of the 1920s for two reasons. Firstly, historians have tended to draw attention to the details of the political events of the 1920s. Secondly, in the debate of the 1950s and 1960s, economists have concentrated almost exclusively on economic issues, and have treated the exercise of integration only in terms of economic costs and benefits. We have thought it important to emphasise the overall picture. While it is necessary to examine political and economic details, such fundamental changes for any society as the integration of separate nations cannot be successfully brought about without the far-sighted vision of deep-thinking men like Grigg and Amery. These men never fail to recognise the interconnection of politics and economics and although one may not approve of either their methods or their ultimate purposes, one should learn from them to view the world as a whole, not as split up between academic disciplines and distinct subjects.

Failure of Closer Union, 1923–31

1. The political controversy

At the beginning of the 1920s the British territories of East Africa were separately administered, but a customs union had been formed between Kenya and Uganda. This meant that there was a free movement of goods between the two territories and that they had a common tariff policy. The aim of federation was to create a complete economic and political union, with a central government for the three territories in East Africa with common laws and policies for the entire area. The settlers in Kenya were willing to support an East African federation only so long as they were assured of a majority of seats in the Legislative Assembly. In this way the settlers would have been able to formulate policy and law for the whole region. The proposal for a single, central government created such widespread debate in East Africa that there were four major reports and commissions on the subject :*

i. East African Royal Commission, 1924 (Chairman, the Hon. W. G. Ormsby Gore);
ii. Hilton Young Commission, 1929 (Chairman, Sir Hilton Young);
iii. the report of Sir Samuel Wilson on his visit to East Africa, 1930;
iv. Joint Select Committee on Closer Unior in East Africa, 1931.

That all these reports were written and that so much evidence was collected over so short a period was due to the vehemence of the internal conflicts which the federation proposals created. The conflicts arose directly out of the fact that, first, it was the white settlers of Kenya who had initiated the planning of a federation. The European settlers in Kenya made up an articulate and politically conscious group and there was widespread fear of white domination among the Asians and Africans and even among some of the colonial government officials throughout all three British territories. Secondly, the proposals stemmed from Kenya, which was already ahead economically, and Uganda especially feared economic domination.

The first steps to bring about federation came from London in 1923, probably originating from Amery at the Colonial Office, although Sir Sydney Henn, a Member of Parliament and a businessman with considerable economic interests in East Africa, had asked for a commission to examine the possibilities of co-ordinating policies and services in the three territories. It is worth noting that, at this point, all the European communities with commercial interests in the region, whether based in or outside East Africa, were eager for economic integration. This keenness for some form of economic union has, in recent years, become even greater. For the reasons discussed earlier, it is in the interest of all businessmen to have as large an economic unit as possible in which they may operate as freely as they can. The business interests in East Africa always tended to function away from public view, either through personal connections in the Nairobi Colonial Civil Service

* For detailed accounts of these, the reader is referred to the following: G. Bennett, *Kenya, a Political History,* chs 6 and 7; M. R. Dilley, *British Policy in Colonial Kenya,* pp. 55–86 (see Bibliography).

or in London through the Colonial Office. Although they did not openly declare their political interests these were an important factor to businessmen running enterprises in East Africa.

The 1923 Royal Commission, under the chairmanship of Ormsby Gore was formed to investigate the truth behind the widespread fears of white domination in East Africa. The Commission recommended that any form of integration would be premature. But one of the results of its recommendations was the setting up of an East African Governors Conference in 1926 under the surveillance of Leopold Amery. A permanent secretariat was also formed. The Conference was to meet annually and to be attended by the governors of Northern Rhodesia, Nyasaland and Zanzibar as well as those from Kenya, Uganda and Tanganyika. The purpose of these conferences was to discuss ways of co-ordinating economic services and policies. Amery clearly believed that in such a series of conferences might lie the foundations of an East and Central African federation on the Milner-Rhodes model. In 1925 Amery appointed Edward Grigg as governor of Kenya intending that Grigg would help him bring about the federation he wanted, using the conferences to gain its acceptance. Grigg could then be made the first governor-general of the united territories. As the federation that Amery and Grigg supported was, in principle, a white-ruled independent one, Grigg backed the main demands of the Kenya settlers. He was anxious to help create the political conditions whereby the settlers would be able to achieve self-government and he worked together with Lord Delamere to this end. It was not unexpected, therefore, that in 1927 Lord Delamere brought up the issue of a Closer Union. Acting on behalf of the settlers he gave support to Closer Union on the condition that the settlers would be guaranteed a majority on the Legislative Council. There is no proof that Grigg and Delamere were actually in collusion over this but there is evidence that such a condition was not out of line with Grigg's political convictions over administration in South Africa. Once again, the Indians in Kenya expressed their fear of a settler-dominated federation. The approval of the British Cabinet was needed for the formation of the federation as it involved a major constitutional change. Leopold Amery therefore attempted to obtain 'some authoritative backing, independent of the view of the Colonial Office, to present to Cabinet. In 1927 he sent the Hilton Young Commission to East Africa which he thought would provide him with the authority he needed. The Commission did in fact give an independent report and found that the conflict between the Asians and the European settlers was as great as it had been in 1922–3. They found, for instance, that the Asian community were against any union of East

African territories because they believed the Commission to be a plot to give Europeans control over the whole of East Africa.

The Hilton Young Commission reported back in 1929, and by then the Indians were not alone in their opposition to the entire proposal of a federation; the Governor of Tanganyika, Donald Cameron, was against it; so too were the Kabaka's Buganda government and the Kikuyu Central Association. Cameron was against it because he feared the European domination of Africans in Tanganyika, a situation that had already occurred in Kenya. The Buganda government feared the loss of Buganda's special privileges. It is interesting that the settlers of Kenya had raised such widespread opposition. The work of the final two commissions need not be examined here. Yet again they collected a mass of detailed evidence, and in the end came to the same conclusion, that virtually all groups in East Africa were terrified of living under a white settler-controlled federation. The election of a Labour government in Britain in 1931 and the onset of the Great Depression put an end, for the time being, to any further ideas or plans for closer political union between the three East African territories and the Milner-Rhodes federation remained a dream.

2. *The economic controversy*

So far we have only considered the politics of federation as seen in the 1920s, but there is another aspect to the problem which in many respects has proved to be the more deep-seated and long-lasting. By the 1920s Kenya's economy was more advanced than Uganda's from many points of view, so that any federation formed on an economic basis might have benefited the Kenyan economy at Uganda's expense.

Two related matters, import duty and railway rates, led to Kenya's economic ascendency in East Africa in the 1920s. The terms of the Congo Basin Treaties had governed trading policies between the territories of East Africa and had regulated their tariff rates until 1918. In that year the Convention of St Germain-en-Laye had revised these terms. Kenya immediately raised her tariffs on many imports from 10 to 20 per cent. After the 1922 Bowring Committee Report on tariff policy, the colonial government of Kenya adopted a policy of protection for suitable settler-owned industries by the raising of tariffs on imports into the country. By 1924 she was charging an import duty of between 30 and 50 per cent on sugar, timber, wheat and wheat flour, butter, cheese, ghee, ham and bacon. In the 1920s it may well have been cheaper to import such goods than to process them in Kenya but the tariffs made it possible for the European settlers to produce these commodities even at higher prices. But, as Kenya and Uganda had had a common market policy since 1917, Uganda still had to buy these Kenya produced goods, paying more than if they had been brought from overseas. However the protection of settler-owned industries led to an overall loss of revenue from import duties for the governments of both Kenya and Uganda. The loss was the greater for Uganda, because she still had to buy goods from Kenya.

As a result of Kenya's economic policies, the Ginners' Association, the Chambers of Commerce and the Planters Association in Uganda joined together in threatening to withdraw from the customs union. They complained that the commodities coming from Kenya were expensive, in short supply and of poor quality and they demanded that the duties on goods from overseas should be reduced. From Kenya's point of view the imposition of these duties was perfectly justified because her 'infant industries needed protection'. She argued that the more developed countries could more easily produce goods cheaply because of their greater experience and more advanced technology. Countries whose development had been later starting needed help and encouragement before they would be able to produce as cheaply as those countries who had been in the field for some time. Therefore, new industries in developing countries should be allowed to protect their goods with tariffs on imports and so monopolise the domestic market until such time as the infant industries would be able to compete on the international market without protection. In Kenya some of the conditions were present which could have supported a limited manufacturing sector. Uganda's economy, on the other hand, was based on an entirely different policy. Uganda wanted to retain tariff barriers against overseas goods, not for protection of infant industries, but for the purpose of raising government revenue. She would, therefore, not wish to discourage foreign imports. Kenya's policy of protection for her new industries was diametrically opposed to this.

Uganda's problem was that, in fact, she was dependent on Kenya for the actual collection of customs duties. Not until 1909 had Uganda received any revenue from British East Africa, who had meanwhile been collecting duties on goods bound for Uganda as well as her own. When, in 1917, the customs departments of the two countries were amalgamated, Kenya took control of the collection of duty paid. Uganda was, therefore, powerless to take any effective action when, in the 1920s, Kenya introduced her protective tariffs. In addition Kenya's exports and her home produce could be transported by rail at lower rates than Uganda's exports. This system had again been designed to assist and encourage European settler-owned industries in Kenya.

Despite objections Kenya's large European and Asian populations were able to make the most of the advantages offered by the common market. Although this early encouragement of local industry did not lead to widespread industrialisation, it did give Kenya a head start in economic development over the other two East African countries and, to date, this lead has been maintained. The growth of foodstuff processing industries has meant that Kenya has been in a more favourable position to benefit from the larger market offered by the three territories together. The controversies of the 1940s and the 1970s have grown out of the fact that Kenya's more highly developed and stronger economy has been able to gain more from a common market than the other two territories combined.

The common market since 1945

1. The institutions

So far we have been concerned mainly with the politics of union. Up to the war economic integration and political union were considered as part of the same issue so that debate centred on the politics. After 1945 the economic aspect gradually gained precedence so that when the argument arose again in the late 1950s the imperial considerations ceased to be of great importance. Up to 1945, apart from the common market a number of centrally organised services were operating in East Africa, including the East African Court of Appeal, East African Posts and Telecommunications, East African Railways and Harbours and East African Airways. There was also a common currency. The Governors Conference which had met regularly since 1926 had discussed matters of common interest for the three countries, relating to the marketing of produce, customs and tariffs and railway rates. As mentioned in Chapter 11, at the start of the Second World War an attempt was made to rationalise production in all three countries; a joint Economic Council was established and for the duration of the War East Africa operated as one economic and commercial unit. After the war it was proposed that a permanent council be set up. This council was to be advised by a central Legislative Assembly, which was to have the authority to administer East African communal services. The colonial government made it clear that they did not envisage this structure as part of a movement towards closer *political* union, thus making it acceptable to the groups who feared political domination by a

European minority. The Europeans living in Kenya objected to the suggestion that the council adopt a policy of non-discrimination on racial grounds and this particular proposal was dropped. The council was set up in 1948 and came to be known as the East African High Commission. For the first time there existed a legally recognised authority whose job it was to supervise the workings of the common market between the territories and to run the common services. We shall only examine the development of the common market here, not because we consider the common services unimportant but because the common market was the impetus behind economic integration and, in principle, it could also have been the stimulus for rapid industrialisation.

2. The common market

The growth of inter-territorial trade between the member countries of the common market was very rapid indeed. Table 12.1 shows the proportion of the total value of the trade within East Africa contributed by each of the three countries concerned.

TABLE 12.1

Percentage of total value of East African inter-territorial exports made up by Kenya, Uganda and Tanzania

	Kenya	Uganda	Tanzania	Total
1945	36·2	41·0	22·8	100
1948	37·5	45·6	16·9	100
1951	50·8	33·5	15·7	100
1954	47·1	44·0	8·9	100
1957	60·7	26·9	12·4	100
1960	60·4	29.5	10·1	100
1963	63·2	26·0	10·8	100
1966	65·7	23·7	10·6	100

From the table it can be seen that Uganda supplied the largest proportion of exports until 1948. This was due to the East African Tobacco Company which was run from Kampala and Jinja. After 1951 Kenya forged ahead. By 1957, Kenya was exporting goods worth almost twice as much as those of Uganda and Tanzania combined. It is worth noting that Kenya's comparatively rapid economic growth began in the mid-fifties. It was at this point in time that branches of overseas industrial firms were established in Kenya. By the time of her political independence Kenya's economy was clearly in a better situation than that of the other territories to take advantage of the larger market.

Not only was Kenya reaping greater proportional benefits from inter-territorial trade, at the same time the total value of trade was also expanding rapidly, as shown in the following table.

TABLE 12.2

Expansion of inter-territorial trade in East Africa, 1944–66
(£K million)

	Kenya	Uganda	Tanzania	Total
1944	1·09	1·98	0·66	3·73
1948	1·93	3·19	0·83	5·95
1951	3·72	4·31	1·15	9·18
1954	5·81	7·54	1·04	11·49
1957	11·43	5·32	2·02	18·77
1960	13·77	6·69	2·33	22·79
1963	19·80	8·24	3·43	31·47
1966	28·90	10·45	4·65	44·00

Table 12.2 shows that Kenya has contributed most to the increase in inter-territorial exports over the twenty-two years considered. The benefits to Kenya's economy were considerable. Kenya was expanding her export trade with Uganda and Tanzania faster than she was expanding her overseas export trade. This meant that she was becoming less dependent on the demand for her primary produce from overseas markets. So there were two sources of profit for Kenya : the overall trade within East Africa was growing faster than East Africa's total overseas trade and Kenya was cornering the largest proportion of the most lucrative areas of it, and the value of her exports to Uganda and Tanzania had multiplied by three in the same period. Kenya's part in the East African common market trade led to her higher growth rates as compared to the other territories in the 1950–7 period. Kenya had become less dependent on overseas markets for her growth, but Uganda and Tanzania found themselves in the reverse situation.

Of course, from Kenya's point of view this trend was vitally important. Instead of becoming heavily dependent on the foreign markets for a few primary products she had captured a high proportion of the East African domestic market. She might, therefore, expect a period of comparative economic growth and stability should her hold on this market be maintained.

But, in a sense, Kenya's success has meant failure for the other two countries. Although the net value of exports from each of the three territories to the other two has increased and in this respect each territory has expanded its production, this must have entailed an increase in *imports*. Kenya has imported fewer goods and so has maintained a better visible trade balance than Uganda and Tanzania, as the following table shows.

TABLE 12.3

Visible balance of inter-country trade (£K million)

	Kenya	Uganda	Tanzania
1959	+ 6·8	−1·38	−5·52
1961	+ 8·9	−0·58	−8·37
1963	+10·6	−1·69	−8·93

Kenya has run a positive visible trade balance for her trade within East Africa since the middle fifties, again unlike Uganda and Tanzania. She has thus been able to reduce her overall trade deficit when overseas trade is taken into account. In other words, her trade with Tanzania and Uganda helps pay for imports from Europe and the United States. The situation for Uganda and Tanzania has been the reverse of this as they both, until recently, had a positive balance on trade with Europe and the United States, which helped pay for their imports from Kenya. Uganda and Tanzania have, in fact, been earning foreign exchange for Kenya. Kenya has had another advantage. A large proportion of the goods destined for Uganda have been sent via Nairobi where most international trading concerns have their headquarters. These goods have been repacked into smaller consignments and sent on to Uganda. In 1957 over a third of all Uganda's imports passed through Nairobi. Kenya was acting as an entrepôt, partly because of her geographical position, and partly because the importers had sited their main offices in Nairobi and Mombasa.

Finally Kenya's international companies have derived the greater benefit from the common market. The majority of firms who have invested in East Africa since the formation of the common market are branches of international companies. These industries, with their modern technology, have found the East African common market very profitable for them. It may be argued that without the common market most of these firms would not have found it worth while to begin production in East Africa because, taken separately, the markets within each country were too small. But they have based themselves in one country only and have chosen the one offering the best services – the best trained personnel, the best staff accommodation and communications services, in fact, the wealthiest city, offering the largest local market. They have kept away from the territories with the weaker infrastructure. Because Uganda and Tanzania were poorer than Kenya in 1945, not having as large a number of European settlers to form a wealthy local market, and because they have been unable to take advantage of trade within a common market, they have been unable to attract the international companies as Kenya has done. Kenya has since become progressively more attractive to overseas companies wanting to locate branches in East Africa. Therefore the main beneficiaries of the common market have clearly been Kenya and the various international companies. Up to the middle of the 1950s most of the inter-territorial trade was in foodstuffs such as wheat, rice, margarine and sugar. Manufactured iron goods were also traded. But since the mid-1950s there has been a marked increase in the manufacture of products other than foodstuffs. The new branches of international companies began production of goods formerly imported from overseas, unaffected by tariff barriers, and so the composition of trade within the common market was altered. The major manufactured items produced in Kenya and exported to Uganda and Tanzania in 1966 are shown below.

	Major Producing Companies	*Country of Ownership*
1. Fresh milk, cream and butter	Kenya Co-operative Creameries	Kenya
2. Wheat (unmilled)	Kenya Wheat Board	Kenya
3. Cigarettes	British American Tobacco (Kenya) Ltd	British
	Rothmans of Pall Mall	British
4. Petroleum products	Kenya Shell	Dutch/British
	Esso Standard (Kenya) Ltd	USA/Switzerland
	Mobil Oil (Kenya) Ltd	USA
	Agip Ltd	Italy
	Caltex Oil Ltd	USA
5. Soap, margarine, cosmetics and dentifrices	East African Industries Ltd (Unilever)	British/Dutch
	Colgate-Palmolive (E.A.) Ltd	USA

6. Footwear	E.A. Bata Shoe Co. Ltd	Canada
7. Clothing	Kisumu Cotton Mills Ltd	India
	Kenya Toray Mills Ltd	Japan
	Kenya Rayon Mills Ltd	Japan
	United Textile Industries Ltd	Japan
8. Beer	East African Breweries Ltd	Kenya
9. Cement	E.A. Portland Cement Co. Ltd	Britain
	Bamburi Cement Co Ltd	Britain
	Association of Portland Cement Manufacturers	Britain

Note: Readers should be aware that the column showing country of ownership is grossly over-simplistic. Company ownership is highly complex so far as all international companies are concerned (cf. *Who Controls Industry in Kenya*, EAPH, 1968). It is now widely recognised that control of these industries is at least as important as ownership. Our justification for using this column is to illustrate the mainly foreign character of the industries with interests in East Africa operating from Kenya.

All other exports were manufactured by overseas companies operating in Kenya. It is therefore not unreasonable to conclude that it was these foreign companies who were interested in the development of the common market facilities in East Africa. The setting up of a common market has made their East African operations more profitable. In a sense, the East African common market represents a close connection between the East African economy and the European and American economies through the companies involved. It also follows that an integration of the East African economies with the European Economic Community would prove to be an integration of the same order. East Africa has become a homogeneous market and European and American investors have been the main ones to benefit. The African sectors of the economies have benefited only in so far as the demand for labour, foodstuffs for home consumption and raw materials has increased. But of course most small-scale peasant farmers have no part in this – no specialised co-operatives have been formed among them. There has been no co-operation among the producers of export commodities, e.g. the coffee and tea producers. Co-operation and integration has been carried out in the main by the branch firms of international large-scale producers and the local large-scale milk and meat industries. The common market in East Africa has served as the base for the expansion of foreign manufacturers. It may be expected that the East African branches of these firms will attempt to monopolise the market, either by taking over smaller companies or by obtaining licences to allow them to operate as the sole manufacturers of their particular product or products. Either way, formation of a common market has increased the tendency towards the centralisation and concentration of production and distribution. Not only has Kenya, particularly Nairobi, become the centre of development for industries producing consumer goods in East Africa, but also Uganda and Tanzania have provided the markets for these goods. In recent years this pattern has become more distinct, with Uganda and Tanzania selling mainly food and raw materials to Kenya* and Kenya exporting finished goods. East Africa has begun to form a small scale version of the international economic scene – expanding and developing centre, based on private capital, exporting its finished goods to the surrounding areas.

Objections to the East African Common Market and its Political Consequences

The colonial authorities of Tanganyika and Uganda in the 1950s were not completely passive in allowing Kenya to take the main share of the benefits of economic union. They saw the situation in the following terms.

1. Kenya's economic boom of the 1950s had led to her rapid economic growth. This boom was due to historical and geographical factors. As a result Kenya had been able to take undue advantage of the common market in East Africa.
2. Although there existed a common tariff barrier against imports from overseas, there were no restrictions governing trade within

* In 1966 Tanzanian exports to Kenya included soya beans, lentils, pears, unprocessed tobacco, oil seeds, oil, nuts, cotton and seed oil. She also exported a few manufactured goods including blankets and travelling rugs and footwear.

East Africa. Kenya's exports to Uganda and Tanganyika had begun to replace the goods that they had previously imported from abroad.

3. These goods were generally more expensive and, initially, were of lower quality.
4. Uganda and Tanganyika were still trading mainly primary produce within the common market. They were buying processed goods from Kenya which they could have obtained more cheaply from abroad. Moreover had these goods been foreign imports there would have been considerable revenue from taxes.

Thus Uganda and Tanganyika found that they were protecting Kenya's manufacturing industry from external competition with little gain for themselves. Most important, they were losing any opportunity they may have had for their own industrialisation. They were falling behind Kenya in economic growth. Therefore they felt that the situation was seriously in need of adjustment. One of the results of these problems has been a great deal of academic argument over the quantifying of gains and losses from such a common market. Although this is useful for small-scale and short-term modifications the major difficulties remain. The essential questions to ask in any discussion of the East African common market is whether the division of activities between the units is to be (*a*) 'vertical' – that is, each unit producing different goods and services or (*b*) 'horizontal' – that is, each unit producing the same goods and services or (*c*) 'mixed' – that is, the units sharing some common services which allow for a limited form of integration.

If the market develops into one with a vertical division, it is to be expected that initially capital and labour will be sucked into the centre of the market, which will to some extent rob other regions of their resources. Undoubtedly the administrative centre will gain but it is a matter for conjecture whether there will be any benefit to the rest. One problem here is that of the three countries forming the economic union, one sovereign state is likely to be the dominant one, and it is in order to ask whether this type of centrally dominated market is appropriate for East Africa. There is the possibility that it would lead to the stronger state swallowing the weaker ones.

The second option of a 'horizontal' type structure is clearly more favourable to the weaker of the three states. It would enable all members of the union to derive equal benefit. The Raisman Report of 1961 and the Kampala/Mbale agreement of 1964–5 supported this solution.

The argument over the form of the common market came to a head at the end of 1959. The Ugandan government had suggested fiscal compensation to counter declining revenues from duty on imported goods that were now supplied by Kenya. Kenya turned down this suggestion. The Colonial Office in London appointed a commission under the chairmanship of Sir Jeremy Raisman to examine the various inequalities in the market. Uganda and Tanganyika wanted an industrial licensing system in order to obtain a 'fair' share of the new industries, in spite of the fact that such a system was in conflict with the aim of internal free trade. The report supported this idea and also recommended a pooling system so that Uganda and Tanganyika would, to some extent, be compensated for their loss of revenue. Very little action was taken on the recommendations of the Raisman report. When Kenya, Uganda and Tanganyika all became independent in the sixties the problems of the common market remained unsolved.

Tanzania suffered most from the unfair system and in 1964 she warned that if more equitable arrangements were not made, she would partially or totally withdraw from the common market. The Kampala/Mbale Agreement was drawn up in 1964–5 to try and ease the conflict. Again an attempt was made to distribute the benefits of trade and industrial location more equally. New industries were to be located by agreement among the three territories and most were to be assigned to Tanzania. Quotas were to be established on the amount of goods one country could export to another. Uganda and Tanzania were to increase the sales of their goods to Kenya. But the Kampala/Mbale Agreement was in direct conflict with the interests of Kenya who, therefore, did not co-operate in the implementation of these resolutions. By 1965 Tanzania had imposed strict quotas on the amount of goods that could be brought in from Kenya. In the same year Tanzania also decided to set up her own central bank and currency system. There was never even any attempt at implementing an industrial 'sharing' scheme.

In 1965 the East African common market came close to breaking up completely. A further investigation was carried out by the Philip Commission in 1966. The report of the commission was published in the same year and the Treaty for East African Co-operation was signed in 1967. The treaty established the East African Community of which the East African common market was a part. The stated goal of the Community was to :

Strengthen and regulate the industrial, commercial and other relations of the partner states for the end that there shall be accelerated, harmonious and balanced development and sustained expansion of economic activities the benefits whereof shall be equally shared.

Here we can see the contradiction between the *aims* of the East African Community and the real situation. Trade within East Africa is more and more being undertaken by the branch companies of international capitalist firms which are in the main based in Nairobi. It would therefore be quite remarkable if the proceeds of this trade were equitably distributed. Yet the goals of the community – to share the proceeds among the member states on an equal basis – remain. National sentiments from Uganda and Tanzania have demanded an equal share of a capitalist community. Each report and commission in the 1950s and 1960s has attempted to solve this long-standing problem of the inequality of benefits and proceeds of the market in East Africa. It seems probable that unless Kenya would voluntarily decide to reduce her own growth rate in order to achieve the goal of community equality, which is hardly feasible, the contradiction between the expectation of the economically weak states and the dynamic of growth of inequality will lead towards greater friction between member states. Finally this contradiction is liable to lead to the break-up of the community itself, as is already beginning to happen.

Part Four

INSTITUTIONS FROM ECONOMIC GROWTH

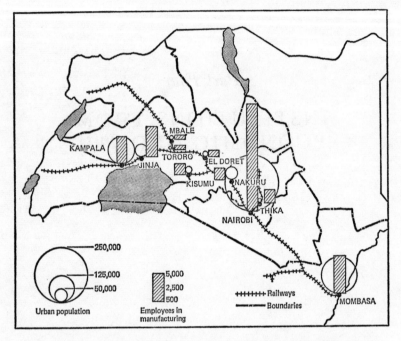

The urban and industrial centres of Kenya and Uganda

This map illustrates a number of major themes in the chapters on manufacturing and industrialisation. It shows the extent of urban development
in terms of the size of the major towns and the number of employees in the
manufacturing industry. It is particularly important because it shows the
definite tendency towards a pattern of concentration in urban and manufacturing development at the time of Independence. By the early 1960s
Nairobi, Kampala and Mombasa were far and away the largest towns in the
entire region, while the number of employees in manufacturing was as
great in Nairobi as in all the other major towns together. It is therefore
not surprising that Nairobi has become the international centre in East
Africa. The map also shows how urban and industrial development has
occurred along the railway line, i.e. along the means of communication
with the sea.

13 Urbanisation

... Kenya's urban population in the short space of 28 years will have swollen from its present level to 9,000,000 (the total population of the country in 1969 was only 10·5 million) ... Problems of urban poverty and unemployment, of inadequacy of housing and urban infrastructure have been recorded throughout history. What most distinguishes the current urban problems ... is their scale and intensity. The severity of the problems reflects primarily the rapidity of overall population growth and the acute shortage of resources.

... The proliferation of squatter settlements and slums and the rising backlog in urban services, have been accompanied by growing recognition that 'developments' implies much more than just expansion of output. Yet with few exceptions, the measures so far undertaken have signally failed to reverse these trends or produce more efficient patterns of urban growth.*

East Africa's 'urban problem' has altered remarkably little since the turn of the century. Poverty, housing shortages, high rents, low wages and slum life have consistently been part of the experience of the rural migrant who has ventured into the towns and cities. What has altered over the years is the *extent* of the urban problem; as the

TABLE 13.1

Urban population growth

	Uganda (1959)	Kenya (1962)
Two major towns:		
Nairobi, Mombasa		440,000
Kampala, Jinja	129,000	
Nine next largest towns[a]	71,000	137,000

[a] *Kenya:* Nakuru, Kisumu, Thika, Eldoret, Nanyuki, Kitale, Malindi, Kericho, Nyeri

Uganda: Mbale, Entebbe, Kabale, Fort Portal, Soroti, Masaka, Tororo, Gulu and Arua

* *Daily Nation* leader article, 14 August 1972, discussing 'The Characteristics of Urban Growth', the potential urban problem in Nairobi in the year 2000.

population in the territories as a whole has grown, the population in the towns has grown even faster. Perhaps the most striking fact has been the unevenness in this growth of the towns, as is illustrated by the figures in Tables 13.1–5.

The two largest cities in both territories have grown immeasurably faster than the other towns. Nairobi and Mombasa together were in 1962 over three times the size of the next nine towns put together and greater Kampala and Jinja in 1959 were just under double the size of the next nine towns in Uganda. The unevenness is perhaps even more striking when one makes a comparison between the sizes of the two capital cities, Nairobi and Kampala.

TABLE 13.2

Growth of total population (in '000s)

	Nairobi	Kampala and Kisenyi
1906	13·5[a]	3·0 (+ approx. 32 in Kisenyi)
1911		
1914	21[c]	—
1921	23[c]	4.0[b]
1928	38[c]	—
1934	47[c]	5 or 6[b]
1948	119	46 (of which 32 in Kisenyi)
1951	222	—
1959	—	99
1962	267	—
1969	509	—

[a] Census taken
[b] Figures do not include Kisenyi
[c] Estimated figures taken from Dr M. Parker's thesis

Up to 1948 there were no proper censuses of the African population so we have to rely on unreliable estimates, and moreover comparison cannot be exact as the boundaries of these towns were continuously expanding. On the other hand Table 13.2 does offer us at least a glimpse of what has been undoubtedly a very rapid growth. Nairobi more than doubled its population between 1914 and 1934, then doubled it again in the following ten years; between 1948 and 1962 it increased by over 15 per cent and the same *rate* of increase has continued since Independence. This pace of growth has been sustained since the origin of the town and is quite remarkable, being rapid even when compared with

TABLE 13.3

Rate of population increase between given dates

	Percentage of increase, total population of Kenya	Percentage of increase, Nairobi population
1921–31	10	100 (1934)
1931–48	40	150
1948–62	54	156
1962–9	24	98

Note: Total population figures between 1921 and 1948 have been taken from D. A. Lury's estimates (see Chapter 1); Nairobi population estimates from Table 13.2 above. Despite potential errors the differences between the rates of the two sets of figures will be in the correct order of magnitude.

the rate of population growth as a whole, as shown in Table 13.3.

It is more difficult to show the rate increase of population in Kampala and Kisenyi. Not only is the origin of Kisenyi different to any aspect of Nairobi but even the roughest historical population estimates are not available. What does appear from Table 13.2 is the low rate of growth before 1934. Kampala's growth rate was probably due to the European and Asian population influx which has always been lower in Kampala town than in Nairobi, as the following figures illustrate:

TABLE 13·4

European and Asian populations in Nairobi and Kenya

	EUROPEAN		ASIAN	
	Nairobi	Kampala	Nairobi	Kampala
1906	642	147	3,581	680
1911	—	—	—	—
1914	—	400	—	800
1921	—	—	—	—
1926	3,712	359	9,589	3,106
1931	7,164	505	17,609	—
1948	—	1,297	—	10,824
1959	—	3,179	—	19,500
1962	—	—	—	—
1969	19,185	—	67,189	—

The very much higher European and Asian population growth rate in Nairobi did not occur by chance. Both Nairobi and Kampala grew initially as administrative cities, as the centres of government services for the export economy. Kenya's settlers required a wider range of complex services, not required by Uganda's peasant-led export economy, and this characteristic is reflected in the urban population figures. Nairobi also acted as a collecting centre for exports where commodities were graded, and as a distribution point for imports, where the goods were sorted into small parcels and sent on. Thus international traders had their headquarters in Nairobi, which increased the foreign element in the population. It would seem probable therefore that up to 1945, the more rapid growth in Nairobi was due primarily to the larger influx of Europeans. They required servants and therefore provided increased job opportunities in the city; they also needed housing and roads and other municipal services which together provided the stimulus for the inflow of people from the countryside which is reflected in the statistics.

Finally, both Tables 13.2 and 13.4 illustrate the increase in the rate of growth of the two cities after 1945. The growth of secondary import industry in the cities and the extension of the pressure of population on the land were concurrent factors leading to the increasing rate of central urban growth in the post-war era. In Kenya the urban growth was at first widely spread among all the urban areas (see Table 13.5 below), but after 1962 the major direction of the growth was towards Nairobi and Mombasa, while the growth of the smaller towns was comparatively slow.

TABLE 13.5

Growth of African population in Kenya's towns (in '000s)

	1948	1962	1969
Nairobi and Mombasa	107	268	608
Percentage of growth		250	225
Nine next major towns[a]	26·2	100	147
Percentage of growth		380	50

[a] See note, Table 13.1

While the growth of the small towns was initially rapid, due probably as much as anything else to the low level from which they began, the continued rate of growth of Mombasa and Nairobi after 1962 and the decline in the rate of growth of the other towns was almost certainly due to the industrial developments in the two main towns and the consequent availability of jobs. Comparable figures for Uganda's main towns for 1948 and 1969 are not at present available.

A further factor in the rapidity of the Nairobi and Mombasa population increases has been associated with the development of the East African Common Market. Nairobi in particular has become the central growth point in East Africa; the city has become the centre of international firms in East Africa, for the international community, for overseas journalists, diplomatic missions and so on. Any overseas organisation concerned with the East African Common Market has tended to become established in or around Nairobi, as the services such as telecommunications, transport and trained staff have been accessible and available. So long therefore as Nairobi continues to play a central industrial and international role the city is likely to continue to attract as high a population inflow as over the past thirty years.

The speed and unevenness of urban growth and its causes are the most important factors in East African urban history. Up to 1948, Africans were poorly represented in the urban process At that time there were only seventeen towns with a population of over 2000 people; together they had a total population of 285,000 of which only 161,000 were Africans. By 1962 the number of towns with over 2000 people had risen to a total of thirty-four with a 671,000 population of which only 442,000 were Africans. This meant that only 7·8 per cent of the total Kenya population, or 5·3 per cent of the total African population in Kenya, were living in towns in 1962. Such figures should be compared to 3·2 per cent of the total population for Uganda and 4·1 per cent for Tanganyika in 1959. The proportion of Africans living in urban areas in East Africa was extremely low in comparison to the urban population in Ghana in 1959 which was 23 per cent of the total, 38 per cent in Egypt, 45 per cent in Brazil or to the 60–80 per cent of people in Europe living in urban centres. East African urbanisation would thus appear to have affected very few of the people, although in practice, due to the patterns of short-term migration, a higher proportion of people than indicated by the statistics will have experienced urban life for limited periods of time.

Yet all the above statistics in some respects give a false impression. Although the total number of people actually living in urban areas on the night of census has been growing over the last seventy years, the total number of people living *permanently* in the urban areas has always been much smaller. Most young people have not simply left their rural homes for Nairobi, but have gone to the nearest urban centre and have progressed from there to larger towns until they have finished up in Nairobi. Until the last few years only a tiny proportion, 2 or 3 per cent, of the people living in the cities was actually born in them. The vast majority not only

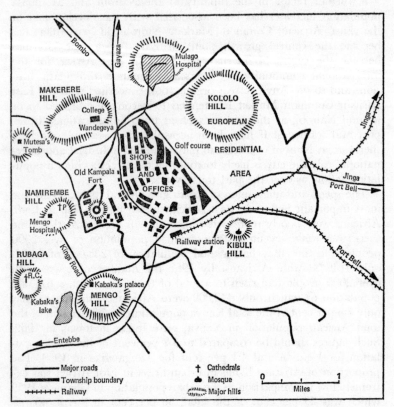

A sketch map of Kampala in 1935

This map shows how Kampala was built on a series of hills and how the roads and the railway line utilised the valleys between them. Most of the hills were topped by important buildings, which dominated the town. For example, the Christian cathedrals and the Kibuli mosque, the Kabaka's palace in the Kibuga, Mutesa's tomb, Makerere College, and so on. This follows the traditional pattern of building in Buganda. This pattern is still observable in Kampala today and was even more pronounced in the early years of the town.

The area between the Old Kampala Fort hill, Kololo Hill and the railway line comprised the municipality of Kampala; note how the commercial and administrative areas in the municipality are concentrated in the valley in the south-west, whilst to the north-east were the European residential and recreational areas. The main African residential areas were situated outside the municipality, in the Wandegeya area around Makerere Hill, and around Mengo Hill, which remained the centre of the traditional Ganda government.

were born in the rural areas but also regularly visit the rural areas, send cash back there monthly and remain as committed to rural as to urban life.

Up to the mid-1950s urban wages were so low throughout East Africa that only a tiny minority of urban migrants could think of bringing their families; thus one of the explanations for the recent rapid increase in urban growth has been that whole families have been coming to the cities rather than single men. Certainly the number of persons of the average family in Kampala and Nairobi has been rising in recent years. Until recently the usual pattern was to spend only a short time in the city before returning home, a pattern called circular migration. With the rise of wages since the late 1950s this pattern has changed. We may thus say that the decline of circular migration, the urban colonial pattern, has been one of the major economic and social changes in towns since Independence.

The origin of urban East Africa

Kampala

In nineteenth-century East Africa the capital of Buganda at Kisenyi and the urban settlement along the coast were the major areas of large scale settlement. Buganda, like many of its neighbouring king-doms, had developed into a centralised and to some extent an autocratic unitary state in the nineteenth century. Political centralisation was associated directly with the authority of the king which was focused in the capital, Kibuga. The capital was the centre of Buganda political and administrative activities, and it was moved from one hilltop to another every few years. Between 1859 and 1890 the capital seems to have been moved at least ten times. The Kabaka's enclosure was on Mengo Hill in 1885 and it has remained there ever since. He lived in a central enclosure with his principal chiefs around him. Likewise each leading chief was surrounded by minor chiefs. Thus all the people in the Kibuga who came from a particular district tended to remain together. Each chief also built a number of houses in his enclosure for the use of his wives and retainers and he would keep some land for cultivation. The entire area was apparently several miles wide, the exact circum-ference varying according to the missionary account to which one refers, but the Kibuga covered up to twelve square miles in all. Estimates of the population of the Kibuga varied from 10,000 to 77,000. In 1911 an official census returned a population of 32,441, which in 1948 had only increased to 34,337, a surprisingly small increase in the period.

It is interesting to note that another town, Mbale, grew up originally with a similar plan to that of the Kibuga, although it started in the early twentieth century. At the very beginning of the colonial era there was no town or settlement on the present-day Mbale site. Mbale began when Semei Kakungulu, a Muganda who had conquered the greater part of Bukedi, was installed by his followers in 1901 as 'Kabaka' of Bukedi. The British colonial authority ordered Kakungulu to retire and move to Lango, as his authority in Bukedi had been established without their consent. He agreed to vacate but only on the condition that he was given a grant of land. He was eventually offered twenty square miles and set up his home with many of his followers on the present site of Mbale in 1902. Within a year a major settlement on the pattern of Mengo had been established. There were gardens, roads, bridges, market places and Kakungulu's own house in the middle. The new town flourished economically and by 1904 it had become a centre for the caravans of the ivory trade. Within a few years it lost its indigenous urban face as the British established an administrative headquarters at the town begun by Kakungulu, so that it acquired the characteristics of a colonial township.

The development of Kampala, which adjoins the Ganda capital, is a growth only of the past seventy years. The site of the actual township dated from 1890 when F. D. Lugard established his camp on a small hill now called Old Kampala. The Lugard camp was fortified by a ditch and palisade and became the centre of British authority and, initially, of administration for the entire territory. A bazaar rapidly sprang up around the fort and so a more spacious site had to be found. The adjoining slopes of Nakasero Hill were used as they had an adequate water supply. In 1905 the British administrative headquarters was moved to Nakasero.

Kampala developed in the twentieth century as a number of centres focused on hill tops. The Church Missionary Society had established themselves in 1884 on Namirembe and the Catholics in 1885 on Rubaga to the west and north-west of Mengo Hill. These urban hilltop developments reflected the central political aspects of Uganda life. The missionaries, the Buganda kingdom and the secular colonial administration had all built their houses on the top of hills, each in its own way symbolised their political power.

The relationship between the Kibuga and Kampala township was defined by the 1900 Uganda Agreement. The Kibuga was included in the settlement which meant that the leading Ganda alone had the power of disposal of urban land within it. The foundations were laid for a powerful land-owning aristocracy who would rule the Kibuga as it was the centre of the Ganda's military, ritual, legal and political life. The Kabaka and Kibuga symbolised their authority and independence. And as the colonial authority had left the entire administration of the Kibuga in Ganda hands, it reflected their political autonomy.

Thus from the beginning of the century there developed two urban administrations : the colonial and the Ganda. The British were legally unable to touch the *mailo* land of the Kibuga which was south and west of the original municipal town, while Crown land extended to the north-east. The Buganda government jealously guarded its *mailo* land and even by 1948, when town planning became an important matter, developmental control was restricted to Crown land.

From the beginning of the century the lack of unitary government over greater Kampala led to a great deal of antagonism, confusion and overlapping. The antagonism was based on the continuous Ganda fear that the expanding municipal authority would take over the Kibuga land while the colonial authority was forever complaining at the disregard by the Ganda authority for the health of its people. The colonial municipality had evolved its own rating system, its services for roads, drainage, lighting, health control and water supply. The overwhelming superiority of the municipality in wealth and the provision of services over Mengo and the Kibuga rapidly developed into a source of friction between the two authorities. The Ganda authorities did very little to regulate developments in the Kibuga. It does not seem that the Kibuga was poor financially, but that the Ganda ruling classes who owned the land of the Kibuga opposed taxing or rating the occupants. Moreover there was no separate Ganda urban authority : the Kibuga was ruled as part of the unitary Buganda government. The unique problems which urban growth inevitably throws up, in particular over health, housing controls and water supply, seem to have been largely ignored by the Baganda.

In effect there developed a duality in greater Kampala, based in some respects on an unintended racial division of the city. There was Kampala municipality, with its strict building rules, a preserve of the European and Asian settlers, in which, until Independence, local Africans had no stake. It was true that large numbers of Africans became urban squatters at Wandegeya and Kagugube, with no secure basis of tenure in the city, but they do not seem to have caused a major problem in the city until the 1950s when attempts began to be made to regularise the situation. No attempt until then was made to accommodate Africans in the municipal area. The African as an urban dweller was ignored. The high rents and enforcement of building standards meant that few Africans could afford to live in the town and provided a positive inducement to the growth of peri-urban slums. There grew up slums on the municipal border, close enough to the sources of employment but outside the expensive municipal boundaries. Thus until the middle of the 1950s the municipality was an exclusive European and Asian administrative and commercial centre where domestic servants were the only large body of the local people living within its boundaries.

On the other hand the Kibuga remained the Ganda capital and developed nearly all the social and economic characteristics of the slum which one finds over the last fifty years in Nairobi as well as in other major capital cities of the world. It had developed relatively free of any effective control of the buildings or settlement. As a result, the area was extremely densely populated, with 23,000 people per square mile or 36 per acre. No local government common services had been developed (like sewage, drainage, water supply or garbage disposal) so that, as with all slums, the area posed a major health problem. The buildings grew up without any organisation. Most were built of mud and wattle and there were few brick houses or concrete floors. As there were no regulations and most people had little cash, people crowded together; 70 to 90 per cent of the people seem to have always lived in the situation where every room in the house was used for sleeping. The social conditions of the Kibuga were similar to those of rural village life with the major exception of the numbers and density of population. It was the density which made all the difference. The Kibuga was an urban village not unlike certain West African towns. The major problem was that urban overcrowding with inadequate provision of clean water, drainage and lack of space created prime conditions for mental and physical ill-health, and in particular provided the conditions for the rapid spread of epidemic disease.

Greater Kampala thus developed throughout the colonial period primarily as a dual or racially divided city. It was a city divided mainly between the Baganda, the Asians and the Europeans; just as Nairobi was divided mainly between the Kikuyu, the Asians and the Europeans, although with the difference that in Greater Kampala a number of Asians rented shops in the Kibuga where they did not have to pay rates or licences. Such practices were not possible in Nairobi. In both territories the geographical base of the dominant 'tribe' was the capital city. And as in Nairobi the areas of growth in Kampala were in the European section. With the arrival of the railway at Kisumu, the opening of external trade with the lake steamers which linked Kampala to the railway, and the production of cotton for export, the European side of Kampala expanded. All the cotton came through Kampala's two ginneries which had been established within the town as early as 1914. The commercial area of the town rapidly became congested and plague, malaria and blackwater fever led to the burning of the bazaar in 1916, as had happened a few years earlier for the same reasons in Nairobi's commercial area.

Racial segregation was also widely recommended around 1914, although it was never legally implemented in Kampala. Yet as the best commercial and residential sites were reserved for Europeans, racial segregation was thus instituted *de facto*, which appears to have satisfied the small European community. In practice all Uganda's towns were racially segregated. Throughout both Kenya and Uganda during the colonial period European urban residential areas remained spacious and well laid out, with avenues of trees, neat murram roads and modest bungalows similar to those of an upper-middle class English suburb.

Nairobi

The origins of urban Nairobi are quite different from those of Kampala and Mengo. There is some evidence to suggest that present-day Nairobi used to be a trading centre for Kikuyu and Maasai women. Ngong was used to obtain supplies by caravans from the coast, but none of this had much to do with why Nairobi has developed on its present site. Nairobi developed because the railway authorities decided that the site should become their head-quarters. The station and sidings were laid out on their present site. The authorities immediately established the residential pattern which is so familiar in Nairobi today; on one side of the track they placed the higher income European houses and on the other side were the lower income groups. Rapidly a bazaar followed the railway headquarters and established itself in the River Road/Tom Mboya Street area. By 1900 the outline pattern of the town was clear.

The Uganda railway administration was a self-contained unit with its legality derived from the Foreign Office. Its jurisdiction extended to a mile on either side of the line. They therefore brought with them their own police force and magistrates. By 1901 both the colonial governor, Charles Eliot, and the provincial administration had moved their headquarters to the railway headquarters.

The railway opened up Kenya to world trade as no other means of transport could have done in 1900. There were few motor cars, for the motor car was still in its infancy in 1900, and was used only by a tiny handful of people in Europe at this time. On the other hand in Europe the railway had been rapidly developed since 1830 and railway engineers had had considerable experience in building

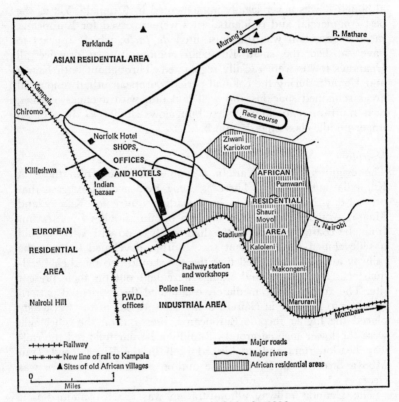

A sketch map of Nairobi in the 1930s

The map opposite shows the main outline of Nairobi in the 1930s. Whereas Kampala had become a zoned city and region as a result of tradition and history, Nairobi became a zoned city in the inter-war years as a result of administrative decision.

In the triangle between the old railway line, the Nairobi River and the railway station was the central commercial and administrative zone, with government offices, European shops and businesses, the Asian bazaar and European hotels.

To the south-east, around the Nairobi River and bordered by the railway line and the race course, were the 'official' African residential areas, including Pumwani which from the 1920s was designated as the residential area to replace the haphazard development of African housing in Pangani and the Parklands area. This area also included the African railway workers' quarters in Makongeni and Marurani.

North of the Fort Hall (Murang'a) road was the main Asian residential area, Parklands.

To the west of the railway line, from Nairobi Hill to Chiromo, was the main European residential area.

After the First World War the area to the south of the railway workshop area began to be developed as Nairobi's industrial zone.

In 1931 the railway line reached Kampala from Eldoret, which provided a direct rail link with Mombasa and a new stimulus for growth. In practice the town appears to have grown very slowly until after 1945. Between 1948 and 1959 the total population of the municipality doubled.

K

cuttings and laying rails in a wide variety of physical environments. It was not surprising that by choosing Nairobi as the centre of the railway network, they were also choosing the site for the capital city. From 1900 to 1940 exports were the mainstay of the growth of the economy, and it was the railway which made this change possible. Hence the centre of the railway was the centre or hub of change in Kenya.

In many respects it was pure chance that Nairobi should have been chosen as it was. From the British point of view it was simply inoperative to rule the vast areas of Kenya from Zanzibar or Mombasa. The logistics of communication were such that some centre had to be established in roughly the middle of the country, but there is no reason to suppose that it could not have been located at Naivasha or Nakuru or elsewhere. But once the railway headquarters were established Nairobi became a powerful centralising agent. The town became the headquarters of the military, the base from which 'pacification' (i.e. conquest) campaigns were waged. The administration moved its offices from Mombasa in 1905. And the branch railway lines which were built in the 1920s ensured that Nairobi became the main distribution point for imports and the collection point for exports. Nairobi rapidly became the centre for the spread of westernisation and the central link between the country and the outside world. This link has become particularly relevant in the 1960s with the development of the international airport and the international satellite communication system.

The growth of Nairobi was fairly rapid, as has already been shown. There was nothing like the Kibuga in Nairobi as there was no existing urban settlement in the area. Yet the dual aspect of urban growth, the contrast between the garden city suburbs of Kampala municipality and the higgledy-piggledy development of the Kibuga has been very much replicated in Nairobi. Developments in the European sector of the city included areas like Karen, Westlands and Ngong, where a house per acre of land was quite normal. The Asian sector of the population has been mainly located in Parklands, while the African sector of the city has grown up in a haphazard manner as at Kampala.

From the earliest years of the city, scattered African villages of huts made from paraffin tins and thatch surrounded the more permanent dwellings of the railway and administration. The problem of sanitation and health, a constant problem in poor areas of cities, hit Nairobi early. In 1902 there was an outbreak of plague in the Indian bazaar as there were no sanitary arrangements in these areas. The most important and largest part of the African squatter villages was Pangani, which was the area where the porters were housed, usually in lodging houses for migrant labour. Other 'squatter' villages at this time were Kaburini, Maskini, Kariorkor, Mombasa villages and Kileleshwa. By 1912 and 1913 there were renewed plague outbreaks in a number of these areas and the embryonic municipal council reacted by passing urban rules which were intended to limit the number of people allowed to occupy a room and to impose standards of cleanliness and hygiene. These rules were never enforced.

All the early villages grew without supervision or organisation and so created a health hazard to the European population. Disease is no respecter of race or class. Urban improvements have often been introduced in different parts of the world simply because the richest section of the community fear the consequences of poor sanitation in the slum areas of their city. In Nairobi the colonial municipal council attempted to solve this problem by destroying the squatter settlements, harassing anyone who appeared to be unemployed, and developing controlled urban African locations on the South African model. To this end, Mombasa, Kaburini, Kileleshwa and Maskini were burnt down in 1923. Pumwani was planned as a model African location and all the residents of Pangani were to be moved to Pumwani. Pangani was planned to be burnt soon after when it became redundant but it took the municipality fifteen years before they found sufficient cash to build the very minimum services in the new village. By 1938, Pumwani was as overcrowded as Pangani had ever been and the health hazards were as great as before. Moreover, as the African population of the city had increased, the numbers of people living on odd verandahs and in the street, people who had not the cash to find a bed, had also increased. It was estimated, probably fairly accurately, that there were, in principle, bed spaces in 1937 for 22,000 Africans in Nairobi, but that there were actually 31,000 Africans in the city. After 1945 the official policy of urban segregation was discontinued, but the growth of African housing, i.e. estates for the large majority of lower paid workers, and of slums has been extremely rapid ever since, so that the early segregated racial pattern of the city remains most apparent.

Over the years the numbers of people living in impermanent urban dwellings in Nairobi has increased and in 1972 somewhere in the region of 170,000 people, or one-third of the city's population, lived in what are popularly known as slums or shanty towns. Nearly all of these people were living in situations of gross overcrowding, with three or four persons per room.

The term 'slum' itself is a hostile one in that the word is used by non-slum dwellers to describe the conditions under which others live. A slum shows a complex of characteristics : low-quality housing, poor social amenities, overcrowding of people, poverty, crime, no jobs, low levels of education. In short a slum demonstrates a range of factors which lead to a circular syndrome of poverty. Although 'slum' is an evocative term which makes people react with the idea of clearance, it is a term for which there is no adequate substitute. A major part of the development of Nairobi has been the development of slums, which has been closely associated with a gross shortage of housing, high rents and low wages.

The duality of the city – between the 'garden' city in the European area and the 'slum' of the African residential areas – developed over the years primarily because the colonial City Council did not accept that Africans had any right to a permanent place in the city. The European municipal authority worked on the basis that Africans had alternative homes in the rural areas, and so they were not concerned with them as residents but as short-term wage labourers. As a consequence of this viewpoint, the segregated urban 'native locations' were designed on the cheapest possible basis. It was argued in two commissions in 1907 and 1913 that the town should be segregated on grounds of health, which in effect was a demonstration that the council was unwilling to spend cash on the African areas. The principle which governed the municipal authority's attitudes to Africans in the town was well expressed in 1930 :

> It seems only right that it should be understood that the town is a non-native area in which there is no place for the redundant native, who neither works nor serves his or her people. The exclusion of these redundant natives is in the interests of natives and non-natives alike . . .

Despite the fact that the natives vastly outnumbered the non-natives in Nairobi, the resources of the town were mainly spent on the white section of the population. Between the years 1932 and 1947, for which figures are available, the City Council spent only between 1 and 2 per cent of its revenue on services for Africans. The council was only spending between £1000 and £2000(?) per year on services for somewhere in the region of 20,000 African people – a pattern of expenditure which was almost a blue-print for the creation of slum conditions.

The problem was that the City Council served roughly 2200 Europeans who were spread out on 2500-odd acres of ground. The whites demanded roads, water, public lighting and sanitary services, and the fact that they were geographically widely spread, meant that (a) the costs per head of the white population for the urban services was extremely high and (b) the African areas were starved of basic urban services like sewage and clean water. Part of the problem was that the Europeans did not like to pay rates (the usual source of income in urban areas). Only a third or less of the revenue was derived from rates, instead of the 60–75 per cent that might have been expected. Hence there was a fairly permanent shortage of municipal finance.

The fact that so little cash was spent on the African location might not have mattered if the inflow of people into the city had been very slow. But as already shown in Table 13·2, the inflow of people into Nairobi was always very rapid and was increasing probably at about double the rate of the population as a whole. We need to ask, why so many people? Until the 1960s the authorities were not aware of the social and political consequences of the continued rate of increase of the population in Nairobi, so that until recently we have lacked appropriate data to explain the movement. The data that we do have from the 1920s suggests that the apparent popularity of work in Nairobi was due to the differences in the wages between the rural areas and the urban areas. So long as potential wages were higher in Nairobi than on the farms, people tended to move towards higher wages.

More exact data has recently become available for all of Kenya's urban areas. This showed that in 1968–70 only 3 per cent of the people living in Nairobi had actually been born there. Few African people had been born in the city, as wages had been so low for so long that people could not afford to bring up families in the city. People had moved into the cities for short periods of work. Then in the late 1950s wages began to rise and people began to consider settling in the city; by 1970 60 per cent of the men sampled were hoping to stay. The people who were coming into the city had the characteristics which are listed in Table 13.6 overleaf.

Thus the tendency of the migration was for the young, the relatively educated, the single, the unemployed, the landless or near to landless to migrate to the towns looking for work. Research undertaken in such areas as Maragoli, an area of very high population density, confirms these findings; the author suggested that Maragoli, despite the fact that the area was over 230 miles from the city, acted as a suburb of Nairobi because the landless young used the city to move backwards and forwards looking for work. It is clear from these findings that although the *pull* of higher wages still is an important factor the *push* from the rural areas to the city is clearly very powerful indeed and provides a major reason why Nairobi has expanded so rapidly. With a growing proportion of the people settling in the urban area, plus the various factors of rural life which encourage migration it is reasonable to expect the existing rate of urban growth to continue.

TABLE 13.6

Migrants to Nairobi, 1970

	Percentage of sample
Had no job in the rural area	60
Owned no land	66
Owned one to five acres of land	23
Were aged below 30	82
(Men) were single	52
Had their wives outside the town	28
Had an education from standard 5 or above	72

Note: All the above percentages include young school-leavers

One of the results of the rapid population expansion has been that many of the young people have been unable to find work. During the colonial period, the colonial authorities made major efforts to control the influx of people into the city by issuing a special urban pass system. Such a pass system was almost inevitably difficult to administer as the people attempted to avoid it by entering the city away from the main roads and keeping out of the way of the police. Moreover the system was expensive to operate, as it required a large number of police and very strict sentences were passed in the attempt to ensure enforcement. The Nairobi pass system never seems to have worked for more than a year at a time in the 1920s and 1930s because the area was so large. In effect, only major access roads could be policed day and night. However employers were always happy to have a pool of unemployed so that wages could be kept down. After 1945, the rate of the influx of people increased and although the numbers of 'bed spaces' increased between 1946 and 1957 by 30,000, the number of bodies increased by 52,000, and this increase was despite massive attempts to control the inflow. In 1949 a new Vagrancy Ordinance was passed. Vagrancy laws had been operative since 1902; they had allowed the police to pick up anyone who appeared to be loitering on the street, apparently without work, and to return him to his home in the rural areas. The Emergency from 1952 provided the Nairobi authorities with the opportunity to do what they had always wanted to do. In April 1954 *Operation Anvil* was put into operation and the city's 'surplus' population were removed. Twenty-eight thousand detainees from Central Province were taken from the city and sent to camps and to the rural areas. Those who remained found barbed wire around their houses, an elaborate pass system and a nightly curfew. At a stroke, massive measures of urban population control had been enforced and the policy of preserving the city for Europeans had been reaffirmed. The standards and provisions for European services could only be maintained if welfare resources did not have to be expended on 'unemployed' Africans.

Since the Emergency influx control has been entirely abandoned, and the Independence government has made no attempt to stop people coming into the city. As the city has grown with such frightening rapidity, the task of influx control except under emergency conditions becomes annually more and more difficult. Yet the city authorities have not simply abandoned the problem; low-priced housing has been a priority, but only those with regular jobs can afford such housing. Very large numbers of people, in the region of 170,000, who do not have a regular income still could not afford the lowest cost housing provided by the City Council even if it were available. Since Independence, squatter settlements have increased both in and around the city boundaries. Clean-up campaigns designed to repatriate 'vagrants' and the burning of shanty houses have become quite common. In the long run only regular work, either in the urban or rural areas, will solve the problem. Yet it must be understood that many of the people who live in the slums are not simply 'unemployed'.

One of the assumptions made by administrators and latterly by academics was that it was necessary to control the inflow of people into the city as so many would be 'unemployed'. The very notion of unemployment is derived from European urban conditions where the people (a) have had no alternative work on the land and (b) where employment statistics have only been gathered in the last forty or fifty years, i.e. during the period of 60 to 80 per cent urbanisation. During the nineteenth century when the people were flocking into the western cities there were no statistics on unemployment. In the same way people have been flocking into Nairobi over the last forty years. Many of the new urban immigrants in nineteenth-century Europe or in twentieth-century Kenya were unable to find work with government or the official companies. In both cases people have reverted to self-help.

Nairobi has had a 'self-help' sector from the origin of the city in 1900. The railhead camps attracted traders from the coast, casual traders, prostitutes, and an apparently 'surplus' population of Indians, Arabs, Somalis and others. As Rev. Andrew Hake has argued,

> from the point of view of the authorities, they were 'surplus' to the needs of the town and its economy, and comprised a menace to health and to law and order. But they themselves had discerned that the railway represented the wave of the future development, and that the little settlement at Nairobi was a place where opportunities would be found for getting, first the pickings of the operation, and later, perhaps, a place within its ranks. Here, in embryo, was the 'self help' city, whose citizens were to live in the interstices and fringes of Nairobi down through the years that followed.

In one sense, as Hake's work on the characteristics of the urban immigrants indicates, it is the young, energetic and slightly better educated who tend to come, and when they fail to find official work, it is not surprising to find that they become small-scale entrepreneurs.

Rev. Hake has documented the character of the self-help city, and it is worth noting here. The new arrival stays with a relative for as long as they will have him or until he is forced to move to another kinsman. After a while, after direct approach to employers, waiting at the gates of building sites, factories and warehouses, he would find himself moving from temporary friend to temporary friend and relying on an ever-widening group of people for food and shelter. Very soon, if the man does not go home, he is forced into one of a whole range of self-help occupations, most of which have always been illegal. Rev. Hake listed over twenty categories of work in this area, as follows : unregistered and underpaid ayahs, brewers and distillers, professional prostitutes, scrap metal and bottle collectors, building material collectors, unregistered shamba cultivators, hand-cart porters, unlicensed shopkeepers, licensed and unlicensed hawkers, woodcarvers, parking boys, maize roasters, scavengers, beggars, car washers, open air barbers, traditional doctors, gaming operators and entertainers. These groups are all outside the law, but in their own way they generate employment; their activities are recorded only with the police and are open to continuous harassment. They are of course part of the free enterprise economy.

In Kisenyi, Kampala, the self-help city has also grown up, probably under very similar circumstances as A. W. Southall has noted :

Initiative in Kisenyi may not be directed into the most laudable channels, but initiative of a kind there is. Besides the tailors, cobblers, 'hotels', beer shops, carpenters, hairdressers, matoke dealers, butchers, brothels and general stores, it is here that numerous hawkers and itinerant traders are to be met. There are the water sellers, the charcoal sellers, the sellers of buns and savoury pies, of palm leaf floor mat weaving or of papyrus rushes, the dealers in old tins . . .

Here is the self-help city, the proof, if any were needed, that private initiative and small-scale private enterprise has existed since the beginning of the century – that in the end whether men *co-operate* to build a town or nation, or whether they operate as *individuals* living on their personal enterprise and wits, depends on structure and opportunities in the community in which they find themselves.

Conclusion

This chapter has emphasised (*a*) the extremely rapid growth of the major towns of East Africa, (*b*) the uneven growth rate between the many small towns and the one or two large towns and (*c*) the different origins of the two capital cities, both of which show a remarkable similarity in their growth – both have developed a duality, an area of large spacious homes for the rich and a cluster of huts for the poor. This picture is over-simplified; the variety of homes between the richest European and the poorest, and between the richest African and the poorest, has always been considerable. The aim has been to try to draw the outlines of the development.

The urban capital cities of both territories, perhaps more today than in the past, represent the unevenness and the disequilibrium in the society as a whole. The fact that they are growing so much more rapidly in terms of total numbers, that the proportion of the dispossessed in the city – the homeless, jobless and landless – is also growing is but an expression of the unevenness in development. The patterns of urban growth, which are illustrated on the map on p. 252, show a definite tendency towards population and industrial concentration. This tendency towards concentration in the capital cities needs to be understood in relation to the growth of concentration in industry, marketing and banking.

These changes are part of the same process of capitalist development, alongside under-development. At one level in both societies, political and economic power has continued to be sucked into the centre, which clearly can benefit only a small proportion of the population. The urban disequilibrium between the slums on the one hand and the garden cities on the other expresses the societies' disequilibrium more openly than any other aspect of development this century.

14 Money and Banking

Introduction

In this chapter we shall examine the history of money in East Africa. First of all we need to understand the nature or the characteristics of money. Money is a universal medium which expresses the value of goods and commodities in the community. Money is universal in the sense that all goods can be valued through the same medium. Thus today we can say that so-and-so is worth so many shillings, thereby not only expressing the value which we place on so-and-so but also expressing its *exchange* value. Money is thus also an expression of the value for which we will exchange one good for another. Clearly therefore, money simplifies exchange as it provides a universal system against which all goods can be valued. Today in East Africa all goods are valued in terms of shillings so that the value of any one good can be compared with that of any other.

Money by itself is valueless. It only becomes valuable when the people who use it are satisfied that when they take it to someone else it will be accepted for the same value as when they first received it. In other words, the public must feel *confidence* that the money they have will keep its value for the period in which they hold it. If this confidence is lacking, people will cease to want to own money at all: they will rather hold their wealth in goods instead.

So long as people have confidence that the money will maintain its value then some will be willing to store it or keep it, in other words, to save money. This is another important characteristic of money: that it can be stored easily, and will not lose its value during the period of storage. This is where the banks begin to come into the picture. In the modern world the banks store money for individuals: the bank is regarded as a safe place to put money. At the same time, the bank may 'borrow' the money it is storing for its customers and use it for investment. In this case, the bank will pay interest to its depositors for as long as the money is left with them. In this way the banks play an important role in the financial affairs of any country: (*a*) as a place in which money can be stored for safe-keeping, (*b*) as institutions which redistribute the surplus wealth of the community and (*c*) as institutions which enable their depositors to accumulate additional wealth through interest on their loans to the banks.

A final question which we can ask about money is, what determines the monetary value of a commodity? There is no fixed monetary value for any good, rather, the value is determined by the ratio between the supply of money available and the supply of and demand for goods in the community. For instance, if the supply of money is ten shillings between ten people, and if there are ten *suffurias* available for sale, provided that each of the ten people wanted a *suffuria* and that each had an equal share of the money available, then the price of each *suffuria* would be one shilling. If these ten people had twenty shillings between them, then the price of *suffurias* would rise to two shillings each. Thus if the supply of money (currency) alters but the supply of and demand for goods remains the same, the money value of the goods will alter. On the other hand, if the supply of money stayed constant but the supply of goods increased, then the value of each good would decline. If for example, our ten men with ten shillings were faced with a supply of twenty *suffurias*, each *suffuria* would sell for fifty cents, other things being equal.

We have argued that money has the following characteristics :

   (i) it provides a universal measure of value for goods;
  (ii) it facilitates the exchange of goods;
 (iii) its value is dependent upon peoples' confidence in it;
 (iv) it can be used to store wealth; and
  (v) the money values of goods are determined by the ratio between the money supply and the supply of and demand for goods.

Let us therefore take a quick look at money in nineteenth-century East Africa. We have already seen from earlier chapters that exchange was widespread before the colonial period. The most widely practised means of exchanging goods was through a system of barter. In other words, one good was exchanged for another good without any form of money coming into the transaction. Barter is a complex and cumbersome method of exchange for a number of reasons. First, the good to be exchanged has to be carried to the market-place before the exchange can take place. Money would be much easier to carry around and easier to transfer from one person to another than, say, a hoe or a goat. In a barter system then, exchange generally only takes place between near neighbours or over short distances. Clearly, the more trading there is in a community, the more need there will be for a portable medium of exchange. Secondly, under a barter system, it is not always easy to get the goods one wants in exchange for the goods one has. If you have beans and you want maize, you must find someone who has maize but wants beans. In the nineteenth century if someone wanted imported goods from the coast it might have been necessary to get ivory to make the exchange and this meant either hunting and killing elephant, or getting tusks from someone who had already done the hunting and killing. It seems probable that it was often necessary to go through a complicated exercise of exchange, involving several different goods before one ended up with what one wanted. Again, it would be much easier if there was some good, or money, which was desired by everyone, so that all exchanges could take place in this medium.

Over most of Eastern Africa there was a shortage of coins as a medium of exchange until the advent of the colonial period. On the other hand, a number of commodities in short supply (salt, cloth, iron and copper – in the form of ingots, bars, wire, weapons and tools) were accepted as a form of currency. Because these articles were in short supply and because they were to some extent durable, they could be used as mediums of exchange and would pass through a number of hands, which eased the mechanics of exchange. From the nineteenth century too, cowrie shells and beads began to be widely used along the major trade routes as a form of currency. The cowrie shells were brought to the coast by dhows. By about 1860, 2500 cowrie shells could be exchanged for a cow around Lake Victoria, but as more and more cowries were imported, they tended to lose their value. They depreciated as the ratio between money or cowries supply, and demand for and supply of goods altered. This meant that *more* cowries were needed to buy the same cow because the supply of cowries increased faster than the supply of cows.

The importance of cowries and beads was that they made exchange easier, as they acted as almost universal forms of value and because they were comparatively easy to carry around. They would be accepted as exchange for almost any commodity and transactions could take place anywhere. In addition they were valued because they were in relatively short supply, they could be divided into small units, they could be safely stored for future needs and finally, they were valued as decoration, that is, they had an intrinsic value beyond their exchange value. These are all important characteristics of exchange mediums.

Capitalist finance and mediums of exchange

1. British money and banking up to 1914
Gold and silver have all the qualities of money mentioned above.

They are in short supply, and have for many hundreds of years played major roles in exchange systems in most parts of the world.

The British used gold in the form of sovereigns as their standard of money until 1914. Specialists in selling gold coin and bullion (goldsmiths) began to play a major financial role from the seventeenth century in England. People soon learnt to keep their gold with the goldsmith for safe-keeping and the goldsmiths gave their clients (or depositors) receipts for the gold they held for them. The receipts could then pass from hand to hand as a form of payment for goods : whoever held a receipt could go and cash it with the goldsmith for gold. In this way, the receipts for gold themselves began to act as a medium of exchange. Thus the goldsmiths were the early bankers, holding gold for people and providing receipts which could circulate freely and which were the original bank-notes. Banks from the earliest times, therefore, were the places where people could store their wealth and from which they could get credit in the form of receipts or bank-notes.

In the seventeenth and eighteenth centuries banks began to issue their own bank-notes; many started to issue notes without the backing of gold because they hoped that not all their creditors would ask to have their notes redeemed for gold at any one time. For this credit service they charged interest, a percentage of the value of the credit extended to their customers. The banks were thus putting more cash into circulation than there was a gold supply to back it. In this way they were increasing the number of commercial transactions which could be carried out in the community and played a very important part in the development of the economy. Everything went well, so long as everyone did not claim the gold equivalent of their bank-notes at the same time. In the nineteenth century a number of financial crises, caused in the main by runs on the banks, had occurred and in 1844 it was decided that only one central bank, the Bank of England, should be allowed to issue bank-notes in England. The Bank was allowed to issue only a limited number of notes without the backing of gold (the fiduciary issue) and, because it had large supplies of gold in its vaults, and because the fiduciary issue was limited, the Bank was always able to meet the demand for gold from its creditors, and thus established a reputation for financial stability and reliability. To say that something was 'as safe as the Bank of England' became a popular way of saying that something could be relied on absolutely. As a result London, with the Bank of England at the centre, became the centre of the banking world and international traders became accustomed to banking in London, using Bank of England notes for security. Traders trusted that the notes could be exchanged for gold on demand, and sterling (British bank-notes and coins) became an international currency in the nineteenth century.

The strength of the banking system in the nineteenth century in England was that it offered safe credit facilities. People could deposit their gold in London banks and would be issued with promissory notes (at a small discount) in exchange, and would know that the bank would not go bankrupt. The banks operated on the basis that they would not have to exchange all their gold for notes at one time and so (with definite limitations) they offered out more promissory notes than they had gold in their vaults. In this way banks increased the supply of money and functioned as financial intermediaries by offering new purchasing power to any industrial or commercial undertaking which they felt could (*a*) repay the credit and (*b*) repay the interest on the loan.

This was a critical factor about the money system operated by British banks in the nineteenth century : they not only reflected the system of exchange but also determined the growth and direction of industry and commerce by directing financial resources (credit) to those institutions which were believed to be good credit risks. This factor is crucial to the understanding of the role of banks in Africa. *The banks had the ability consciously to direct financial resources in this direction or that, within the confines of profitability, to stimulate the development of some productive resources and to leave others alone.*

At the period of colonisation, therefore, London was the centre of the financial world, operating a system of gold against sterling notes. Thus the monetary system introduced into East Africa reflected not the indigenous system of exchange, but an entirely different system. It was one based on gold and sterling and a subsidiary dependant on the British system. It was a colonial monetary system tied to British sterling.

2. *The colonial financial system*

A colonial financial system was one which was implanted by the imperial authority. The following characteristics of the financial systems in use up to 1962–3 in Kenya and Uganda were typical of such a colonial financial system, and were all four created and controlled by the metropolitan centre :

  (i) the currency in use;
 (ii) the rates of exchange of the currency in use with the metropolitan currency (sterling);
(iii) the bank structure and loan policies; and
(iv) the determination of the supply in cash.

Until the early 1920s the currency in use in East Africa was the Indian rupee. The Indian currency system, like its counterpart, the Indian legal system, was lifted wholesale into East Africa. There was a certain logic about introducing rupees into East Africa. By the end of the nineteenth century Indian bankers dominated the Zanzibar ivory and caravan trades. Indians were the earliest financiers in the area. Then with the rapid expansion of Indian trading activities, moving up along the line of rail, rupees became the currency of commerce at the turn of the century. It was the currency which was most readily available and acceptable to the traders. Hence the British made the Indian silver rupee into the standard coin for British territories in East Africa. The anna, pice and rupee were made legal tender in Kenya in 1898 and in Uganda in 1906. In order to make the rupee in East Africa exchangeable into sterling the exchange rate was fixed at fifteen rupees to the British gold sovereign. Anyone wanting to bring foreign cash into the country simply exchanged the foreign cash for rupees through the Currency Board in Nairobi.

In 1910 the anna and pice were dispensed with and the rupee in East Africa was divided into 100 cents, and new fifty, twenty-five, ten, one and half-cent coins were created. While this new coinage was being introduced, the cowrie shell currency continued in use for a number of years. In 1901 800 cowries could be exchanged for one rupee in Uganda, and in the meantime the colonial government accepted cowries for tax payments. The cowries finally went out of use round about 1909.

The first bank to be set up was not unnaturally the National Bank of India, in Zanzibar in 1893 and in Mombasa in 1896. Rapidly the National Bank of India (a colonial British-owned bank, despite its name) established branches in Entebbe, Kampala and Jinja. The Standard Bank of South Africa (also a British colonial bank) came soon after and by 1910 it had seven branches in Kenya, two in Uganda and eight in Tanganyika.

These two banks, together with Barclays D.C.O. (Dominions, Colonial and Overseas, originally called the National Bank of South Africa) which began to operate in East Africa during the 1914–18 war, all had their headquarters in London and their main offices in their British colony of origin. They were specialist banks in that they dealt with British overseas currency and banking. As their reserves were held in London, they were tied firmly to sterling although they were concerned with trade to and from British colonies. They were established primarily to service British overseas colonial capital, that is, to provide banking services for the export and import of British goods and capital, which from the 1850s had been invested all over the world. These banks thus financed the needs of British industry for food and raw materials, the export of consumer goods and capital equipment and they financed the development of mining and export crop production in the colonies. Not surprisingly therefore, they dealt almost exclusively with an expatriate clientele in their dealings in finance, commerce and production. Also not surprisingly these banks preferred short-term rather than long-term loans to their clients as business tended to be risky. These banks, then, operated straightforwardly as outposts of London, with concern for the host country. Their terms and the level of credit offered were determined by the London money market.

In Kenya loans were offered to white farmers and in Uganda the banks entered the Asian bazaars. They offered overdrafts to traders against the security of trade bills. They also provided mortgages (credit on the security of title deeds of property) for farmers and ginners. Essentially the early financial structure in the two territories reflected the basic economic aims of colonial development : the encouragement of export crop production for the European market and the encouragement of the import of British finished goods. This was the basis of the banking system up to 1918.

Financial development in East Africa, 1918–1940

1. The financial crisis of 1919–20 and the establishment of the East African Currency Board

Again we must return to the world financial scene in order to make sense of the financial crisis which hit East Africa in 1919–20 and which led to the creation of the East African Currency Board, the institution which ordered the financial affairs of the territories until Independence.

In the world as a whole, up to 1914, the gold standard was the basis of financial dealing and systems. In Britain all Bank of England notes were in theory exchangeable into gold. Gold was valued at (sterling) £3 17s. 10½d. per standard ounce, from 1844 to 1931. However, during the 1914–18 war economic activity in Europe was greatly expanded and the Bank of England printed more notes than it had gold stocks in its vaults in order to finance the war effort. Thus for the duration of the war Britain left the gold standard and simply printed money according to her needs and did not guarantee to exchange bank-notes for their gold equivalent. During this period the amount of paper money printed by Britain increased faster than the increase in the amount of goods her industries were producing. The result was inflation : prices of

goods rose as the supply of money increased faster than the supply
of goods and the purchasing power or real value of money therefore declined. For instance if a bicycle cost an individual buyer £10
in cash in 1914, by 1918 that same bicycle might have cost as much
as £20. In fact the purchasing power of sterling declined by 40 per
cent between 1914 and 1920.

In India up to 1914 the silver rupee was the basic unit of currency. In 1914 the silver rupee also ceased to be tied to gold and
sterling. As a result the paper rupee inflated in the same manner
as sterling as more rupees were printed in India than there were
goods available. Because the rupee after 1914 was not tied to gold
the value of the rupee altered *separately* from the value of sterling.
Thus the pound sterling inflated according to conditions in Britain
and the Indian rupee in India inflated according to conditions in
India. This situation was difficult for East Africa as she was, in a
financial sense, in the the middle of these two systems; she used
the silver rupee as her basic currency coin, but imported sterling
in large amounts from selling coffee, sisal, cotton and so on to the
London market. So long as the value of silver was determined in
relation to the value of gold, East Africa could take the silver rupee
with confidence and exchange it for pounds sterling. During the
war however, the rate of exchange between sterling and rupees
altered separately as neither was tied to a common gold standard,
and this put the East African currency in a difficult position.

As we saw above, the Indian silver rupee had been made the
standard coin in East Africa from 1898. In 1905 the exchange value
between Indian silver rupees and the British gold sovereign had
been set at fifteen rupees to the sovereign. At this time one paper
pound sterling was exchangeable for one gold sovereign, so sterling, and rupees in East Africa, enjoyed a stable and fixed rate of
exchange (15 rupees = 1 sovereign = £1). But as we have seen, sterling and Indian rupees ceased to be tied together after 1914 and
the exchange values of the two currencies began to alter. By
1918–19 £1 sterling was worth only ten rupees at the banks and
by November 1919 less than eight rupees were being exchanged
for £1. The reasons for the changing exchange rates were due to
conditions outside East Africa, and therefore do not concern us
here, but the consequences of the changes in the exchange rate were
of great importance to East Africa. As the rates changed, some
people began to gain and some to lose, and as long as the
rates continued to alter, no one could be sure what would happen
next. A situation of insecurity was created.

The rapid changes in the exchange rate between sterling and
rupees might have been avoided if Britain had returned to the gold

standard at the end of the war. In that case, the paper pound would again have been fixed in terms of gold and then in terms of silver. However, in 1918 when Britain wanted to return to the gold standard, she was unable to do so at the old pre-war level because during the war she had lost stocks of gold, mainly through buying goods in the United States, and she no longer had enough stocks of gold to support her paper currency (which had increased in quantity during the war) at the old rate. A return to the gold standard therefore could not be made immediately, and as a result currencies such as rupees were able to alter in value in relation to sterling.

In East Africa some groups of people suffered from the altering exchange rate, as follows:

1. Those who had borrowed money in rupees and had to repay the loans and pay the interest on them in sterling, which had to come from London. In effect in 1918 they were paying *more* for their loans than previously.

2. Those who exported goods to Britain for sterling, and who then had to change their sterling into rupees for local expenses. By 1919 they could only get eight rupees for every pound instead of fifteen as in 1913.

3. New settlers who were coming to East Africa in 1919 and who brought sterling assets with them and then had to get rupees for their local expenses (a soldier-settlement scheme in Kenya coincided with the currency crisis). In other words, anyone who was getting their money in sterling and had to convert it into rupees to pay local wages or to obtain other services and goods was suffering. During the war labourers' wages had remained constant in terms of cents and rupees and the changing exchange rates meant that in effect employers were paying more in terms of sterling for their labour even though the number of cents and rupees had not changed. This was a major problem for the settlers and the government.

Other groups gained from the situation, as follows:

1. Those people who sold their exports to India for rupees and then changed them to sterling to buy goods in Britain.

2. Those people who had bought land when the value of the rupee was fifteen to the pound (before the war) and sold it after the war when the value of the rupee had appreciated in terms of sterling.

3. Banks who held rupee debts and who were taking sterling in repayment.

4. Labourers whose wages remained unchanged.

While the exchange rate continued to alter, the extent to which any individual gained or lost depended on the point of time at which he made his transactions. Thus someone exchanging pounds for rupees in 1919 got less rupees than he would have got in 1918, and if the situation continued unchecked, he might well have got even fewer rupees for the same number of pounds in 1920. As we have seen above, many settlers were losing on the currency exchange market. At the same time other factors were causing them hardships. By 1920 the prices they received for their exports had declined rapidly. In that year, export prices were between 300 and 800 per cent lower than they had been a few months previously. Thus their supply of sterling was declining at the very time when they needed more to buy rupees. As we saw in Uganda it was these conditions (unfavourable exchange rates and the fall in prices of exported goods) which caused the collapse of the Uganda white settlers.

There is no doubt that, from the point of view of the colonial officials and the settlers, what we have been describing was a major financial crisis. The outcome was to affect the monetary arrangements and the financial structure of East Africa until 1967. At the time anyone who had a stake in holding or using money as a part of their daily affairs felt a loss of confidence in the value of the currency which they were using. The imperial authority, in conjunction with the colonial authorities, decided to try and stabilise the situation by pegging the rupee to sterling in East Africa by law. After considerable argument it was decided to fix the rate of exchange at 10 rupees to the pound sterling. At first the settlers seemed to be reasonably satisfied with this proposal. Although settlers with debts to repay would, under the new arrangements, have to pay more shillings and pounds for their debts (£1 for every 10 Rs debt, instead of £1 for every 15 Rs debt) than under the pre-war arrangements, they might have been worse off if the rates had continued to change. But then two things happened. First the exchange rate of rupees to sterling on the open market (in India and outside East Africa where the exchange rate was not fixed by law) altered in the opposite direction, so that rupees *lost* their value in exchange for sterling. Between June 1920 and February 1921 the value of the rupee against sterling declined until it once again reached the old 1913 level of 15 Rs to £1 sterling. Secondly, as a result of this downward movement in the value of rupees on the open market, people found that they could exchange rupees for sterling in East Africa at the rate of 10 to £1 and then exchange the sterling back to rupees on the open market at £1 to 15 Rs and so make a 50 per cent profit. As a result, rupees began to flood the East African market so that the colonial authority retaliated in February 1921 by declaring the rupee to be no longer legal tender in East Africa, substituting in its stead two East African shillings for one rupee. From then on, until 1923 in Kenya and 1926 in Uganda, the demonetised rupees were collected in and replaced by shillings.

When the rupee on the open market began to decline in value against the pound after June 1920 the settler community began to feel that their original agreement to the new fixed rate of exchange in East Africa was against their interests and they attempted to campaign for a return to the old exchange rate of 15 Rs to the pound sterling. This campaign, however, failed. They then tried to reduce the effective value of the rupee from another direction. At the time of the change-over to a shilling currency the two-shilling piece, or florin, was divided into 100 cents, just as the old rupee had been divided into 100 cents before. The settlers, apparently in league with the Governor, attempted to get the shilling piece as the new unit of account, divided into 100 cents, hoping that by continuing to pay wages in cents at the new rate they would effectively halve their wages bills. They failed to bring off this subterfuge, although they did manage to reduce wage rates by other means by 33 per cent throughout Kenya between 1921 and 1923.

After 1921 and until Independence East Africa remained on a shilling standard and the East African shilling was exchangeable with the British shilling on a one-to-one basis. During this period of time sterling was one of the two international trading currencies, so that a stable exchange with sterling offered stability to holders of East African currency, and it was stability above all else that the British government wanted for their colonies.

In fact Britain never returned fully to the gold standard after the 1914–18 war; in 1926 she went onto a 'gold bar standard' and then finally went off the international gold standard in 1931. In 1936 Britain made an agreement with the United States to exchange £1 for 2·4 dollars, an exchange rate which remained until 1949. The United States dollar became the world's dominant currency during the inter-war period and since then until recent years all capitalist countries have taken the ultimate value of their currencies from the dollar. The East African shilling took its value from sterling which meant in practice that the East African economies were tied to the British economy until 1967. Thus when sterling inflated so too did the East African shilling. This system of exchange provided security for British investors in East Africa, which was the intention, but ignored any changes in East African production which differed from changes in the British economy. Thus the monetary system reflected in a very real manner East Africa's dependency on the British economy throughout the colonial period.

To return to the 1920s. In April 1920 the East African Currency Board was set up to supervise the monetary system in East Africa. Basically the Board had the following functions:

(i) to organise the change from the rupee-based currency to the shilling-based currency in East Africa by 'buying up' all the rupees in circulation;

(ii) to issue East African notes and coin against sterling at the rate of 20 East African shillings to £1 sterling; and

(iii) to obtain British and colonial government securities for the sterling it collected from the exchange.

The Board worked in this way: if you were a settler or a trader and you wished to bring into East Africa £100 sterling, you placed the £100 with a commercial bank, say, Barclays; Barclays then sent the £100 to the East African Currency Board who then printed and coined another £100 in East African notes and coins which was then sent back to Barclays. Barclays would then give you the £100 East African. The £100 sterling which the Currency Board held was then used to buy government securities. The idea was that the newly-created East African currency issue would be backed 100 per cent by British securities in the form of government bonds. The aim was to create *security* for currency holders and investors who would know that the Board could always sell their securities to raise sterling should the investors wish to reconvert their East African currency holdings into sterling.

In practice the Board did not have 100 per cent security because (a) it inherited a deficit of £246,000 as the existing East African currency in circulation in 1919 was in excess of sterling assets and (b) the Board had undertaken to convert the whole of the existing rupee currency in East Africa into shillings. The Board made a loss on the conversion because until 1927 it exchanged 1 rupee for 2 shillings in East Africa, but when it then exchanged the rupees collected on the open market (i.e. to India) it had to accept the open market price for rupees which from 1921 was considerably less than 2 shillings each. By 1925 the Board had created £5·61 millions in East African currency, but its actual reserve fund in sterling assets was only £2·45 millions; by 1940 the figures stood at £6·93 millions East African and £3·74 millions sterling.

The Currency Board had its headquarters in London with a government advisory board in Nairobi which consisted of the bank managers of the three main commercial banks operating in East Africa. Between 1927 and 1930 they dealt with £9–10 million sterling going in and out of East Africa annually. Most of this cash flow came to and from London while the rest moved around the world.

2. *The commercial and merchant banks*

In the 1920s and 1930s the economic development of the settlers in Kenya and the cotton ginners and distributors in Uganda was financed through the commercial and merchant banks operating in the territories. The commercial banks were branches of British banks which provided some mortgage facilities for settler farmers and overdrafts to suitable clients in Uganda. There was no thought of extending credit facilities to the indigenous peoples during these years because few Africans had registered land which they could offer as security against a loan from the banks. In Uganda the Kabaka was supposed to have had a bank account, but he was virtually the only African in that position. The commercial banks understood their role within the successful but generally conservative British banking tradition, which involved offering relatively short-term loans to people whom the local bank manager knew personally – in other words, to expatriate whites.

Most bank loans in this period went to Kenya settlers. They were able to mortgage their land as security against loans from the commercial banks and they could offer their future incomes from export crops as security for loans from the merchant banks. The banks demanded between eight and ten per cent interest on loans to settlers. Although today we would not consider these rates to be very high, at the time they were comparatively high rates of interest, principally because the banks thought of farming as a risky business. The settlers, therefore, had a comparatively high interest burden to carry. Moreover. the commercial banks lent credit to settlers on the basis of the future value of their total land-holdings rather than on the value of the land in productive use. As only about one-third of most settlers' land was in productive use this meant that settlers tended to borrow more than they could possibly hope to repay in the short run. The settlers were, therefore, over-borrowing and this led to severe indebtedness which built up during the 1920s and hit the farmers particularly hard during the depression of 1930–6. Many banks had to foreclose on their mortgages during this time, and found themselves owners of land. Roughly about 25 per cent of the settlers went bankrupt during this time.

The merchant banks offered loans on the security of settlers' export crops. They provided credit against future sales on the understanding that the borrowers would sell their crops through the bank. The more important banks involved in these transactions were Arbuthnot Latham, Dalgety, Mitchell Cotts, J. Gilliats and Jardine Matheson. They were concerned to obtain the crops, and ship and sell them in Britain and elsewhere. They would offer farmers six or nine months loans on the expected value of the crops which then had to be sold through the merchant banks.

The banking structure therefore was organised to provide short-term, high-interest loans. What the settler farmers needed, however, was long-term, low-interest loans. Many of them had little in the way of capital resources of their own, so that if they wished to develop their land, they had to rely on borrowing. If the settlers tried to use short-term loans to finance long-term improvements, they had to pay back the loans before the improvements had taken effect. Neither the commercial banks nor the merchant banks saw it as their purpose or in their tradition to provide the long-term interest which the settlers needed. What the settlers needed was a special land bank to provide for their special credit needs, in other words, an institution which would provide them with long-term, low-interest credit for developing and improving their farms. The importance of a land bank was well understood by many officials and the proposal for such a bank with a loan capital of £1 million was made in 1919. However the commercial banks did not support such a development and the Colonial Office refused to support the idea without the approval of the commercial banks. If the commercial banks had agreed to the idea, and had been prepared to put up some of the capital, probably the Colonial Office would have approved also. It was not until the 1930s that a land bank was finally established in Kenya.

3.   *The Land Bank*

The setting for the establishment of the Land Bank was the depression of the early 1930s. By this time the slump in world prices of primary commodities had seriously reduced the economic viability of settler farming. This, together with the settlers' increasing indebtedness, led the commercial banks to refuse to offer further credit to the settlers. Without some form of financial aid, it looked as if settler farming was doomed. In Uganda where the same situation prevailed, and where government support was not forthcoming, this is what happened; most settlers were unable to continue to farm without commercial bank credit, and they had to abandon farming. In Kenya the Land Bank saved the day for many farmers.

The Land Bank had originally been planned to provide loans to pastoral settler farmers for fencing and dipping facilities but it soon came to have a much broader function. Unlike the commercial and merchant banks, the Land Bank did not get its funds by mobilising local savings from individuals or institutional depositors. The Bank obtained its funds by borrowing on the London money market under government guarantee at about $4\frac{1}{2}$ per cent interest and then it re-lent the money to settler farmers at $6-6\frac{1}{2}$ per cent, well below the existing commercial rates. The Bank began its operation with a loan from London of £240,000; in 1933 another £260,000 loan was negotiated and three years later in 1936 yet another £500,000 was obtained. These loans brought the capital of the Bank to £1 million. Roughly one-fifth of all the settlers who approached the Bank for loan facilities had no security to offer against their loans. Very often, they were already in debt to the commercial and merchant banks. The majority of these settlers asked the Bank to take over part or all of their existing debts and to obtain their mortgage deeds from the mortgagees. By 1938, just under 40 per cent of all monies lent by the Land Bank had been used solely for the purpose of discharging settlers' debts and it is probable that a considerable portion of the rest had been used likewise. In short the major function of the Bank in this period was to relieve indebted settlers of their debt burdens and thus it helped to maintain impoverished settlers on their farms.

The support offered by the Land Bank was not the only source of aid that the settlers could draw on in the 1930s. In 1930 the Agricultural Advances Ordinance provided over £200,000 in loans to settler farmers, and the Mortgages Relief Ordinance of 1936 stopped the commercial banks and other lenders from foreclosing on white farmers' property in lieu of annual interest repayments. In Kenya it was these special banking facilities which supported the settlers in their hour of greatest need and ensured the continuance of white farming in the colony.

Money and Banking, 1945–1970

In the period after the Second World War up to 1970 the financial structure of East Africa altered considerably. After 1945 the money and banking institutions expanded rapidly, in line with the growth of marketing and industry: by 1970 the pre-1940 structure was hardly discernible. Three major schemes ran through the changes which occurred. First, financial activity increased. For instance, the number of commercial banks operating in East Africa increased rapidly; the loan policies of the old private banks were also expanded and there was a marked rise in the inflow of foreign funds to finance both public and private ventures. Secondly, the old East Africa Currency Board was replaced by a central banking organisation. Finally the commercial banks were careful to restrict their lending to secure and profitable enterprises, and this left major areas of the economy under-financed as they could not guarantee the security and profitability demanded by the banks.

1.   The growth of the banking structure

Between 1918 and 1951, apart from the Land Bank, no new banks were established in East Africa. Through the 1950s and early 1960s, however, a number of banks began operations in East Africa, creating between them a new network of banks in the major cities. In 1951 the Nederlandsche Handel-Maatschappi came to East Africa, followed in 1953 by the Bank of India and in 1954 by the Bank of Baroda. In 1956 the Habib Bank started operations, then the Ottoman Bank in 1958, the Commercial Bank of Africa in 1961 and the Bank of Pakistan in 1962.

Likewise during the 1950s and early 1960s, the older–established commercial banks (mainly the three old British banks) expanded very rapidly by setting up new branch banks in the smaller towns. Between 1949 and 1960 in Kenya alone the number of towns with a banking service increased from 12 to 65 and the number of branch banks from 22 to 139. The three major commercial banks owned 85 per cent of all the banking offices in East Africa. Kenya, with its greater number of expatriates and its more successful policy of industrialisation, had exactly 50 per cent of the expansion of branch banking. By 1964 Kenya had 164 bank offices as against 91 in Tanzania and 70 in Uganda.

Another development in banking which occurred before Independence was the growth of hire-purchase and housing-finance companies. Both types of institutions are banks in so far as they hold money deposits and lend cash for specific purposes. Unlike the commercial banks, however, they do not operate current accounts. In the field of hire purchase the Credit Finance Corporation was set up in 1955, Lombard Banking (East Africa), National Industrial Credit and the United Dominion Corporation around 1959. For housing finance, The Kenya Building Society and Saving and Loan Society were established in 1949, followed in the 1950s by the Housing Finance Corporation and the Permanent Building Society. All these hire-purchase and housing-finance companies were branches of larger companies in Europe which set out to mobilise funds in East Africa. It is important to note that this flurry of international financial activity in the private sector in East Africa occurred at a time of industrial and marketing growth, in the 1950s, a period of rapid expansion in East Africa.

After Independence the main growth areas on the banking and finance scene were in the sphere of government-organised banking. Agricultural finance for the large estates, small 'progressive' farms, co-operatives and settlement schemes were all initiated by government-backed parastatal finance organisations. In the early 1960s all the private banking institutions were hit by falling-off of financial confidence in East Africa as a great deal of money was repatriated to Europe. However, the banks, like industry, picked up again after 1965.

2. Loan policy

Throughout the 1950s and 1960s commercial activity in East Africa increased, and the bank's policies on loans reflected this growth. Both bank deposits and bank advances (loans) rose substantially, with advances increasing even more rapidly than deposits, as the following table shows:

TABLE 14.1

Bank deposits and advances in Uganda, 1938–1968

	Deposits U£ (millions)	Advances U£ (millions)	Advances ratio (percentage)
1938	1·8	0·6	33
1948	6·4	3·0	45
1958	17·5	11·5	66
1968	42·0	33·0	75

Source: Background to the Budget, Government Printer, Kampala.

The same picture could be seen in Kenya's statistics for bank deposits and advances.

From the table above it is clear that (a) both deposits and advances have been rising very rapidly, (b) advances have been rising even more rapidly than deposits, hence the increase in the advances ratio, and (c) up to 1948 (in fact up to 1952) the ratio of advances to deposits was annually below 45 per cent but after 1952 the ratio increased even more rapidly. Up to 1952 the East African commercial banks had been borrowing (i.e. receiving deposits) more money than they needed in East Africa and so they re-lent in Europe. In effect from 1900–52 savings mobilised in the colonies were being used for economic development in Europe. From 1954–5 the ratio of advances to deposits began to increase very rapidly – to 78 per cent and up to 94 per cent by 1970. This meant that banks were lending domestically (i.e. in East Africa) nearly as much as they were borrowing in East Africa and in fact the table under-represents the extent of the increase. This situation was felt to be unsafe because there was little cash left in the bank reserves for cases of emergencies, so the banks began to borrow from Europe in order to increase the amount of cash available for loans in East Africa. Thus from about 1955 until 1972 the situation was reversed in the sense that bank credit ceased to flow out of East Africa and began to flow in instead.

The advances and deposits refer to the activities of locally-established banks and so to money which has been mobilised from domestic sources, in East African currency. The other side of the same story was the growth of loans from overseas, mainly from Europe and the United States. This cash, which has so often gone under the euphemism of 'aid', is usually lent at 5 per cent or more, like any other bank loan.

Foreign borrowing accelerated in the 1950s for two major reasons. First, public revenues, taxes and local borrowings had not grown fast enough to pay for official investment projects (schools, hospitals, roads, etc.) and secondly, trading currencies (like sterling) were needed in large quantities to pay for the growing burden of imports (see Chapter 10). If foreign currency was not obtained through foreign loans, the only alternative would have been to raise cash domestically through higher taxes (forced saving). If people were forced to pay higher taxes it would have meant a lower consumption rate for everybody, including the newly-rich, the petty bourgeoisie of East Africa, who placed such a high value on social status and style, as expressed in the possession of foreign radios, cars, clothing, etc. In fact the annual inflows of foreign cash over the last fifty years, as we saw in the chapter on foreign trade, have closed the gap between the differences in domestic savings and domestic investment, while allowing a comparatively high rate of consumption for the colonial and post-colonial elites.

3. *The central banks*

Central banks were established in all three East African territories within a few years of Independence. The move from the East African Currency Board to central banks as a means of financial and monetary control was a reflection of the generally increased financial activity and the demand for local financial control in each country. Central banks are, in principle, concerned to provide a central control mechanism for a country's financial system. They should control the supply of domestic cash, administer the flows in and out of the country of foreign monies, and operate as the central bank for all the commercial banks in order to create stability in times of crisis. Central banks can also expand or reduce the commercial banks' credits through control of the rate of interest at which they lend to commercial banks and they can place legal controls on the level of credit in relation to the level of deposits. The basic purpose of a central bank, therefore, is to adjust the level of financial activity in the society, and they can play a creative role in regulating the money supply.

For many years the East African Currency Board had played only a passive role in financial affairs. It issued East African currency, but in no way affected the level of domestic credit. Thus the Board had simply supported short-term fluctuations in movements of foreign exchange and was unable to cushion the domestic market. During the 1930s and late 1950s, for instance, there had been a large outflow of foreign capital. During these outflows of cash the total amount of currency in circulation had decreased very considerably. Between 1956 and 1962 the currency held by the East African banks decreased from £9·6 million to £3·2 million. Before 1955 the Board had to increase the cash available to the community by creating new credits. In 1955, for the first time, the Board was allowed to offer credit to the government, up to £20 million and in 1960 this sum was raised to £25 million. By lending heavily to the governments during the period when money was leaving the countries, the Board was able to increase the flow of cash in the East African countries. Thus it was helping to offset the economic disadvantages created by the loss of confidence of the private investors.

The commercial banks at this time did not have their credit levels controlled from East Africa as there were no central banks. Their credit policy was controlled from their head offices in London, so that in a crisis of confidence they might either accelerate the crisis or act to offset it, according to the central office's policy. In practice the commercial banks helped to offset the outflow of money between 1956 and 1962 by increasing their own credit facilities. As a result of these operations, both the commercial banks and the Currency Board helped to limit the effect of the fall-off in confidence of the private capitalists in the years running up to Independence and immediately afterwards. By 1964 the private foreign investors' confidence in the viability of the East African economies had been re-established. The events of 1956 onwards showed that the level of financial activity and the goodwill of foreign investors had played a large part in determining the financial stability and growth of the East African economies. To release the economies from this dependence on the outside world local financial control seemed to be essential.

4.   Credit security and profitability

Since 1945 and particularly since Independence, the extension of
credit facilities and the expansion of the banks have reflected the
growing industrial activity of both Kenya and Uganda. As credit
has increased since 1945 the commercial banks have been plagued
by the problem of how to lend to institutions and individuals so that
profit can be maximised and security of repayment ensured. One
means to overcome this problem has been to reduce the competition
between commercial banks. A collective agreement was signed
between the big three commercial banks which was called the 'Summary Banking Arrangements in East Africa'. Not surprisingly this
document is closely guarded and is unknown to the general public.
It was designed to reduce competition between the banks over rates
of interest and other charges to customers. As new commercial
banks were set up, they are said to have signed the agreement.
Thus despite the diversity of commercial banks the services they
offer have been remarkably uniform.

There is some evidence to suggest that agricultural production
has received a low proportion of commercial bank credits in East
Africa since the 1930s. Up to 1929 the main commercial banks had
financed the international traders and the white farmers. The
depression illustrated that large-scale farming was neither a safe
investment nor profitable except over short periods. In Uganda,
where the proportion of large foreign-owned estates was comparatively small, it was not surprising that bank credit was so limited.
In Kenya the Land Bank, established in 1930, took over many of
the settlers' debts. Thus after 1945 the colonial government took
over the main responsibility for the provision of settler credits. It
organised the Cereals and Sugar Finance Corporation which
offered short-term finance for cereal producers before planting and
provided minimum annual payments. The Land and Agricultural
Bank continued to provide the long-term loans and it developed a
Rehabilitation Fund and a Development Loan Scheme for specific
agricultural purposes. Finally the government nominated the Agricultural Settlement Board to provide loans for new settlers. By the
1960s £9·5 million was being provided in credit. The volume of
cash directed to the large farmers through these government banking agencies rose from £9·5 million in 1960 to £11·2 million in
1964 and to £21·6 million in 1970. The commercial banks have
thus played a comparatively small part in Kenya's agricultural
development after 1940 and the government has taken over the
provision of credit to the less secure areas of the economy.

It is in line with these developments that the commercial banks
have been unwilling to lend to peasants. Until the early 1960s

nearly all lending was confined to Europeans and a few Asians: credit facilities were simply not available to Africans. The commercial banks were unwilling to lend to Africans for a number of reasons. Banks were unwilling to lend to small-scale concerns, particularly for peasant farming. This was against their British traditions. Most of the banks were branches of British banks with British managers and their policies were, therefore, based firmly on the interests of the head offices and their traditions; nowhere did British traditional banks offer credit services to peasants because it was not considered that peasant activities would be very profitable. Secondly, the commercial banks' original role was to finance the large farmers and the export–import trade; they were not interested in small-scale business, which was in any case a more difficult and insecure area of business. Thirdly, the commercial banks argued that the soundness of their banks (no bank had ever collapsed in East Africa) was based on their policies of applying a uniform standard of credit-worthiness to all their customers, whatever their race. The banks demanded a regular money income and property as security so that if the loan were not repaid, they could take the property instead. The problem was that many Africans could not provide such security, either in the form of property, registered land or stocks and shares, or in the form of a regular money income. The settler farmers in Kenya could not show a regular money income. They had property in the form of registered land but even so they could not always reach the banks' standards of credit-worthiness. The fourth reason that the banks gave was that Africans had not developed a 'banking habit' which meant that repayments of interest on loans was often forgotten. However, the 'banking habit' develops with experience, and as a result of the other three reasons which restricted credit to Africans, this habit was given little chance to develop. The argument was circular. Africans were represented as lacking banking assets, having a low credit-worthiness, and a low business mentality. Thus there was a vicious circle which prevented the development of credit facilities for Africans.

In practice therefore, the system was discriminatory because although the requirements for credit were the same for all peoples, the situations of the peoples were vastly different. Not only could the bank staff not communicate with local people but the level of security required for loans was too high for them to meet. Added to this there were government restrictions placed on Africans seeking credit. After 1948 any African who wanted credit from the banks for more than K£10 had to get permission from his District Officer. In 1955 the East African Royal Commission suggested that the law was made in order to protect the man who did not understand how the banking and credit systems worked; 'there is a manifest failure', the Report stated, 'on the part of many Africans to understand the essentially negotiable nature of any acceptable security'. Moreover the Land and Agricultural Bank and other government loans schemes applied in practice only to Europeans. The entire financial system was loaded against African participation until 1960.

In Uganda the Credit and Savings Bank, established in 1950, was the exception. It had a capital of half-a-million pounds sterling and was intended to promote small-scale African enterprises. However it lacked the expertise required for small-scale peasant banking and it rapidly ran into problems of loan repayments. However, it did manage to maintain itself in existence.

Conclusion

Two outstanding political events have occurred in East Africa during the last one hundred years. The establishment of colonial rule was the first. The achievement of independence of the East African states was the second. Can we estimate the economic significance of these two events for the peoples of Kenya and Uganda?

Any estimation of the significance of colonial rule has to start with an understanding of the dynamics of the pre-colonial economies. Before the colonial period, capitalist commodity relations of production had not affected production in East Africa to any great extent. This meant that the economic systems were not designed for planned annual growth, although there was surplus production and some accumulation of wealth. It seems probable that trade was central to accumulation, and thus an important dynamic within the pre-colonial economies. Trade provided for the exchange of goods between different regions and it occurred on a more or less equitable basis, with surpluses in one area being exchanged for surpluses in another. Everywhere one finds that while one area might specialise in goats, another would specialise in iron hoes, a third in fishing, a fourth in boat-building, a fifth in salt production, a sixth in arable crop growing, and so on according to ecological and climatological conditions. Small-scale specialisation of production and the exchange of surplus production between specialist producers were essential dynamics of the pre-colonial economies. In the lacustrine kingdoms accumulation through trade and specialised production was organised in a highly sophisticated manner with regular markets throughout the country. In other societies trade was also widespread although it was on a smaller scale and it was not regulated into organised markets to the same extent. Nevertheless, in these smaller societies, accumulation of wealth was certainly an important feature of the economy. For the pastoralists accumulation of animals was amongst the most important of all pursuits; even among agriculturalists animal accumulation was important.

Another important dynamic in the pre-colonial economies was population expansion: as the original units expanded in size the clans would subdivide and new pastures and agricultural lands would be opened to accommodate the growing populations. All societies seem to have been on the move, slowly expanding from one area to another, and we can see the importance of this expansionary process in the care with which the traditions of origin and migration have been kept in each group. Land tenure rights and systems of social and political control were everywhere legitimised by reference to these traditions, and formed the basis for production relations within the societies.

A third dynamic was technological change, but unlike the process of technological change in the modern period, here change was very gradual, a characteristic of pre-capitalist societies all over the world.

In the nineteenth century the penetration of Eastern Africa by Arab trade imperialism added a new dynamic factor to some pre-colonial economies. Unfortunately our knowledge of the effect of Arab trade on the pre-colonial economies of Kenya and Uganda is still meagre. In Tanzania some of the economic effects of Arab trade are more clearly seen : the rise to political prominence of Mirambo and other trader chieftains and the felt need to control the trade routes and to tax the trade had a major political and economic effect over a wide geographical area. In all the areas where they operated the Arab caravans introduced a new element into the pre-colonial economies. They wanted ivory, slaves, copper and a few other less important commodities. In return they offered consumer goods, from articles for personal adornment to cloth and luxury goods. So far as the local economies were concerned the Arab caravans represented the first stage of capitalist imperialism : local raw materials were exchanged for imported finished goods. The linkages between the Arab caravans with their Indian financiers and European shippers and traders, and the European and American demand for ivory and copper indicate clearly the economic connection between this trade and the imperialism of the nineteenth century. However, these linkages do not appear to have integrated the pre-colonial economies into the system of the world market in any fundamental way except perhaps along the coast where plantation production and commerce was geared towards the international economy. Elsewhere the Arab trade undoubtedly served to stimulate production, not only of items for export, but also of a range of intermediate goods. Salt and iron goods, for example, were often obtained by the caravans so that they could be traded for foodstuffs and export commodities at other stopping places. However the emphasis appears to be on producing more with the same techniques, rather than on developing new techniques of production. The new demands could be met almost everywhere within the context of the old economies, and the dynamics of accumulation through trade and expansion remained virtually unaltered.

Compared with the Arab trade imperialism, the European colonial invasion was traumatic for East African society. The invasion itself and the military resistance which followed throughout Kenya and Uganda was certainly less destructive of life than the new diseases and the inter-European war which came in the wake of the invaders. Between 1890 and 1923 hundreds of thousands of people died from disease, starvation, warfare and other pestilence, as was seen in Chapter 1. The initial effect of colonisation on the peoples of East Africa must have been demoralising and debilitating from a physical point of view. Its impact on local economies was equally devastating.

The new dynamic for economic growth was in effect a major expansion of the type of trade introduced by the Arabs, but a trade which was far more systematically organised. Food- and raw material-producing enclaves were intentionally introduced into Kenya and Uganda, while finished manufactures were imported on a far larger scale than ever before and the import–export economy thus created was centrally controlled by the invading power. This process effectively destroyed the dynamic factors of the older economies without giving them adequate access to the new dynamic. The old techniques of production of consumer items which had been refined over the years collapsed under the impact of the imported goods from the technologically advanced West and as a result, local trade declined rapidly. The traders themselves were replaced by the incoming Asians who had access to the new goods and the capital to finance their distribution. The dynamic of population growth was stopped dead and the development of 'tribal' reserves and boundaries stopped the associated geographical expansion and the opening up of new lands.

Did the imposition of the colonial economy introduce technological change as a dynamic in the local economies? For the Baganda, the demand for cotton stimulated a change in the relations of agricultural production and among those people who entered the market economy for domestic or export goods, the range of agricultural goods produced was modified; but as far as the techniques of production were concerned, few changes occurred. Apart from the introduction of the use of the imported *jembe*, which was probably a small improvement on the older, locally produced hoe, the techniques of production were little affected by western science and knowledge for about twenty years. The old problems of drought and famine had in no way lessened and may in some instances have became greater.

The direct result of this situation was that the old forms of accumulation continued, in particular the aggregation of livestock as a mark of wealth. With the introduction of coin as the medium of exchange cash was used to strengthen the old forms of accumulation, rather than to replace them. The old men remained the fount of wisdom and the deciders of planting time and other important events. Thus, while a great deal of the substance and the dynamics of the old economies had been destroyed, many of the old forms remained in operation.

The above generalisations probably held for the majority of the people of East Africa until the late 1940s when the export economy was expanded and commodity exchange intensified. Some people found themselves more involved in the colonial economy than others; the Kikuyu, the Baganda and the Chagga of Tanganyika were the most obvious groups who became integrated into the colonial economy. Many of the farmers in these groups took up new crops and farming methods, found themselves short of fertile land, involved themselves in co-operative marketing and established improved dairy herds. It is not surprising therefore that in these areas one finds that social differentiation between rich and poor has become more sharply defined than in other areas.

Thus some of the predominantly agricultural peoples had benefited from the introduction of the colonial export economy, and this served to encourage the growth of regional differences of wealth. The differences which grew up were in marked contrast to those of the pre-colonial period when the predominantly pastoral people had been economically and militarily the strongest groups. The colonial invasion had fundamentally altered the pre-existing balance of productive forces in East Africa and a major consequence of the colonial export economy was that it heralded the end of pastoral dominance in East Africa as a whole and directed new growth into agricultural pursuits.

During the first forty years of the twentieth century East Africa experienced the establishment of what could be called the classical structure of a colonial economy. The colonial economy was a geographical extension of the metropolis; the so-called development was no more than the growth of production of crops for export which was tied to the demand structure of the metropolitan market. Essential to the continuance and expansion of this system were the new political and administrative structures which were introduced to East Africa in this period: the centralised state, the communications system and the administrative machinery.

By about 1945 however, this classical period was beginning to come to an end. A new growth factor had entered the scene. This was the establishment in East Africa of branch companies of international firms. While in one sense the branches provided just one more attachment between East Africa and the metropolis, at the same time they operated to introduce a whole range of new factors. They provided a new and important area for inflows of finance capital where previously capital flows had been mainly from imperial to colonial government. They provided a new system of control of the means of technical knowledge and thus in many respects they took over the roles of the colonial governments themselves and became the major instrument for contemporary imperialism. As we show in Chapter 7 this was in many respects the outgrowth of the centralising tendencies of capitalist industry in Europe and the United States which took place after the Second World War. In East Africa it led to the growth of branches of international firms, like Brooke Bond, who controlled production, processing, packaging, shipping and marketing of their goods.

From the 1950s the colonial governments of both Kenya and Uganda were going all out to attract branches of the international corporations. Their strategies for development depended on the attraction of international capital and provided the conditions for yet another phase of imperialism as the international corporations took over many of the purposes of the colonial administration. In the 1960s the colonial governments were able to retreat strategically before the pressure of nationalist politics, leaving their politically independent successors with the conviction that development rested on their continued ability to attract international finance capital.

By the 1970s it was clear that international capital had become a dominant force in the direction and structure of the Kenyan economy. Kenya had been able to mobilise considerable quantities of foreign capital and to distribute a portion of it to the national petty bourgeoisie. Nearly all agricultural land had been registered and enclosed since 1963 and a self-confident group of leaders had grown up to take the place of the settlers as the leaders of the country. With the growth of the export orientation of the Kenyan economy after Independence, a deepening of the colonial structure did indeed occur, but more significant has been the process of change which originated with the Emergency and which led to a new level of capitalist production relationships. The old racial relations of capitalist production have been utterly destroyed and commodity relations have penetrated even the most intimate of the old pre-colonial social practices. Thus while the external direction of the colonial economy has been enlarged, the internal productive relations have been fundamentally altered as the whole society rather than a select group has followed the capitalist path.

Uganda, on the other hand, was far less successful in attracting capital from abroad in the 1960s. As a consequence she was unable to satisfy the expectations of the incipient petty bourgeoisie. The Tanzanian government faced much the same problem after Independence when foreign capital and companies were not entering Tanzania in significant force. The Tanzanian government was able to respond to the situation in 1967 by attempting to move towards a socialist orientation with the propounding of the Arusha Declaration but Ugandan politics did not allow for such a basic change of direction. The Common Man's Charter was a compromise document and Uganda remained dependent on foreign capital for her development until the overthrow of Obote's government when the remaining foreign capital deserted.

These are some of the major changes and continuities which have characterised the East African economies over the last one hundred years or so. Two other features have also shown themselves to be characteristic of both Kenyan and Ugandan economies in the colonial and Independence periods. The first of these is the continuing unevenness of growth. Differences in the levels of wealth of the nation states, differences in the regional distribution of wealth within each country and differences in individual holdings of wealth have increased rather than declined. The political and social consequences of these growing inequalities since Independence have been that people have struggled, argued and fought along ethnic, religious, and now along military lines. The rich have attempted to maintain the differences and the poor have attempted to catch up, or to alter the balances in their favour.

The second feature has been the concentration, centralisation and monopoly of institutions and power. The marketing parastatals were the most obvious expression of this movement in the economy from the 1930s; and more recently this growth of central power has become a dominant feature throughout East Africa. This general movement is the consequence of an existing powerful and wealthy ruling class. In Uganda the monopoly marketing institutions provided a method for extracting the maximum surplus from agricultural exports which was then directed towards the agency of government, which represented a bureaucratic colonial ruling class. In Kenya the marketing board surpluses were directed towards the settlers, the aspiring ruling class of the country. This general movement towards monopoly institutions, initially in marketing and then in finance, grew in intensity over the last thirty years of colonial rule and has rapidly accelerated over the first ten years of Independence. This growth in concentration of economic and political power has been diversified outwards into growing areas of the production process; into all areas of distribution (including domestic as well as export distribution); and into exchange and banking. Furthermore the political institutions have grown in the same direction, as authority has become centralised and the legislative bodies have become less powerful than the executive organs of government. Similarly, as population and industrial concentration has focused on Nairobi, Mombasa and Kampala, urban growth has shown the same tendencies.

The features we have been describing have occurred in societies which are based on peasant, small-scale agricultural production. It would seem that this growth in centralisation, side by side with peasant structures, is characteristic of export-oriented economies. The centralised structures have allowed those who control political power to direct surpluses produced by the community towards themselves and their friends. This distribution has been used to reinforce the existing political structure and to consolidate the development of a ruling class. In the First Republic of Uganda the incipient ruling class was unable to accumulate sufficient surpluses to consolidate its position: in Kenya the process has been much more successful.

Concentration of power within the new institutions of industry, urban centres and even the East African common market has grown rapidly over the last ten years, alongside differential growth patterns between rich and poor, town and country and between agricultural and pastoral areas of the countryside. Rather than being the consequence of the maintenance of pre-colonial modes of production, poverty has resulted from the widespread effects of peripheral capitalism. Wealth and power have become concentrated among certain groups while poverty remains the predominant condition of most of the people. It seems likely that although a few individuals will rise out of their poverty this division is likely to become ever more deeply embedded.

Bibliography

Introduction

Few references appear in the text of this book because we felt that most of our readers would be more concerned with the text itself than with referring to the sources of our information. However we realise that there may be a number of teachers and scholars who will wish to refer to our sources, either to find more detail than has been possible to present in this short book or to check our interpretations against the data. We have therefore listed our major sources below, arranging them chapter by chapter, including in our lists both published and unpublished works from a wide range of sources. We would add that the bibliography is by no means exhaustive but we hope that our selection will enable the interested scholar to make a start on the wealth of material which is scattered around and to which new papers, articles, books and the results of research currently being undertaken are constantly being added.

List of abbreviations commonly used in the bibliography

EAISR	East African Institute of Social Research, Makerere University, Kampala (now Makerere Institute of Social Research)
EALB	East African Literature Bureau, Nairobi
EAPH	East African Publishing House, Nairobi
EASSC	East African Social Science Conference (annual)
EDRP	Economic Development Research Project, MISR, Kampala
HMSO	His/Her Majesty's Stationery Office, London
IDS	Institute for Development Studies, Nairobi
JAH	*Journal of African History*, published by Cambridge University Press
NCCK	National Christian Council of Kenya, Nairobi
OUP	Oxford University Press
RDP	Rural Development Project
UKASA	United Kingdom African Studies Association
UNESCO	United Nations Educational, Scientific and Cultural Organisation

Chapter 1   *Population*

Barbour, K. M. and Pothero, R. M. (eds), *Essays on Population* (Routledge & Kegan Paul, 1961).

Blacker, J. G. C., 'Population Growth and Urbanisation in Kenya', in L. N. Blomberg and G. Abrams, *United Nations Mission to Kenya on Housing* (1964).

Cipolla, C. M., *The Economic History of World Population* (Pelican, 1970).

de Walle, E., 'The Economic Implication of Increase in Rural Density', cyclostyled, University of Nairobi Library (1969).

East Africa, *Population Census* (1948).

East Africa Statistical Department, 'Geographical and Tribal Studies' (1950).

East African Royal Commission 1953–55 Report, Cmd. 9475 (HMSO, 1955).

Etherington, D. M., 'Projected Changes in Urban and Rural Population in Kenya', *East African Economic Review* (June 1965).

Fazan, S. H., 'Report of the Committee on Native Land Tenure in Kikuyu Province' (Government Printer, Nairobi, 1929).

—— 'Memorandum on the Rate of Population Increase of the Kikuyu Tribe', cyclostyled, Kenya National Archives (1932).

Fearn, H., *An African Economy* (OUP, 1961) ch. 2.

Foster, W. D., *The Early History of Scientific Medicine in Uganda* (EALB, 1970).

Gilks, J. L., 'The Incidence and Character of Syphilis and Yaws in Kenya', *Kenya & East Africa Medical Journal* (Aug 1931).

Gilks, J. L. and Orr, J. B., 'The Nutritional Condition of the East African Native', *Kenya & East Africa Medical Journal* (June 1927). Also published in *The Lancet* (Mar 1927).

Goldthorpe, J. E., 'Attitudes to the Census and Vital Registration in East Africa', *Population Studies*, vol. VI (1952/3).

Goode, C. M., 'Salt Trade and Disease . . .', *African Historical Studies*, vol. V, no. 2 (1972).

Heisel, D. F., 'The Rate of Population Change as a Variable in Development Planning', discussion paper (IDS, 1966).

Hill, K. H., 'Population Trends in Africa', conference paper (UKASA, 1972).

Humphrey, N., *The Liguru and the Land* (Government Printer, Nairobi, 1947).

Huntingford, G. B. W., *Nandi Work and Culture* (HMSO, 1950).

Kenya, *Population Census* (1962; 1969).

Langlands, B. W., 'Sleeping Sickness in Uganda 1900–1920', mimeographed (Kampala, 1967).

—— 'The Demographic Conditions of Uganda as a Developing Country', occasional paper no. 9, Department of Geography, Makerere University, Kampala (1970).

Leys, N., *Kenya* (1924; repr. Cass, 1973).

Lury, D. A., 'Population Data in East Africa', discussion paper (IDS, 1966)

—— 'Population Estimates: Back Projections of Recent Censuses', *East African Statistical Review* (1967).

Martin, C. J., 'The East African Population Census 1948. Planning and Enumeration', *Population Studies*, vol. III (1949/50).

—— 'Some Estimates of the General Age Distribution, Fertility and Rate of Natural Increase of the African Population of British East Africa', *Population Studies*, vol. VII (1953/4).

Morris, K. R. S., 'Studies on the Epidemiology of Sleeping Sickness in East Africa', *Transactions of the Royal Society of Tropical Medicine and Hygiene*, vol. LIV (1960).

Odingo, R. S., *The Kenya Highlands* (EAPH, 1971).

Ominde, S. H., *Land and Population Movement in Kenya* (Heinemann, 1968).

Paterson, A. R., 'Memorandum on Development in Kenya', cyclostyled, Kenya National Archives (1926).

—— 'Population in Kenya', *Kenya Medical Journal* (Feb 1926).

Pool, D. L., 'The Development of Population Policies', *Journal of Modern African Studies*, vol. IX, no. 1 (1971).

Richards, A. I., *Economic Development and Tribal Change* (Heffer & Son for EAISR, 1952).

Soff, H. G., 'Sleeping Sickness in the Lake Victoria Region of British East Africa 1900–1915', *African Historical Studies*, vol. II, no. 2 (1969).

Spencer, P., 'Social and Demographic Processes among the Rendille and Samburu', conference paper (UKASA, 1972).

Sutton, J. E. G., 'Cattle Keeping in the Kenya Highlands', cyclostyled, School of Oriental and African Studies, London (1970).

Uganda, *Population Census* (1959; 1969).

Wrigley, C. C., 'Population Density, Political and Economic Change in Precolonial Africa', conference paper (UKASA, 1972).

Chapters 2, 3 and 4   *Agriculture*

Allan, W., *The African Husbandman* (Oliver & Boyd, 1965).

Beattie, J., 'Bunyoro', *Journal of African Administration* (1954).

Brown, L. H., *Agricultural Change in Kenya 1945–1960*, Food Research Institute, Stanford University (1968).

Buganda Planning Commission to the Kabaka's Council of Ministers, 'The Economic Development of the Kingdom of Buganda', report (1964).

Clayton, E. S., *Agrarian Development in Peasant Economies* (Macmillan, 1964).

Cone, L. W. and Lipscomb, J. F. (eds), *The History of Kenya Agriculture* (University Press of East Africa, 1972).

Cowen, M. P., 'Differentiation in a Kenya Location' (EASSC, 1972).

East African Royal Commission 1953–55 Report, Cmd. 9475 (HMSO, 1955).

Ehrlich, C., *The Uganda Company. The First Fifty Years* (Kampala, 1953).

—— 'The Uganda Economy 1903–1945', in V. Harlow, E. M. Chilver and A. Smith, *History of East Africa*, vol. II (OUP, 1965).

Elkan, W., *The Economic Development of Uganda* (OUP, 1961).

—— *Crops and Wealth in Uganda* (OUP, repr. 1970).

Fallers, L., *Bantu Bureaucracy* (University of Chicago Press, 1965).

Fearn, H., *An African Economy* (OUP, 1961).

Girling, F. K., *The Acholi of Uganda* (HMSO, 1960).

Green, R. M., 'The Kenya Land Commission 1932–33 and the Dorobo Land Issues', seminar paper, Department of History, University of Nairobi (1972).

—— *The Economic Development of Uganda* (Johns Hopkins Press, 1961).

International Bank for Reconstruction and Development, *The Economic Development of Kenya* (Johns Hopkins Press, 1963).

Jameson, J. D., *Agriculture in Uganda* (OUP, 1970).

Karuga, J. G., 'Land Transactions in Kiambu', working paper no. 58 (IDS, 1972).

Kenya Colony, 'Despatch from the Governor of Kenya commenting on the East African Royal Commission' (Government Printer, Nairobi, 1956).

Langlands, B. W., 'On the Disparities of Economic Development in Uganda', paper (EASSC, 1968).

Lawrence, J. C. D., *The Iteso: Fifty Years of Change in a Nilo-Hamitic Tribe of Uganda* (OUP, 1957).

Leys, C., 'Politics in Kenya : The Development of Peasant Society', discussion paper no. 102 (IDS, 1970).

Manners, A. J., 'Economic Processes and Power Structure : The Impact of Colonialism in Buganda', paper (EASSC, 1972).

Manners, R. A., 'The Kipsigis Culture Change in a "Model" East African Tribe', *Contemporary Change in Traditional Societies*, ed. J. H. Steward, vol. I (1967).

Matheson, J. K. and Bovill, E. W., *East African Agriculture* (OUP, 1950).

Middleton, J. F. M. and Greenland, D. J., 'Land and Population in West Nile District, Uganda', *Geographical Journal*, vol. cxx (1954).

Mitchell, Sir Philip, *The Agrarian Problem in Kenya* (Government Printer, Nairobi, 1948).

Mohiddin, A., 'Notes on the Colonial Background of Sessional Paper No. 10 of 1965', paper (EASSC, 1972).

Mukwaya, A. B., *Land Tenure in Buganda*, East African Studies (EAISR, 1953).

Muriuki, G., 'A History of the Kikuyu to 1904', Ph.D. thesis (London, 1969).

Odingo, R. S., *The Kenya Highlands* (EAPH, 1971).

—— 'Settlement and Rural Development in Kenya', *Studies in East African Geography and Development*, ed. S .H. Ominde (Heinemann, 1971).

Powesland, P. G., *Economic Policy and Labour* (EAISR, 1957).

Randall Baker, P., 'Agricultural Change in Bunyoro, 1954–1968', *Studies in East African Geography and Development*, ed. S. H. Ominde (Heinemann, 1971).

Richards, A. I. (ed.), *Economic Development and Tribal Change* (Heffer & Son, 1952).

Ruthenburg, H., *African Agricultural Production Development Policy in Kenya, 1952–1965* (Munich, 1966).

Seidman, A., 'The Dual Economies of East Africa', *East African Journal* (Apr, May, June, July 1970).

Sorrenson, M. P. K., *Land Reform in Kikuyu Country* (OUP, 1967).

—— *Origins of White Settlement in Kenya* (OUP, 1968).

Swynnerton, R. J. M., *A Plan to Intensify the Development of African Agriculture in Kenya* (Government Printer, Nairobi, 1954).

Uganda, *Report on the Uganda Census of Agriculture* (Entebbe, 1966).

Uganda Statistical Abstract (1969).

van Zwanenberg, R., 'Primitive Capital Accumulation . . .', D. Phil. thesis (Sussex, 1971) ch. 5.

Vincent, J., *An African Elite* (Columbia University Press, 1971).

Wagner, G., *The Bantu of Western Kenya*, vol. ii (OUP, 1970); reprint of 1949 ed., entitled *The Bantu of Northern Kavirondo*.

Whisson, M., *Change and Challenge* (NCCK, 1964).

Wilde, J. C. de, *Experience with Agricultural Development in Tropical Africa*, 2 vols (Johns Hopkins Press, 1967).

310   *Bibliography*

Winter, E. H., *Bwamba Economy* (EAISR, 1955).

Wrigley, C. C., 'Buganda, An Outline Economic History', *Economic History Review*, vol. i, no. x (1957).

—— 'Kenya : The Patterns of Economic Life, 1902–1945', in V. Harlow, E. M. Chilver and A. Smith, *History of East Africa*, vol. ii (OUP, 1965).

—— *Crops and Wealth in Uganda* (OUP, repr. 1970).

Yeld, R., 'Land Hunger in Kigezi, Southwest Uganda', *Land Settlement and Rural Development in Eastern Africa*, ed. R. Apthorpe (n.d.).

Chapter 5   *Pastoralism*

Baker, P. A., 'A Geographical Appraisal of Karamoja as a Beef Production Area', unpublished manuscript in Makerere University Library, Kampala.

Barber, J., *Imperial Frontier* (EAPH, 1968).

—— 'The Karamoja District of Uganda', *JAH*, vol. iii, no. 1 (1962).

Brandt, R., 'Rinderpest or Cattle Plague' and 'Pleuropneumonia', *Agricultural Journal of British East Africa* (1908, 1909).

Chambers, R. J. H., 'Report on the Social and Administrative Aspects of Range Management Development in North Eastern Province of Kenya', cyclostyled (1969).

Daryll Ford, C., *Habitat, Economy and Society* (Methuen, 1963).

Dyson Hudson, H., *Karimojong Politics* (OUP, 1966).

Ehret, C., *Southern Nilotic History* (Northwestern University Press, 1971).

Gulliver, P. H., 'Nomadism among the Pastoral Turkana of Kenya', *Nkanga*, no. 4 (n.d.).

—— 'A Preliminary Survey of the Turkana', mimeographed, University of Cape Town (1950; repr.1963).

Halderman, J. M., 'An Analysis of Continued Semi-Nomadism among the Kaputie Maasai Group Ranchers', working paper no. 28 (IDS, 1972).

Heady, H. F., *Range Management in East Africa* (Government Printer, Nairobi, 1960; rev. ed., 1972).

Henning, R. O., 'Range Management in the Pastoral Areas of Kenya', *Journal of African Administration*, vol. xiii, no. iv (1961).

Henriksen, G., 'Preliminary Report on the Fieldwork Conducted in Turkana in the Period May through November, 1972' (unpublished).

Hill, J. H., 'Native Cattle and their Relations to the Future Stock Industry', *Agricultural Journal of British East Africa* (1908).

Hill, P., *Studies in Rural Capitalism in West Africa* (OUP, 1970).

Huntingford, C. W. B., *Nandi Work and Culture* (HMSO, 1950).

Jacobs, A. H., 'African Pastoralists: Some General Remarks', *Anthropological Quarterly* (July 1962).

—— 'A Chronology of the Pastoral Maasai', *Hadith*, 1 (EAPH, 1968).

—— 'Memorandum on the Political and Economic Development of the Maasai', cyclostyled, private circulation from Dr Jacobs.

Kenya Colony, *African Land Development in Kenya, 1946–1962* (Government Printer, Nairobi, 1962).

Kenya National Archives, 'A Visit to Elgeyo-Marakwet', *Ministry of African Affairs* (July 1938).

Kenya. Report of the Northern Frontier Commission, Cmd. 1900 (HMSO, 1962).

Report of the Land Commission of Kenya. Evidence & Memoranda, Cmd. 4556 (HMSO, 1934).

King, K. J., 'The Maasai and the Protest Phenomenon, 1900–1960', *JAH*, vol. XII (1971).

Lambert, H. E., 'The Pressure on the Land', private papers of Mr Lambert, University of Nairobi Library.

Lewis, I. M., 'Somali Conquest of the Horn of Africa', *JAH*, vol. VI, no. 2 (1960).

Leys, N., *Kenya* (London, 1924).

Maher, C., 'Soil Erosion and Land Utilisation in Kamasia, Njemps and East Suk Reserves', cyclostyled report (1937).

Massam, J. A., *The Cliff Dwellers of Kenya* (repr. Cass, 1968).

Mbithi, P. M. and Wisner, B., 'Drought and Famine in Kenya', working paper no. 46 (IDS, 1972).

Newland, R. N., 'Review of the Cattle Trade in British East Africa, 1904–08', *Agricultural Journal of British East Africa* (1908).

Nsubuga, H. S. K., 'Dairy Farming in Busoga, West and East Mengo', RDP no. 61 (1968).

Ogot, B. A., *History of the Southern Luo*, vol. I (EAPH, 1967).

Pole Evans, I. B., 'Report of a Visit to Kenya', Agricultural Department Library (1938).

Richards, A. I., *Hunger and Work in a Savage Tribe* (Routledge, 1935).

Rigby, P., 'Pastoralism and Prejudice: Ideology and Rural Development in East Africa', *Nkanga*, no. 4 (n.d.).

Ruthenberg, H., *African Agricultural Production Development Policy in Kenya, 1952–65*, Ifo Institute, Berlin (1966).

Smith, A., 'The Economy of the NFP and the Italian Abyssinian War', *East African Journal* (Nov 1969).

Soja, E. W., *The Geography of Modernisation in Kenya: a Spatial Analysis* (Syracuse University Press, 1968).

Stanner, W. E. H., 'The Kitui Kamba . . .', Ph.D. thesis (London, 1939).

Sutton, J. E. G., *The Archaeology of Western Kenya*, memoir no. 3 of the British Institute in Eastern Africa (1973).

Theiler, Dr, 'Diseases of Livestock in Africa', *Agricultural Journal of British East Africa* (1909).

Tignor, R. L., 'Kamba Political Protest and the Destocking Controversy of 1938', *African Historical Studies*, vol. IV, no. 2 (1971).

Uganda, *Beef and Cattle Ranching Development* (Government Printer, Entebbe, 1968).

—— *Report of the Committee on the Marketing of Livestock Meats and Fish and their Products in Uganda* (Government Printer, Entebbe, 1969).

Uganda Veterinary Department, *Annual Reports* (1920–60).

Webster, J. B., 'Pioneers of Teso', *Tarikh*, III, 2 (1970).

Webster, J. B., Okalany, D. H., Emudong, C. P. and Egimu-Okuda, N., *The Iteso During the Asonya* (EAPH, 1973).

Welch, C. P., 'Pastoralists and Administrators in Conflict : A Study of Karamoja District, 1897–1968', M.A. dissertation, University of East Africa (1969).

Wilson, F. O. B., Correspondence (24.8.1932) from Nanyuki, among Lady Wilson's private papers.

Chapter 6 *Nineteenth-Century Craft Industries*

Birch, J. P., 'Madi Blacksmiths', *Uganda Journal*, vol. V, no. 1 (1937).

Brown, J., 'Iron Working in South Mbere', *Mila*, vol. II, no. 2 (1971).

Casati, G., *Ten Years in Equatoria and the Return with Emin Pasha*, 2 vols (London, 1891).

Fallers, L., *Bantu Bureaucracy* (University of Chicago Press, 1965).

Gilleband, M., Correspondence on Keiyo blacksmiths.

Haden, J., 'Okebu Iron Smelting', *Uganda Journal*, vol. XXXIV, no. 2 (1970).

Johnston, H. H., *The Uganda Protectorate*, 2 vols (London, 1902).

Lamphear, J., 'The Kamba and the Northern Mrima Coast', *Precolonial African Trade in East and Central Africa*, ed. R. Gray and J. Birmingham (OUP, 1970).

Lanning, E. C., 'Bark Cloth Hammers', *Uganda Journal*, vol. XXIII, no. 1 (1959).

Roscoe, J., *The Northern Bantu* (1st ed. 1915; repr. Cass, 1961).

—— *The Banyankole* (OUP, 1923; repr. 1968).

Routledge, S. K. and K., *With a Historic People* (1st ed. 1910; repr. Cass, 1968).

Shiroya, O. J. E., 'Northwestern Uganda in the Nineteenth Century. Interethnic Trade', cyclostyled seminar paper, Department of History, University of Makerere, Kampala (1970).

Sutton, J. E. G., 'Iron Working in Tanzania' and 'Traditional Salt Production in Tanzania', *Kwale* (1972).

Thomson, A. D., 'Barkcloth Making in Buganda', *Uganda Journal*, vol. vi, no. 1 (1934).

Trowell, K. M., 'Some Royal Craftsmen of Buganda', *Uganda Journal*, vol. xxiii, no. 2 (1941).

Trowell, K. M. and Wachsman, K., *Tribal Crafts of Uganda* (OUP, 1953).

Wagner, G., *The Bantu of Western Kenya*, vol. ii (OUP, repr. 1970).

Webster, J. B., 'Migration and Settlement of the Northern Region', cyclostyled, Department of History, University of Makerere, Uganda (1972).

Were, P. O., 'The Origins and Growth of the Iron Industry and Trade in Samia', B.A. dissertation, Department of History, University of Nairobi (1972/3).

White, R. G., 'Blacksmiths of Kigezi', *Uganda Journal*, vol. xxxiii, no. 1 (1969).

Chapter 7 *Industrialisation in the Twentieth Century*

Amsden, A., *International Firms and Labour, 1945–70* (Cass, 1971).

Arrighi, G., 'International Corporations, Labour Aristocracies and Economic Development in Tropical Africa', *Imperialism and Underdevelopment* (Monthly Review Press, 1970).

Barclays Overseas Review, 'Private Foreign Investment in Africa' (Aug 1971).

Brett, E. A., *Colonialism and Underdevelopment in East Africa* (Heinemann, 1973).

Daily Nation (11.2.72, 23.2.72, 14.6.72).

East African Royal Commission 1953–55 Report, Cmd. 9475 (HMSO, 1955).

East African Trade and Industry, vol.vii (June, Oct 1955).

Economic Commission for Africa, *Statistical Yearbook 1970*, 'Economic Statistics for Africa' (UNESCO, 1970).

—— 'Summaries of Economic Data for Kenya' (UNESCO, 1971).

The Economic Development of Kenya, report of a mission organised by the International Bank for Reconstruction and Development (Johns Hopkins Press, 1963).

Ghai, D., 'Employment Performance Prospects and Policies', discussion paper (IDS, 1970).

Green, R. H. and Seidman, A., *Unity and Poverty* (Penguin, 1968).

Hall, S., 'Some Aspects of Economic Development in Uganda', *African Affairs* (1952).

Herman, B., 'Some Basic Data for Analysing the Political Economy of Foreign Investment in Kenya', discussion paper (IDS, 1971).

Kenya, 'Manufacturing', *Annual Report for the Colony and Protectorate of Kenya* (1947–60).

—— *Growth of the Economy 1954–62* (Government Printer, Nairobi, 1962).

—— *Economic Survey* (Government Printer, Nairobi, 1971).

—— *Statistical Abstract* (Government Printer, Nairobi, 1971).

'Kenya : Strategy for Investment', *Africa* (June 1972).

Leys, C., 'The Limits of African Capitalism : The Formation of the Monopolistic Petty Bourgeoisie in Kenya', *Development Trends in Kenya*, mimeographed proceedings of a seminar, Centre of African Studies, University of Edinburgh (1972).

Maitra, P., *Import Substitution Potential in East Africa*, occasional paper no. 2 (OUP for EAISR, 1967).

Oursin, T., 'Development and Structure of Industry in Uganda', *Studies in Production and Trade in East Africa*, ed. P. Zajadacz (Munich, 1970).

Pearson, D., *Industrial Development in East Africa* (OUP, 1969).

Penrose, R. T., 'Multinational Corporations in East Africa : Policies and Problems', paper (EASSC, 1971).

Ruchett, H., 'The Chemical and Allied Industries in Kenya', *Studies in Production and Trade in East Africa*, ed. P. Zajadacz (Munich, 1970).

Safier, M., 'Patterns of Industrial Location and Urban Growth in East Africa, 1945–1985', paper (EASSC, 1968).

Seidman, A., *Comparative Development Strategies in East Africa* (EAPH, 1972) ch. vi.

Soper, C. D., *Jinja Transformed* (EAISR, 1955). Reviewed in *Uganda Journal*, vol. xxi, no. 1 (1957).

Stoutgerdigk, F. J., *Uganda's Manufacturing Sector* (EAPH, 1967).

Theuman, R., 'Political and Economic Consequences of Kenya's Development Strategy', paper (EASSC, 1971).

van Arkadie, B., 'Private Foreign Investment : Some Limitations', *Private Enterprise and the East African Company* (Tanzania Publishing House, 1965).

Wilson, G., *Owen Falls: Electricity in a Developing Country* (EAISR, 1967).

Wilson Ord, H., 'East African Companies', *East African Economic Review* (June 1960).

Chapter 8   *African Trade in the Nineteenth and Twentieth Centuries*

Bohannan, P. and Dalton, G. (eds), *Markets in Africa* (Northwestern University Press, 1962).

Goode, M. C., *Rural Markets and Trade in East Africa* (Washington, D.C., 1970).

Gray, R. and Birmingham, D., *Precolonial African Trade in East and Central Africa* (OUP, 1970).

Hill, P., 'Markets in Africa', *Journal of Modern African Studies* (1963).

Kamuhangiri, E. R., 'The Precolonial Economic and Social History of East Africa with special reference to South Western Uganda Salt Lakes Region', conference paper, Historical Association of Kenya (1972).

Lonsdale, J. M., 'A Political History of Nyanza 1888–1945', Ph. D. thesis (Cambridge, 1964).

Memon, P. A., 'Some Geographical Aspects of the History of Urban Growth', conference paper, Historical Association of Kenya (1972).

—— 'The Spatial Dynamics of Trade and Urban Development in Kenya during the Early Colonial Period up to 1915', working paper no. 78 (IDS, 1972).

Ngumu, D. M., 'Trade during the Precolonial Time in Nyeri District', B.A. dissertation, Department of History, University of Nairobi (1973).

Ochieng', W. R., 'Trade Contacts and Cultural Connections between the Gusii and the Luo in the Nineteenth Century', conference paper, Historical Association of Kenya (1972).

Quiggin, A. H., *Trade Routes, Trade and Currency in East Africa*, occasional paper, Rhodes-Livingstone Institute (1949).

Ssekamwa, J. C., 'Factors Mitigating against the Development of Retail Trade among Uganda Africans', paper (EASSC, 1971).

Sutton, J. E. G., *Early Trade in Eastern Africa* (EAPH, 1973).

Sutton, J. E. G. and Roberts, A. D., 'The Salt Trade in the Nineteenth Century', *Azania*, vii (1968).

Uzoigwe, G. N., 'Precolonial Markets in Bunyoro-Kitara', *Comparative Studies in Society and History*, vol. xiv, no. 4 (1972).

Vansina, J., 'Long Distance Trade Routes in Central Africa', *JAH*, vol. iii, no. 3 (1962).

van Zwanenberg, R., Research into the Lake Magadi Salt Trade and Trade along the Eastern side of Lake Victoria (unpublished).

Wagner, G., *The Bantu of Western Kenya*, vol. II (OUP, repr. 1970).

Were, P. O., 'The Origin and Growth of the Iron Industry and Trade in Samia', B.A. dissertation, Department of History, University of Nairobi (1972).

Chapter 9   *Nineteenth-Century Arab Trade*

Alpers, E. A., *The East African Slave Trade* (EAPH, 1967).

—— 'The Nineteenth Century: Prelude to Imperialism', *Zamani*, ed. B. A. Ogot and J. A. Kieran (EAPH, 1968).

Austen, R. A., 'Patterns of Development in Nineteenth Century East Africa', *African Historical Studies*, vol. V, no. 3 (1971).

Beachey, R. W., 'The Arms Trade in East Africa in the Late Nineteenth Century' (EAISR, 1959).

Bennett, N. R., *Studies in East African History* (Northwestern University Press, 1971).

Berg, F. S., 'Mombasa Under the Busaidi Sultanate', Ph.D. thesis (Wisconsin, 1971).

Clayton, A., 'Labour in the East African Protectorate 1895–1918', Ph.D. thesis (St Andrews, 1971).

Collister, P., *The Last Days of Slavery 1870–1900* (EALB, 1961).

Cooper, F., 'The Treatment of Slaves on the Kenya Coast in the Nineteenth Century', *Kenya Historical Review*, vol. II, no. 1 (1973).

Coupland, R., *The Exploitation of East Africa* (Faber & Faber, 1939).

—— *East Africa and Its Invaders* (OUP, 1965).

Fitzgerald, W. W. A., *Travels in the Coastlands of British East Africa and the Islands of Zanzibar and Pemba* (London, 1898).

Gavin, R. J., 'Palmerston's Policy Toward East and West Africa 1830–1865', Ph.D. thesis (Cambridge, 1958).

Gray, R. and Birmingham, D., *Precolonial African Trade* (OUP, 1970).

Harris, J. E., *The African Presence in Asia: Consequences of the East African Slave Trade* (Northwestern University Press, 1971).

Hartwig, G. W., 'The Victoria Nyanza as a Trade Route in the Nineteenth Century', *JAH*, vol. XI, no. 4 (1970).

Holmes, C. F., 'Zanzibari Influences at the Southern End of Lake Victoria', *African Historical Studies*, vol. IV, no. 3 (1971).

Jackson, M. V., *European Powers and South East Africa* (Longmans, 1962; rev. and extended, 1967).

Lugard, F. D., *The Rise of Our East African Empire* (repr. Cass, 1968).

Lyne, R. N., *An Apostle of Empire: being the life of Sir Lloyd William Mathews* (Allen & Unwin, 1936).

Nicholls, C. S., *The Swahili Coast* (Allen & Unwin, 1971).

Oliver, R., *The Missionary Factor in East Africa* (Longmans, 1967).

Salim, A. I., *The Swahili Speaking Peoples of the Kenya Coast, 1895–1965* (EAPH, 1973).

Sheriff, A. M. H., 'The Rise of a Commercial Empire. An Aspect of the Economic History of Zanzibar 1770–1873', Ph.D. thesis (London, 1971).

'Slavery in Africa', special supplement in *Trans-action* (Jan/Feb 1967).

Stanley, H. M., *Through the Dark Continent*, vol. I (London, 1899).

Turton, E. R., 'The Pastoral Tribes of Northern Kenya 1800–1916', Ph.D. thesis (London, 1970).

van Zwanenberg, R., 'Anti-Slavery, the Ideology of Nineteenth Century Imperialism in East Africa', conference paper, Historical Association of Kenya (1972).

Whitely, W. H. (trans.), *Tippu Tib – Dairies* (EALB, 1966).

Chapter 10   *Foreign Trade in the Twentieth Century*

Cutajar, M. Z. and Franks, A., *The Less Developed Countries in World Trade*, Overseas Development Institute, London (1967).

East Africa, *Trade Reports* (annual).

Economic Commission for Africa, *Summaries of Data: Kenya* (UNESCO, 1971).

Emanuel, A., *Unequal Exchange: A Study of the Imperialism of Trade* (Monthly Review Press, 1972).

Frank, B., 'Terms of Trade or Unequal Trade', *Bulletin of the Institute of Development Studies*, vol. III, no. 4 (1971).

Frankel, S. H., *Capital Investment in Africa* (OUP, 1938).

Haslemere Group, 'Coffee : The Rules of Neo-Colonialism' (1972).

Kenya, Department of Agriculture, *Annual Reports*.

—— *Statistical Abstracts* (annual).

Kyesimira, Y., *Agricultural Export Development* (EAPH, 1969).

Myint, H., 'The Gains from International Trade and the Backward Countries', *Review of Economic Studies*, vol. XXII, no. 2 (1954–5).

Oloya, J. J., *Coffee, Cotton, Sisal and Tea in the East African Economies* (EALB, 1969).

Rweyemamu, J. F., 'International Trade and the Developing Countries', *Journal of Modern African Studies*, vol. VII, no. 2 (1969).

Seidman, A., 'Prospects for Africa's Exports', *Journal of Modern African Studies*, vol. IX, no. 3 (1971).

Uganda, Department of Agriculture, *Annual Reports*.

—— *Background to the Budget* (Government Printer, Entebbe, annual).

—— *Statistical Abstracts* (annual).

West, R. L., 'An Estimated Balance of Payments for Kenya 1929–1939', *East African Economics Review*, vol. III, no. 1 (1956).

Wickijer, V. D., *Coffee, Tea and Cocoa* (Stanford University Press, 1957).

Wrigley, C. C., *Crops and Wealth in Uganda* (OUP, repr. 1970).

Chapter 11   *Marketing and Distribution*

Ehrlich, C., 'The Marketing of Cotton in Uganda, 1900–1950', Ph.D. thesis (London, 1958).

Engholm, G. F., 'The Decline of the Immigrant Influence in the Uganda Administration, 1945–51', *Uganda Journal*, vol. XXXI, no. 1 (1967).

Heyer, J., cyclostyled paper on marketing in Kenya, no title, Department of Economics, University of Nairobi (1968).

Karani, H., 'Pricing and Marketing of Maize in Kenya', discussion paper (IDS, 1965).

Kenya Coffee Board, *Monthly Bulletin* (1931–7).

Kenya Food Shortage Commission Report, 1943 (Government Printer, Nairobi, 1943).

—— *The Kenya Sisal Board Bulletin*, no. 20 (1957).

Kijubi, S., 'The Introduction of Cotton in Uganda', M.Sc. dissertation, Chicago University (1956).

Klemm, M., 'Some Aspects of Milk Marketing', discussion paper (IDS, 1966).

Knowles, O. S., 'Agricultural Marketing in Kenya', B.Litt. thesis (Oxford, 1955).

—— 'The Development of Agricultural Marketing in Kenya', *East African Economic Review*, vol. III, no. 1 (1956).

Kyesimiro, Y., 'The Production and Marketing of Maize in Kenya', EDRP no. 65 (1965).

Leubuscher, C., *Bulk Buying from the Colonies* (OUP, 1956).

Livesage, V., 'Control of Produce Buying in Africa', *Empire Journal of Experimental Agriculture*, vol. VIII, no. 32 (1940).

—— 'Trusteeship', unpublished MS. held at Rhodes House, Oxford.

Llewellyn, G. W., 'Government Marketing Control – The Case of the Maize Industry in East Africa', EDRP no. 144 (1968).

Makerere University, Department of History, B.A. student essays :

Kazibwe, M. N., 'The Social and Economic Effects of Cotton and Coffee on the Growth of Population in North Singo 1903–54'.

Mugwanga, K. S., 'Social and Economic Transition through Cotton and Coffee Growing in S. E. Kyazwe'.

Munakukaama-Nserek, J., 'The Traits of Economic Paternalism in Mityana Area 1908–60 Regarding Cotton-Growing'.

Sekamwa, S. K., 'Peasant Chief and Cotton Buyer in the Cotton Industry in Kyaddondo County of Buganda 1903–49'.

Sonko, S. K., 'Agrarian Life in Gombe, 1903–50'.

Marani, R., 'The Asian Trading Frontiers in East Africa and the Asian Sources', History Department, Makerere University, Kampala (1969).

Massell, B. F., Heyer, J. and Karani, H., 'Maize Policy in Kenya', discussion paper (IDS, 1965).

Okerere, O., 'The Role of the Co-operative Movement in the Economic Development of Uganda', M.A. dissertation, University of East Africa (1968).

Thomas, H. O., 'A Brief History of the African Highland Produce Company', kindly lent by the Company.

Walker, D. and Ehrlich, C., 'Stabilisation and Development Policy in Uganda : An Appraisal', *Kyklos*, vol. xii (1959).

Walters, A. R., 'Change and Evolution in the Kenya Coffee Industry', *African Affairs*, vol. lxxi, no. 283 (1972).

Yoshida, M., 'The Historical Background to Maize Marketing in Kenya', EDRP no. 91 (1966).

Chapter 12   *East Africa and Economic Federation*

Amery, L. S., *My Political Life*, vol. ii, 1914–1926 (Hutchinson, 1953).

Bennett, G., *Kenya: A Political History* (OUP, 1963).

Dilley, M. R., *British Policy in Kenya Colony* (New York, 1937; repr. Cass, 1966).

Doimi di Delupis, I., *The East African Community and Common Market* (Longmans, 1969).

Elkan, W. and Nutty, L., 'The Economic Links Between Kenya, Uganda and Tanganyika', discussion paper no. 143 (IDS, 1972).

Ghai, D., 'The Territorial Distribution of Benefits and Costs of the East African Common Market', *East African Economic Review* (June 1966).

Grigg, E. M. W. (later Lord Altrincham), *Kenya's Opportunity* (Faber, 1955).

Harlow, V., Chilver, E. M. and Smith, A., *History of East Africa*, vol. II (OUP, 1965).

Huxley, E., *White Man's Country*, vol. II (Chatto & Windus, 1935; repr. 1968).

Kassim Guruli, G., 'Equality in the East African Common Market', *East African Journal* (Sep 1971).

Kennedy, T. A., 'The East African Customs Union : Some Features of its History and Operation', *Makerere Journal*, no. 3 (1959).

Leys, C. and Robson, P., *Federation in East Africa* (OUP, 1965).

Mawani, Z. S., 'The East African Community', private paper.

Ndegwa, P., *The Common Market and Development in East Africa* (EAPH, 1968).

Nimcock, W., *Milner's Young Men: The Kindergarten in Edwardian Imperial Affairs* (Duke University Press, 1968).

Nixson, F. L., 'Industrial Location and the East African Common Market', EDRP no. 148 (1967).

—— 'The Reshaping of East African Economic Co-operation', *East African Journal* (Aug 1967).

Robson, P., *Economic Integration in Africa* (Allen & Unwin, 1968).

Rothchild, D., *Politics of Integration* (EAPH, 1968).

Chapter 13   *Urbanisation*

Clayton, A., 'Labour in the East African Protectorate, 1895–1918', Ph.D. thesis (St Andrews, 1971).

Daily Nation (14.8.72).

Economic Commission for Africa, *Statistical Yearbook* (UNESCO, 1970).

Elkan, W., 'Circular Migration and the Growth of Towns in East Africa', *International Labour Review* (Dec 1967).

—— 'Urban Unemployment in East Africa', *International Affairs* (1971).

Gutkind, P. C. W., *The Poor in Urban Africa*, McGill Center for Developing Area Studies (July 1970).

—— *The Royal Capital of Buganda* (Mouton & Co., 1963).

Hake, A., *History of Nairobi* (forthcoming). Chapters on: 'The African Metropolis'; 'The Control of the City'; 'An Underworld Rising'.

Hoselitz, B., 'Generative and Parasitic Cities', *Economic Devopment and Cultural Change*, vol. III (1955).

Kenya, *Official Census* (1948–69).

—— 'Land Development and the Squatter', Government paper (1968).

McMaster, D. N., 'The Colonial District Town in Uganda', *Urbanisation and its Problems*, ed. R. P. Bechuirale and J. M. Houston (Blackwell, 1970).

Myers, D., 'Nairobi's First Thirty Years', *Kenya Past and Present*, vol. II, no. 1 (1973).

Parker, M., 'Political and Social Aspects of the Development of Municipal Government in Kenya', Ph.D. thesis (London, 1949).

Rempel, H., 'The Rural and Urban Migrant in Kenya', *Urban African Notes*, vol. VI, no. 1, African Studies Center, Michigan (1971).

Safier, M., 'Patterns of Industrial Location and Urban Growth in East Africa, 1945–1985' (EASSC, 1968).

Southall, A. W., 'A Study of Social Differentiation in Kampala' (EASSC, n.d.).

Southall, A. W. and Gutkind, P. C. W., *Townsmen in the Making* (Kegan Paul for EAISR, 1957).

Sunday Nation (24.9.72).

Temple, P. H., 'Kampala and Influences Upon Its Growth and Development' (EASSC, 1963).

Tribe, M. A., 'Urban Population Growth in Relation to National Resources in Uganda', EDRP no. 145 (1968).

Uganda, *Official Census* (1948–69).

van Zwanenberg, R., 'History and Theory of Urban Poverty in Nairobi', discussion paper no. 139 (IDS, 1972).

Weeks, J., 'An Exploration into the Nature of the Problem of Urban Imbalance in Africa', conference on urban unemployment in Africa at the Institute of Development Studies, Sussex.

Yahya, S. S., 'The Changing Pattern of Land Use and Land Values in Suburban Nairobi', Department of Land Development, University of Nairobi (1969).

Chapter 14   *Money and Banking*

Bosu, C. R., 'African Business Financing Schemes in Uganda', EDRP no. 118 (1962).

Colonial Office, London, documents in the Public Record Office : PRO.CO.533 : 388.15680, 394.16000, 399.16164.

Dillon, B., 'Financial Institutions in Kenya 1964–71 : A Preliminary Analysis', working paper (IDS, 1971).

East African Royal Commission 1953–55 Report, Cmd. 9475 (HMSO, 1955).

Henry, J. A., *The First Hundred Years of the Standard Bank* (OUP, 1963).

Kenya National Archives, *Ministry of African Affairs*, 10.83.6.1428 (The Land Bank in the 1930s).

—— *Ministry of Financial Development*, 1.3479.21.1459, 1.3701. 34.1464 (The Land Bank).

Kratz, J. W., 'The East African Currency Board', International Monetary Fund Staff Papers, vol. xiii (1966).

Loxley, J., 'The Development of the Monetary and Financial System of the East African Currency Area, 1950–64', Ph.D. thesis (Leeds, 1967).

McWilliam, M. D., 'Banking in Kenya 1950–60', *East African Economic Review* (June 1962).

Martin, P. (ed.), *Financial Aspects of Development in East Africa* (Munich, 1970).

Newlyn, W. T., *Money in an African Context* (OUP, 1967).

Newlyn, W. T. and Rowan, R. C., *Money and Banking in British Colonial Africa* (OUP, 1947).

Nwankwo, G. O., 'British Overseas Banks in the Developing Countries Until 1945', *Journal of the Institute of Bankers* (June 1972).

Scott, Lord Francis, private papers, 'Statistical Research', File ix G; 'Analysis of Bank Statistics for BEA', 1927–31 (1932) memoir no. 4.

Uganda, *Annual Report* (1905/6, 1907/8, 1919, 1946).

—— *Background to the Budget* (Government Printer, Entebbe, annual).

van Arkadie, B., 'Central Banking in East Africa' *Federation in East Africa*, ed. C. Leys and P. Robson (OUP, 1965).

van Zwanenberg, R., 'Primitive Colonial Capitalism . . .' D.Phil. thesis (Sussex, 1971) ch. 2.

Index

Self-help, 271–3
Slavery, 166, 175–80
Smith, Adam, 227, 229
Soil erosion, 47–8, 97, 99–100
Somali invasion, 88
Squatters, 30–1, 42, 95
Stock
  development, 93, 102
  importance of, 86
  routes, 100
  sales, forced, 101
  and white settlement, 95–7
Swynnerton Plan, 49, 53

Tanning, 120
Technology, xvii, 124, 136–8
Tobacco, 71
Tractor services, 72
Trade
  African, **145–62**
  Arab, **163–82**
  exports and dependency, 229
  foreign, xxii-xxiii, 183–200
  and foreign capital, 196
  imports, 197

in animals, 95
Indian, 160
licensing, 162, 212–13
long-distance, 147
nineteenth-century, 148–52
subsistence, 146
visible balance, 195–6
and war, 154–5, 170

Uganda Company, 207
Uganda Development Corporation,
  131
Urbanisation, 140, 247, **253–74**

Vagrancy, 270–1

White settlement
  African resettlement, 52
  and Closer Union, 238
  continuity in 1960s, 51–2
  in Kenya, 38
  in Uganda, 61–4
  increase in, 45
  and marketing, 204, 218–19
  and world slump, 209